The MUHLENBERGS of PENNSYLVANIA

Other books by the author

CONRAD WEISER
Friend of Colonist and Mohawk

THE WHITE ROOTS OF PEACE

HENRY MELCHIOR MUHLENBERG

The MUHLENBERGS of PENNSYLVANIA

by

PAUL A. W. WALLACE

Philadelphia
UNIVERSITY OF PENNSYLVANIA PRESS
1950

Manufactured in the United States of America

To

my sons, Tony and David

ACKNOWLEDGMENTS

The author wishes to thank the members of the Muhlenberg family who have made available their family papers and portraits. Mrs. Jesse Wagner, Mr. Frederick A. Nicolls, Mr. Charles H. Muhlenberg, Mr. David M. Gregg, and many others have been more than generous in their help.

I owe much to the American Philosophical Society, especially to Dr. William E. Lingelbach, Librarian, and to Dr. L. P. Eisenhart, Executive Officer. A grant from the Society's Penrose Fund, together with leave of absence from Lebanon Valley College, enabled me to devote the necessary time to the completion of the work.

To Dr. Luther D. Reed, Librarian, Dr. Theodore G. Tappert, Dr. John W. Doberstein, and Rev. Karl Schild, I am indebted for permission to use, and assistance in using, the Muhlenberg papers in the Library of the Lutheran Theological Seminary, Mt. Airy, Philadelphia.

It is a pleasure to acknowledge the help received from the staff of the Historical Society of Pennsylvania, the American Philosophical Society, the Krauth Memorial Library, the Pennsylvania Historical and Museum Commission, the Manuscript Division of the Library of Congress, the National Archives at Washington, D. C., the New York Historical Society, the Library of Haverford College, the Library of Franklin and Marshall College, and many other institutions. Very particular thanks are due to, among others, the following persons: Dr. E. D. Merrill, Dr. John H. Powell, Mr. J. Bennett Nolan, Mr. Wayne Andrews, Rev. Russell H. Zimmerman, Rev. Harry Julius Kreider, Rev. Henry H. Bagger, Dr. L. H. Butterfield, Capt. Victor Gondos, Mr. George Allen, and Rev. Harry T. Richwine.

CONTENTS

ILLUSTRATIONS

CHAPTER I

MISSION TO AMERICA

The story of the Muhlenbergs must begin with the church at Trappe, the scene of much, and the symbol of all, that the family did. Its brown stone walls (long since covered with roughcast to keep out the damp, for the church has no heating) look down across the fields to where the old Muhlenberg house sits in a small hollow beside a spring.

If Henry Melchior Muhlenberg, who built the house for Anna Maria, his bride, in 1745, were to return today, he would hardly recognize the place. New porches, a turret on the roof, and the walling up of the handsome old south doorway have changed its outward appearance.

But Old Augustus Church remains as it was when the campfires of Washington's army shone round it in 1777, and as it was when young Pastor Muhlenberg held the first services within its walls on September 12, 1743.

It is only the forest around it that has changed. The wall of trees that once threw back echoes of the preacher's voice has gone. The church now stands on the edge of a field, in a small grove of scattered trees, looking for all the world like a great boulder brought down by some ancient glacier from the mountains.

Today its old-fashioned German-rural architecture may seem out of place beside the stream of Philadelphia suburban traffic that flows past on the modern highway. But it fits in well enough with its own east Pennsylvania landscape—

> . . . the pleasant land behind
> Unaltered since Red Jacket rode that way—

where grainfields, meadows, and woodlands dip into winding valleys, and the horizon is everywhere blue with distant hills.

Its compact strength and integrity of form make it the best possible memorial of Henry Melchior Muhlenberg and the family he founded.

Henry Melchior Muhlenberg was born on September 6, 1711, at Einbeck in the Electoral Principality of Hanover, a state whose Prince, George Louis, on the death of Queen Anne three years later, was to become King George I of England.

Henry Melchior's father was Claus (Nicolaus) Melchior Muhlenberg, a shoemaker by trade, a lay deacon in the church, and a town councilor. Whether Claus Muhlenberg was descended from the once powerful Von Mühlenbergs (named for Mühlberg, the mill town on the Elbe in Saxony where in the tenth century Prince Ziracka, founder of the family, had his seat) need not concern us. The fortunes of the Von Mühlenbergs had been broken by the Thirty Years' War, and the remnants of the family made no effort to have the title restored.

His mother was Anna Maria Kleinschmidt, daughter of an army officer.

Henry Melchior's early years were spent in the ancient town of his birth, and he drew into his blood the traditions and loyalties of the place. One of these was a passionate attachment to the Lutheran Church. Citizens of Einbeck had been among the first followers of Martin Luther; and, as early as 1528, they had invited a Lutheran pastor to serve them in the Market Church. During the Thirty Years' War, Einbeck was twice besieged and once taken. The scars it received at that time were not entirely obliterated until 1718, when King George of England, who was at the same time Electoral Prince of Hanover, restored it.

It is small wonder that in after years the man whose boyhood had been spent here should feel a prime loyalty to two institutions: the Lutheran Church and the House of Hanover. His loyalty to the former remained to the end and was the mainspring of his life. His loyalty to the latter remained until it was shaken by the storms of the American Revolution.

When he was seven years old, he was sent by his father to a classical school, where he laid the foundations for that mastery of Latin which enabled him in later life to speak and write the language with fluency. At the age of twelve he was confirmed and received into the Lutheran Church.

There was no sudden conversion, no moment of ecstatic vision, to mark the beginning of his religious life. He grew into religion. As a child he took it for granted, as he took for granted other mysteries of the universe, such as the glory of daylight, the beauty of the rainbow, and the play of the human imagination. When he was thirteen years old, on the death of his father and as a result of his own great grief, he tells us that a door was opened in his mind and he had his first glimpse of the spiritual world. It was not, however, any

> . . . dim and undetermined sense
> Of unknown modes of being

that came to him then, leaving him moved but groping and wondering. His mind was precise and liked exactitude. The clean-edged statements of the Lutheran Church's Augsburg Confession satisfied his intellectual curiosity. But to say that his religious experience came to him wrapped in the catechetical garments of the church to which he belonged, is not to say that religion, as he apprehended it, was merely a matter of assent to a set of propositions. It was much deeper than that. Behind the handed-down dogmas (which were, after all, no more than attempts to explain something *known at first hand*), he had felt a Presence.

For a time after his father's death, his schooling was interrupted and he turned to support himself by manual labor. But soon friends of the family, who had marked his quick and eager mind, interested themselves in putting him forward. Herr Alberty at the minster began to instruct him, during the evenings, in organ playing. Thereafter he was never without a patron.

The list of these patrons is long and revealing. It will be well for the reader to run his eye over some part of it. The very names and titles carry with them a flavor of the lavender world Henry Melchior did not entirely renounce when he came to America.

There was, first of all, His Worthiness Herr Rector Johann Joachim Schüssler, superintendent of the best classical school in Einbeck; then the Reverend Dr. Joachim Oporin, Dean of the Faculty and Professor of Dogmatic and Moral Theology at the University of Göttingen, as well as author of *The Ancient and Only Rule for a*

Convincing and Effective Manner of Preaching (in two parts)—a saintly person who did much to deepen and direct the young man's religious life; His Excellency Herr von Münchausen, High Sheriff of Hanover; His Grace Count Wernigerode; His Grace the Twenty-fourth Count Reuss of Köstritz; His Grace Count Erdmann Henckel of Pöltzig; His Excellency Privy Councilor von Gersdorf and his good Baroness; the pious Gotthilf Augustus Francke and the rest of the "Right Reverend Fathers" at Halle; and, finally, His Reverence Friedrich Michael Ziegenhagen, German Lutheran Chaplain of the Royal Chapel of St. James in London.

It is a company to remember—not individually but in the mass. It represents more than just the friendly and paternal society in which he grew up. It represents the mold in which he did his thinking, his frame of reference. Even after he had come to Pennsylvania, his instinctive reliance on European patrons for encouragement and sanction colored his first impressions of the New Land. For long years, also, it tempered his judgment; and, as we shall see, it led him finally into such a severe mental conflict as took the tempest of the Revolution to resolve.

His politics (when he ruminated at all on such "Machiavellian matters") he took from his patrons and from the comfortable system that gave them their titles and him their patronage. Government, he believed, is the Great Patron, established by God and sanctioned by His Word. Romans 13.1: "Let every soul be subject unto the higher powers. For there is no power but of God: the powers that be are ordained of God."

What twist this text was to receive under the impact of the American Revolution will be considered in due course.

Order, decorum (in the best sense), and harmony—these were the most valuable gifts he received from his early German environment. These, as he saw it, were the marks of God's presence in the world. These were the steps to the Temple—the steps by which he himself, as he believed, was ordained to lead men to the altar.

At the age of twenty-two, he began to support himself by teaching children at Zellerfelde in the Hartz Mountains writing, reckoning, catechism, and the clavichord.

He was born to be a teacher (*Lehrer*), which means, in German, also a *preacher*. With a passion for learning (from boyhood he spent his spare time with books) he possessed also a passion to instruct. He preached his first sermon, if family tradition is to be trusted, to the bare walls in a barn.

But he was not destined to spend his life teaching children clavichord at Zellerfelde in the Hartz Mountains. In 1735 he entered the University of Göttingen, where he studied Greek, Hebrew, Logic, Mathematics, and Dogmatic and Moral Theology. At Göttingen he met two missionaries who had been laboring among the Jews, and was inspired to join them. They stipulated, however, that he should first prepare himself by study in the great citadel of Pietism, Halle, famed for its educational work and for the many missionaries it had prepared for the foreign field.

To Halle, therefore, he went. Before he had been there a year, "the Fathers at Halle" (it was thus he always spoke of them) proposed that he go as a missionary to India, and he prepared to forsake the Jews for the people of Bengal.

There was some little delay before he was ready to go. After he had been at Halle for a time, teaching in the great orphan school, inspecting the sick wards, conducting classes in Theology, Greek, and Hebrew, and studying for himself in the evenings Bible and Paraenetics, he was called away to the diaconate and inspectorship of an orphans' home maintained by Baroness Gersdorf at Grosshennersdorf in Upper Lusatia. In 1739 he was ordained to the ministry in the city of Leipzig.

It was on his thirtieth birthday, September 6, 1741, after his return to Halle, that Bengal lost him. On that day His Reverence Doctor and Professor Gotthilf Augustus Francke, Director of the Orphan House and member of the Society for the Propagation of the Gospel in Foreign Parts, presented to him a call to Pennsylvania. Three forlorn Lutheran congregations, without proper church buildings or a pastor, one at Philadelphia, one at New Providence (more frequently called Providence and now known as Trappe), and one at New Hanover, had sent through Court Preacher Ziegenhagen in London an appeal to Halle for a man to come over and help them.

"If it is the Lord's will, I will go," said Henry Melchior Muhlenberg.

CHAPTER II

THE GEORGIA PACKET

On July 10, 1742, when a day's sail beyond Land's End, the *Georgia Packet,* bearing Henry Melchior Muhlenberg on his mission to America, lost its escort. The captain of H. M. S. *Launceston,* having spied a sail and supposing it very naturally to be a Spanish privateer, signaled the two vessels under his protection a "happy voyage," and turned off to pursue the stranger over the horizon.

The *Georgia Packet's* partner, a merchant vessel bound for Philadelphia, was a better sailer than her Savannah-bound companion, and, before evening, had drawn so far ahead as to be out of sight. The *Georgia Packet* was alone on the wilderness of waters, and Henry Melchior aboard her was alone with Original Sin. It was his introduction to the wild, free life, unbeautiful but challenging, of men uprooted from their traditions, which he was to see more of in the land of his mission.

He had left the shores of Europe behind him forever. But not its memories. And a few of these memories must be glanced at, since they contain the secret springs of much that would otherwise be difficult to understand about his later life.

To begin with, there were memories of all the leave-takings.

There had been a considerable flurry among his patrons and benefactors when they heard he was about to forsake Grosshennersdorf for America. Her Gracious Ladyship, the Baroness von Gersdorf, former patron of the orphan institution, deprecated his decision to give himself to the wilderness (especially the Pennsylvania wilderness, whither the nephew of whom she disapproved, Count Zinzendorf of Moravian sympathies, had betaken himself), and advised him to seek counsel from his high patrons the Gracious Counts Reuss and Henckel, which he did immediately. Count Reuss in particular, who had been responsible for his call to the diaconate of the Grosshennersdorf orphans' home, wished him to remain. His Grace the Baron von Burgsdorf, Assistant Judge of the Superior Court, who, now that the Baroness von Gersdorf had relinquished her estates, had become the "gracious ruler" of Grosshennersdorf and its orphans, also wished him to remain.

On maturer considerations, however, His Excellency, the Twenty-fourth Count Reuss, agreeing that it was easier to find someone for Grosshennersdorf than for America, released him; and, on December 9, the second Sunday in Advent, Henry Melchior preached his farewell sermon at Grosshennersdorf on a text from Hosea 11.7-8: "And my people are bent to backsliding . . ."

Taking leave at the castle of Her Grace the Baroness von Gersdorf and her family, he set off, as obligation demanded, for Pöltzig to take leave of Count Henckel, and to Köstritz to take leave of Count Reuss. At Halle he said good-bye to His Reverence Dr. Gotthilf Augustus Francke, and at Wernigerode to His Excellency the Gracious Count of said name.

His friends were all regretful to see him go, but sympathetic with his missionary projects for the great new land across the sea. To the young evangel, these leave-takings were, for the most part, encouraging and happy.

But there was unpleasantness, too; and it came where it would hurt the most, in Einbeck, his home. His rapid rise to notice had there been marked by jealous eyes. The local clergy could not easily forgive him his noble patrons, the réclame his dedication to foreign missions had brought him, and his pietistic tendencies. That was it: Pietism! They had him there. *Pietismus* was a word that in Hanover connoted matters of the deepest prejudice. It was a foreign thing, Saxon, rooted in Halle. The Pietists were "do-gooders," full of cant about orphans, elementary education, Bible societies, and missions. Pietism and conventicles! They would get him on that if there was law in the land.

Muhlenberg came home to Einbeck on February 17, 1742, to take leave of his old and ailing mother. He said good-bye to her and to his twenty-four brothers, sisters, nephews, and nieces. The house was crowded with visitors: old friends, neighbors, and members of the Ministerium who had come to spy on the man who was *homo pietismi suspectissimus.*

On Oculi Sunday, February 25, he preached from Isaiah 61.1: ". . . He hath sent me to bind up the brokenhearted, to proclaim liberty to the captives, and the opening of the prison to them that are bound."

In the evening many friends came to the house to converse with him about his work and the Gospel he was carrying abroad.

That was the opportunity for which his enemies had been waiting. The pastor of the Market Church and others of the local Ministerium invoked the law. They accused him of being an "itinerant fanatic" and of holding "forbidden conventicles."

The burgomaster sent a constable. On March 10 Muhlenberg was forbidden the use of the pulpit. The town broke into factions, some championing him as a persecuted preacher of God's truth, others denouncing him as a pietistic heretic. A rescript against him was procured from the Consistory in Hanover. The burgomaster read it to him and threatened him with imprisonment.

Muhlenberg knew how to stand up for himself, and he did so now. He loved position and titles, but was not afraid of those who held them. He asked the burgomaster what he thought of the whole procedure, whether it was "*juridice, politice, philosophice,* or *theologice.*"

The burgomaster, who was a man of sense caught in the meshes of a bad law, defended himself with spirit and good Latin. The whole affair, he said, had been conducted properly "*ab exsequutione ad cognitionem causae,*" i.e., from the corpse to the coroner's inquest.

Muhlenberg replied that it looked to him more like the Spanish Inquisition.

It was an unpleasant ending to the Einbeck pastoral. But it had one good effect. It enabled the missionary to leave the burgomaster, his mother, his twenty-four brothers and sisters and nephews and nieces, his friends, neighbors, and the Ministerium, with less anguish than he had anticipated.

It was a nasty lesson he had just learned, but it was well that he had learned it. The lesson was this: that even in the best-ordered societies, the old Adam can still find an outlet; and the more tightly organized the society, the better opportunity there is for jealousy and cunning to work anonymously through the law. The burgomaster himself admitted that the law against conventicles had apparently been used in this instance to satisfy a private grudge.

But if Muhlenberg felt a momentary spark of revolt against the tight social system he was putting behind him, it was soon extinguished by the spray of the ocean, for on board ship he was to see what man free and unconstrained could be like, and it frightened him.

Because the call to "the western wilderness" had come to Halle through the Court Preacher in London, with whom the Lutherans of Pennsylvania had been in correspondence, it was protocol for the missionary to accept it formally at the hands of Master Ziegenhagen himself. To London, therefore, he now addressed himself.

He went first to the city of Hanover, where he took leave of "Her Grace, the consort of His Excellency, the High Sheriff von Münchausen"; and he stopped long enough in the city to submit to the Privy Council, whence the rescript had come, a report on the incident at Einbeck—not, as he said, in any spirit of revenge, "but only to vindicate the pure truth." It was a characteristic act. His enemies, throughout his life, got small change out of Henry Melchior Muhlenberg.

From Hanover he proceeded into Holland by way of Osnabrück and Narden. At the latter place he boarded a horse-drawn canalboat and had his first boat ride—two miles down the canal to Amsterdam. From Amsterdam another canalboat took him, by way of Leyden and Rotterdam, to Briel; and from Briel he rode in company with a Hungarian courier who cheered him with converse in English, French, and Latin, to Hellevootsluis, where he took the packet boat for England.

The tedium of the two-day trip across the North Sea was broken by a violent attack of seasickness, an ailment to which his constitution seemed to be peculiarly susceptible. Once ashore in England, he managed to climb into a coach, and proceeded by this conveyance across country from Harwich to Colchester and thence to London. He arrived at six o'clock on the evening of April 17—by his calendar, that is, or April 6 according to the English calendar, which was still Julian and therefore eleven days behind. It was not until 1752 that England and her colonies caught up.

Being a stranger in London, without lodging and with not too great familiarity with the language spoken there, he entertained hopes of reaching *Herr Hofprediger* Ziegenhagen's residence in Kensington before nightfall. He accordingly climbed into a hackney coach, saw his baggage put in beside him, and drove off.

The coachman, as it turned out, was a hearty, free spirit who carried the keys of the City of London in his pocket—a type Dickens was to make familiar to the world three-quarters of a century later. Sam Weller's father might have appreciated his vagaries somewhat better than the German missionary was at that moment in a mood to. On the box beside him Jehu took up a bibulous companion, stopped at various pubs to refresh himself with what

> . . . does more than Milton can
> To justify God's ways to man,

and made himself so roaring drunk that he could not find Kensington. For comparison, let us imagine a New York taxi driver who could not hit upon Central Park. Bewildered but hopeful, the coachman drove, shouting, for miles about the London streets, until the young missionary (as he tells us) was driven to prayer.

Such was Muhlenberg's introduction to the "Land of hope and glory, mother of the free."

Fortunately he had a sense of humor, and the evening ended happily. When he arrived at Ziegenhagen's in Kensington Square, the anxieties of the drive were obliterated by the warm and considerate welcome he received from his fatherly host.

The weeks spent in Kensington and London were a delight to the young missionary. A comfortable lodging had been prepared for him near-by. He took his meals regularly with the Court Preacher, day after day discussed church doctrine with him and the need of a correct and final catechism (they shared the German love of tidiness and finality), heard him expound Revelation 5, verses 6 to the end, on Good Friday, and, on Easter morning, heard him preach in the Court Chapel on the works of the angels at the Resurrection. On the "second Easter Day" he heard the Second Court Preacher, Master Butjenter, preach. Muhlenberg himself preached at the Court Chapel on the afternoon of April 25, and at the German Evangelical Lutheran Church of St. Mary's in the Savoy on the afternoon of May 9. He talked, dined, and walked in the fields, always with the best and most stimulating companions. He reveled in the services, the preaching, the music. Above all, he enjoyed the conversation of his good host, who expounded important passages of Scripture to him, presented him with the key to "the difficult third chapter of John," and explained to him the danger of separating from one another "the High Priestly Office and the State of Humiliation . . . and likewise the State of Exaltation and the Kingly Office of Christ."

It must be confessed that the class of problem in New Testament exegesis which engrossed religious minds in the mid-eighteenth century has lost its fascination even for the initiated today. Though Muhlenberg was a product of his time, he, too, became aware that his scholarly preceptor had carried the expository method somewhat beyond the limits of sublunary intelligence. On May 2, after hearing Ziegenhagen in the Court Chapel dilate on John 10.16, he wrote in his Journal, "This text was so profoundly drawn out and developed that even the chief points became too strong to be comprehended at one time." He noted elsewhere in the Journal a frequently experienced regret that the Court Preacher in the pulpit was not blessed with a greater number of "hungry and eager listeners."

Never again was Henry Melchior to be so happy, so filled with ardor for the great work ahead, so conscious of an enveloping atmosphere of friendship, security, and support.

If he missed something in London, he was unaware of it. To judge from his Journal, he was too intent on plans for the salvation of those in what he afterward led a friend to call "Pennsylvania—throne of Satan" to receive any impression at all of the literature, painting, politics, and gentlemanly society of Pope's, Hogarth's, Walpole's, and Lord Chesterfield's England. What spare time he had was spent in perfecting himself in the use of the English tongue and in writing letters to his family and patrons in the Hanover and Saxony behind him.

The time came for his departure. On May 24 he received from Ziegenhagen's hands the formal call and his credentials to Philadelphia, New Hanover, and Providence. Passage had already been taken for him on a ship, the *Georgia Packet*. The Court Preacher, in his "right fatherly way," had taken care of all the arrangements.

Muhlenberg was not to go straight to Philadelphia. He was to go first to Georgia, where, at Ebenezer, name of grace, he was to present Ziegenhagen's greetings to the Salzburgers (Protestant refugees from the archbishopric of Salzburg in Austria). Afterward he was to travel north by coastal vessel, taking the Salzburgers' "dear Pastor Boltzius" along with him to be his introduction to the Pennsylvanians.

He went down with the tide boat, on June 12, to Gravesend, where, on the following day, he boarded the *Georgia Packet* and met the company that was to share the voyage with him during the next three months and a half. On the thirteenth the *Georgia Packet* lifted anchor and set sail.

From the soft way of life to which books, lectures, and congenial religious conversation had accustomed him, Henry Melchior was rudely torn by life on board this ancient, overladen little two-masted vessel, which betrayed such a propensity for getting herself involved in whirlwind, tropical calm, and contrary winds that the captain's reckonings were found to be hopelessly out when the ship did finally get herself into fathomable water off the coast, not of Georgia, but of South Carolina.

Since England was then at war with France and Spain, and the ocean was filled with privateers, the *Georgia Packet* was armed to the teeth. It carried ten medium-sized cannon, besides an assortment of swivel guns, muskets, swords, and sabers, to say nothing of a drum—which latter turned out to be the most serviceable weapon on board. There was a drummer boy to handle the drum, but unfortunately there were no soldiers to handle the more lethal weapons. The Georgia Trustees, who had dispatched the vessel with supplies for Governor Oglethorpe, had hoped the navy might provide a warship to convoy her across the ocean; but the fortunes of war decreed otherwise. The navy could give help to Land's End, but no farther. The *Georgia Packet* must do the main hop on her own.

There were seven sailors in the crew—good fellows, on the whole, and not much given to mutiny, though once when in liquor they did slash the captain rather badly. There was a boy steward, and a captive Spaniard (a Roman Catholic) who served as cook and talked good-humoredly about religion with the Protestant missionary. In the steerage were two pious Salzburgers, Matthias Kulk and Anna his wife, with their three young daughters. There were also four tailors (one of whom, when the first powder drill was sounded, hid himself and had to be hauled out with ropes before he could be quartered to his gun), and a married woman whose husband knew how to look after her—if attempting to tear a sailor's throat out is evidence.

The captain of the warship that convoyed them to Land's End said he did not think the *Georgia Packet* would reach America. But the sea dog who captained her was a more cheerful gambler, and he thought she would. So did the rats. They stuck by the ship—stuck by it in such increasing numbers that before the voyage was over, as Muhlenberg tells us, he had to take out his handkerchief and shoo them away like flies.

The eight passengers who shared with the captain his table and the one cabin on the ship were tough morsels for the young parson to cut his eyeteeth on. Tobias Smollett, who was on the ocean himself at this time, gathering materials for his *Roderick Random,* would have found them meat more to his taste.

We can afford to spend a little time making their acquaintance, because it was in their company that Muhlenberg had his apprenticeship to the turbulent life of men adrift in more ways than one. The uncompromising method of religious attack, first fully displayed by him here on the *Georgia Packet,* was (with modifications) to become habitual with him, and we can best understand it if we see the primitive circumstances that originally provoked it.

Between him and the other passengers, when he came on board, was a wall of noncomprehension. To reach them, Muhlenberg put his head down and charged. Bluntly he told them to give up their sins. He admonished and even threatened them.

The results amazed him as well as everybody else. The wall went down. The encounter left him bruised—more convinced than ever of the depravity of man—but triumphant: the method had worked, and he would use it again. It left the others astonished and respectful. Muhlenberg and his cause were evidently something to be reckoned with. A few of the noisier ones grew silent and began to think.

It would take Geoffrey Chaucer's pen to do justice to the company of sundry folk into which the bull-necked parson with his heavenly concerns had so uncompromisingly thrust himself.

To begin with the captain: This tough-skinned worthy had little in common with the august commanders of our modern Atlantic *Queens.* He was a boisterous, rough-and-ready sea dog whose philosophy was not to stint sailors their whisky or passengers their fun. He was a "good mixer" and ready for anything: a fight in the steerage, a bawdy song on deck, or a Sunday-evening service in the cabin. He was emotional in his way, and shed tears when the crew first got soundings off the American coast. To judge from his language, he had a devil in his tongue, but he was no bully and no tyrant. There was singular equanimity in his conduct when some overliquored sailors one night tried to beat and cut him up. He took their frolic without rancor, had them put in irons (with the help of the passengers), and let them sleep it off. He relieved the Parson's constipation with small beer.

There was a London lawyer on board, a Freemason, who said he was leaving England because he found his wife and relatives there a drag on his advancement. But he was a moral man—when company, as he said, let him alone. He believed that eating the apple in the Garden of Eden betokened the sin of "irregular cohabitation." The Masons of London, he said, were respectable people who met to drink beer and discuss the Bible. He had a fencing tongue, and when Muhlenberg spoke at too great length about such things as the true meaning of conversion or the sins of dancing and "throwing ball," he asked the Parson to locate for him the Bible text, "Be not too righteous nor too ungodly." He sang off-color songs, but he read prayers well for the Pastor on Sunday evening.

Then there was a lieutenant—a bit of a blade, frolicking, joking, railing to the point of nuisance when in health, but modest and tractable, as the Pastor found, when he was seasick.

The merchant on board was a thoughtful man, with some knowledge of the human heart. He was a reformer in his way, but not one after Pastor Muhlenberg's model. He believed it better to guide and direct human nature than to try to shackle it. He enjoyed watching a good boxing bout (even though the men were, as Muhlenberg noted with pain, stripped to the waist), provided it was carried on "in an orderly and Christian way." This was not the kind of man Muhlenberg found it easy to understand, but he grew to like him.

Before the voyage was over, the Pastor observed (perhaps more as the result of his own shipboard awakening than of the merchant's) that the man of trade had signs of grace in him.

A "freedwoman" shared the cabin with the men. She had formerly been captured by the Spaniards, and was now returning home. When she came on board, there was more than a touch of the Wife of Bath about her. One night when the company in the cabin proposed to marry her to a sailor in sport, it seems not to have been the woman herself but Muhlenberg who put a stop to the foolery. She cursed and swore with the best of them when they left Gravesend, but before the voyage was over she had grown quiet. She avoided the "whoopee" and guarded her tongue.

There was to her something arresting about Muhlenberg's way. She had little reason at first to like him. In reproving sin he was sharp-tongued and persistent. But she could understand him when he stood to his gun on sight of a Spanish sail; and she could understand him, also, when he said that anything spoken against the honor of his greatest Friend, the Savior of the World, hurt him more than "a knife driven into his breast."

Loyalty to a friend—that was something within the freedwoman's experience and comprehension. As a former prisoner of war, she knew what it meant to have a friend behind the scenes. Was this religion? She had never thought of it in that way before. The idea captivated her, and she became, in her own queer way, God's champion. During the latter part of the voyage, when her tongue got loose —and it still slipped its moorings at times—it was in rebuke of those who said anything "against God."

In the cabin there was a custom's officer who had a smattering of gentility. But the Pastor found him more interested in his "honor" than his salvation. It seemed to Muhlenberg wholesome enough when he found this man one day disputing with the lawyer about "the spiritual meaning of the law"; but not when, as happened on occasion, he showed himself inclined to press argument with the aid of powder and ball. Twice Muhlenberg had to intervene to prevent a duel between the collector of customs and the exponent of the law.

The Pastor was at his best when, one day, he found a challenge had been presented and accepted between the two. He took them both by the hand, saying, "The wiser of you should beg the other's forgiveness." The simpletons, in their haste to beg pardon, forgot the quarrel.

Muhlenberg himself needs no introduction, unless it be to say that with all his faults of speech and manner (his English was still heavy and his exhortations were oppressive) he made Christian standards so real and palpable to the company on board that they came to wonder if they might not after all be the miserable worms he so frankly indicated they were. He had made the *Georgia Packet* a floating citadel of conscience in the North Atlantic.

Bad food, bad water, bad air (there was heaven's plenty of fresh air about them, if they could get to it; but to walk on deck when the wind was fresh was, as the Pastor said, like walking on the roof of a house)—all these did nothing to mollify the severity of his judgments. Not even the medicines he took to keep all snug below prevented, as he said, the expulsion of everything *per vomitum.* He was fearful of death, fearful of continuing to live. And yet he was no coward. Actual peril did not bother him. It was no boast when he noted in his Journal that the smell of powder, after they had been firing the guns one day, helped him to eat the first meal in a week with any relish. He remained to the end cheerfully interested in the military preparations on board.

There was always the expectancy of being boarded by a Spaniard. The sight of a strange sail brought at once to their ears the sound of the captain's bell, the drum, and a call to action stations. No one, of course, had much doubt about the outcome if they ever got into a fight. But it was hoped this show of preparedness would deter an enemy from coming close enough to see how little the *Georgia Packet* was to be feared.

At Portsmouth they had seen the sinister black shape of the *San Sebastian,* with its record of thirty-nine British ships taken, brought in by three English warships. But there were other privateers still roaming these waters, and the *Georgia Packet's* convoy had broken up at Land's End. Between July 10, when the *Launceston* left them, and September 23, when the sailors found bottom, at twenty-five fathoms, off the American coast, the cry "a sail" was the most dreaded of all sounds.

Their course at first was southerly, running parallel with the coast of Spain. On the evening of July 16, four large ships came into view. The captain thought it was all up with the *Georgia Packet,* but he kept his head. He had the lights extinguished, the fire put out; and he sailed a cunning course in the hope of eluding them. There was little sleep that night. In the morning the strangers were still with them. But soon they veered off, for whatever reason, and the Pastor made the ironic comment in his Journal, "We let them go quietly."

It was the same again on the nineteenth, when at noon the cry came that two ships were driving down on them before the wind. The Pastor, though sick, got up, buckled on a sword, went to his post, loaded his swivel gun, and prayed. He admitted to fear when the strangers came irresistibly down on the weather side, but he tried to cheer himself with the reflection that at worst he would soon be with his Maker. Cabin windows were barred, the cannon were pulled into position, and the captain ran up the English flag.

He held his fire until the foremost ship came within hailing distance, when he challenged it. Receiving at first no reply, he was about to fire; but fortunately the answer came in time. They were English ships, he was told, one from Genoa and the other from Gibraltar, and they had chased him only because they thought the *Georgia Packet* was a Spaniard.

A lesson was learned from this encounter that served to save their lives two months later. It happened in this way. After the *Georgia Packet* had wallowed its way, week after week and month after month, in the general direction of the southern English colonies, the drinking water gave out. It had long been in a stinking condition, for weeks it had been rationed, and more recently it had been eked out by rain water, olive oil, and vinegar. For the last few days it had been doled out drop by drop. Even the rats were desperate. Muhlenberg tells in all seriousness how they bit the corks out of vinegar bottles and dipped their tails in to lick. At night they licked the moisture off human faces. He assures us that he himself was awakened one night by a rat licking the sweat off his face. With the Salzburgers he sang songs of death and resurrection.

On September 16 they consumed their last drop—not much more than moist mud from the bottom of the water casks. That same day, they sighted two warships on the horizon, "and saw by their flags that they were English."

The problem was to get near them. A few days before, they had passed a large ship at a distance, but it had not bothered to stop. There was little hope that these vessels would take time off from their weightier war business (Spain had recently invaded Georgia) to pass the time of day with a friendly merchantman.

But the captain of the *Georgia Packet* had an idea. He turned his ship toward the Spanish parts, concealed his English flag, and showed a disposition to escape. That did it. The two warships took the bait, chased and overhauled him, and the foremost fired a shot across his bow. Then the *Georgia Packet* hove to and bawled explanations.

There were no recriminations. Immediately the two warships sent over three tuns of what Muhlenberg thankfully called "nectar."

Five days later the *Georgia Packet* reached harbor and cast anchor at Charleston, South Carolina.

But before Muhlenberg steps ashore (which he did on September 23), it will be well to look back for a moment and see what the voyage had contributed to his education.

If he was, as he called himself, "the restless conscience" of the company, they were as certainly his schoolmasters. He learned much from them.

First, was a knowledge of what he calls "the abominable and unfathomable Fall of Man." This was an impression that was to ride a little more easily on his mind after years had made him more used to it and he had nerved himself to "accept the universe." A wife and family also introduced him to some mysteries that made his outlook more tolerant and his convictions more bearable.

Second, was a realization of his own shortness of patience. That he never quite succeeded in correcting this fault was due less to lack of will than to lack of imagination: he had difficulty in putting himself in the other person's place.

And, third, was the lesson borne in upon him toward the end of the voyage, after he had observed that his exhortations and objurgations had not sufficed to make men over in a day: that it is not wise, as one of the passengers put it, "to force the fruit too much."

It was the first lesson, unfortunately, that for a time was to have the deepest influence on him in America.

CHAPTER III

PENNSYLVANIA AT LAST

A little over two months elapsed, "under the patience of God," between Muhlenberg's arrival at Charleston and his advent, half dead from exposure, in Philadelphia. The pain and disappointment which filled the interval served only to prepare him for the worse shock awaiting him on his arrival.

It had been pleasant enough in Charleston harbor, when the *Georgia Packet* sailed past the two friendly English warships anchored there, fired her cannon in salute, and received in reply a thundering welcome from the commodore's flagship. But it was different when he went ashore. Evidences of the slave trade—black slaves and half-black—depressed him.

He was informed that there were fifteen slaves to every white man in the place. He heard of revolt and massacre, of the white man's fear and consequent hatred of his black chattels, of the refusal to give them Christian teaching lest they turn upon their masters, and of the recent suppression by the authorities of a mission.

"A horrible state of affairs," he observed, "which will entail a severe judgment."

His mind was filled with longing for the three happily named stations of his call: Philadelphia, City of Brotherly Love; New Hanover, recalling the wooded hills his boyhood had known in Germany; and Providence, named for God's loving care. But the Pennsylvania of his dreams was still far away. It was not so much the miles of coastal waters that separated him from it, as the directions of Court Preacher Ziegenhagen, which were to visit first the Salzburger colony in Georgia. Savannah was a good many miles south of Charleston; and Ebenezer, where dwelt the good Pastor Boltzius, who was to accompany the young missionary to Pennsylvania and help get him settled there, was some thirty miles inland from

Savannah. Time was getting short. The season was closing. Coastal travel during the fall and winter was next to impossible.

The *Georgia Packet* needed recuperation after what she had been through. Muhlenberg learned that she would not be ready to venture the last leg of her journey to Georgia for another two weeks. He was impatient to be off, and persuaded the captain to make arrangements with the skipper of a small sloop then in harbor to have him taken down the coast at once. Accordingly, the missionary and the Salzburgers were taken over in a rowboat to the other craft with all their belongings.

On his way to the sloop, Muhlenberg had an adventure—small but ugly enough to a sensitive man. A twelve-year-old black girl tried to escape by concealing herself in Muhlenberg's company, seating herself between two of the Salzburger children, who were burned almost as black as she was by the sun, wind, and salt water of three months on the Atlantic. She was detected by Muhlenberg's innocently asking who she was. He saw her thrashed and returned to her master.

The voyage to Savannah was trying. The sloop meandered among the islands, when contrary winds permitted it to advance at all, and "lay by" when they did not. These pauses gave Muhlenberg an opportunity to visit the plantations, which he found interesting, but the delay was irritating and he grew querulous. He admonished an Irish passenger against the foulness of his language until the old fellow was driven for solace to his bottle.

"When I began to recommend the medicine for his sores and get at his conscience, he quenched it with strong drink," wrote the Pastor.

Even the Salzburgers, with whom in these narrow quarters on the sloop he was thrown much more closely in contact than he had been on the *Georgia Packet*, came under his displeasure. "Observing a number of faults in the discipline of the children," as the young bachelor records, he "kindly" brought it to the attention of the parents, who received it as kindly, albeit somewhat coolly, and promised to pray for better guidance in the future.

Mosquitoes plagued him, and on warm evenings he had to seek the shelter of the "cow-dung" smudge on deck.

It took six days to reach the town of Beaufort on Port Royal. For the skipper, this was journey's end. His home was here. He accordingly transferred Muhlenberg and the Salzburgers to a rowboat for the remaining fifty miles or so of their voyage. The rowboat proved to be a faster means of transportation than the sailboat had been, but even so it was not exhilarating. The inner channel they chose for safety went dry when the tide was out. They climbed the bank and sat under the trees till the water came back. At eleven at night they came to a trading vessel anchored in the channel. With the captain's permission they clambered aboard to enjoy a snatch of sleep. But they were on their way again by three o'clock. Their oarsmen did so well that the party reached Savannah at eight o'clock in the morning. It was now October 2.

There was delay in Savannah while Colonel Stephens, to whom Muhlenberg had a letter of introduction, made arrangements for a boat to take the party of six with their belongings up the Savannah River to Ebenezer. Muhlenberg was too impatient to wait, and went on by himself in a small boat, reaching Ebenezer on October 4.

It was no pleasure to him to learn afterward that the boat into which Colonel Stephens had stowed the Salzburgers, with all their as well as Muhlenberg's baggage, had sprung a leak and nearly sunk. Lives and goods were saved, but all Muhlenberg's things were soaked.

At Ebenezer the joy with which "dear Pastor Boltzius" greeted him was tempered somewhat by the reading of Ziegenhagen's letter, which indicated to the comfortably-settled Boltzius the hard path of duty he must take in accompanying the new missionary through the equinoctial storms to Philadelphia. Boltzius was resigned. If it was the Lord's will, he would go. But first he must take steps to assure himself it *was* His will. He and the congregation, therefore, submitted Ziegenhagen's instructions to the Lord in public prayer "for His final decision."

It is impossible to tell from Muhlenberg's Journal whether he was relieved or not at Boltzius' final defection. Certainly it cannot have been exhilarating to the newcomer to find the man appointed to be his sponsor in Pennsylvania so little eager to go with him. On the other hand, Muhlenberg recognized that Boltzius had a number of very good reasons for his hesitation. He had in Ebenezer a frail wife, two sick children, a devoted congregation, vines to plant, and other business to attend to. Besides, if he went now, he had the prospect of a most unpleasant journey.

The net result of the public prayers was that Boltzius must shoulder his cross and go. But Muhlenberg (by this time not unready to dispense with so very lukewarm a companion) did a little praying of his own.

"I saw even more difficulties," he wrote, "and therefore prayed the faithful God that He might reveal His gracious will more clearly, even if it should be in the midst of the journey."

Muhlenberg and Boltzius together took the river boat to Savannah. From there, finding no other craft to take them on, they continued in the same conveyance, with hired oarsmen and a steersman, to Charleston, where they hoped to pick up some kind of craft sufficient to take them up the coast to Philadelphia.

But at Charleston they were told the shipping season was over, and that it was unlikely they could get a boat for Philadelphia before spring. To travel by land was next to impossible, unless they were content to go without baggage, since the roads were long and swampy.

Dear Pastor Boltzius read the signs, purchased a horse, and returned to Ebenezer.

Muhlenberg stayed on, and his persistence was rewarded when, on November 1, a small sloop arrived from Philadelphia, and it was learned that the skipper planned to set out on the return journey in a few days. The skipper agreed to take the missionary along, if he insisted on it; but in all honesty, and with the backing of everyone else whose advice Muhlenberg asked, the skipper warned the Pastor against it. The ship was too small to be safe in the equinoctial storms, and it had no weapons, not even a pistol, for protection against the Spaniards. Besides, it had no conveniences. The cabin was barely large enough for three people, and, with Muhlenberg, there would be nine.

But Muhlenberg was not going to be stopped now. The worst the Spaniards and the elements could be imagined to have in store for him should no longer separate him from the pleasant land of Pennsylvania. When the ship sailed on November 12, he was aboard.

It was not a pleasant journey. The ship's company, he soon found, offered him what he called "a foretaste of hell." The men were of all nationalities, but no faith. Several of them "had been prisoners of the Spaniards and were now returning to their homes in Philadelphia." Their language, though consonant with what he afterward heard defended as "the custom of the country," was beyond anything he had met with up to that time, and there was no escaping it. There was no Spanish cook on board to match him in religious conversation, and there were no Salzburgers with whom he could sing songs of death and resurrection.

Muhlenberg's description of the voyage is one of the most vivid pieces of writing that ever came from his pen. He had entered upon the journey with earnest and prayerful determination. God's hand, he said, could be with him as surely on a small vessel as on a large one. After the voyage was over, he acknowledged God's mercy in bringing him through alive. But he admits that, before they reached Cape Henlopen, he thought God's hand might better have been employed in sinking the ship and taking him directly to His presence.

November 17, Wednesday. Rain and stormy wind continue. Our sailors have been out the whole night in the rain and sea water and are half-frozen and half-dead. . . . Our little cabin is about large enough for three men. The crew had nothing else to do, however, but to creep in with us, and they lay on top of each other, treading and pushing and jostling one another. I have been lying in my nest with all my clothes since Saturday, vomiting continually day and night. I dare not take off my clothes because of the cold, nor can I change my clothing because of the horrible movement of the ship; nor do I even have the room and the strength.

November 18, Thursday. The wind became very favorable for us and so strong that we sailed nine English miles in one hour, but the waves are too great and come into our little ship in such quantity that they threaten to sink it. Since Friday evening I have not been able to eat or drink anything whatsoever, and now I have a high fever. I asked the captain whether it were not possible to put me ashore somewhere, but he said that he could not get ashore even if I were to give him £100 sterling.

November 19, Friday. During the past night the wind was so violent that we sailed more under the water than on it. The crew again lay all over us. My fever was not so high, however, that the crew could dry themselves with it. Oh how long the minutes and quarter-hours were for me! Around me I had the soaked sailors and dreadful blasphemers, from above the rain fell on me, from below and from the sides the sea water came into my bed. In my stomach the fear of vomiting tormented me; in my blood the fever raged; on my body preyed the vermin which were an accumulation of my own and those of the crew. Only one thing comforted and sustained me in patience, and that was the thought that if the ship cracked, it would go down and carry my wretched sinful body down into the depths and let my soul come to my Redeemer. Today the wind abated and the sun shone several times.

On Thursday, November 25, Henry Melchior Muhlenberg stepped ashore in Philadelphia. The long journey was over, the goal attained.

Childe Roland to the dark tower came.

CHAPTER IV

THE HOLY WAR

Muhlenberg landed in Philadelphia at about eight o'clock in the morning. There was, of course, no one to meet him. He found an inn and deposited his baggage while he looked around. He had no letters of introduction, but, having heard in Georgia of a certain Mr. Zwifler who had gone from Ebenezer to Philadelphia some five years before, he looked him up and found him.

He could not have happened on a more communicative person. Mr. Zwifler knew all about Lutheran church affairs in Philadelphia. The congregation, he said, had split up. Most of the members (and certainly the more spiritually minded among them, said Mr. Zwifler) had gone over to Count Zinzendorf, the Baroness von Gersdorf's unfavorite nephew. Mr. Zwifler himself had written a call to that gentleman. The members of the anti-Zinzendorf party had attached themselves to the Reverend Valentine Kraft, recently arrived from Germany (after being removed, as Muhlenberg knew, for good cause from his church offices in the Duchy of Zweibrücken).

Valentine Kraft had also harnessed himself to the congregation at Providence. As for New Hanover, the third station on Muhlenberg's call, a quack doctor named Schmid (who dipped more zealously into the bottle than into the Scriptures) had got himself hired to preach. The three congregations were already supplied. Muhlenberg's certificate from Göttingen, his ordination from Leipzig, his letter from Ziegenhagen, were impressive but out of place. It would appear that the women liked Kraft, the topers liked Schmid, and for those who wanted religion there was Zinzendorf. Muhlenberg was *de trop*.

It did not appear amusing to Muhlenberg. It was for this that he had left family, patrons, and a distinguished career in Germany.

Here he was now in Pennsylvania, unwanted, alone, without a wife or intimate friend to confide in.

All his life Muhlenberg was subject to overwhelming fits of despondency. What he had just learned from Mr. Zwifler was more than enough to cause him such a spasm. But at the same time Muhlenberg had fighting blood in his veins. He was capable of a quick rebound, especially if the shock of disillusionment was a desperate one.

It is not surprising, therefore, that the news of his enemies' victorious advance did not bow the "strong thick neck" which Henry Melchior had brought with him to America. He went at once into action. That same night he left the comfortable room he had engaged in Zwifler's lodging, and went out into the rain and cold, mounted on a hired horse, in company with a stranger who knew the road to Providence and New Hanover. He was determined to reconnoiter his enemies' positions without delay.

Providence was only twenty-seven miles from the city, and New Hanover only nine or ten miles more. But deep roads and flooded streams made the journey a bad one. They got only ten miles on their way the first night. Late the next afternoon Muhlenberg had his first glimpse of Providence (or "the Trappe," as the inhabitants called it), but he scarcely noticed it. He was intent on reaching New Hanover before night, and, besides, he was suffering from cold, having been half immersed in the waters of Perkiomen Creek when his horse lost its footing at the ford.

Conferring with the deacons at New Hanover next day, he learned that Preacher Schmid was not a universal favorite. Indeed, he had pretty well broken up the congregation. Some of the members, disgusted with his "scandalous life," had renounced churches and parsons forever. Others said the fellow might drink to excess, but you had to admit he did preach "edifying sermons." No doubt it was these latter who held the opinion that a man of such proven capacity for spirituous wares should not be turned off for an interloper whose credentials said something about "salary." The way to pay a minister, these people thought, was to give him cash for services performed. Schmid was paid when he pulled a tooth, or married a couple, or baptized their child, or buried the old folks. He was paid cash for administering the sacraments. He was satisfied with this business-like procedure, and their interests were protected. If they did not want him, they did not pay him. What could be fairer?

It all seemed ridiculous to Muhlenberg. But was it so ridiculous to the community? He did not know. Humor implies a norm that has been departed from, but where was the established norm in Pennsylvania? The province had no state church, such as he was accustomed to in Germany, and no government regulations to preserve religious standards.

"In religious and church matters," he wrote, everyone has the right to do as he pleases. The government has nothing to do with it and will not concern itself with such matters. . . . A preacher must fight his way through with the sword of the Spirit alone. . . ."

Without patrons to guide him or the law to back him, yet firmly resolved to clean up the unholy mess into which Lutheran church matters had drifted in Pennsylvania, Henry Melchior picked his weapons with care, and in a few days was ready to take on all comers. He had decided not to try to rout his opponents, Kraft and Schmid, by too direct an assault upon their moral character. Their easy manners had made them popular with too many.

"Be very merry," said Valentine Kraft to him (no doubt with a glint in his eye), "lest the people mistake you for a Pietist."

The chief weapon he chose was one that came naturally to the hand of a native of Hanover: the principle of derived authority. To explain this it will be necessary to glance for a moment at something fundamental in Muhlenberg's character.

He was an evangelical, but at the same time he had a strong admixture of eighteenth-century conservatism, with its extravagant respect for authority. In the Lutheran Church, as he had known it in Germany, each branch rested for its final authority on the civil ruler and the Consistory (composed of theologians and jurists) which advised him. In Hanover the head of the church at this time was Prince George, who was at the same time King of England and sovereign of Pennsylvania.

Over Kraft, Schmid, Zinzendorf, and all the other contestants in the clerical arena who challenged his title, he claimed superior authority. He had been *sent* by His Majesty's Chaplain, Friedrich Michael Ziegenhagen. It is true that Ziegenhagen, knowing British law in the colonies, made no other claim for his own authority in sending Muhlenberg than the fact that certain Pennsylvania congregations had asked him for a pastor. That did not concern Muhlenberg. Ziegenhagen could explain his authority as he liked. It was enough for Muhlenberg that he could claim Ziegenhagen's.

We are not, of course, to suppose that Muhlenberg for ever after thought it necessary to defer to overseas authority. On the contrary, as soon as he could establish a synod in Pennsylvania, which he did in 1748, it became the recognized authority, with power to ordain, make constitutions, and try offenders against church discipline. But without such authority from Europe in the first place, he felt he could not have got himself or his church properly planted on American soil.

On Sunday, November 28, at New Hanover, Muhlenberg preached his first sermon in the Province of Pennsylvania. He recalled that it was exactly a year (making allowance for the change in calendar) since he had preached his farewell sermon at Grosshennersdorf. The congregation consisted of backwoods people from "plantations" scattered here and there, for miles around, through "the bush." Not many attended, for the weather was bad, and those who came were on horseback. They could not come on foot because the roads were too deep in mud and the streams were high and difficult to cross.

"Schmid the empiric," who had expected to preach himself, was content to take a chair by Muhlenberg's side and listen. Schmid was an amiable rascal who knew his own limitations. He put up small fight, was very polite, and said he did not want to be in Muhlenberg's way. Later Muhlenberg met him pulling teeth and preaching in Maryland.

On Monday he traveled to Providence (the Trappe) to discuss the situation with one of the deacons there. Valentine Kraft, he was told, had arrived from Germany only a few weeks before, claiming to have authority from the Consistory of Hesse-Darmstadt. His "windy boasting" had gained him quite a following among the looser-minded folk who gape at words, and the deacon, though not unfriendly to young Muhlenberg, thought he had better come to an arrangement with Kraft and divide up the congregations with him. There was room for both.

On December 1, in Philadelphia, he had his first meeting with Valentine Kraft. Kraft's weapons were the big smile and the glad hand. He welcomed Muhlenberg with pompous paternalism, saying, in the presence of others, that he would take care of the newcomer and place him in such charge as he found him best adapted to. Later Muhlenberg learned that this unspeakable "worthy," who was reported to be engaged to a teen-ager in Philadelphia and a widow in Lancaster, and at the same time to have a wife still living in Germany, had already organized a presbytery for Philadelphia and a consistory for Pennsylvania—the purpose of which, as it seemed to Muhlenberg, was to let the rascal travel round the country and carry on a lucrative "trade with the Holy Sacraments."

When Kraft proposed that Muhlenberg join his consistory and help ordain a "worthless schoolmaster" (the ordaining of "lazy and drunken schoolmasters" seemed to Muhlenberg to be Valentine's peculiar craft), the young man declined. Kraft then went into action. Finding Muhlenberg indisposed to be received as an ally, he determined to get rid of him by sending him out into the country and fixing him there. He made a show of authority and wrote a consistorial rescript ordering Muhlenberg to preach successively at Providence, New Hanover, Oley, and Lancaster. Lancaster was a long way off. The Lutherans there were looking for a preacher, and Kraft hoped the congregation would swallow the newcomer as a pike swallows a minnow.

Muhlenberg did, in fact, preach in Providence on December 12, in the senior deacon's barn. Valentine Kraft was there, bustling about with the air of a benignant factotum setting up a young protégé in life. Kraft even went so far as to read the letter from Ziegenhagen to the congregation, and they seemed to be pleased. Next day Kraft went on to New Hanover, soliciting the advice of a deacon's wife on the question of Muhlenberg's marriage: would it be best to accommodate him for wife with a city girl or "a farmer's maiden from the country." Muhlenberg, who followed his tracks, soon found out what the old sinner was up to. Kraft offered, on his own authority, to give New Hanover Muhlenberg as their pastor; but he said all arrangements must be made at once, or else he would take him away and install him at Lancaster.

This was too much. Muhlenberg assembled the congregation, showed them his call and his letter from Ziegenhagen in London. Valentine Kraft, he informed them, had not even a shadow of authority over him. The only authority he recognized was that of his London instructions and his Pennsylvania call. The congregation said they would abide by Ziegenhagen's arrangements.

He spent Christmas Day in New Hanover. In the morning he held services in the log church. In the evening he gathered the deacons and elders of the congregations of both New Hanover and Providence in his room and submitted to them "for their consideration and signatures" a document which he had written in English—the language of the country:

> We, the Elders and Presbyters and the other members of the Lutheran Protestant Congregations at New Hannover, Providence and Philadelphia
>
> (1) We testify in God and affirm by Subscription, that we have accepted with a thankful Heart the Rev. Heinrich Melchior Mühlenberg as a lawful called, ordained, and by our Supplications Sent and represent Minister of the Gospel and the Augsbourg Confession, by the Reverend Frederick Michael Ziegenhagen his Maiestis German Chaplain and Member of the Society for promoting Christian Knowledge.
>
> (2) We promise to furnish our Minister with all Necessaries what is required for his living in the lawfull Vocation. . . .
>
> (3) While we live in the last Days and in perilous Times, we will turn away from Such a Sort of Preachers, which are Lovers of their own Selves, Covetous Boasters proud, Blasphemers, unholy, having a form of Godliness but denying the Power thereof, creeping into Houses and Congregations without Vocation, 2 Tim. 3. vers. 1-6 . . ."

Those who bothered to look up their II Timothy 3.1-6, especially verse 6, would find Valentine Kraft (with a wife-to-be in every parish) so neatly impaled that his reputation has remained fixed to this day: "For of this sort are they which creep into houses, and lead captive silly women . . ."

The two flanking redoubts had now been captured, Providence and New Hanover. There remained the citadel itself, Philadelphia.

Muhlenberg carried his "acceptance" (containing the "silly women" citation) to the city, and issued a call to all German Lutherans to meet in the Swedish Lutheran Church and determine which of the two, Kraft or himself, had the better call and the better credentials. Kraft himself was invited to attend but he, having possibly looked up his II Timothy 3.6, discovered pressing business in the country. The non-Zinzendorfian German Lutherans responded to Muhlenberg's invitation, heard the reading of Ziegenhagen's letter, acknowledged Muhlenberg's ordination and call, and signed the acceptance.

Then the young champion, having disposed of Kraft, turned his attention to a more serious contender, the great Count Zinzendorf himself.

The Count was a man of stature: blameless of life, wealthy, well-born, self-sacrificing; a devoted Christian, a man of vision, and a properly ordained Lutheran minister. But Zinzendorf had his weak points, chief among which was the fact that he was not "regular." He was a Christian first and a churchman second. He was neither right Lutheran nor narrowly Moravian. Though himself an ordained Lutheran minister, he had been ordained a Moravian bishop by a minister of the Reformed Church. He subsequently renounced his bishopric, just as he renounced his title, von Zinzendorf, lest it impede his work for Christian unity in America. But the meaning of this straddling of church boundaries seemed clear to the suspicious eyes of young Henry Melchior Muhlenberg. Zinzendorf was not the man to rally the scattered Lutherans under the single banner of the Unaltered Augsburg Confession.

In temperament the two men were utterly unlike. Muhlenberg, trained in logic, devoted to form, hard in his thinking, and narrow in his loyalties, was infuriated by the expansive boldness of the Count's schemes and by the variableness of the moods in which he pursued them. Besides, the Count was passionate and he minced no words.

When they first came together, on December 30, in Zinzendorf's room, Muhlenberg met the Count's arrogance with a pertness that would seem to us today utterly inexcusable if it were not for the provocation he received.

Zinzendorf was wild with impatience at the young stranger who presumed to threaten the success in Philadelphia of the Count's noble dreams of a united Christendom—in the Moravian spirit if not exactly under the Moravian Church. Muhlenberg, on the other hand, feeling himself to be the embattled champion of the church and creed the Fathers in Halle and the Court Preacher in London had sent him to defend, was aghast at the Count's attack on the very authority on which he had staked the success of his own mission.

A few passages from the interview, presented as Muhlenberg records them, will give us a whiff of the atmosphere.

ZINZENDORF. "Mr. Zigenhagen is an archliar and hypocrite! . . ."
MUHLENBERG. ". . . I have often heard in Germany that you yourself were a liar."

ZINZENDORF. "Are you such a Lutheran as Mr. Zigenhagen is?"
MUHLENBERG. "If you had a heart or spirit without guile, you would not ask such questions."

MUHLENBERG.. "You are just what your aunt told me you were."
ZINZENDORF. "Hold your tongue about my aunt."

As a test of Muhlenberg's ability to hold his own in verbal rough and tumble with the great ones of the world, the interview was a success. But as anything else, especially as an example of the Communion of the Saints, it yielded points to a good bullfight. Muhlenberg, responding to a "polite" invitation to come and see the Count, had expected a private meeting. When he arrived he found the Count seated at a table and surrounded by his followers ("toadies," Muhlenberg called them, for he could never speak of Moravians without bile). The visitor was given a seat facing his inquisitor.

The interview opened with Zinzendorf's very natural inquiry: On what authority had the newcomer set himself up against the Count's already-established church organization in Philadelphia? The question gave Muhlenberg the opportunity to say what he continued to repeat throughout the meeting, that the authority rested on two things: Pennsylvania initiative and English sanction.

ZINZENDORF. "On what conditions are you here?"
MUHLENBERG. "I have been called and sent through the Reverend Court Preacher Zigenhagen, who had a commission from the congregation."

"Called and sent." That the call had been issued some three years past, and that it was the better part of a year since he had been sent, laid him open to the reminder that during the interval between the call and Muhlenberg's arrival, the Count had organized the Lutherans in Philadelphia on their invitation. But in his pocket Muhlenberg had a final, triumphant document, the acceptance. It was signed, it is true, by only a part of the Lutherans, and those, chiefly, who had formerly allied themselves with Kraft. But any weaknesses there may have been in the signatures to the acceptance were more than offset by the seal of overseas authority.

"My call has been signed," he said (signed, that is, by Ziegenhagen), "and I shall trouble myself no further, but just follow the instructions of my superiors in Europe."

"I hope, by God's grace," he added, "to establish some order."

These last words give the key to his life and especially to his church career in America.

CHAPTER V

THE LORD'S SHEEP DOG

The world outside Pennsylvania knows the Keystone State best for two things: the religious and political idealism of William Penn, and the industrial efficiency of modern Pittsburgh. Between these two, in the moving pageant of history, is a Pennsylvania (now all but forgotten) neither lovely nor efficient. It was a period of jostling adjustment, marked by much wrangling and quarreling, during which time the Goddess of Liberty, not yet elevated to a statue in New York harbor, was passing through the pains of adolescence.

It was this Pennsylvania, and not William Penn's, to which Henry Melchior Muhlenberg came in 1742. A brief sketch of its mental atmosphere is necessary to provide the background for the story of his life.

Since his equanimity had been much disturbed by the manner of his introduction to the colony, we might expect him to have a somewhat jaundiced opinion of it. It is well, therefore, for us to take our first impression from another source, from a traveler whose dispassionateness is less likely to be called in question. A passage from the *Travels* of Johann David Schöpf (Erlangen, 1788) will serve our purpose:

> Penn, as it seems, felt and sought to avoid all hardships which inequality among men entails, those conditions described by Rousseau, in so masterful a fashion, only long after. But experience soon taught that universal love may be easily imagined and preached, but, in a growing colony, may not so easily be practiced. However, the world had to be told in this way to what lengths brotherly love may go—of which all hearts are not equally capable, and over which self-love still holds dominion. Certainly, laws would be necessary in a society of saints, and perhaps would be nowhere more needed than where people so easily become habituated to think eccentrically—

When Muhlenberg first came to the province, the seeds had already been sown of that complex life which amazes and delights the traveler of today if he stays long enough in the Commonwealth to understand it. Among the "free inhabitants" were men of all nationalities: Englishmen, Irishmen, Scotsmen, Swedes, Frenchmen, Hollanders, Germans, "yellow Indians," and "black Africans." And there was no less variety of religious affiliations: Quaker, Church of England, Presbyterian, Mennonite, "Saturday and Sunday Anabaptist," Schwenckfelder, Zinzendorfer (Moravian), Roman Catholic, Reformed, Lutheran, and so on.

Muhlenberg found the American atmosphere "variable," and the men "unbridled." There are, he wrote, two religions in America, the Messianic and the Satanic; and he noted that the Prince of Darkness had by far the larger number of adherents.[1]

Among the Christians themselves, he found more church partisans than followers of Christ. Disputation was everywhere. Even the Plain People, the pacifists, used their tongues as swords. The Lutherans were disunited, bewildered, and bitter. Everywhere among his people he found turmoil and confusion.

"The English authorities," he wrote, "hear of tumult, strife, and quarrels among the Germans on all sides and do not know where the *nodus* lies."[2]

It was to the cleaning up of this situation that he devoted all the energies of his honest, emotional, and combative nature.

As we have already seen, he got off to a bad start in Pennsylvania. The circumstances of his arrival fixed in his mind (for some time, at least) the conviction that the province was peopled by devils. At every crossroad he found himself tilting with Apollyon, who disguised himself variously as a Moravian, Quaker, Dunker, Mennonite, or even a fellow Lutheran who had got a bee in his bonnet about some point of doctrine or church politics. His letters and journals leave no doubt about the matter.

"If a preacher or catechist has not been thoroughly converted in Europe," he wrote sadly, "we can entertain but poor hopes of him in Pennsylvania."[3]

"Pennsylvania," he wrote again, "cherishes the rottenest, subtlest sinners who in other parts of the world would be scummed off and swept out."[4]

"I well see," wrote Acrelius in answer to his letters, "that the place in which you dwell is the Throne of Satan. I shudder at your dire contestations with false brethren and false Apostles! I rejoice at the report of your victories and congratulate you on them."[5]

False apostles! There were plenty of them. No one but Rabelais could do justice to the race of vagabond preachers who at that time infested Pennsylvania, but Henry Melchior has given us some pen portraits of them that may at least serve to fasten them in our minds.

Pennsylvania teems, he said, "with a wicked and frivolous rabble and vagabond preachers and students, and the devil is raging and carrying on his slanders and calumnies against the poor Hallenses."

The tooth-pulling Schmid and the much-marrying Kraft, whom we have already met, had given Muhlenberg only a taste of the comedy to come, in which men like Magister August Wolf, "a capricious character, full of pride and self-importance,"[6] with a gift for "rhetorical flourishes," were to play important parts. There was, for one, "that filthy rag called Parson Andreae,"[7] and, for another, "that blemish,"[8] Carl Rudolph, self-styled Prince of Württemberg.

For some time the last-named bobbed up like a grinning Jack-in-the-box in Muhlenberg's face wherever he went. The fellow, wrote Muhlenberg, "passes himself off as a Lutheran preacher and roves about the whole country, whoring, stealing, gluttonizing, and swilling during the week, and on Sunday in his sermon he reviles us as horrible Pietists and refutes the Moravians in the manner of a charlatan."[9]

To drive off these wolves and herd the scattered sheep: these were the two heads of the task he had set himself.

And this was the work for which he was best qualified. Indeed, it was the only work for which, by temperament and training, he was fully prepared. He suggests as much in his own Journal, where a certain modest candor appears at times in the midst of the self-assertiveness of a man engaged in perpetual combat. Comparing himself with his colleague Handschuh, who was weak of body but strong in things of the spirit, he notes that he himself had "the strength of a horse but few spiritual and ministerial gifts."[10]

He reported a remark made to him by Mr. Gute at Pöltzig when he was about to leave for America: "When I look at your strong, thick neck, I can imagine that it will take a great deal to get a sword or ax through it."[11]

It was one of Muhlenberg's best qualities that he knew his own limitations and could (when not in combat) describe them to us with frankness and clarity.

One of the best pictures of himself he has left was written in old age and in terms describing his special aptitude for the work he actually accomplished: "The sainted 24th Count Reuss once said: 'Our Lord Jesus, the Head Shepherd, needs not only under shepherds but also sheep dogs, who must round up the sheep and goats on the pasture by barking at them, and herd them into one flock.' "[12]

If we think of Muhlenberg as the Lord's sheep dog, barking his scattered people into the proper Lutheran fold, we shall perhaps take less offense than we might otherwise do at the more than occasional nip he administered to those he regarded as straying.

His methods of work were various, but they all showed an understanding of human nature and were well adapted to the pioneer environment in which he found himself. To get rid of the "notorious rascals" who disfigured the pulpits in this "wild free land" where anyone, as he said, with enough cash to buy a black vest could set himself up for a preacher, Muhlenberg knew that his first step must be to get good trained men on the ground. "For people," as he once wrote to Pastor Hartwick in another connection, "must first have something better before they will give up what is worse."[13]

His never-tiring correspondence with the Fathers at Halle served to keep alive in Europe an interest in American missions, with the result that a long line of trained and devoted men like Brunnholtz, Schultze, and Kuntze crossed the Atlantic to help Muhlenberg lay the foundations of a strong, educated ministry for his church.

He was not himself a great preacher, but his congregations were pleased enough with what he gave them. It was his custom, as he tells us, to preach for three-quarters of an hour and then "catechize the whole congregation on the sermon."[14] The people seemed to like it. They felt they were getting something. A catechism has clear edges, and, as Muhlenberg said, "is as much a necessity for us as our daily bread . . . it is important to have a uniform set of *phrases.*"[15]

The sermons themselves, while not inspiring, were thoughtful and pleasing in the light of their day. He usually avoided personal controversies in the pulpit, for that, as he said, drove the people away. His discourses were well organized, comfortably orthodox, and well pointed in the "application." People crowded to hear him. He records that when he preached at Providence on January 16, 1743, the numbers who came to hear him were too great to be accommodated in the barn that then served for his services, and he had to preach outside under the sky, where the forest that walled in the clearing threw back a strong echo of his voice.

He was master of several languages, and preached in German, English, Holland Dutch, and Latin as occasion demanded. He was quick to adapt himself, in matter, style, and manner of illustration, to his hearers.

His greatest enthusiasm was for the building of churches, and it was an enthusiasm that was catching. Almost as soon as he reached Providence and preached in the barn, he set plans in motion for the erection of a stone church, "54 shoes long and 39 shoes wide,"[16] with a bell to summon his widely scattered people for the service. Nothing could have been better calculated to unify the congregation by exciting in them pride in their common efforts and their achievements. As early as January 5, 1743, Muhlenberg could report that they were already hauling stones to the site and had subscribed half the cost of the erection, which it was estimated would run as high as £200 sterling. Ziegenhagen in London, when he heard of the project, raised a subscription to help.

In Philadelphia it was the same. An £800 building was there projected, seventy feet in length and forty-five feet in breadth. There was to be an eighty-five-foot steeple for bells. On March 12, 1743, a lot was purchased at the corner of Fifth Street and Appletree Alley. By the beginning of June, the masons had almost completed one story. The cost, however, was frightening. Money had to be borrowed, and when enemies circulated a rumor that the church was going bankrupt, it became difficult to keep workmen on the job. Four deacons pledged their credit.

Slowly the building of St. Michael's advanced. The first public service was held within its walls on October 20, 1743, though at that time the windows were not in, the floors were not laid, and there were no seats but boards set on blocks. As late as 1745, when in January Brunnholtz preached his first sermon in St. Michael's, the windows were still not in place, and the Bible on the pulpit was covered with snow. It was August 14, 1748, before the building was finally consecrated.

But back in Providence, a *gemütlich* little town that held Muhlenberg's heart from the first, the church rose rapidly. By April, 1743, the masons were at work. On May 2 the cornerstone was laid, and the church was named Augustus, after Augustus Hermann Francke, founder of the Halle institutions and father of the Gotthilf Augustus Francke who had first given Muhlenberg his call to Pennsylvania. By August 31 the roof was completed, and on September 12 the congregation held the first service within its walls.

Two years later, on October 6, 1745, the church was consecrated, Muhlenberg conducting the service, assisted by Peter Brunnholtz, Tobias Wagner, Lawrence T. Nyberg, John Helfrich Schaum, and John N. Kurtz. A stone bearing a Latin inscription was placed over the entrance.

Sub remigio Christi . . .
Under the auspices of Christ,
Henry Melchior Muhlenberg, together
with his Council, I. N. Crosman,
F. Marsteler, A. Heilman, I. Mueller,
H. Haas and G. Kebner, erected
from the very foundation this temple
dedicated by the Society holding
the Augsburg Confession.
A.D. 1743

It is not the purpose of this book to trace the course of Muhlenberg's labors as an organizer of the Lutheran Church in America. There are many church histories that have already done that very well. It is sufficient for our purpose to say that within ten years after his coming to Pennsylvania he had gathered together and put into some order, as he tells us, twenty congregations, and that before the Revolution he was called upon to guide, advise, and organize churches of his denomination in other provinces, New York, New Jersey, and Georgia especially. Though his authority was, strictly speaking, local to Pennsylvania, it may truly be said that he did actually preside, during its formative period, over the whole Lutheran Church in America.

When he came to Pennsylvania, the great need, as he saw it, in the religious community which he was to serve was not more sentiment but more firmness: better organization, more careful discipline, and above all honesty. The German Lutherans were then in a pitiable condition. Differences in language and political background separated them from the main stream of American life. There was no administrational tie with the Lutherans either in Germany or in England, and no sound native organization had as yet grown up to take the place of the authority to which they had been accustomed in the state churches across the sea. In consequence they were scattered, milling around without much sense of cohesion or direction.

When he died, he left behind him a tightly (but democratically) organized church, which had its own authority *on American soil* for ordaining, supervising, and if necessary disciplining its ministers; a body adhering, for the most part without intolerance, to the Unaltered Augsburg Confession, and ready to join other denominations, when the time was ripe, in the modern crusade for Christian unity.

In accomplishing his mission to drive off the wolves and round up the flock, the methods he used, let us admit, were often crude. The suspicions and jealousies he felt within himself sometimes stirred up in others a bitterness that could not be assuaged. He was unjust to some men, notably Count Zinzendorf, and, to a lesser degree, Caspar Stoever. But he left behind him a sound church body capable, under gentler hands than his, of developing among its members certain spiritual qualities he himself only dimly apprehended.

AUGUSTUS CHURCH

CHAPTER VI

ANNA MARIA

There were two Henry Melchior Muhlenbergs. One was the great church organizer, stern, precise, and logical, a devotee of order and decorum, the Patriarch of the Lutheran Church in America. The other was the man who fell in love with Anna Maria Weiser.

If he had married, as he tries to make out in his letter on the subject to the Fathers at Halle,[1] solely with a view to the advancement of his church work in Pennsylvania, he would surely not, in 1745, have married a daughter of Conrad Weiser.

Weiser, it is true, had standing with the powers that be. In after years Muhlenberg could say with pride to Chief Justice Delancey of New York, "My wife is Conrad Weiser's daughter."[2] Weiser was a man of ability and integrity, with a high reputation in government circles for his understanding of the Indians and for his success in dealing with them, especially with the formidable Six Nations of New York, who held suzerainty over the Indians of Pennsylvania and title to much of the land in the province. But he was a freedom-loving child of nature: grotesque, original, incalculable; a man of variable temperament, explosive in his angers, adventurous, romantic, and, as far as Lutheran conformity was concerned, simply a backslider. He had left his mother church, the Lutheran, to join the monastic cult of the Seventh Day German Baptists at Ephrata, where he became "a priest after the order of Melchizedek"; and later he left the "Seventh Dayers" to associate himself with Count Zinzendorf and the Moravians. In 1745, although his attachment to the "Zinzendorfers" was waning, he was still devoted to the ideals they preached, and assisted in the establishment of their Indian missions. At the same time he was in some measure attracted by the religion of nature practiced by the best of his Indian comrades, and he remained all his life deeply suspicious of the formal creeds and disciplines of the established churches.

Anna Maria had been educated among the Moravians. Her brothers and sisters had little of intellectual companionship to offer a student from Göttingen and Halle. It was Anna Maria herself that he wanted, not a connection with her family. His choice was sound, because she appealed to the inarticulate best side of his own nature. Besides "the imperishable richness of a meek and quiet spirit"[3]—that "ornament of womanhood" which his conscious mind recognized and approved in her—she possessed other qualities which touched a still deeper chord. She had her father's warmth, boldness, and generosity of outlook. She carried within her a spark that was to give flame to Henry Melchior's children.

If he had married a wife less nervous and imaginative, it would be difficult to account for his sons, Peter, Frederick, and Henry Ernest. All three boys began their careers as their father wished them to do. They were clergymen, efficient within the narrow circle of duties their father had prepared for them. They preached and catechised and immersed themselves in the petty politics of congregational factions. But there was something within them that could not be bound by the walls their father thought sufficient to contain them. To his great grief, Peter became a Revolutionary soldier, Frederick a Revolutionary politician; and Henry Ernest, though he never forsook the church, reached out to enlarge the bounds of science. They could not help themselves. Through their mother's blood they had inherited the dynamism of Conrad Weiser.

Little is known of Muhlenberg's courtship. His Journal, designed for the information of the Fathers in Halle and the edification of his descendants, leaves no record. Anna Maria, although unlike her mother she could read and write, has left neither journal nor love letters to satisfy our curiosity.

The best picture of the courtship is a not too romantic sketch found in a letter written in 1768 by Henry Melchior to his friend Pasche on the other side of the ocean, requesting that his two younger sons, then at Halle, should be taught singing and piano:

"I earned my board, made friends, and convinced old Weiser's sensibilities, so that he gave me his daughter as a wife, or helpmate, because at my first visit, I played and sang the edifying Halle songs on his house-organ. Sometimes a hard heart can be thus softened and an entrance gradually won for the word of God."[4]

We know that his courtship was not a long drawn-out affair. One can imagine that the heart of the maiden, who lived "back of beyond" on the wrong side of the Schuylkill River, in the Tulpehocken Valley, was quickly touched when the protégé of Count Reuss and Baroness von Gersdorf, the emissary from the Fathers at Halle and Court Preacher Ziegenhagen in London, began to show her attention. She may not have been much impressed by narratives of his victories over Zinzendorf, from whom she had received much kindness, or by stories of his discomfiture of Kraft and Schmid and Stoever and the rest of those who opposed him. But she was certainly interested in his accounts of the stone church he had built in the Trappe, fifty-four "shoes" long and thirty-nine "shoes" wide, beside the Great Road to Philadelphia, and of the near-by thirty-three acres he had acquired for his own estate. There was a spring there in a hollow, like the Weiser's spring at Tulpehocken, and beside it a perfect site for a home. The house would be built, said Henry Melchior, as soon as she consented to preside at his table.

If Anna Maria was like her father in this as she was in other ways, she made up her mind quickly. But again, if she was like her father (who, in important matters, said Henry Melchior, "has a wise head and does not commit himself"), she did not disclose her mind too suddenly. Muhlenberg's feeling of triumph at the outcome of his suit, a feeling which penetrates the cold report of these proceedings later sent by him to Halle, is evidence that there was grave competition for her hand. Pyrlaeus, who had studied Mohawk in her father's house, thought she should have given her hand to a Moravian. But in the end Maria and her father gave their consent. On Friday, April 22, 1745, she left her father's house and was married to Henry Melchior by Pastor Tobias Wagner in Christ Church, which stands in a grove near Stouchsburg, between Womelsdorf and Myerstown on the Benjamin Franklin Highway.

The house at the Trappe (her husband *would* call the place Providence) was all she could have dreamed of. Her father's house, built soon after his arrival in 1729 in Pennsylvania, was large for the time and its community. But, in accordance with the custom of the country, it had only one room besides the attic. Her new mansion at Providence had five rooms besides the attic. This was the house, built with Conrad Weiser's assistance during the summer after the marriage, where eight of her eleven children were to be born.

Her father's home had been a hospitable one—always full to overflowing. Besides the large family that grew up in it, there was a constant stream of visitors from the outside. The Indians who stopped there on their way to conferences in Philadelphia preferred to sleep out under the trees in the orchard, where the ventilation was better. But many a trader, missionary, and soldier, and even the Provincial Governor himself, spent the night at "Weiser's," which was for years the best-known spot between the Upper Schuylkill and the Susquehanna. The new house at Providence, besides containing the large family that grew up around her, welcomed many a distinguished visitor. The Honorable Richard Peters, Provincial Secretary and President of the Academy in Philadelphia, condescended to spend the night there before preaching, "very soundly and edifyingly," to a large congregation in Augustus Church. Another distinguished visitor (of a somewhat different stamp) was the Reverend Charles Magnus Wrangel, Provost of the Swedish Churches on the Delaware, Pastor of the Wicaco Gloria Dei (Old Swedes) Church in Philadelphia, and former Private Chaplain to King Adolphus Frederick of Sweden. He spent two days and nights under the Muhlenberg roof and delighted the Pastor and Anna Maria with his gentleness and humility.

Other visitors of all sorts drifted in and out: ministers, traders, government officials, Indians, troubled souls of all walks in life, wanderers, the homeless—"My house," said Muhlenberg, "was a sort of guest house for the scattered."[5]

Before the Muhlenbergs in 1761 left Providence to take up their residence in Philadelphia, this first Muhlenberg home, with Augustus Church near-by, had become the center of Lutheranism for all Pennsylvania. It is still a shrine to be visited not only by Lutherans but by Americans of all persuasions, because it was the home of Peter Muhlenberg, Frederick Muhlenberg, and Henry Ernest Muhlenberg, whose fame is nationwide and still growing.

Henry Melchior was proud of his house and the tract of land he owned beside it. "Although it put me somewhat in debt," he wrote,

"I now have a fairly good residence where I can raise the necessary grain for my bread, keep a horse and several head of cattle, and keep house with less trouble and work. Here, then, we have our earthly abode where we can dry our clothes a little after we have been out in the storm and rain; and we rejoice that the lot has so fallen that our home should be in Providence until we reach the true Fatherland and peace at last."[6]

Nine years later he could write with pride to Ziegenhagen and Francke, "My whole family, including children and the help who look after house and land, comes to 13 souls."[7]

He did not live in luxury—unless it be the luxury of seeing a happy and united family growing up around him, and of knowing himself to be secure in his finances and able to save a little for himself and the rest of them against the future. His parishioners at the Trappe could pay him little in the way of salary, but they were lavish enough with gifts of "victuals, grain, and household provisions."

"The dear people," he wrote, "are glad to give corn, wheat, chickens, and the like, but money is rare."[8] Elsewhere he said: "They offer so many kind gifts in the form of meat and drink that there is superabundance. They do not know how to make their good-will toward me sufficiently manifest."[9]

Providence was a good place in which to bring up the boys. There were woods to roam and rivers to fish in. John Peter Gabriel, the first child, who was born October 1, 1746, seems to have grown up with a gun and a fishing rod in his hands. He was a shy lad. In later years he was remembered as the congressman who never made a speech. As a boy his father found him diffident but not flabby. He could be patient under provocation but at the same time he was capable of surprises when his sense of justice was touched. Nature was his teacher. He learned more from the woods and the people he met in them than he did from his books.

Henry Melchior was proud of this tall, strong youth growing up on his doorstep; but at the same time he was puzzled by him and haunted by the fear that his own sins might be visited upon him in the guise of a frivolous son. Rod and gun, which seemed to symbolize the boy's ruling passion, savored too much of the world—like the ball play for which he had reprimanded the passengers on board the *Georgia Packet*.

The next child was a daughter, Betsy (Eve Elisabeth), born January 29, 1748, at a time when the physical pains of the mother were as nothing to the mental pains suffered by the father, who was undergoing one of his recurrent attacks of melancholy.

"I shall doubtless not live long enough to bring up the poor children,"[10] he wrote.

The Lord, however, had better plans for him than he supposed. He lived to see all of Eve Elisabeth's nine children born—one of whom, John Andrew Schultze, was twice to become Governor of Pennsylvania.

The second son, Friedrich, was born on the night of January 1, 1750. It was poor Anna Maria who, along with her physical pain, suffered depression this time, for her husband was away on pastoral duty. It so happened, however, that this very night her father, Conrad Weiser, returning from a journey, stopped in at the parsonage; so that, as the good Pastor said, the daughter had "some visible support at any rate."

To Europe, the proud father recording this event, wrote: "I humbly entreat His Reverence, Court Preacher Ziegenhagen and also His Reverence, Doctor and Professor Francke, graciously to condescend to allow me to give their names to my son at his Baptism, and to add to them the name of my father-in-law, and thus call the boy Friedrich August Conrad."[11]

On January 15, assisted by the Reverend Mr. Brunnholtz, Mr. Conrad Weiser, Mr. Vigera, and Mr. Marsteller, he administered Holy Baptism to the child with the above battery of commemorative names—a child who was to grow up to become a member of the Continental Congress and Speaker of the House of Representatives in the First Congress under the Constitution.

Sons and daughters continued to arrive regularly and with due alternation of the sexes. After Frederick came a daughter, Peggy (Margaret Henrietta), born September 17, 1751, who grew up to be a high-spirited, hot-tempered, loyal consort to the Reverend John Christopher Kuntze, founder of the German Department in the University of Pennsylvania and a professor of Oriental Languages at Columbia University in New York.

The fifth child and third son to enter the family circle was Gotthilf Henry Ernest (born November 17, 1753), who grew up to be the most like his father of all the boys—after, that is, the storms of his youth were past, for Henry Ernest had much of his grandfather Weiser's explosiveness of temper and openness of attack.

Then came Polly (Maria Catharine, born November 4, 1755), who grew up to be a quiet, gentle, considerate girl, but, as a woman, more romantic and headstrong than her family found proper. She is the "Mrs. Mary Swaine" whose virtues are recorded ("affectionate wife . . . indulgent parent . . . mild and gentle . . . of feeling") on a stone slab under the walls of Augustus Church at the Trappe.

After the birth of Polly, four of Anna Maria's children died in infancy, two in Providence and two in Philadelphia. Anna Maria never liked the city. The only one of the Philadelphia brood who survived was Sally (Maria Salome), who was born on July 13, 1766. She was still only a child at the time of the Revolution, but she fell in love with and married a Revolutionary soldier, later to be known as Congressman Matthias Richards.

Peter, Frederick, Henry Ernest, Betsy, Peggy, Polly, and Sally—these were the children by which Henry Melchior and Anna Maria gave the Muhlenberg name to all America.

CHAPTER VII

SADDLEBAG PREACHER

Henry Melchior Muhlenberg won his greatest fame as a church organizer, but it is as a country pastor that he is most to be loved. The sixteen years (1745-61) spent in his first home at the Trappe were not only the busiest but also the healthiest, happiest, and best in his career.

He loved the Trappe from the day of his arrival in Pennsylvania, even before he had seen the place. There was something folksy about the very name that appealed to him. He tells us that when he first set foot in Philadelphia and inquired the way to Providence, no one seemed able to tell him a thing about it. They had not even heard of the place. At length he ran into a German who explained the mystery: the former Providence was now popularly known as "the Trapp."

The piece of folk etymology that went with the name amused him. It seems that some early inhabitants, a man named Schrack and his wife, had built themselves a hut and dug a cave beside it in which they did their cooking and kept a small shop and a tavern. One night an English settler, having stayed over long in Schrack's cave, found himself afterward protesting to his wife that if he was late coming home it was because he had "fallen into the trap."

"Such learned etymologies we have here!" said Muhlenberg.

In Muhlenberg's congregation at the Trappe there were some fifty families scattered around through "the bush" in every direction. Writing to Pastor Boltzius in Ebenezer, Muhlenberg described the rigors of a Pennsylvania pastorate.[1] His two country churches, he said, lay ten miles apart, and the district they drew from was wide. East and west, the two families farthest apart were thirty miles from each other; north and south, eighteen miles. Preaching, catechizing, visiting the sick, baptisms, funerals—all these the Pastor had to attend to among the members of his two churches and their several filials. And traveling in these back parts, though only some twenty or thirty miles from Philadelphia, was not easy. In going about his district, he had several large streams to cross—the Schuylkill River and Perkiomen and Skippack creeks—without the aid of bridges. So many were the demands upon him that he had scarcely a day at home. Most of his time was spent on horseback.

Besides attending to the regular duties of his wide parish, he was constantly answering calls from other congregations who wanted assistance—usually against the Zinzendorfers. There were Upper Milford and Saccum, for example, in the mountains thirty miles from his home; Tulpehocken, fifty miles away; Lancaster, forty-five miles; "Yorktown" (across the Susquehanna), sixty-six miles; Raritan in New Jersey, seventy miles.

Making special visits to these distant places, as he said, "tires the body, distracts the mind, and leaves little time for meditation. . . ."[2]

"Everything has to go at full speed in this vast country,"[3] he wrote in his Journal. There was no time for books and scholarship. These he had left behind him in Germany. In America, only the "book of nature" remained open to him—things seen, heard, and felt. It is amazing that so bookish a man should have adapted himself so quickly to their teaching. He soon learned to understand—well enough, at least, for the cultivation of sympathy—the world outside the college halls he loved.

> When we study in warm rooms [he wrote], hear lectures, and work with books, we are trained in a soft way of life. We learn little of the trials and the life of poor people in their households, little of the disadvantages and advantages of their way of living. Accordingly we are not in a position to judge how hard or how easy it may be for them to combine secular and spiritual callings. . . .
>
> When I first arrived in this land, still had warm, European clothes, and was younger than I am now [he was writing in 1753], I preached in barns or transparent wooden churches during the cold winters. The poor people assembled from miles round about. They were cold and wet and wore poor, thin clothes. When I preached rather long, keeping warm as a result of my earnest preaching, I noticed that the people who sat still became increasingly restless. I was depressed and supposed that they had no real hunger for the Word of God, until I had an opportunity to put myself in the position of an auditor and listen to the preaching of one or another of my colleagues. . . .[4]

He grew milder as he grew older. But in his first years in Pennsylvania, even in his beloved Providence, the foibles of his fellow men did not merely grieve but sometimes infuriated him. The man who said he hoped his soul at death would enter the body of a favorite horse, he called a "dung worm"; and he noted with satisfaction that the horse was struck dead by lightning and the man "hanged himself in his own house."

Reprimanding a Germantown churchgoer for the drunkenness and unchastity of his wife, he was surprised to find with what difficulty it was that he escaped the husband's cane.

> The art of our necessities is strange
> That can make vile things precious.

Such experiences were a blessing to him. He learned by them that, as he said, "zeal for the truth must be moderated by Christian wisdom, and prudence seasoned with love and gentleness; otherwise it lacks judgment and causes harm."[5]

Both a sense of duty and the pressure of his own restless and uncontrollable energy drove him to travel all over the Province of Pennsylvania and far beyond her borders to investigate the so-called "confusions" that so bedeviled the Lutheran communities of the time. Sometimes these confusions developed into "tumults," as when one party in the church locked the doors against another, and, when the lock was broken (as almost invariably happened), beat up their opponents and so forced the matter into the law courts. Muhlenberg was what today is called a "trouble shooter." In that capacity he stepped into the Tulpehocken Confusion (where his father-in-law, Conrad Weiser, played an erratic supporting role), the Lancaster Confusion, and confusions in Rhinebeck, New York, Germantown, Philadelphia, the Swamp, Bedminster, Molatton, York, Pennsylvania, and Ebenezer, Georgia.

Not that he loved confusion. On the contrary, confusions made him ill.

"They spoke of the strife," he wrote of a conference held in his house. "I had a headache."[6]

But his passion for order was so strong that he presided over many a gladiatorial show in the church vestry.

"Where freedom is, there is my home," said Benjamin Franklin.

"Where freedom is *not,* there is *my* home," retorted the revolutionary zealot, Tom Paine.

So with Muhlenberg, zealot for organization. Where order was not, he made his home. And he left things better than he found them. It is true, he did not change human nature, and quarrelsome people still quarreled after his departure. But he had a gift for probing under the festering nonessentials of a dispute and exposing the cause of the infection. A surgeon is to be commended who skillfully probes and cleans a wound, even though the process may be unpleasant to the patient. Muhlenberg usually put his hurt congregations on the way to recovery—and then, half sick himself, rode home and went to bed. He was more sensitive to the sight of church uncleanness than his enemies, or even his friends, were aware.

He wore himself out by these skirmishings about the country in all seasons and weathers, making night journeys through rain and snow while his body was plagued with fever or dysentery, sometimes suffering agonies from hemorrhoids while on horseback, arriving at his destination so nearly speechless with weariness and catarrh that he could admonish angry elders and deacons only from a bed and in a whisper. When his horse could no longer carry him through the snow, he got off and walked, leading the animal. One day when the ferryboat could not get him across the Second River because of the swift current and the floating ice, he plunged his horse off the boat into the water and swam with it ashore.

Through rain and shine he kept his appointments, fearing lest the enemies of religion might cite him as an example of the parsons who "promise much but keep little."

His enemies were always very real to him and never long out of his mind. He prayed:

> Give strength that I may valiantly
> See every battle through;
> And in the struggles still to come
> Help me my foe subdue.[7]

Once during a stormy crossing of the Susquehanna, he prayed the Lord to save him lest the Moravians, who were popularly reputed to have skill in praying their enemies to death, should find cause for unholy triumph in his disappearance.

He rode to Monocacy (to fight, as he believed, the Moravians' black devil of slander and white devil of pride) through roads so deep in water that the horse had to wade almost up to its knees. He arrived at midnight "half dead, completely tired out, wet, and ill, having covered thirty-six miles within ten hours in a continuous downpour of rain."[8] After cleaning up a confusion in Saccum and Upper Milford, he rode home, making thirty miles on the last day "through rain and cold winds," in a physical condition which he calls a "muddle" of fever and convulsions.

On another trip to Saccum and Upper Milford, on a bitter cold night, he became lost in the deep snow and fell with his horse in a snow-covered swamp. He managed to get himself out but, finding the horse by now utterly exhausted, had to go ahead and make a track for the poor animal. He came so near to collapse himself that he would have given up had it not been for the thought that, if he were discovered frozen to death, his enemies would say he must have died drunk.[9]

One November night in 1748, while on the way to New Hanover, his horse got stuck on the edge of a marsh. He dismounted, fell waist deep into the bog, pulled himself out, and wandered about for two hours without knowing where he was going until at last he found a fence and followed it to a house. After a short rest there, he went on and completed his journey.

No wonder he wrote, after six years in Pennsylvania, "I am worn out from much riding; I am incapacitated for study; I cannot even manage my own household . . ."[10]

On his way to Birkensee, one night in August 1749, with two companions who had come to show him the way, he got lost on a mountain ridge. The three of them led their horses through the dark, and "crept around" miserably for hours in the bushes. He got himself stuck in wild grapevines and had to be cut loose. Tempers were lost. One of his companions, a man of pious lips, much given to interlarding his conversation with quotations from "edifying books," scratched his face in the thickets, forgot himself, and cursed his horse.

Muhlenberg, who had learned much about human nature since the days of the *Georgia Packet*, was as much offended by the man's obtrusive piety as he was by his abusive tongue, and observed to him sharply that "a good fountain does not yield both sweet and bitter water."

The real hero of many of these adventures was his "old, faithful horse," growing stiff in its joints in Muhlenberg's service during seven hard years. The Pastor nearly lost this companion one night in the icy Perkiomen. The story deserves telling in Muhlenberg's own words, betraying, as it does, an anxiety for a suffering fellow creature—with no soul to save—which does the Parson's feelings credit.

Muhlenberg was returning with a guide from Birkensee, where he had been trying to evoke order out of the confusion caused by "a rude, wild group, who had been corrupted and hardened in wickedness by the vagrant preachers."

We were soon overtaken by night and thus were unable to ride very fast; so it was eleven o'clock at night before we reached the Perkiome Creek, which is still a mile and a half from my house. To our great surprise we found that the cold weather had frozen the stream hard and that it was covered with ice. My guide's horse was unshod, so I had to go ahead and break the ice. I did this at great peril to my life, but I remained in the saddle despite the leaping and rearing of the horse. I let my companion follow in the footsteps and holes which my horse had broken. In breaking the ice my horse had always to rear up in front, and at the same time break a hole with his forefeet and keep the piece of ice on the bottom until he leaped forward with his hind feet, and in this way continue to go forward. I got over safely but, owing to the darkness of the night, I missed the outlet on the other side and came with my companion to a bank which was absolutely perpendicular and about again as high as a man.

I did not dare to risk going back again because my horse in leaping had not made an open path, but only a series of holes. We took off the saddles and with the help of some bushes clambered up on land. We resolved to make an attempt to get the horses up also. We tied the saddle girths to the bridle of my companion's horse and made him stand on his hind feet so that he could reach the top of the bank with his forefeet. We pulled, and the horse, being young and nimble, bravely helped himself with his hind feet and safely reached the bank. But when we tried to do the same thing with my horse, that was old and stiff, and had him half way up, the bridle broke and the poor beast fell backwards with all his weight into the ice and lay on the bottom in the water with his legs in the air, locked in by the ice. He will surely drown, I thought, and I gave up the poor, faithful beast for lost because I could see no way to help him. But my companion would not give up. In great haste he cut off a branch of a tree with a small knife to make a lever, sprang down with it, made a large opening in the ice, helped the horse get on its side and finally on its feet in the water. Then the horse started to go back across the creek again, breaking through the ice, but in its weakness got stuck in the middle. We put our saddles and baggage upon the one horse and set out to go the rest of the way home on foot, but we got lost in the dark thickets. We wandered around in a circle for about a half-hour, until finally the stars appeared in the sky and showed us where we were. We arrived at my house about three o'clock. Early in the morning I sent several neighbors to the stream and they found the horse still in the ice in the middle of the creek. They got him loose and brought him home half dead. I felt well enough to take care of the service on that same day, but was later stricken with illness.[11]

Muhlenberg was sorry next year to have to dispose of this same horse, which had carried him "for seven years over mountains and valleys, through thorns and thickets"; but it had to be. The Pastor had made a journey, with Conrad Weiser as his guide, to Rhinebeck on the Hudson, in order to probe the wound of a confusion. Conrad Weiser went on to Onondaga for a conference with the Six Nations Confederacy, and Muhlenberg was left to return from Rhinebeck by himself. He was afraid to attempt the wilderness without a guide, and so took the boat downriver to New York—where, indeed, another confusion was in need of the surgeon's skill. The captain of the river boat would allow no horse on board. The Pastor, accordingly, before he embarked, gave the animal to a poor man as a gift. Let us hope it had found a good master. Muhlenberg did not cease to regret its loss. He was never again to have so sure and faithful a companion for difficult ways.

Always and everywhere on his travels, Muhlenberg complained of the drinking and profanity that made night hideous around him. The inns at which he stopped and the people he met in them, gave him, as he had said before of his ship's company in November 1742, a foretaste of hell.

If his disgust seems overfastidious to us now, we should read more widely in the travel literature of that day. François André Michaux, who traveled through Pennsylvania as late as 1802, speaks of the inns he encountered with something less than enthusiasm. He found the taverns in the small towns very numerous and very bad. At Bedford his lodging was "filled with drunkards, who made a frightful uproar, and yielded to excesses so horrible as to be scarcely conceived. The rooms, the stairs, the yard, were covered with men dead drunk, and those who were still able to get their teeth separated uttered only the accents of fury and rage."[12]

Muhlenberg's travels were not all unpleasant. He had a love of natural beauty and, when pain, weariness, or danger had not subdued his taste, he found delight in Pennsylvania's Endless Mountains, as the Indians called them with an eye to their horizon-sweeping rims. Unhappily for us, it did not often occur to him that such sentiments would interest either the Fathers at Halle or his own posterity, for whom the Journals were written.

One day in March 1751 he climbed Eagle Peak in the South Mountains behind Conrad Weiser's home, and described his experience in a passage as full of genuine nature poetry as the times have to show.

> We wanted a little exercise and some fresh air, so with our friends we climbed three miles up to the highest peak of the great mountain from which we were able to see about thirty miles in all directions. The sun shone pleasantly, bright and clear, and the huge split rocks sheltered us from the raw March winds. Three eagles which probably had their nest in the rocks flew over our heads, gradually wheeling upwards in circles and climbing ever higher into the golden sea of the streaming springtime sun, becoming smaller and smaller to our eyes until finally they were almost lost from sight. The hearts and minds of us all were inspired by the sight.

He was reminded of a picture of an eagle in flight toward the sun, which he had seen in the Orphan House at Halle. Isaiah 40.31: "But they that wait upon the Lord shall renew their strength; they shall mount up with wings as eagles."

"We felt that it was good to be there," he continued, "and that we should build tabernacles, but we had to climb down again laboriously and carefully, for we were still in the world and in an earthly tabernacle."

CHAPTER VIII

PETER AND THE CHRISTIAN DRUGGIST

Henry Melchior Muhlenberg, who had so confidently offered advice, before his marriage, on the bringing up of children, found the difficulties of parenthood greater than inexperience had led him to suppose. The problem was bad enough at Providence. After the Muhlenbergs had moved to Philadelphia, where the Pastor hoped by his presence to allay the troubles simmering in the congregation of St. Michael's, it seemed to grow worse. The intoxicating air of "this wild free country" was more menacing to adolescent minds in the city than in the country.

Peter especially frightened him. Peter was a quiet, somewhat withdrawn, boy of fifteen, with none of the marks of the Einbeck scholar upon him. He was a reader, but he was not fond of his schoolbooks. He had no love of tradition, and he had little of that sense of decorum that flows from it. At the Trappe he had liked nothing so much as wandering off by himself in the woods with a gun, or exploring the fords of the Schuylkill. Now that the family had moved to Philadelphia, and the boy, entered at the Academy, was exposed to corruption "among the impudent and emancipated youth of this city," his father was deeply worried about him—and about himself. "It would be a great scandal and offense in my position, and to the ruin of his own soul, if he should fall into wild ways."

Henry Melchior wrote after this fashion as early as January 10, 1762, to Ziegenhagen in London, on whose fatherly interest he relied for help in his present difficulties. Peter himself was uncertain what he wanted to do with his life. He had been confirmed in the Lutheran Church, but there were as yet no marks of the preacher upon him. If he could not make his living by rod and gun, he leaned to medicine or business of some sort.

He had romantic dreams also of soldiering. His grandfather, Colonel Conrad Weiser, had with his battalion during the late war held Pennsylvania's Blue Mountain line against the Delawares and Shawnees. Peter, while on a visit to his grandfather's farm at Tulpehocken, had had an actual taste of war. Rumor having come that the Indians, after passing the Gaps of the Swatara, had crossed the Kittatinny or Blue Mountains and were now pouring down into the valley with rifle and scalping knife, Mrs. Weiser, in the absence of her husband (who was marching at the head of a small army of men raised overnight to meet another threat from the direction of Harris's Ferry), had fled with her children and her grandchild Peter to the town of Reading for safety. It had all been very exciting, and, nobody having at the moment been hurt, was pleasant to look back on.

The extent of the father's fears for his shy and impulsive son may be measured from a letter he wrote to Ziegenhagen after the boy had been sent to Europe. In this letter the Pastor expressed regrets that his own official duties had prevented his giving Peter as much fatherly care as he should have done. Certainly, he observed, the boy while in America had betrayed no signs of vice, "his chief fault and evil bent" being "toward hunting and fishing but not toward the gen[us] foem[inum]." However, continued the father, anticipating the worst, "if the Reverend Fathers observe the slightest evidence of that kind of thing, I humbly beg you to put him in some place where there are disciplined soldiers, under the name of Peter Weiser, before he causes any more trouble and scandal. There he can obey the sound of the drum if he will not follow the Spirit of God."

An education for the boys in Europe had for some time been Pastor Muhlenberg's dream. He wrote to Ziegenhagen, January 10, 1762, asking if he knew of any openings in London for Peter "to learn surgery, or even an honest trade," or if he thought it possible "the blessed institution" (the Orphan House at Halle) might possibly be willing to take him as a student.

This modest suggestion bore fruit. A reply came that Halle would take not only Peter but also his brothers; and the Fathers at Halle, especially Dr. Francke, would make themselves responsible for the boys. It was hoped the lads might thus be prepared to follow in their father's missionary footsteps.

Plans went ahead at the sober speed to be expected in days when an exchange of letters between America and England took from four to six months. But, by the spring of 1763, arrangements were complete. The boys were first to go to Ziegenhagen in London, from there to their father's old home at Einbeck, and thence to Dr. Francke in Halle.

On April 27, 1763, they said good-bye to their father, who prayed with them at home, and to their mother, who accompanied them to the ship. Henry Melchior had church business to attend to with Provost Wrangel of the Swedish Lutherans and could not come down to see them off. On board Captain Budden was there to receive them, and also Chief Justice Allen in whose care they were to be during the voyage. At four o'clock in the afternoon they sailed.

Henry Melchior has been criticized for sending his boys abroad at so early an age (Peter was sixteen years old, Frederick thirteen, and Henry Ernest nine), and for interesting himself too little in what happened to them afterward. The criticism (which is based on the evidence of his own Journals, in which he commonly shows himself in the worst possible light) is unjust. He sent them to a European school in order to give them the advantages of a better education than was available to them at that time in Pennsylvania. To keep them abroad was a severe and continuing drain on his resources, but he met it cheerfully. In order to pay their expenses, he had to sell all but a small part of the property he loved so much at the Trappe. While they were in Europe, he watched over them as carefully as he could from so great a distance, keeping a check, and a double check, on their welfare. The first hint we have of Peter's troubles comes from a sympathetic letter written by Henry Melchior to London.

The voyage took seven weeks. The boys landed in London on June 15, received six guineas from "His Reverence, Court Preacher Ziegenhagen"—accompanied, no doubt, with sound catechetical instruction. Crossing to Rotterdam by fishing boat on June 21, they went on to Einbeck to visit their father's family; and thence, under escort of a relative, Bense, they proceeded to Halle, where they arrived about September 1.

They were placed in the Orphan House where their father had taught. Frederick and Henry applied themselves to their books, especially languages—French, Latin, Greek, and Hebrew. But Peter's mind was elsewhere. He was averse to studying, as his brothers planned to do, for the ministry. He wanted a life of action, if not as a soldier like his grandfather in Pennsylvania and several great-grandfathers in Germany, then perhaps as a doctor (he had always been interested in the Halle medicines his father dispensed with professional skill), or even as a merchant like his father's friend, Henry Keppele, in Philadelphia.

The Fathers at Halle were kindly enough disposed to this young wildling from America. Indeed, His Reverence Doctor and Professor Francke knew just the position for him. It was providential, and he warmly presented the facts as he understood them.

It seems that the pious Archdeacon Niemeyer of Halle had a cousin, the worthy Herr Leonhard Heinrich Niemeyer, who owned and operated a mercantile establishment dealing in drugs and groceries in the great city of Lübeck, formerly one of the Hanseatic towns. Herr Leonhard Niemeyer was known to be willing to take the American youth as an apprentice, giving him food and drink, and instructing him in business and good morals, Latin and arithmetic. When the apprentice's time (six years) was up, the "worthy Herr" was prepared to outfit the boy with a journeyman's suit (coat, waistcoat, and breeches, with hat, cane, shoes, and stockings thrown in for good measure)—or one hundred marks as an equivalent.

When the contract was signed on Michaelmas Day, September 29, 1763, Peter Muhlenberg, in return for all these putative benefactions, bound himself "to serve as trade apprentice to Leonhard Heinrich Niemeyer, of Lübeck, for six years from Michaelmas this year, 1763, until Michaelmas of the year 1769, D.V., to perform faithfully his master's business and any other affairs undertaken by him, . . . arrange everything in an orderly manner in the shop, accost, and serve everyone in an obliging, polite, and cordial manner, so that their custom shall be maintained. . . . And in order to become more clever, he must pray to God diligently for His Grace and assistance . . . ; when he is sent to church, he must attend duly and reverently to the service, returning home immediately after the sermon and hymns, to read religious books and thus to end the day of the Lord in a manner well pleasing to God."

The language of the contract was well pleasing to the Fathers at Halle.

Doctor and Professor Francke, who bound himself for Peter's fulfillment of the contract "in every particular" (which included some small items about spying on his fellow servants and never leaving the house without his master's permission), was to supply the youth with clothes, at his father's expense. It was stipulated in the contract that the boy was not to be allowed pocket money. The significance of these last details will be apparent as the story of the pious grocer-druggist unfolds itself.

It was a complete "take-in." When Peter arrived at Lübeck, he found Niemeyer's mercantile establishment to be a very small grocery store with a little drug business appended. Niemeyer attended to the paregoric while Peter attended to the groceries—pouring out a glass of brandy for one customer and tying a packet of tea or sugar for another, standing on his feet at this business every day (including Sundays) till ten o'clock at night. He took his meals with the servants and attended, perforce, their "frolics," which were not always edifying. The commercial details of such a business he mastered in a month, and not another tap of knowledge did he gain in his years at Lübeck—unless it be a knowledge of human nature, and of just how much it is best to take before rebelling.

Niemeyer had memorized some pietistic patter (the *clichés,* without the "power," were easy to pick up), and he had an affability that fooled the young man, who found his master kind and accommodating with his lips.

There were, of course, times when the mask was dropped. Peter, standing in an open shop, exposed to the wind, found his thin, ragged clothing gave him little protection. Dr. Francke, who had the oversight of his clothing, had apparently forgotten that winter comes in north Germany. When Peter begged his mistress to have something mended for him, she replied that if his father did not send money he could "go naked." When he appealed to his master to let him learn bookkeeping, as promised in the contract, the old fox gave him such an answer, said Peter afterward, as he "did not wish to hear again."

If we wonder why he did not complain earlier (he told the truth in a letter to Pasche, January 2, 1766, in answer to some direct inquiries), the reason is clear enough. For one thing, he was afraid of putting complaints on paper in a letter to his father, since he knew no way of sending letters to America except through Halle, and he had good reason to believe that Their Reverences opened his mail. He was afraid that anything said to Francke might reach Archdeacon Niemeyer and through him get back to his master. He was allowed no freedom to leave the shop, no freedom even to hold a friendly conversation with customers who came into it. He was spied on. He knew he was in a trap; but, being ignorant of the ways of hypocrisy, he was at the same time actually miserable at the thought of hurting his smiling, much-promising master, who had the name of the Lord always on his lips.

Peter had no pocket money and could not even pay for any outside washing. The Niemeyer family washings were not any too frequent, and Peter, with only two shirts to his back ("one for superfluity, and another for use"), was hard put to it to keep clean—especially in winter, since it was the custom in Lübeck to dry clothes on the ground, and in a frosty winter the process was long and uncertain. Peter had to wear his shirt without change anywhere from four to six weeks.

It is difficult to believe that Peter, if he had wanted to, could not have found some way of exposing the whole wretched business to his father. But the lad was proud. He knew that he had already hurt his father by leaving Halle. It is not recorded that the Prodigal Son corresponded freely with his parents about his diet. Peter was a good sport. He ate his husks and said nothing.

Herr Niemeyer, on the other hand, was not at all averse to corresponding with the American Pastor. He wrote to him with all appearance of fatherly solicitude for the youth under his care, and asked for money to buy the boy some clothes. Henry Melchior replied generously, sending fourteen pounds on one occasion and thirty marks on another. Peter saw nothing of the money and very little of the clothing. Indeed, he heard of the transaction only by accident. Niemeyer asked also for some American "curiosities" to give to his friend, Herr Edler, another "learned apothecary" of Lübeck. Henry Melchior went to a great deal of trouble and sent some interesting things, among others a garter once worn "by an Indian King"—a relic, perhaps, preserved by Anna Maria of her father's friend, Shickellamy, the Iroquois vice-regent at Shamokin.

Henry Melchior's heart was touched by Niemeyer's religious vocabulary. The good Pastor wrote to Francke expressing gratitude for his having put Peter under so good a man, who cared for the boy's soul as well as his body. To Peter himself he sent such gifts as a cap and a snuffbox—small things but all that seemed called for after the youth's needs had been so thoughtfully attended to by the pious druggist.

The wife of Professor Francke, who was as badly taken in as the good Doctor himself, wrote encouragingly to Frau Muhlenberg in Philadelphia, August 26, 1765, after Peter had been living under prison conditions for nearly two years: "We hear constantly good accounts of your oldest son, who is in Lübeck; he is happy and his employer, Herr Niemeyer, a Christian druggist, is well contented with him. Now may the Lord rejoice the worthy parents . . ."

This hocus-pocus could not go on forever. In time "Daddy" Muhlenberg became suspicious, and made it his business to find out what was happening.

However much it hurt him to think in any way but reverently of Francke, Muhlenberg had learned enough to feel constrained to write a letter, a very secret letter—"*sub rosa rosarum,*" as he said—to the Reverend F. W. Pasche in London, telling him that the arrangements made in "all fatherly love" by His Reverence Herr Doctor Francke had not turned out well. He tabulated his reasons for the opinion:

1. A young man could learn Niemeyer's petty business in four weeks, not six years.

2. Peter had had to go in rags through the winter, wearing a shirt for weeks at a time.

3. He had been bound for six years, when four was the usual time for such apprentices.

4. He had not learned bookkeeping as promised. He had not learned Latin. He had not even learned to spell German correctly.

5. He had to eat in the kitchen, clean shoes, and listen to the servants' idle chatter.

"And," he added, in what one is pleased to recognize as the growl of a bear about to protect its young, "his master has even been heard to say in company that it cost him an anker of wine to get the American for six years."

When this last juicy morsel had traveled from London across the North Sea, as it did in good time, for the edification of the Fathers at Halle, it caused such a stirring in the dovecotes as had scarcely been heard since the Thirty Years' War.

It might be indecorous, but it would not be incorrect, to say that His Reverence Herr Doctor and Professor Francke "blew up":

> It seems as if young Mühlenberg had been set on by others, and also that some people from envy had tried to influence his father's mind against Herr Niemeyer. A plain proof of this is the fabrication that Herr Niemeyer was overheard to say that it cost him an anker of wine to get this American for six years, which is plainly and positively false, for neither the Reverend Doctor Francke, nor Herr Niemeyer, is capable of such corruption, moreover neither of them received the slightest present of coin from him. Herr Niemeyer is not a mere grocer, but a druggist, a learned apothecary. . . . In the enclosed letter of young Mühlenberg's to his father (which has been opened, in order to get more particular information of his circumstances), it is incorrectly stated that Doctor Francke had overpersuaded him. He himself had a great fancy for business. . . .

Professor Francke tried to control his simmering wrath, but it boiled over. Indeed, the fires that made it bubble seemed to get hotter as time went on (there was never a brisker fuel than these ten gallons of wine), until the mere name of Muhlenberg made the good Doctor tremble with rage. Of this we shall see more in the next chapter.

Meanwhile it is enough to observe that Professor Francke, who in 1742 had sent Henry Melchior as a missionary to America, was now, a little more than twenty years later, helping to prepare him for American independence by destroying his reverence for overseas sanctions.

Peter had vast reserves of patience, but he had his boiling point, too. It was reached when his master, the "learned apothecary," received from Francke a letter dated April 3, 1766, and relayed its contents to the victim. The letter indicated that, in the opinion of His Reverence, Peter's complaints had no real foundation; that he, Francke, admonished the boy "to give his heart entirely to the Lord";

and that he enjoined Niemeyer to instruct the lad to mend his own clothes, see that they were properly washed, keep himself clean, and eschew wearing cuffs, which he said were "unnecessary finery."

The fact that the Fathers at Halle, especially Inspector Sebastian Fabricius, began a serious investigation of the matter did not help very much. When Peter was informed that Dr. Francke had offered to pay Niemeyer a sum of money (to be charged to his father) if he would let the boy off in four years instead of six, and when Peter was again reprimanded about his washing and the wearing of cuffs, he determined to leave. The merchants of the town, he said frankly, had informed him that, under the circumstances in which he found himself, no magistrate could bind him or force him to buy time from his master.

Peter was becoming more than a little tired of the Fathers at Halle. It seemed to him that they were all so intent on protecting one another that they had lost the inclination, if not the power, to protect innocent people dependent on them. The fact is, they were too innocent themselves to believe that the honey-mouthed hypocrite, Niemeyer, could be anything but what he claimed to be: an earnest, well-meaning, but much-abused Christian gentleman, trying to do the best he could for an ungrateful apprentice.

Niemeyer's mouth, when his face was turned toward Halle, continued to dribble honey. He wrote to the Fathers in praise of his apprentice, whom he said he treated like a son of the house. The boy, he was happy to observe, never really complained and was perfectly contented. There was, of course, as there had to be, a practical note, too, in the letter. If the boy wished a change in the contract, Herr Niemeyer must be satisfied. A man has to think of his dependents. In a word, he was willing to give up as many of the remaining years of apprenticeship as Peter desired, for an indemnity at the rate of fifty thalers a year.

When he turned his face to Peter, however, its lines grew hard. He held him by force of the law, he said, and would make him serve out his time.

He presented him with a letter and instructed him to sign it:

> Since last Easter, when our oldest apprentice left, my principal has had the great kindness to allow me to eat at his table, and has also promised that, when my four years of apprenticeship are ended, he will make me

a journeyman, at the same time requiring me to remain in his shop without salary as a journeyman for those two years. I have accepted this offer with pleasure and am resolved, with God's help, to remain in Lübeck for that length of time, and I can moreover assure Your Reverence that I am now content and give up my will, by Divine Grace. . . .

Peter declined to put his name to this pious claptrap. Instead, he sent it, unsigned, to Fabricius. By this time, however, the befuddled Fathers at Halle seem to have lost all power of reading evidence or distinguishing good from evil except as a set of metaphysical propositions. They admonished Peter to look to his conscience.

Negotiations drooled on. In Philadelphia, Henry Melchior was called on to do justice to Niemeyer. The Pastor offered to pay the apothecary handsomely. Halle wrote to Peter, advising him to "commit all to God diligently in prayer." A Lübeck firm, asked to investigate Herr Niemeyer, reported him to be "a pleasant man."

In July Uriah Heep consented to sign a new contract, setting Peter free by the following Easter—on payment of one hundred thalers. In the meantime the boy was to be given four hours off every week for instruction in arithmetic and bookkeeping. Niemeyer was all smiles again (as well he might be, for one hundred thalers was a good bargain); and Peter, generous by nature, forgot the bitterness of the past months and pronounced his master in a letter to Fabricius "a very quiet and peaceable man." And, he might have added, 'umble.

The new contract was signed July 16. On August 13, a confidential clerk of the firm in Lübeck which had been handling the negotiations for Halle sent the contract to the Fathers and with it some private thoughts about the business, among other things suggesting that one hundred thalers was excessive and that Niemeyer was not to be trusted to fulfill that part of the contract which specified free time for Peter's education.

It would seem that on this same night Peter also had been doing some thinking, and that he put his thoughts into action. At least it appeared so next morning to the worthy druggist.

At four-thirty in the morning, Niemeyer's house door was heard to bang. The maid came flying to her master's bedroom with news that the American boy had gone. Springing out of bed and hurrying to Peter's room, the learned apothecary saw for himself that the ungrateful apprentice, with his clothes and his trunk, had vanished.

"It mortified me greatly," he wrote to Halle, "to have to undergo such treatment on the part of an apprentice whom I loved and esteemed so much, and to whom I had shown so much kindness and courtesy. Moreover, as is well known, the injury to my business is exceedingly great: but that I hope with certainty your Reverence will indemnify me for . . ."

What hurt the "Christian druggist" most, as appears from his letter, was that now, without the apprentice to look after his shop in his absence, he would be unable to go to church.

Dr. Francke gulped it all down, hook, line, and sinker. He wrote fiercely to Pastor Muhlenberg in Philadelphia, condemning him for having put into his son's head what he called "the idea of English liberty." He hinted at hidden and sinister reasons for Peter's sudden break: Peter had "gone astray"; he was headed for "destruction."

To turn now to the American side of the question, Peter, having once made up his mind to leave his master, had acted with decision, speed, and efficiency—qualities which George Washington was later much to admire in him, and Lord Cornwallis to deprecate. Before leaving the house, Peter had completed the details of his plan of campaign. He had somehow got in touch with a certain Captain Fiser, who was in Lübeck enlisting soldiers for a British regiment soon to sail, on garrison duty, for America. Captain Fiser knew the Muhlenbergs and was glad to help this scion of the family, who was evidently in a tough spot. He would make him "Secretary to the Regiment," ship him to America, and let him get his discharge there as soon as he landed.

On leaving Niemeyer's house at four-thirty in the morning, Peter went at once to the recruiting office, accepted the King's shilling, and sent a messenger back to the house with a note advising Herr Niemeyer not to endanger his health "by useless anger."

Niemeyer pursued his apprentice, and was at the recruiting office almost as soon as the birds were up; but it was already too late.

Captain Fiser was very accommodating, and said he would release Peter and let him go back to the shop *if he wished to go.* He enlisted no man against his will.

But Peter, when appealed to, said he would not stay in Germany "for two hundred ducats." And that was that. Peter was now the King's man.

"He would listen to no entreaty," said Niemeyer afterward. The "Christian druggist" found nothing better to do than go home and tell everyone how badly he had been treated—which he did with a piety that was not unmixed with thoughts of revenge.

He read Peter's letter of farewell. One sentence in it he pondered slowly: "Reassure for me my dear parents, whom I should certainly not have done anything in opposition to, if I had not had weighty reasons which God alone knows."

"God alone knows." That would do it, thought Niemeyer. Just a hint, and those words could be made to look like Old Scratch. He sent a copy of Peter's letter to Doctor Francke (whose susceptibility, if not to ten gallons of wine, at least to more subtle forms of influence, he knew very well), "so that," as he said, "you can see Muhlenberg's motives. . . ."

The poison worked. The sin-probing (and projecting) imagination of Doctor Francke, quick to scent evil in those who disturbed his equilibrium, toyed with the idea.

He began to write. "Secret reasons . . . infatuation . . . destruction"—the thoughts poured into his mind and he wrote them down in a letter to poor Pastor Muhlenberg in Philadelphia—a letter the consequences of which we shall consider more fully in the next chapter.

There was another passage in Peter's letter which the good druggist may have read without realizing its full significance. "I shall thankfully acknowledge, as long as I live, what you have done for me."

Niemeyer had done this for him: He had taught Peter Muhlenberg that there is a time to pray and a time to fight.

CHAPTER IX

BROKEN MIRROR

It all worked out as Captain Fiser had arranged. On September 12, 1766, Peter Muhlenberg left Lübeck for Ratzeburg. By September 29 he had reached Hamburg, from which port he sailed with Colonel Prevost's recruits for Philadelphia on the ship *Venus*, Captain Rogen.

Meanwhile, Doctor Francke had written a letter, dated August 28, 1766, to Henry Melchior Muhlenberg. We need not follow it at any length. A few barbed and poisoned sentences here and there will be sufficient to make the reaction of the Pastor and his family understandable.

"I heartily pity your Reverence," wrote Francke, "for I can well conceive the sorrow which afflicts your old age [Henry Melchior was fifty-four]. For my part, I know that I have omitted nothing, and have nothing to reproach myself with. Meanwhile I hope that the prayers and tears of his beloved parents may bring back this erring son, and that, by God's grace, you may experience more joy in your two dear sons who are here, for nothing is impossible with Him."

The somewhat dubious anticipations and consolations hinted at in the last half of the last sentence were explained a little later when the good Francke observed that Henry Ernest had threatened to run away, but that the Fathers at Halle would continue to bear their burden—in the form of Henry Ernest and Frederick Augustus.

Never did a bomb explode more neatly over its target. The boys' mother, Anna Maria, was broken by the shock and never completely recovered. She suffered the first of those recurrent seizures or paroxysms which were thereafter to make her life a misery. Henry Melchior suffered no such physical catastrophe. But his first reaction to Francke's letter was, as might have been expected of a man who was constitutionally so apprehensive and so fearful of shame, one of abject and complete humiliation. He prostrated himself before God and before Halle.

Philadelphia, December 9th, 1766.

Right Reverend, most esteemed Herr Director

Dearest Benefactor!

From your Reverence's two last letters of August a[nno] c[urrente], I see today, the 9th of December, a. c., with sorrow that my eldest boy has allowed himself to be overcome by the world, the flesh, and the devil, and gone headlong to destruction, and that the youngest one is not far behind. On the one side it mortifies and bows me to the ground with shame to find that Your Reverence and other children of God have been caused so much care, anxiety, and vexation by the sending abroad of my perverse offspring, all of which I am in no condition to make amends for. . . . What I dreaded here, has taken place in Europe. The enemy [i. e., Satan] has attained, and more than attained, his object; he has made me unfit for my office and an offense to the children of God in Europe. . . . There is nothing left for me to do but, under God's mercy, to repair to a remote congregation in the country, and there, as my nearest and most pressing duty, to keep my children at work and prayer, while I may be enabled to devote my few remaining powers to the service of a heedless congregation. Lest the cause of God should suffer harm or injury through me and mine, I shall be obliged to sever my connection with the church. . . . I recognize this as a Divine leading and as my bounden duty under the circumstances—not to flee but simply to follow the sign, and betake myself to a place where I can bring up my children rightly, and devote the rest of my strength to the good of the most abandoned of mankind. . . . If my boy had played me this trick here and enlisted, I would have sold him as a servant until his majority, or have put him in the House of Correction. . . . If he had been overcome by homesickness and longing for American garlic, he could have written to that effect, and his return after Easter, 1767, would not have been taken so amiss as this infamous desertion. And, as I am very anxious about my youngest son, who does not improve, and, as the middle one, F. A., might get homesick if he remained behind alone, I humbly beg that Your Reverence will be pleased to direct that they shall both be sent back to me at my own expense, with the new missionaries to Pennsylvania or to Ebenezer. . . . In the meantime, God's gracious providence will give me a small place, *aut in, aut sub, coelo,* where I can serve Him proportionately to my strength, can govern my household, and devote my last hours to preparations for eternity. . . . On account of this sorrowful adventure of my children, I must say, as Luther does in his translation: "Look not upon me, because I am black, because the sun hath looked upon me; my mother's children were angry with me; they made me the keeper of the vineyards; but mine own vineyard have I not kept." . . .

Your
Mühlenberg.

But that was not the end for Henry Melchior. It has been noted already, on the occasion of his landing at Philadelphia to find his three congregations stolen from him, that Henry Melchior, after one of the overwhelming fits of disillusionment and despondency to which he was prone, had the faculty of rebounding valiantly.

It should be added that these alternating waves of feeling were not the mechanical reactions of a manic depressive. They were a developing experience. In the depths he found illumination and new life.

When Muhlenberg wrote to Francke, his world was in ruins. His self-respect was gone, his career seemed to be at an end. The only reality he could grasp was the blackness that overspread his brain. It is under such conditions that some men commit suicide. But life was strong in Pastor Muhlenberg, and something within him (call it the instinct of self-preservation, religious faith, or what you will) spoke out against the blackness and called for light. It came, only a glimmer at first, and never concentrating at a definite point so that he could describe it to others or even to himself. It was an illumination rather than a point of light, or perhaps we should say a new kind of seeing rather than a fresh illumination.

Hitherto he had looked at things, even American things, obliquely, through a mirror set up in Halle. The mirror was no longer there. It had been shattered. There was no recourse but to look at things now directly, for himself.

He turned his eyes. It took a moment to adjust his focus. But when he had done so, he was surprised to find how clearly and with what sharp appraisal he could see. There was no blackness after all.

The boys were all right! But they were American boys, not German, not English, not European. It was best to see them against their own background and to judge them by American standards, which were not those of any other country under heaven.

Henry Melchior had passed through a not uncommon experience. He had, as the saying goes, "accepted the universe." With it, he had also accepted America. There was much about "this wild free country" he still disliked. Its people were restless. They swore, drank, fought, and fell in love too much. But here they were, vital, with souls to save. And it was men who understood them who could save them.

Peter came home. On January 15, 1767, he landed at Philadelphia. His father paid Captain Fiser £30 sterling to meet an advance Peter had received for clothes and maintenance, and the young man was given an honorable discharge.

Peter had liked wearing the uniform, and he had made good friends in the army. But he was satisfied to say good-bye to it. Soldiering served a purpose, but it was not a way of life Peter would choose to give himself to permanently. There was other and perhaps more congenial work to be done—where should he turn?—in business, medicine, or even (our Lady of Darkness having touched his heart as well as his father's) the Christian ministry.

Henry Melchior Muhlenberg wrote with spirit to his friends abroad, not concealing pride in John Peter Gabriel. He wished his friends in Halle and London to know that they were mistaken if they supposed the young man's measure had been taken by a petty grocer-druggist in Lübeck.

"I have sent him to a private English school here," he wrote to his good friend Pasche in London, March 29, 1767, "where he is learning bookkeeping, and making some progress. He keeps himself quiet and retired, and yet is popular among friends."

The Pastor was now confident that God's hand was resting on his son, and he was glad to have Peter stand beside him as an ally in the Holy War still raging in Pennsylvania.

He wrote again to Pasche, May 23, 1767: "Satan had bent his bow, using my son for the arrow, and was shooting off all his weapons, thinking to set the whole house on fire. But an invisible hand watched over and protected it. . . ."

Friends in Philadelphia came to Peter's assistance. It was proposed by some of them that he keep an alehouse, and Peter thought he could make a go of it. The "Christian druggist" at Lübeck had taught him the tricks. "He can make all kinds of *aqua vitae* of brandy," said his father. But Henry Melchior did not really wish to see a son of his doling out liquor in an alehouse, and Peter himself was not enthusiastic.

Other friends wanted to set him up in the grocery-drug business, with the famous Halle medicines as his specialty. For this there was some enthusiasm, especially on the part of Henry Melchior, who took pride in the cures he worked with Halle prescriptions. Henry Keppele, the Pastor's staunch friend and Peter's, offered to stand security on Peter's behalf for four hundred thalers worth of medicines from Halle.

But it was not to be. The "dear Doctor Francke," as Henry Melchior wrote to Pasche, "in a fatherly letter" (for which may the Lord forgive him) was "pleased to announce that they would not place any medicines from the Institution with such a one as Peter."

Other doors opened. The Reverend Richard Peters, after the Treaty with the Indians at Fort Stanwix in 1768, thought Peter might be useful as a missionary teacher among the Six Nations, who still held his grandfather, Conrad Weiser, "in solemn remembrance." Peter referred the matter to his father, who, however, was reluctant to see his son go, lest, as he wrote to Richard Peters, the young man might himself "turn Indian" sooner than turn the Indians Christian.

The next door that opened, Peter entered. Provost Wrangel of the Swedish Lutherans proposed to train this earnest and personable young man as a catechist and launch him as a native teacher in the American church. Henry Melchior was content. If his son did not have the scholarly background a European university might have given him, he had other qualifications which were no less important. For one thing, he knew his people.

Provost Wrangel took Peter into his home, taught him the foundations of theoretical and practical religion, and set him to taking down sermons as the Provost delivered them in his church. He gave him a tutor—Christian Streit, "a worthy youth of poor and pious parents"—who instructed him in Latin and Greek. Within a few months Peter was sent out to some of the country churches to deliver "a memorized catechetical discourse." Provost Wrangel even allowed the young man to preach in the Swedish Church at Wicaco—the Old Swede's Church.

The result was gratifying, especially to Peter's father. The church was crowded and Peter won much praise. With pride—not unmixed, however, with perturbation—the elder Muhlenberg ventured to let the young catechist preach for him at Barren Hill and Pikestown.

The results were overwhelming. Wherever Peter went, invitations were pressed on him to return. Even the Pastor's own congregation in Philadelphia petitioned to be allowed to hear him.

On the evening of Good Friday, 1768, Peter preached his first sermon in St. Michael's. His father, half sick with anxiety, stayed at home, "praying with tears to the Chief Shepherd and Bishop of our souls, that He would . . . not allow His cause to be injured through me or mine."

The church was crowded as it had never been before. After the sermon, the Elders came to Henry Melchior to congratulate him.

"Thank the Lord!" he reports them as saying among themselves, "for when the old man, now standing on the edge of eternity, retires, the Providence of God points out to us an offshoot, who will serve and comfort us in case of necessity."

This is what Pastor Muhlenberg wrote "to the Fathers in London and Halle" (attention Doctor Francke!): "Impartial, intelligent, and experienced people say that he has a pleasant tenor voice, a clear and distinct delivery, puts emphasis in the right place, is polite, quiet, and guarded in his conversation, and will have nothing to do with strong drink. . . . If a thing is of God, it will stand. . . ."

I have dwelt at length on this Halle episode, not from any desire to exploit the weaknesses of the second generation of Halle Pietism, but the better to take the measure of Henry Melchior Muhlenberg. By comparison with the men at Halle whom he had once revered, he stands out as a giant: a man with courageous common sense and the honesty of an intelligence in which self-interest has not obliterated the distinction between good and evil, and which is capable not only of seeing the facts of a given situation but of recognizing also the instruments *ready to hand* by which to deal with them.

The work which Muhlenberg did in America is the more remarkable because he had to cut the fibers of one part of his brain in order to do it. He had to renounce his reverence for Halle and his instinctive reliance on overseas sanctions. Europe, and especially Halle, had helped him to get started. But in the end he built his church on what was best in America.

CHAPTER X

FEED MY SHEEP

The years spent at Halle and Lübeck were not wasted on the Muhlenberg boys. At Lübeck, under the ministrations of Herr Niemeyer, Peter had learned how to look after himself. It is true, he might have learned the same lesson elsewhere, for apprenticeship in the eighteenth century gave opportunities, in America as well as in Europe, for sharp practice. But at Lübeck, distance from home and from the watchful care of friends who might at once have protected him put Peter on his own responsibility and taught him both patience and resourcefulness. At the same time it introduced him, with the aid of an enterprising soldier of the King, to the technique of rebellion.

The knowledge gained by Frederick and Henry Ernest at Halle was of quite a different kind. Their school and college careers gave them a good foundation in scholarship and some useful training in team play. Despite their high spirits, which offended some of their pietistic professors, they were essentially earnest youths who profited more from their training than their mentors ever knew.

Of the two, Henry Ernest made the better use of his academic preparation, the study of facts and principles. He became in America one of the leading scholars of his day. Frederick, on the other hand, profited most from the talk of professors and students, in classroom and hall. He applied this experience later to the guiding of public debate in the many legislative bodies over which he presided in America.

To both of them the habit gained at Halle of adapting themselves, in lectures or conversation, to men of equal minds but differing tastes and backgrounds, laid the foundation of their success among politicians from the thirteen colonies and scholars from all over the world.

Henry Ernest has left a list of his studies which shows what foundations Halle gave him at school and college.[1] It is of some interest to know that he had only one year of university training.

In Latin he read Eutropius, Nepos, Terence, Justin, Julius Caesar, Cicero, Livy, Ovid, Virgil, Horace, etc.

In Greek he read the New Testament, Herodotus, Thucydides, Homer, Callimachus, etc.

He read the Hebrew Bible.

At the University he attended lectures in Logic, Biblical Criticism, Theology (Dogmatic and Moral), General and Ecclesiastical History, etc., etc.

Besides these more strictly "academic" subjects, their father wished them to have training in music.

"If there is time and opportunity," he wrote, December 16, 1768, to Pasche, "I would desire them to be practiced in singing, chorals, and thorough bass on the piano, besides the *studio catechetice*. . . ."[2]

He reminded Pasche that he himself had won his wife by music.

Meantime in Philadelphia Henry Melchior was becoming worried again. The flurry of 1766, it is true, had passed, and the Fathers at Halle had for several years thereafter continued to bear the burden of Frederick Augustus and Henry Ernest with what measure of cheerfulness they could. But Pastor Muhlenberg feared Dr. Semler's lectures in the Higher Criticism might be disturbing to young and impressionable minds. Besides, Henry Melchior's strength was bending under the burden of his official duties, and he needed help. Would it not be well to bring at least Frederick back from Europe, as some friends advised, to assist his father in Philadelphia? On second thoughts, might it not be best to bring them both back? He wrote to this effect, August 23, 1769, to Pasche. "I heartily wish that, if it is the will of God and the judgment of the Reverend Fathers, my two boys could come here, the sooner the better, for I look for some support from Friedrich August, and could make Heinrich useful in the school work, for I am in a sad case, and, in my weakness, have no help for Philadelphia and Whitemarsh."[3]

It may be supposed that the Fathers at Halle were not averse to this change, for they were frankly disappointed in the Muhlenberg boys.

Director Knapp, Professor of Theology, wrote a letter dated May

14, 1770,[4] saying that he was now sending the Pastor's "two dear sons" home. They were not being dismissed, he assured their father; but there were, nevertheless, six good reasons why the Professor of Theology thought it "not wrong" to let them return immediately to America.

1. Their parents wanted them to come home.

2. The sainted Doctor Francke had, before his death (which loss to Pietism had occurred September 2, 1769) said they would be better at home.

3. The boys themselves wanted to go home.

4. It was expensive to keep them at Halle.

5. An opportunity now presented itself for their safe return home in the "desirable company" of a missionary on his way to America, the Reverend Christopher Kuntze.

6. Their souls were being endangered by some new ideas they were picking up in their studies at Halle.

Neither boy, said Director Knapp, was "fitted for the pastoral office." Henry Ernest, in particular, had too much pride:

> On a certain occasion, he was so carried away by pride and insolence, as to ill-treat an innocent little boy who stood near him, although in the presence of the preceptors and all the orphans. He had to be punished by confinement. . . . He has an unparalleled spirit, in which the elder, too, is not wanting; but the latter is by nature more tractable, and I cannot say that he has given those in authority over him any trouble. But no real earnestness has been observed in them up to this time, indeed, on the contrary, from their associates, etc., their minds appear to incline to frivolity.

What tricks the "innocent little boy" may have been playing on Henry to make him explode with such characteristic openness before all the world, the good Director does not say. He goes on to lament Frederick's and Henry's "want of sufficient knowledge" and the absence of any signs in them of real conversion. He admitted that they had "naturally good talents," and might, with industry assisted by prayer (i.e., on the part of others), be trained to venture an occasional country sermon at some such place as Barren Hill. "But as to trusting a church to them, before they are roused to greater seriousness, I could and would not advise it."

This was straight from the shoulder, and, however quaintly expressed, was on the whole sound criticism. All three boys may, like Peter, have felt God's hand upon them; but His call was not primarily to the church. Peter was cut out to be a soldier, Frederick a politician, Henry Ernest a scientist.

If Henry Melchior's theology was right, God's hand may sometimes be seen even in our blunders. All three boys entered the secular careers in which they were to be so distinguished, through the doorway of the church. They brought "altar, sword, and pen" to the service of a new nation. And it is well for us, who enjoy the fruits of that service, that their experience at the altar preceded their other careers and determined in large measure the quality of them.

From Hamburg, Frederick and Henry, in company with their destined brother-in-law, Kuntze, took ship for London, which they reached on June 21. There, on July 29, they embarked on the *Dutchess of Gordon,* Captain Win, for New York, where they arrived nine weeks later, September 22.[5] Early on the morning of September 26, they reached their father's home at Philadelphia, in what Henry calls the "very blessed land" of Pennsylvania.

Their home-coming was celebrated in a manner not quite conformable to the advice of Director Knapp, who had proposed an interval of time, industry, and prayer before they should venture a sermon at so humble a place as Barren Hill. At the earnest desire of the congregation, they were invited to hold Thanksgiving services in the newly erected Zion Church in Philadelphia, Frederick in the afternoon and Henry Ernest in the evening.

The father, as usual, was disturbed at thought of the opportunities for failure thus opened to them. The boys were young. The mature members of the congregation were undoubtedly well affected to them, but what about the great outside world, especially the boys of their own age who had once played with them and now, on the return of these polished scholars from seven years' study abroad, might be tempted to play jealous tricks and raise a tumult in the church to discredit them?

He wrote to Samuel Shoemaker, telling him of his fear lest "a Concourse of unruly Apprentices and wicked Boys might disturb us in the Worship of God Allmighty," and requesting His Worship to provide special constables "to prevent Disorder, and tumultuous Noise and Disturbance about or near the said House of Worship."[6]

On Sunday, October 7, 1770, in Zion, at the corner of Fourth Street and Cherry, Frederick Augustus and Henry Ernest preached their first sermons in America, with all necessary police protection.

"Thousands filled the church," wrote Pastor Muhlenberg to the Fathers at Halle (attention Director Knapp!), "and listened and looked as attentively as if they had never seen or heard the like before."[7]

Ordination soon followed. At Reading on October 25, Frederick and Henry Ernest received a preliminary examination in Scriptural Latin, Greek, and Hebrew. "According to the unanimous opinion of all," as it is recorded in the minutes of the Synod, "the knowledge of the younger Mühlenberg is especially admirable, considering his age and the time of his stay in Halle, that being only seven years."[8]

There followed an examination in the doctrines of the church. Questions were asked, to be answered by passages read from the Scriptures in the original tongues, and elucidated. The questions bore upon Holy Baptism, "the Being, qualities, unity, and Trinity of God," and Original Sin. The examination was carried on at first in German and afterward in Latin. Then, in the name of the Triune God, the two young men were ordained to "the holy ministerial office," and received as *Collaboratores Ministerii.*

Frederick was moved almost to tears when Pastor Jung preached on the text "Lovest thou me? Then feed my sheep."

He traveled next day to Tulpehocken, where he took up residence with his uncle, Frederick Weiser, and began his Journal.

DIARY
of
FREDERIC AUGUST CONRAD MUHLENBERG[9]

Commenced October 25, 1770, to wit, the important day of my ORDINATION to be Assistant to the Senior of the United Evangelical Lutheran Congregations in Pennsylvania.

Tulpehocken, Oct. 26, 1770.

25th. This day is and always will be to me the most important day of my life, because on it I was ordained as a co-laborer in the United Evangelical Lutheran Congregations here. Although the whole proceeding was very impressive to me, the admonition of the Rev. J[ung]: Lovest thou me? Then feed my sheep—my congregation—was peculiarly so. Lord Jesus grant me thy help; else all my efforts and labors will be in vain.

Peter, instead of coming to Reading for ordination with his brothers, remained behind in Philadelphia to attend to the congregations. It was to be two years before he was ordained, and when ordination did come to him it was in England, at the hands of the Bishop of London, and into the Church of England.

Various attempts have been made to explain this curious twist in the religious life of the Muhlenberg family. For the moment it will be sufficient for us to notice two very plausible interpretations put upon it by Dr. William Germann, who suggested, first, that Peter Muhlenberg avoided ordination in 1770 because of "a certain alienation from the Lutheran Church, born of his experience . . . with the people at Halle,"[10] and second, that his father held him back from ordination, finding him not so strict a Lutheran as his brothers.

In Frederick and Henry, whatever lingering respect for the judgment of Halle may have lain in his mind, Pastor Muhlenberg felt more confidence.

Frederick, he wrote to Pasche, "has by nature an honest heart, some experience of God's grace, a tolerably clear head, a sound stomach and moderate bodily vigor. He can endure hardships and is more accustomed to the American climate than a born European; he has a fine, clear, penetrating voice for Zion. . . ."[11]

The same voice, in after years, was to sound very well in the halls of Congress.

Henry, wrote his father, was liked for his catechization—"he can deal so wisely with young people." The father admitted that his unruly spirit had "never been rightly broken," and he feared harm from his quickness at taking up new ideas; but he hoped that the scars which Dr. Semler's lectures had left on his mind would disappear and his intellectual difficulties be smoothed out "by grace and trouble here," that is, by the practical exigencies of pastoral experience in America.

The boys were soon to have trouble and stir enough to smooth out any of the wrinkles left on the brain by Dr. Semler's Scriptural variants and emendations. Frederick soon found himself settled at the far end of the Tulpehocken region, in Schaeffers Stettel (Schaefferstown), some seventy miles from Philadelphia, with five churches in his circuit, most of them from six to ten miles distant from his lodging. Henry Ernest, after some years spent at New Germantown and Bedminster in New Jersey, was called to Philadelphia to assist his father. He took care of the outlying congregations which had been such a drain on the older man's energies. He made regular journeys to preach at Frankford ("6 Miles from here"), Barren Hill (twelve miles), Pikestown (thirty miles), and Cohansey (forty miles).

Peter, meanwhile, had received an invitation, dated May 4, 1771, to a parish at Woodstock in Virginia. His ability to preach in two languages, German and English, suited the needs of the mixed congregation in the Shenandoah Valley. Woodstock made an attractive offer which appealed alike to his love of adventure and his desire to settle down. The living, he was informed, "as established by the Laws of the Land with the Perquisites, is of the Value of Two Hundred and Fifty Pounds Pennsylvania Currency, with a Parsonage House and a Farm of at least two Hundred Acres of Extreme Good Land, with every other Convenient Out House belonging to the same, which will render it Very Convenient for a Gentlemans seat."[12]

A curious condition was attached to the call: that the incoming pastor be ordained by a bishop of the Church of England. The explanation was that the Anglican Church was the state church of Virginia, and only a minister ordained into that denomination could enforce the collection of tithes from his congregation.

It was necessary, therefore, that Peter should go to London for ordination. To Peter this was no serious obstacle, at least in point of conscience, since his father had often said that there were no doctrinal barriers between the two churches. Peter could receive ordination into the Church of England without ceasing to be a good Lutheran.

Peter sailed for London on the *Pennsylvania Packet,* Captain Osborn, Commander. He left Philadelphia, March 2, 1772,[13] after saying good-bye to his parents, wife, and other relatives—his sister Polly in particular, who, poor soul, seems to have been having emotional difficulties of her own at the time, and perhaps felt a special kinship with a brother who had had his own spell of rebelliousness at Lübeck.

After a quick voyage, Peter reached Dover, April 10, and traveled thence overland by coach. He rattled through Canterbury, Rochester, and Chatham, and between these cities enjoyed the "delightful prospect" of southern England's "gardens, fields and meadows." Arrived in London, he found lodging on Tower Hill, from which he moved in a few days to a place near the Savoy, where his father had preached in 1742.

During the weeks that followed, he made good use of his time. On April 13 he visited Thomas and John Penn, the Proprietors of Pennsylvania, and, presenting a letter of introduction from Richard Peters, was, as he says, "received very kindly by both." On Easter Sunday, April 19, he heard Mr. Pasche preach at the Savoy.

On Tuesday the twenty-first at Mayfair Chapel, in the presence, as he records, of "some of the nobility," he was ordained a deacon by the Bishop of Ely. In the King's Chapel on Saturday the twenty-fifth, he was ordained a priest by the Bishop of London.

Two days later he dined with Court Preacher Ziegenhagen, with whom his father had so long corresponded, and discussed with him the propriety (which the aging Ziegenhagen would not allow) of a Lutheran's being ordained by a bishop of the Church of England.

The very young Peter had a little difficulty in adjusting himself to Ziegenhagen's years, but he wrote that he found his father's friend "very kind, and considering his age extremely pleasant."

There was something a trifle ghostly to Peter in renewing thus his father's ancient friendship with people who were already grown "old calendar," like the traditions, the decorum, the propriety that oppressed him in the mellow but damp air of old England. He longed for the intoxicating air of the wild, free country of his birth. He haunted the Virginia Coffee House and the Philadelphia Coffee House, which the sea captains frequented.

There was delay about his return passage. While waiting, he amused himself visiting Westminster Abbey to see the monuments. He called on the Archbishop of Canterbury, with a message from the Reverend Dr. Richard Peters. On the afternoon of May 3, he preached, as his father had done before him, in the German Chapel at the Savoy. Crowds came to hear the young American.

At the Philadelphia Coffee House, on the seventh of May, he spoke with Captain Osborn, on whose ship he had hoped to return to America. Finding that the Captain could not sail before the latter part of June, he made arrangements with Captain Harry Peddington for a passage to Philadelphia at the price of twenty-five guineas.

Before he left London, Captain Osborn made up a party and took him to see "the celebrated Garrick"; but Peter does not tell us what he thought of player, playhouse, or play. His diary and correspondence have none of the color we find in the effusions of the more emotional and less inhibited Frederick.

At last, on the twenty-fourth of May, he sailed on Captain Peddington's ship from the docks of Deptford, London. There was a little accident at starting. Their vessel ran afoul of a Jamaica ship. But there was no serious damage done, the ship went on its way, and after a two months' voyage Peter found himself once more in Philadelphia, making preparations for a further journey, by land, to Virginia.

On the twelfth of August he sold his furniture, and on the thirteenth he bought a sorrel horse.[14] On his way south, he paid a visit to Frederick in the Tulpehocken region. We find that his Woodstock salary commenced on September 6, the day he left Frederick's house and started on the long journey south. It was the beginning for the young parson of ten years of the most stirring adventure.

CHAPTER XI

BLESSED BE THOU, THE LAND OF MY MOTHER

No one can be a good world citizen who is not first a good citizen of his own country, since what has no center can have no circumference. And it is universally conceded, except among the inhabitants of Bachelor Hall, that the best citizens in any country are the parents of a large family.

Henry Melchior Muhlenberg and Anna Maria, his wife, had eleven children, of whom seven grew to maturity, married, and became very good citizens in their turn.

The first of the seven children to marry was Betsy (Eve Elisabeth). On September 23, 1766, Provost Wrangel officiating, she was married to the Reverend Christopher Emanuel Schultze, one of the missionaries sent out from Halle by Francke and Ziegenhagen in 1765 to assist Pastor Muhlenberg in the American mission field.

Betsy and her husband remained for five years in Philadelphia, where Emanuel Schultze was second pastor of St. Michael's Church. Then she went with her husband to the parsonage at Tulpehocken, near the present Stouchsburg. From this center, during the remainder of his life, Pastor Schultze ministered to a number of small churches, declining, when it came, an invitation to return to Philadelphia. He was an extremely busy man, loved, trusted, overworked, and uncomplaining, the confidant of all the Muhlenberg family, especially of his father-in-law, whose letters to him provide us with much of the best information we have of the Patriarch Muhlenberg's inmost thoughts—even on so delicate a subject as the Revolution when it threatened to sweep him from his moorings.

Betsy was a tireless consort, strong-minded, patient, hard-working, and at the same time tender and sensitive to an unusual degree.

Betsy and Emanuel between them brought up as sound a race of young folk as ever came out of a country parsonage. One of the children, John Andrew, grew up to be twice Governor of Pennsylvania.

Peter was the next one to marry. On November 6, 1770, he took to wife Hannah (Anna Barbara Meyer), daughter of a successful potter. The impressionable Frederick has left us the best account we have of the wedding.

Frederick was at this time living at Tulpehocken, where he had a number of back-country churches to attend to and no helpmate to look after him in the parsonage—though he had some hopes.

On the first of November, 1770, Frederick received a letter from his brother,[1] inviting him to attend the wedding in Philadelphia as groomsman. On Sunday morning, November 4, after dosing himself with several raw eggs to relieve a cold and hoarseness, he conducted a nine-to-twelve o'clock service; and then (without eating any dinner because, as he says, in the matter of eggs he had overdone the thing and was now definitely sick) he conducted another service which commenced at half-past one. After that, he rode five miles farther to Frederick Weiser's farm (the old Weiser farmstead under Eagle Peak), where his brother Henry joined him.

Next morning the brothers set off at five o'clock, enjoyed a golden sunrise (they were both sensitive to such things), and jogged on past Pottstown and the Trappe, again without dinner, till they had put fifty-five miles behind them. Next day at noon, after traveling heavily all morning over wet and slippery roads, they reached Philadelphia, to find everyone well, excited, and happy, making a vast turmoil in the house, which had been turned quite upside down in preparation for the wedding festivities.

By evening the house had settled down to respectability, and the guests assembled. Everyone made much of Frederick, who, they had supposed, could not possibly have got down in time from his back-country parsonage. Frederick himself was shy and embarrassed. Just back from Germany, where he had spent his adolescent years, unacquainted with American customs (he had never been to a wedding), and tired after his long journey, he found the part of groomsman, which as he says was thrust upon him, a frightening one to play in the presence of "so many city gentlemen and ladies." But he carried it through playing the part of "a very important personage" to everyone's satisfaction, and enjoyed a good wedding supper afterward.

So far so good. But Frederick found the days that followed gloomy. After this small glimpse of city life and marital bliss, he found Bachelor's Hall in the country bleak. When there was no proper home of one's own to return to, country visiting could be a depressing experience. At Northkill, where he preached on Sunday, November 18, he found his parishioners uncouth. Not having read Rousseau, he thought it must be the influence of the hills and rocks upon them. The literary cult of nature, it must be remembered, had scarcely come into vogue (1770 was only the year of Wordsworth's birth), and Frederick did not look to find "beauty born of murmuring sound" in the faces or manners of his country parishioners.

He did not know whether he should be amused when a countryman, as he approached, blew his nose into his hand and then shook hands with the preacher without waiting first to wipe his fingers on his breeches. Frederick was startled, too, when, on being invited to dinner, his host berated him for not bringing his own knife for the victuals.

"You, a preacher, and do not even have a knife!"

It distressed him to see that, when the chicken appeared, the members of the family each took hold of a joint and pulled. Though this was a way to quick service, Frederick longed for the more leisurely habits of city tables.

But there was plenty to occupy him. The colonial country pastor may have suffered much, but it was seldom from ennui. He preached, catechized, confirmed, married, baptized, visited the sick, listened to gossip, was berated by the sects, and dabbled (though unwillingly) in church controversies. He traveled endless miles on his country circuit.

Frederick was a friendly soul who liked people, and enjoyed the chances and changes of what he found on the whole to be a "very good world." When in congenial company, no adventures or misadventures were too much for him. But he could not stand being alone.

At Tulpehocken he was becoming restless and despondent. He noticed the change in himself. Early in December he wrote in his diary, "I find I am becoming quite nervous, because of being left alone here."

In April 1771, he visited Peter at New Germantown. But it seems that by this time his loneliness was too deep even for his brother to lift him out of it. Its quality was changing. He was homesick for Pennsylvania, where his heart was. At the moment it was doubtful if even the gates of Paradise would have appealed to him—unless they had been located in Pennsylvania.

On returning to his native province, he wrote in his diary for April 29, 1771: "I must confess that I do not like New Jersey. It is true it was pleasant to be with my brother. But the mode of life among the Jersey people does not suit me. How glad I was when my feet again trod the soil of our highly favored Pennsylvania. Blessed be thou, the land of my mother. In Philadelphia I found everything all right."

He might well say so. In Philadelphia there was a sugar refiner's daughter. David Schaeffer, the sugar man, was an important official in Zion Church. His sons were mundane, eccentric, and to Frederick tedious; but his daughter Catharine was made in God's image.

Frederick left Philadelphia a few days later, as he tells us, "with a heavy heart." Perhaps it was the sight of the Reverend J. C. Kuntze's blessedness that depressed him with a sense of his own insufficiency. Kuntze was about to marry Frederick's sister Peggy (Margaret Henrietta).

Peggy was a spirited young damsel of nineteen, strong, practical, a good housekeeper, fond of butter and cheese. She had in her the makings of a marvelous wife and mother, but she had also a will of her own and the spunk of a Tartar.

On June 12 Pastor Kuntze wrote in haste and anguish to Betsy and her husband, with whom Frederick was then staying in Tulpehocken.

"*Die* Miss Peggy *Mühlbg,*" as it appears from Kuntze's letter, was displeased with him because he had (at the suggestion of her own mother) sent a letter to the Schultzes inviting them to his wedding. And now, it seemed, "*die Peggey*" (his spelling could not keep pace with his panic, and he misspelled Peggy's name in one way or another every time he introduced it) was "really angry" and said she would not hear a word about marriage.[2]

Marriage! To Frederick the very word was like a knell. Everyone else was getting married. Every coign of the woods round Schaeffer's Stettel echoed "marriage" to his ears. From his new but lonely parsonage here, which he entered June 17, 1771, he rode next day to Tulpehocken to attend the marriage of Frederick Weiser's daughter. On returning, July 2, from the excitements of a trip over Indian paths to the Mahanoy and the Shamokin region, "marriage" seemed to echo across the Tulpehocken Valley from the Kittatinny to the South Mountains.

Frederick received the formal announcement from his father, written July 16, that the pastor whom the worthy Fathers at Halle had not long since ordained and sent to America, where he was now third preacher in St. Michael's, John Christopher Kuntze by name, had proposed marriage to his daughter, Margaret Henrietta, and gained the consent not only of Peggy herself but also of her "poor parents" and the congregation.

Peggy's tempest was over. Again Frederick traveled to Philadelphia to witness the bliss of persons more happy than himself. This time (if we interpret rightly the meager entry in his diary) he was too overcome by melancholy to make a story of it as he had done on the occasion of Peter's and Hannah's wedding. Perhaps he found that "a sorrow's crown of sorrow" is looking on at happier things. There is nothing in his diary but this laconic entry for July 22: "This evening Peggy was married."

This could not go on forever. One last resource is left to the melancholy, desperate lover. Of this Frederick was aware, and of this he took courage to avail himself. He resolved to ask the girl he loved to marry him.

He remained at his post in the country long enough to get himself established properly at the fifth church in his circuit, Lebanon, and then on Sunday, September 15, after preaching at Schaefferstown in the morning and at Warwick in the afternoon, he set out for Philadelphia with his life's peace at stake.

He reached the city on the sixteenth and, two days later, held an interview with the sugar refiner's daughter.

The simple entry in the diary is packed with a lifetime of anxiety: "*18th.* Stopped with Miss Catharine Schaeffer to get her consent to marry me. This I secured several days later."

The next entry we find in the diary is also short, but it reads like a peal of bells:

"*22nd.* Preached in Zion."

The wedding was held on October 15, John Christopher Kuntze officiating. For their honeymoon, the couple went back to Tulpehocken.

Catharine was packed with her maid in a stagecoach along with Mr. Kucher, Mr. Kucher's wife, and Mr. and Mrs. Kucher's three children. Frederick rode on horseback by himself.

The journey was slow, the horses struggling through roads deep in mud; but the party got as far as Heidelberg in time for Frederick to preach there on Sunday afternoon.

From this point, Frederick's diary changes its tone. One no longer hears the wail of loneliness. Instead, a healthy note of comradeship is struck.

"*28th* [October]. With my wife went to Lebanon on horseback."

There are no more despondencies in the diary. Indeed, there is not much more diary. Frederick had now a better confidante than its pages had ever given him.

In September 1773, he received a call to the Swamp Church (Christ Church), at the northwest corner of Frankford and Williams streets, New York.

"In November," he wrote, "papa gave his consent. I announced this to my congregations. Soon thereafter I departed with bag and baggage, almost in midwinter. Lord bless my going out and my coming in.

"*Dec. 16.* Came to New York with my family. . . .

"*May 29th.* Trinity Sunday. A daughter, Mary Catharine, was born to me, and baptized June 3rd by Rev. Schwerdfeger. . . .

"*8th* [*August*]. Wrote to Rev. Schulze, John Gaetley, David Shaefer, and having a favorable opportunity, to Rev. Schwerdfeger, to whom I forwarded 3 pounds of snuff."

That was the last entry. The cares of a growing family, a vigorous church, and a coming revolution, put a stop to it.

Meanwhile, Henry Ernest, the youngest brother, had been established in Philadelphia with a roving commission to do the outside work. As his father had done before him, he rode up and down the country, through mud and snow, swimming his horse when the water at the fords was high, supplying for Peter when Peter traveled, supplying for Frederick when Frederick was ill, supplying for anyone else who needed him, and taking care of congregations that had no regular minister.

Henry Ernest was a strong man: an earnest, learned, dogged preacher and scholar, less imaginative than Frederick and better balanced than Peter—both less patient and less explosive. He had little sympathy for waywardness in others, as his romantic sister Polly knew only too sadly. At the same time he spared himself as little as he spared anyone else, and managed with all his preaching, riding, and catechizing to find time for his books. He was the scholar of the family.

But he was more than the scholar. He was also a man. The first hint we have that he had pondered his Genesis 2.18 ("It is not good that the man should be alone") is found in a letter from his mother to Betsy Schultze, April 5, 1774,[3] informing her (in Anna Maria's characteristically bold, flowing hand and style, running without punctuation from one page to another, but with a bounding positiveness that is a delight to all lovers of life and light) that "henrich" wanted to marry Miss Cathy Hall, soon.

Evidently Miss Cathy encouraged him, for the marriage took place on July 26 of the same year.

Henry Ernest now had a partner for life. Cathy bore him eight children, and outlived him by twenty-six years.

The marriage of the third sister, the gentle and dutiful, but also romantic and passionate, Polly, came out of the blue. At least its announcement came out of that element. It was suddenly discovered in 1775 that there was a Mr. Swaine in the family, and that he had entered it through marriage with Polly, though just when the marriage had taken place no one ever seemed to know.

There had been, it is true, some warning. Early in 1772 Henry Ernest in a cryptic letter[4] had admonished Polly against taking up with engaging strangers. Such people, he indicated, come to a bad end. Some time later Frederick wrote to Peter in Virginia, telling him that Polly had made a fool of herself and eloped.[5] But, even with such warning, the appearance of Francis Swaine in 1775 as a member of the Muhlenberg family circle was undoubtedly a shock to everyone but Polly.

Francis Swaine, without whom Polly could not live, had parents in Cork, Ireland. Little else is known about his past. He appears, when we meet him, to be a gentleman who cut quite a figure. It is true that he was very much of a ne'er-do-well, and for long years failed in everything he undertook (marriage with Polly excepted); but he failed so charmingly and with such an air of distinguished unconcern that everyone wanted to help him and everyone did. He had an infectious friendliness about him that in time captivated the rest of the family as it had already captivated Polly. At the same time he had a distinctly genteel manner, easy but superior, which constrained them all to call him "Mr. Swaine." He gave the family something to laugh at, and at the same time he gave them tone.

Little Sally, the youngest daughter, viewed all these marriages with round eyes. She was only two months old when her sister Betsy was married, and only eight years old when Henry Ernest tied the knot. But Sally's bright eyes took notice, and she launched out on the sea of matrimony at the earliest age of them all. She was only fifteen when, on May 8, 1782, she was married to Matthias Richards, a prosperous saddler of Boyertown, Pennsylvania, who had a future before him. We find him in Congress, from 1807 to 1811, and dining with Presidents Jefferson and Madison.

CHAPTER XII

EBENEZER

By 1774 Henry Melchior Muhlenberg, now in his sixty-third year, had come to feel himself in his less cheerful moods already grown old and useless. He liked to call himself at such times "a fifth wheel on the wagon."

His unsparing labors as a saddlebag preacher during his early years in America had undoubtedly worn him down. The perpetual quarrels of his congregations were a torture to his tired nerves. It seemed as if his people could make no decisions without getting into rages.

The church council at Philadelphia had split into three factions over the appointment of a third pastor. One party was for bringing in Mr. Helmuth from York, Pennsylvania; another was for calling Frederick Muhlenberg down from the Swamp Church in New York; a third was for getting Henry Ernest Muhlenberg in from New Jersey, where he was at this time serving the congregations of New Germantown and Bedminster. All this was in the open. Secretly, other divisive pressures were being exerted by Patriots and Loyalists, as the incidence of civil war began to be felt by the congregation. The rumormongers were busy. Someone who signed himself "Tacitus" left a letter at Muhlenberg's door hinting at dark reasons for the Pastor's "correspondence with Europe."

It was like a breath of fresh air to him when a request arrived from Court Preacher Ziegenhagen in London and the Reverend Johann August Urlsperger of Augsburg to undertake a journey to Ebenezer, Georgia. The purpose of the journey was to settle another confusion or, as the Fathers more tactfully expressed it, to restore the former "blessed state of the congregation."

Muhlenberg was pleased to be offered the commission, not only because it brought assurance that the Fathers still recognized him as a power in world Lutheranism, but also because it promised to give him renewed acquaintance with some of the exciting scenes of his youth. On his arrival in America, thirty-two years before, he had made the journey from Charleston to Savannah under very primitive conditions. He had visited the newly established mills of the Salzburg community and had held services in the congregation of "dear Dr. Boltzius." Dr. Boltzius was now gone, but it would be pleasant to see what progress had been made since his day in the Salzburg settlement. And it would be particularly pleasant, after all these years of routine labors in Pennsylvania, to be once more the missionary, one *sent,* especially since his old patron and friend Ziegenhagen had once again signed his credentials.

Urlsperger's original authorization had been sent as far back as December 20, 1772, empowering Muhlenberg, first, to hear the charges preferred by the two quarreling preachers, Rabenhorst and Triebner; second, to reduce to a few major heads the innumerable complaints that emanated from them—complaints about the administration of the mills, about the deed of purchase of the plantation, and from each pastor about the personal character of the other; third, to judge all matters impartially and, as far as possible, to evolve peace and order out of this, the greatest of confusions.

In further instructions, Urlsperger advised Muhlenberg to adjust the disputes over precedence which further complicated the warfare between these two disciples of the Prince of Peace.

Urlsperger's instructions, and Muhlenberg's cautious comments on them (preliminary to the investigation), may perhaps prompt some cynical reflections upon a religion of peace which occasioned the effusion of so much bad blood. Muhlenberg was to learn something in Ebenezer which it behooves the cynic also to keep in mind, namely, that while it takes two or more to keep the peace it takes only one to start a war; so that in whatever circle we may find ourselves—whether in the Lion's Club, a church, or the Assembly of the United Nations—the disturbers have an influence out of all proportion to their numbers. It is this which keeps the gentleman with the forked tail smug.

There were not, as Muhlenberg soon discovered, two disturbers at Ebenezer. There was one, Triebner. This rascal used the familiar technique of the bully: he accused Rabenhorst of the faults he wished to conceal in himself, forced his co-worker to defend himself, and then tried to get him on points. Triebner was a man of better education than some of the creatures Muhlenberg had had to root out on his first coming to Pennsylvania; but, if he had more learning, he had no more spirituality than Schmid, Kraft, Prince Rudolph of Bohemia, or the rest of the bats that flew by night in the church loft.

But Muhlenberg could not know in advance how clearly the issue was to be defined after he had been a little time on the ground. While making preparations for the journey, he was full of forebodings:

> Whoever has had experience in these matters will readily agree with me that it is extremely difficult to bring about a reconciliation and mediation between parties involved in religious disputes . . . , because each has his own proselytes who become ignorantly zealous and are inclined to argue with hands, feet, and tongue, especially in an absolutely free country where there is no such thing as subordination and the arbitrator has no power to carry out impartial and excellent decisions.

There were other deterrents to the journey. One was the problem of finding someone to take his place in the Philadelphia congregations. This difficulty was soon overcome. The three-cornered fight over the appointment having been won by the adherents of the First Pastor's youngest son, a formal invitation was sent to Henry Ernest, and, after some pressure from both of the young man's parents, was accepted. Henry Ernest came down from New Germantown to become third pastor in Philadelphia.

Another difficulty was presented by the outbreak of the Indian war, which made travel to Ebenezer hazardous. There was a possibility that Ebenezer might find itself in the danger zone. Certainly a trip by land from Pennsylvania to Georgia, such as the Pastor had at first thought of making so as to avoid the seasickness he suffered on every voyage, was now out of the question. He must think of his scalp before his stomach. If he went at all, it must be by water, memories of the hideous journey from Charleston to Philadelphia in the fall of 1742 notwithstanding.

His age, too, and the weakness that followed two serious illnesses in 1773 and 1774, were all against the trip.

But the greatest of all impediments was Anna Maria, his "poor, sick, overwearied, hysterical wife," who refused to be separated from her husband. Ever since the news had come from Halle of Peter's running away and enlisting as a soldier, and after the further shock of the Barren Hill Church affair, when Henry Melchior had very nearly gone to prison because he had underwritten a considerable part of the church debt, she had suffered from *passio hysterica*, epileptic paroxysms. The sudden seizures were always alarming, and she often injured herself in falling. Besides, it took strength to look after her when the paroxysms came.

Henry Melchior talked with her frankly. It seemed unwise for her to accompany him. On the ship and in strange houses there would be no conveniences. While on board, he himself would be ill and perhaps too weak to look after her. Without proper attendance, she might die.

But Anna Maria had a strong will and utter loyalty. Henry Melchior, "*lieber Mann*," was her husband. She would not leave him. If it was the Lord's will that he go to Ebenezer, she would go with him.

Henry Melchior tried to reason her out of this resolution. He admitted that it would be unwise to leave her with Betsy or Peggy, since their children would likely be frightened by her illness. For the same reason it would be unwise to leave her with strangers. But he proposed that she go to her mother in Reading, the "Widow Weiser," "for nursing and care."

Anna Maria would not hear of it. And we can understand her reasons. She feared to inflict herself on her mother, who was old and not strong, and might not be able to bear the burden. Indeed, the health of Ann Eve Weiser was more to be concerned about than Anna Maria herself. Daily at the Trappe the Muhlenbergs apprehended bad news from old Mrs. Weiser at Reading.

Besides, Anna Maria had made some inquiries for herself about the effect of sea voyages on such illnesses as hers. Several English women told her the sea had given them relief. That settled it.

She would go.

Henry Melchior was pleased enough with her resoluteness, in so far as it was a mark of affection; but he did not share her hopes of a cure and, knowing (as she did not) what coast travel was actually like, he was frankly apprehensive of the outcome.

What was he to do? There was the Lord's call, there was the marriage contract, and there was Anna Maria.

"But what is the profit," he wrote, "of much arguing with the weaker vessels, especially with hypochondriacs and hysterics, either with valid or invalid arguments."

A final thought came to him which seemed to answer all arguments against the journey. Perhaps this voyage was the means chosen by the Lord to deliver Muhlenberg's worn-out self—"a screech owl and bittern in the American wilderness"—and his "sick helpmate" from the ills of this world.

"Thirty-two years ago," he wrote, "divine Providence ordained that your best friend and beloved Father Ziegenhagen should send you to Eben Ezer, and now once more. Since upon your arrival in this part of the world you said 'Good morning' at Eben Ezer, it may very well be that you will also say 'Good night' in the same place."

Anna Maria went. And with her went Polly to attend her.

Through the Reverend Richard Peters, Henry Melchior obtained a passport signed by Governor John Penn. This precaution, he felt, was necessary in view of the disturbed political conditions along the seaboard, which tended to keep men's minds inflamed and suspicious.

"Even respectable people," he noted, "are occasionally looked upon as spies."

He would have been too incredulous to be disturbed if he had been told in advance the mad rumors which his own departure for Georgia was to set flying.

On August 27, he took his "sick and swollen wife" in a chaise to the port, and they went on board Captain Sam Wright's brigantine bound for Charleston. For sixteen pounds and six shillings he had bought passage and three berths, for himself, Anna Maria, and Polly. Food for the voyage, the passengers had to provide for themselves. When they came on board, they found a supply of provisions had been sent on ahead for them as a gift from their good friends Mr. and Mrs. Henry Keppele.

The Muhlenbergs received a heart-warming send-off. Members of their own family were there, and some of their oldest and best friends in Pennsylvania, including the Keppeles. Mrs. Keppele took a particularly affectionate leave of Anna Maria. They had long been close friends. Henry Keppele joined the party of fourteen who, attaching three skiffs to the brigantine, accompanied the Muhlenbergs for a distance of "five or seven" miles down the river. Peter, home on a visit from Virginia, was among them. So were Henry Ernest and Peggy's husband, Christopher Kuntze. It was a jolly party. But there were tears shed when in the afternoon Peter, Henry Ernest, Christopher Kuntze, Henry Keppele, and the rest bade them another farewell and got into their boats to row back to Philadelphia.

The Henry Melchior who entered upon this voyage was a very different man from the missionary who had come over on the *Georgia Packet* in 1742. Thirty-two years in the "American wilderness" had matured him and taken off some of his asperities. He might still call himself (in a moment of depression) "an object of loathing to the world of refined taste," but he was now more tolerant, more sympathetic, and more generous—expecting good as well as evil from his company; in a word, a more friendly and Christlike person, and a better ambassador for the religion of Jesus. He had learned to eat gracefully with publicans and sinners.

On the *Georgia Packet* he had behaved like an animal trainer in a cage, armed with a bristling chair and a whip. On Captain Sam Wright's brigantine he was more modest. He took his place as one of the group, and when he entered the general conversation he listened before he spoke. He had even learned to laugh at himself.

On the first Sunday out, he held no service, partly because, as he tells us, he was unwell, and partly because he did not wish to obtrude himself. When, on passing Cape May, they reached the open sea and ran into contrary winds, "fiendish seasickness" overcame him and Polly, but not his wife—though she, poor soul, had "just that many more attacks of *passio hysterica.*" He was too ill to write much in his Journal, too ill to observe and note down "the winds and variations." But that, he added quaintly, would "do no harm to the commonwealth," since foul and contrary winds in abundance were to be found in the writings of Voltaire and the journals of the Higher Criticism.

On the second Sunday out, having received a request from "the entire ship's company" (passengers and crew alike) to conduct a service, he found himself able to preach for three-quarters of an hour before he had to be helped down to his cabin. The passengers thanked him warmly with words, the sailors, with a mess of food sent down to his bunk—not prepared in the most refined taste, as he observed, but refreshing because it was "sweetened with good will, salted with sincerity, and seasoned with faithfulness."

They anchored at Charleston on September 8, and the three Muhlenbergs went ashore. They found much hospitality in the city and many friends, but the Pastor was as much disturbed and oppressed as he had formerly been by the evidences of slavery about him. The situation, indeed, seemed to have grown worse. Whereas in 1742 he had been told the proportion of whites to Negroes was one to fifteen, now it was one to twenty.

The journey to Savannah was interrupted for six weeks at Charleston while they waited for a boat to take them on. It was impossible to go overland to Georgia with Anna Maria in her condition. The roads were very bad. There were too many streams and rotten bridges to cross. Besides, there were no post or stage coaches. They must complete their journey, as he had done in 1742, in a small boat.

Henry Melchior felt he was fortunate in being able to arrange for their transportation in a schooner. He had had to use a rowboat in 1742. But they waited some time for the schooner to sail. By October 4 the Pastor learned that the captain of the vessel had an "inflamed" eye, and did not know when he could leave. The Muhlenbergs would have to wait.

The Pastor occupied part of his time picking up information about the Ebenezer Confusion. He learned among other things of the attempted poisoning, by putting arsenic in their coffee, of Pastor Rabenhorst and his wife. No suspicion, it seems, attached to Mr. Triebner. For the crime a Negress had been condemned by the authorities to be burned alive.

Storms beat upon the coast. None of the small vessels engaged in traffic with Savannah dared venture out. But on October 18 Captain Churchill's eye being now well enough for him to sail at two o'clock that afternoon, the Muhlenbergs packed up in a hurry and sent their things on board.

Their vicissitudes were not over yet. Toward evening they were informed that the captain's goods had been attached for debt and the vessel was not sailing. It was with difficulty that the Muhlenbergs got their own goods, which had been included in the arrest, off the ship. They picked another schooner and sent their things on board on Monday, October 24.

That same day Henry Melchior received a commission that occasioned him a good deal of embarrassment. A coach stopped in front of the Muhlenberg lodging. Out of it stepped a woman of their acquaintance, and with her a very fine lady, "widow of an English High Church minister," who was going to Savannah by the same boat and wanted Pastor Muhlenberg's "protection and attention."

The Pastor, who showed a blessed streak of shyness when confronted with furbelowed Christianity, tells us he had to do a little coughing before he could collect his wits. When he looked at the fashion plate before him, he was moved to say that he and his wife were simple people, unacquainted with the refinements of etiquette, old and infirm, and subject (he had to out with it) to such attacks of seasickness as rendered quite illusory any hopes the High Church widow might entertain of his attentions.

In his heart, Henry Melchior was amused. He knew what life was like on board these matchbox coastal vessels during the stormy season. He had sympathy for the lady, with all her finery a fellow Christian, thinking how intolerable such conditions must be to anyone so sensitively brought up as she had been. But as to dancing attendance upon her—"How would it ever be possible for me to attend to her and set things right if that artistic headdress and those innumerable folds and ribbons should ever be put out of place?"

Polly, of course, could help her, provided, that is, Polly herself were spared from seasickness.

No one was spared. But Henry Melchior remained sufficiently in command of his intellect to learn something about people. He learned that fine ladies are women first, with a woman's courage as well as her frailties. On board ship the High Church widow proved less fragile than her headdresses had seemed to presage. She was a mother (she brought her little son on board with her) and therefore not at all as unfamiliar with discomfort and pain as Henry Melchior, blinded by her ribbons, had supposed.

In the ship's cabin, which had four bedsteads "ingeniously contrived like cow cribs," the High Church lady shared one with her child. An old English sea captain took the second, Polly the third, and the Muhlenbergs, husband and wife, had the fourth.

The narrow trough assigned for their habitation was found to be too small to hold them both together. They arranged, accordingly, to share it for the one night of their passage by occupying it in turn. From eight to twelve at night it was his to lie down in (sleep was impossible), and she took his place and counted the hours from twelve to six.

As soon as they crossed the bar, which was at seven o'clock in the evening, the waves hit them and the English widow went down. Polly followed and was unable to help. Henry Melchior would gladly have played Sir Galahad, but, as he writes, "this seasickness, like yawning, is catching, and I myself had to flee the cabin on my knees and, in the dark, seek some place on deck where I could practice *invertus motus peristalticus.*"

Downy sleep was far enough from all eyelids. Henry Melchior found plenty of causes for this phenomenon without invoking the laws of "inverted peristaltic action." There was, first, "the overpowering stench"; second, the "swarm of poisonous, stinging gnats, called musquitoes"; third, the "cackrotsches" flying about the floor in search of victuals; fourth, vermin: "Beneath, above, and on all sides of the cabin, between the old wainscoting, the rats and mice scampered and fought and squealed"; fifth, the motion of the vessel, "like a drunken Frenchman dancing a rustic minuet."

"Watchman, what of the night?"

Morning brought no relief. A fog came up and fresh winds drove the captain out of his course. The situation called for seamanship. The sailors cast the lead:

"Five fathoms." Too shallow.

They turned the ship about and cast again: "Four fathoms."

They tried again and again: "Three fathoms—two fathoms."

The captain went to pieces. He wrung his hands and cried, "We are between the rocks and the sandbanks."

All sail was lowered and the rudder was loosened. The ship was left to wallow in the trough of the waves. Everyone expected she would strike at any moment and go down. The one boat on board would hold but four people, and there were thirty or forty souls to be saved—if the batch of Negro slaves in the hold, just brought over from Africa, counted as souls.

There seemed no escape. Anna Maria found comfort in the Bible:

"The Lord went before them by day in a pillar of cloud, to lead them the way; and by night in a pillar of fire." But Henry Melchior was frightened and frankly said so. He would gladly have had the faith of the disciples on the Sea of Galilee—but, as he says, they had great work to do, and besides, they had the Almighty Redeemer with them in person. Therefore they could not perish. "This did not apply to me, an unprofitable servant."

He justified his fears in another way. To say that no true Christian fears death is simply not true. Whatever bliss may await the faithful in the next world, the wrench of parting from this one is nevertheless painful. Anna Maria was right when she said that God could save them. But were they sure that God wanted to? Perhaps He had other plans and meant to take them now to himself.

"I know well what the Lord can do," he wrote, "but I do not know what He will do, and where and when and how He will call away the children of men."

It was not the call, but the parting, that frightened him.

"It is and always will be a momentous transition to depart spiritually from time to eternity!"

But happily their anxieties were soon over. In an hour and a half, at half-past eight o'clock in the morning, the mist broke and the sun came out. The sails were run up, the captain picked up their course, and by two o'clock that afternoon they had anchored and landed at Savannah.

Early in the morning of November 2, while still in Savannah, Anna Maria had a dream. It is worth recording here, since both the Muhlenbergs took their dreams seriously and were able to point to some interesting coincidences (if they were nothing more) to justify their faith in them.

She dreamed that she was driving to a wedding, through a beautiful country. Beside her was her old friend, Mrs. Keppele, dressed in wedding clothes, and looking very lovely. When Anna Maria awoke and remembered the affectionate, consoling way in which her old friend and benefactress had talked with her, she believed Mrs. Keppele had meant to comfort her for the death of some member of the family. Her own mother, Ann Eve Weiser, came at once to her mind.

A month later a letter arrived from Henry Ernest in Pennsylvania which gave them the key to the dream. On November 3 (the day after the dream), Mrs. Henry Keppele herself had died.

"We may presume," writes Henry Melchior, "that before her death Mrs. Keppele thought of my poor, sick wife, and we can in some measure observe in such instances that there must be a mental correspondence between bosom friends, however far they may be physically separated from each other."

Since this chapter is a travelogue rather than an excursion into the field of church history, we shall not follow the long, intricate, cautious, but ultimately conclusive examination which Muhlenberg made of the Triebner-Rabenhorst controversy, or give any detail of his findings. It is enough to observe that sight of this "sinful confusion" made him depressed and on occasion actually ill. Mr. Triebner he found to be a clerical go-getter: a grasping, plotting, hypocritical rogue, who made it his policy to elicite slander without precisely launching it himself, and spoke the language of piety where he thought it would do most harm to the innocent.

"May the Lord preserve me," wrote Muhlenberg, "from co-workers, colleagues, and brother ministers who speak a pious language but do not act according to the dictates of humanity and philosophy, much less the A B C's of the Christian religion."

He advised the Reverend Fathers in Europe to appoint Mr. Rabenhorst first minister, and to warn Triebner that, unless he conducted himself like a Christian, his salary would be cut off. That was language Triebner could understand.

It turned out, however, that the Reverend Mr. Triebner was endowed with enough stupid cunning to serve his purposes for a little time longer. He knew how to fish in the troubled waters of the Revolution. When Henry Melchior learned that Triebner had cast in his lot with the Tories, usurped Rabenhorst's place, got his hands on church money, and decamped with it when the place became too hot for him, it helped him to make up his mind about the Revolution. The British, it might be added, when they found what a sticky substance they had got on their hands, tried to wash Triebner off. But not before he had done a vast deal of harm to all concerned.

Meanwhile such words as "vile," "vulgar," and "currish" came readily to Muhlenberg's pen whenever he wrote about Triebner.

Since the fellow was a newcomer to the American scene, Muhlenberg recalled an admonition that the venerable Ziegenhagen had once given: Missionaries ought not to send home reports during their early years in the field, before they had had time to gain comprehension. A newcomer is blind, so to speak, "and he judges, as a blind man does, only by the color of things."

By the end of January, Henry Melchior had done all he could to bring peace to troubled Ebenezer. His next concern was how to get Anna Maria and the unobtrusive Polly safely back to Pennsylvania.

They were caught on the horns of a dilemma. A winter voyage would be uncomfortable and dangerous. He knew, as he said, that the Lord *could* provide him with a pleasant passage, but he was too modest to think that God would, for their sole benefit, alter the course of nature, change the prevailing northwest winds to southern ones, and waft them home by a miracle. On the other hand, he expected that by spring the strife between the colonies and "their angry mother" would have burst out into war, with the consequent interruption of shipping. If he and his wife and Polly waited till spring, they might never get back.

It seemed best to go at once. But he recoiled from the prospect. The perils were too great. He wrote in his Journal that he was not quite ready yet to meet his Maker, since, as he said, "for many years past I have had to live in the midst of all sorts of distractions and constant strife, eating polemical straw and thistles instead of nourishing food, and have little time to collect my thoughts and properly prepare myself for the supremely important transition from time to eternity."

But Anna Maria had the deciding voice.

She would go now.

Early in February they drove to Savannah. Henry Melchior visited the Governor, and, on February 14, the Honorable Chief Justice Anthony Stokes called on Muhlenberg at his lodging.

The Chief Justice's visit was something of an embarrassment. Stokes, being a teetotaler, could not be regaled with wine; and the Muhlenbergs could not serve him with tea because that drink had been abolished by the colonies as something to be viewed "with horrour," being "the detestable instrument which laid the foundations of the present sufferings. . . ."

But the visit went off comfortably nevertheless. The Chief Justice was sociable, spoke good Latin, discoursed with the Pastor about "Leibnitzian, Aristotelian, and Wolfian philosophy," as well as about the Thirty-nine Articles, Lutheranism, Germans, and the Protestant religion; and he drank water.

"He speaks very slowly and deliberately," commented Muhlenberg, "which is a good trait in a chief justice; quick to hear, slow to speak, and slow to wrath."

They sailed on the seventeenth of February. There were only four passengers on board, the three Muhlenbergs and a tailor. So far so good. In addition to five sailors, there was a captain who knew his business, and a steersman who did not: he had never made this passage before. The Pastor entertained himself with reflections on what might happen to the ship if the captain died and left the course to the steersman.

But fears about their course were soon driven out by others derived from the motion of the ship, which developed an eccentric and violent lurch. The Pastor was once catapulted, head over heels, across the cabin against Anna Maria, "poor wretch," sitting on a chest, and nearly broke her legs.

Long dark nights of sickness in their "civil prison" reminded him of Jonah in the belly of the whale. When they were within sixty miles of Cape Henlopen a fierce norwester sprang up and drove them out to sea. Sails were hauled down to save the masts, the rudder was secured, and the ship left to ride it out as best she could.

> The little ship quivered [wrote Muhlenberg] with strange epileptic paroxysms and made such wild and erratic leaps, upwards, downwards, sideways, backwards, and forwards that it was impossible to walk, stand, sit, or lie, and one knew not how to live or die. We had secured the window shutters, but we nevertheless shipped waves several times from above and were partly soaked. Each of us passengers grasped something secure in the cabin and held on to it, as in ancient times they grasped the horns of the altar and let themselves be killed. . . .
>
> I cannot deny that I prayed in the depths of my heart: "O Lord, suffer the tree to remain this one more year." . . .

By morning they had been driven a hundred miles before the gale. But a favorable wind soon came up and brought them to the Cape. They sailed up the Delaware River, delayed by only one more misadventure. A sailor casting the lead unknowingly got the line tangled and shortened, so that, when he called, "Five fathoms," the depth was really only three or four. The pilot in consequence ran them on the sands. They were so firmly stuck that even at high tide four shallops could not pull them off until they lightened ship by the removal of five thousand weight of barreled rice.

On March 6, they stepped off the boat at Philadelphia to be greeted by their children.

But what a change they found in the city! The political atmosphere was unrecognizable. Before he left, the Pastor had been able to shut his eyes to the Revolution, but now the noise of it was all around him. He himself was the focus of rumors, wild and ridiculous to any sober judgment, but believed in by many with fanatical frenzy. He was said (by the more moderate rumormongers) to have been conducting a correspondence with the court chaplains in London with a view to the levying of a tithe in Pennsylvania. Others, less moderate, said he had left for Ebenezer because he had been "tarred and feathered, driven about in a cart, and drummed out of Philadelphia." Some believed he had fled to escape being hanged by the people. Others said that God had pursued him with vengeance: he had been shipwrecked and drowned somewhere between South Carolina and Georgia.

But the prize rumor was this: "The King has become a Papist, and old man Mühlenberg has gone abroad to celebrate mass for him."

"All the foul vapors from the father of lies," observed the Pastor, "were let loose and spread *methodo mathematica* in every direction."

Even in some Lutheran circles the belief had taken root that Pastor Muhlenberg "had betrayed the country to the King."

Should a pastor take sides? Could a man be neutral? The questions were thrust on him every moment.

When it was charged to his face by a visiting Virginian that the Lutheran clergy had "betrayed the liberty of the country," he replied confidently that he and his colleagues cherished "civil and religious liberty as a precious gift vouchsafed from God."

But when he slept one night in an inn occupied by the militia, and heard some of them engaged in drunken conversation "with heavy tongues and half-closed eyes," on the state of the world;

when he saw others lying on or under the table to sleep off their liquor, and smelt them—he tells us he felt seasick.

"If America has no better patriots and heroes than these," he wrote, ". . . our priceless liberty of conscience will be in a bad way."

What was a pastor to do? All voices cried out against neutrality. This was a time for decision. But how was a God-fearing pastor to decide?

England had done wrong in losing her temper. The patriots were right when they pointed to her angry and tyrannical acts in handling the American problem. Men had a right to defend their liberties.

But England, bulwark of Protestantism and mother of free institutions, was surely, he thought, still sound at heart; and her help was needed by young America in a world threatened by warring autocracies.

Perhaps each side was half right. But dared one think, much less speak, in such fashion? In time of war, such views were held to be treason. If you said a good word for the colonies, the Tories called you a rebel; if a good word for England, the Patriots called you a traitor.

What was to be thought? What was to be said? What was to be done? In the past he had avoided any political involvement. God's word had been sufficient guide for him: "The powers that be are ordained of God." But who now were the powers that be? Where were they? People talked about the Rights of Man, of responsible government. Could power reside in the multitude? Were they the state? It was all very puzzling, but on answers to these questions depended his career, his life, and the future of his church. To chart a safe and correct course through these storms would take much reasoning, Bible reading, and prayer.

"It is a question," he wrote, "whether reason and revelation counsel us to conjugate in the active, passive, or neuter. . . ."

The great debate was on throughout the nation, in public halls, within the mind of each man and woman. For the next eight years the genus *americana* was to think of little else.

CHAPTER XIII

"THIS UNNATURAL WAR"

Henry Melchior Muhlenberg decided to be neutral. Throughout his life he had made it a principle to keep out of politics. In heaven there are neither Whigs nor Tories, and his duty was to prepare men for heaven.

This does not mean that he was indifferent to government. On the contrary, he believed that loyalty to government was one of a good man's best qualities. Henry Melchior exercised his franchise in Pennsylvania. But, like Samuel Johnson, he was not interested in abstract theories of government, and he feared that preoccupation with such philosophical speculations was the road to "Atheism, Naturalism, Enthusiasm, Superstition, Division, Disloyalty, and Confusion."[1]

His prime interest was in matters of individual right and wrong, in a man's relations with his fellow men *within the frame of the government in which he found himself*. By training and temperament he was a nonrevolutionist, a conservative, who believed government to be sacred, and who rested his case on the Scriptures, Romans 13.1: "Let every soul be subject unto the higher powers. For there is no power but of God: the powers that be are ordained of God." In Hanover he had accepted the semifeudal rule of the Elector of Hanover; in England the constitutional monarchy under King George; and after coming to America, the Republic (as he called it in 1753) of Pennsylvania.

Not only was he conservative by temperament, but he was strongly attached to the government of Pennsylvania and to the power that had given it its charter: the English King, the English Parliament, and, behind them both, English tradition. In particular he was pleased with the liberty of conscience guaranteed to the colony in the name of the King and the Proprietaries.

A document he prepared in June 1766 for preservation in the cornerstone of Zion Lutheran Church, Philadelphia, told posterity "how we, your ancestors, . . . set out from various parts of Europe, particularly from Germany, how we made the arduous and dangerous journey, under the shadow of almighty God's gracious wings, across the vast ocean to this western world, and how we were received as free subjects under the protection of the glorious Protestant King of Great Britain and admitted as free inhabitants and citizens by the noble proprietors of this *province*, the honorable Penns and their lawful heirs. Among other benefits and privileges, we have accordingly enjoyed, without molestation, the precious liberty of conscience and religion, and shall continue to enjoy it as long as it pleases God."[2]

He was not unaware—who could be?—of the political fermentation already pointing toward a revolutionary explosion; but he hoped and believed (in 1766) that such an explosion could be avoided. In the Zion cornerstone, he asked posterity to pray for "your lawful Protestant King of Great Britain," and to "allow no disunity, dissension, party spirit, or division to arise among you," but always to "smother the first sparks with Christian love and forbearance."

His motto, as he tells us, was "Fear God, honor the King and those in authority, and love thy neighbor." From 1742 to 1773 he kept up a steady correspondence with the members in London of the Society for Promoting Christian Knowledge. In a letter of 1772, he speaks of "the mild and blessed Government" of the Proprietaries, and its "inestimable Blessings."

Until July 4, 1776, he continued to pray publicly for King George.

It is not surprising, therefore, that in his Journals, through the years leading up to Lexington and Concord, there is very little reference to the momentous events taking place in the political world. This does not mean that he was indifferent to what was going on in Parliament and the colonial assemblies, or careless about the preservation of colonial liberties. However much he might regret the excesses to which freedom sometimes tempted men, he wished to see no diminution of the statutory privileges to which Americans had been accustomed. In 1766 he preached and published a sermon of thanksgiving for the repeal of the Stamp Act, and he deprecated the truculence of some British manifestoes and parliamentary resolutions.

But his fear was less for the harm that might be done by temporary acts of reprisal, on one side or the other, than for the loosening of the principle of government itself if the quarrel should be allowed to deepen into civil war or revolution. He distrusted the mob, with its phobias. He had no illusions (the Augsburg Confession has a strong passage on the subject of Original Sin) about the state of nature or the infallibility of the crowd. *Vox populi,* he said, can be *vox diaboli* as well as *vox Dei.* "It is not the Multitude of disorderly people that maketh a state," he wrote, January 9, 1752, "but the law and the Rulers."[3]

There was another reason for his hesitation in taking sides. As a practical statesman of the Lutheran Church he thought it expedient to avoid doing anything that would cause whichever side came out on top in this "unnatural and inhuman war" (he was frankly unsure of the outcome) to take reprisals on the institution of which he was the head.

That neutrality would be difficult, he knew very well. As he said afterward, "If a preacher wished to be neutral, he found himself between two fires: if he wished to join one party, the other party declared him an outlaw and put him under the ban."[4] The Loyalists suspected neutrals to be "rebels" at heart; the Patriots were sure they were secret Tories.

But Henry Melchior Muhlenberg, though a shy man and in some things timid, was no coward. Having chosen to "see both sides" and steer a neutral course, he stubbornly adhered to his decision as long as honesty permitted.

As late as 1775 he believed that the differences between the mother country and the colonies could be quietly and reasonably adjusted—if people would only recall what it was they had originally been quarreling about. He thought it was the frayed ends of the dispute, the accidental circumstances and the reprisal-breeding reprisals that inflamed men's minds and incited to bloodshed. But, as the quarrel deepened and the guns began to roar, he became convinced that the burden of responsibility for the disaster lay with the mother country. She, as the older and stronger party, had the greater obligation to keep a cool head and an understanding heart. Yet she had lost her temper and taken action which, considering, as he said, the climate of America and the temperament of its people, made going back impossible and war inevitable. As Frederick Muhlenberg wrote to his brother Henry Ernest in 1785, "The character of the American people, as you and I showed at the Orphan House, is such that they are better won by kindness than severity."

Even so, despite the deepening of Henry Melchior's private sympathy with the cause of the colonies, he tried to preserve an official neutrality. He prayed for both sides—though one suspects that, as time went on, he came to believe that God lent a more attentive ear to the American half of his prayers.

Nothing could better show the differences in temperament among the four Muhlenberg men—Henry Melchior and his three sons—than the effect of the Revolution upon them.

To begin with, there was the natural difference between the generations, Old Calendar and New Calendar. They all had had European training, but differences between father and sons in the matter of early environment caused a marked difference in outlook. Henry Melchior had his roots in Europe. He still looked upon America as a "wilderness," and feared the high free spirits of her people. The boys, on the other hand, had grown up to take both American high spirits and American freedoms (in politics, manners, and speech) for granted; and while abroad, all three of them had acquired a sharp feeling of separateness from Europe which drew them closer together and made all the broadsides and oratory in America preceding the Revolution seem like an echo of their own feelings.

By 1777, they were all, the boys and their father together, united in their American loyalty. But, whereas the boys had never been anywhere else, their father had had to think his way to that position.

The war, when it came, found the boys serving pastorates in three different colonies: Peter in Virginia, Frederick in New York, and Henry Ernest in Pennsylvania. Its first blasts in each locality interrupted their careers. When the storm had passed, Peter and Frederick had been swept out of their churches and had entered public affairs. Only Henry Ernest remained in the ministry.

Peter, as we have already seen, had gone in the autumn of 1772 to Virginia, to take charge of a bilingual church at Woodstock, county seat of the newly established Dunmore County in the Shenandoah Valley. There he made a success among the German settlers from Pennsylvania, and at the same time made golden friendships among the English of the neighborhood. His taste for hunting and fishing did him good service in the Old Dominion, bringing him friendships with such men as Taverner Beale and, if tradition is to be credited, with George Washington.[5] At the same time he took a manly interest in the political matters which were then occupying the attention of all thinking men in Virginia, and he became a follower of Patrick Henry.

Peter did not separate himself from the world as his father tried to do. Peter believed that a clergyman has duties as a man and a citizen which, in a democratic society especially, must be discharged with as sincere a reverence as if he were administering the sacraments. The particular dispute between England and the colonies concerning the manner in which the latter were to share the expenses of the Seven Years' War had developed while Peter and his brothers were in Europe. When they returned to America, the trouble had already gathered head, and men were disputing, not about the Seven Years' War, but about "the rights of Englishmen."

Peter had been in Virginia only a year when there occurred in a faraway port the incident known as the Boston Tea Party, which received such a good press as to make it an event of world importance. The Boston Tea Party provided for all the colonies a dramatic symbol of some of the deepest issues involved: to begin with, taxation without representation; and, behind that, "the sovereignty of the people," the right of revolution, the right of secession—in a word, the rights of man.

The Boston Tea Party, moreover, set off a chain of reactions that led straight to the Declaration of Independence. It was this chain that swept Peter Muhlenberg into his revolutionary career.

On December 16, 1773, citizens of Boston dumped the tea into the harbor. In reprisal, the British Parliament in March passed the Boston Port Bill, closing the port of Boston to general shipping, beginning with June 1. When the news reached Williamsburg in May, the Virginia Assembly set aside June 1 as a day of mourning.

"The effect of the day," as Thomas Jefferson noted, "thro' the whole colony was like a shock of electricity."

The Reverend Peter Muhlenberg, who held the office of magistrate at Woodstock, felt the shock. When, on June 16, the freeholders of Woodstock met "to consider the best mode to be fallen upon to secure their liberties and properties" against such inroads as the Boston Port Act, Peter Muhlenberg was elected moderator or chairman. He headed a committee, on which were Francis Slaughter, Abraham Bird, Taverner Beale, John Tipton, and Abraham Bowman, appointed to draw up "Resolves." The committee presented the following resolutions, which had already been voted by the freeholders of Frederick County:

1st. That we will always cheerfully pay due submission to such Acts of Government as his Majesty has a right, by law, to exercise over his subjects, as Sovereign to the *British* Dominions, and to such only.

2nd. That it is the inherent right of *British* subjects to be governed and taxed by Representatives chosen by themselves only; and that every Act of the British Parliament respecting the internal policy of *North America,* is a dangerous and unconstitutional invasion of our rights and privileges.

3rd. That the Act of Parliament above mentioned, is not only itself repugnant to the fundamental laws of natural justice . . . ; but, also, a despotic exertion of unconstitutional power, calculated to enslave a free and loyal people.

4th. That the enforcing the execution of the said Act of Parliament by a military power, will have a necessary tendency to raise a civil war, thereby dissolving that union that has long happily subsisted between the mother country and her Colonies. . . .

5th. It is the unanimous opinion of this meeting, that a joint resolution of all the Colonies, to stop all importations from *Great Britain,* and exportations to it, till the said Act be repealed, will prove the salvation of *North America* and her liberties. . . .

7th. That is the opinion of this meeting, that Committees ought to be appointed for the purpose of effecting a general Association, that the same measures may be pursued through the whole Continent; that the Committees ought to correspond with each other, and to meet at such places and times as shall be agreed, in order to form such general Association. . . .[6]

A Committee of Correspondence was accordingly appointed, with the same members as on the Resolutions Committee, Peter Muhlenberg being chairman.

Shortly thereafter he was elected one of two representatives from Dunmore County to the Virginia Convention, which met August 1-6 in Williamsburg. There Patrick Henry sounded his disturbing note of urgency, and George Washington offered to raise a thousand men and march them to help Boston.

This same month, however, brought to Peter a temporary dampening of revolutionary ardor. He made a trip to Philadelphia to see his father off on the long voyage to Ebenezer. There is no record of what his father said to him on this occasion; but from what we know Henry Melchior thought of Peter's radical activities, and from what happened afterward to Peter, it is apparent that the father, before leaving Philadelphia (perhaps, as they both thought, never to return), gave his son advice. His argument, as we find it scattered through his journals and letters, must have run something like this:

To begin with, hasty action of whatever kind was to be deprecated. It was true, tempers had been lost on both sides; but the British, no less than the Americans, were proponents of liberty, as their long history had shown. The essential freedoms on which Americans prided themselves were a part of English tradition, and were not permanently threatened by momentary outbreaks of indignation on the part of the Mother of Parliaments. As for talk of civil war, that was plain foolishness. The colonies were far too weak to match strength with a great power, especially with one that controlled the seas on which they depended for their commerce. At all costs peace should be striven for, and a political dispute should not be permitted to rise to the emotional intensities (as some hotheads seemed to aim) of an ethical, almost a religious, "fermentation." In a word, leave the jurists to work out the constitutional details of what was, after all, a jurisdictional dispute. No essential issues were involved.

Peter, always earnest, honest, and forthright, and at the same time much influenced by the last speaker and the last turn of events, resigned all his political offices. It has been suggested that he did so in protest against the absence of more spirited action in Virginia.[7] It seems more probable that it was his father's influence that caused him to withdraw. It might, after all, be the part of wisdom to let the situation develop and see what came out of it. Perhaps, in the course of events, he might discern more clearly a sign from on high.

Meanwhile, things were moving rapidly in Virginia, and preparations for war were seen everywhere. Independent companies of soldiers were forming in every county, and politics, as Peter wrote to his brother engrossed all conversation.

Early in January 1775 appeared the sign for which Peter had been waiting. An election was held in Dunmore County, and Peter Muhlenberg found himself, willy-nilly, reëlected chairman of the Committee of Correspondence and Safety.

"Whether I choose or not," wrote Peter to his brother Frederick, "I am to be a politician."[8]

It was Lübeck all over again: revolt, acquiescence, revolt—the second one decisive. Peter Muhlenberg for the next eight years was to devote his energies to the Revolution.

He went up to the famous Convention held in St. John's Church, Richmond, beginning March 20, 1775, the purpose of which was to "prepare a plan for the embodying, arming, and disciplining such a number of men as may be sufficient" to secure "our inestimable rights and liberties from those further violations with which they are threatened." Since he was never a talker in political assemblies, we have no means of knowing what influence he had on the Convention; but the influence of the Convention on him we know to have been profound.

It was on March 23 that Patrick Henry delivered his "liberty or death" oration, which pressed upon men the sense of urgency and at the same time, by simplifying the issues, made it easier for them to make a decision.

In matching himself against the cautious minds of the gentry from the southern Virginia counties, Patrick Henry used arguments which met and overthrew the very reasoning Peter Muhlenberg had heard from his father. The speech was perfervid, and time has made what record we have of it (all at second hand) sound hackneyed. But if it is read again in its original context, read with the hesitations of such men as the conscientious Peter Muhlenberg in mind, we may recapture something of the quality that caused Thomas Jefferson to say of Patrick Henry, "He was far before us all in maintaining the spirit of the Revolution." In time of emergency it still stirs the blood, not only of Americans, but of free men all over the world.

> This is no time for ceremony. The question before the House is one of awful moment to this country. For my own part, I consider it as nothing less than a question of freedom or slavery. . . .
>
> I have but one lamp by which my feet are guided; and that is the lamp of experience. I know no way of judging the future but by the past. And judging by the past, I wish to know what there has been in the conduct of the British Ministry, for the last ten years, to justify those hopes with which gentlemen have been pleased to solace themselves and the

House. . . . There is no longer any room for hope. If we wish to be free; if we mean to preserve inviolate those inestimable privileges for which we have been so long contending; if we mean not basely to abandon the noble struggle in which we have been so long engaged, and which we have pledged ourselves never to abandon until the glorious object of our contest shall be obtained—we must fight! I repeat it, sir, we must fight! An appeal to arms and to the God of Hosts is all that is left us!

. . . Sir, we are not weak, if we make a proper use of those means which the God of nature hath placed in our power. Three millions of people, armed in the holy cause of liberty, and in such a country as that which we possess, are invincible to any force which our enemy can send against us. Besides, sir, we shall not fight our battles alone. There is a just God who presides over the destinies of nations, and who will raise up friends to fight our battles for us. The battle, sir, is not to the strong alone; it is to the vigilant, the active, the brave. Besides, sir, we have no election. If we were base enough to desire it, it is now too late to retire from the contest. There is no retreat but in submission and slavery. Our chains are forged. Their clanking may be heard on the plains of Boston. The war is inevitable. And let it come! I repeat it, sir; let it come!

It is in vain, sir, to extenuate the matter. Gentlemen may cry peace, peace—but there is no peace. The war is actually begun! The next gale that sweeps from the north will bring to our ears the clash of resounding arms! Our brethren are already in the field! Why stand we idle here? What is it that gentlemen wish? What would they have? Is life so dear, or peace so sweet, as to be purchased at the price of chains and slavery? Forbid it, Almighty God! I know not what course others may take, but as for me, give me liberty, or give me death.

Patrick Henry has been called "a spirit fitted to raise the whirlwind." With this speech, the Revolution may be said to have begun in Virginia—and in the heart of Peter Muhlenberg. He needed no further sign. He knew now that he had been called to serve this cause—though whether as a chaplain or a soldier time was not yet ripe to disclose.

Meanwhile Frederick Muhlenberg, from the Swamp Church in New York, had been watching uneasily the signs of approaching storm. He had little desire to mix himself in politics. He was a native American, with an instinctive and deep loyalty to the land of his birth. He disliked the arrogance of some who called themselves Loyalists, and his observance of the ways of the world, in high English circles in New York, left him with distaste and a little fear. He has given us an amusing account of the King's College (Columbia) commencement in 1774, and the subsequent banquet at Hall's Tavern to which he was "unexpectedly" invited, and which he attended, as he says, "in fear and trembling," in company with members of the English Church clergy and representatives of the town and colonial officialdom. So many healths were drunk that, after escaping as soon as he could with any decency, he prayed God to preserve him from such company in future.

His sympathies were for Boston in her troubles. But, with all his enthusiasm, he was a man of some detachment and had a keen, critical eye which enabled him to detect fustian wherever he saw it, whether among friends or foes. He disliked the note of rhetoric that had crept into Peter's correspondence, and expressed disapproval of the belligerence that inspired it. He believed, as his father did, that a pastor should keep out of the political ferment.

"You have become too involved," he wrote to Peter, "in matters with which, as a preacher, you have nothing whatsoever to do and which do not belong to your office. . . . Nothing can excuse you . . ."[9]

But circumstances took care of Frederick's hesitations. When, in the late summer of 1775, a British warship dropped shells into the city of New York in an effort to dislodge the militia, Frederick's wife and two children fled with some fifteen hundred other refugees for safety outside of the city.[10] Cathy and the children took refuge with the grandparents in Philadelphia. Frederick himself stayed behind, watching developments. But his mind was made up. Those who made his wife a refugee made an enemy of Frederick. When the British finally occupied New York in 1776, Frederick fled to his father's house in Pennsylvania.

Henry Ernest, meantime, Third Pastor in Philadelphia, said little but nursed his wrath against the Loyalists.

CHAPTER XIV

"A TIME TO FIGHT"

Early in January 1776 Peter Muhlenberg burned his bridges. It had been his intention to join the army of Virginia as a chaplain, but on January 12 he accepted appointment by the Convention at Williamsburg as a colonel, and immediately went home to recruit his regiment.

At the Convention in August preceding, only two regiments had been provided for. Now six more (and soon a seventh) were added, one of these, the Eighth Virginia Regiment, to be raised among the Germans of the Shenandoah Valley. To officer this regiment, men from the Valley were nominated by the Convention on January 12, and next day the *Virginia Gazette* printed in its "List of Field Officers" the names of "Peter Mulenberg, Abraham Bowman and Peter Helvenstone" as Colonel, Lieutenant Colonel, and Major of the Eighth.

It was a remarkable compliment to pay to the twenty-nine-year-old parson, who had previously had no more army experience than sufficed to get him transportation across the Atlantic. But his undoubted popularity among the people of the Valley, and his active (though not voluble) association with "patriots" on the Committee of Correspondence and in the Virginia conventions, made it seem worth while to gamble on his capacity to master enough military science within the next two or three months to justify giving him a command.

The one thing which the public at large remembers about Peter Muhlenberg is his dramatic leave-taking of the congregation at Woodstock. Story, song, and drama have preserved the incident in many versions. Its climax in the words "There is a time to pray and a time to fight" has become a symbol, not only for America but

JOHN PETER GABRIEL MUHLENBERG

for all the world, of the faith that does not flinch from committing itself to action.

It is not known with certainty when the sermon was preached. Peter Muhlenberg himself tells us nothing about it. But there is evidence which points to the morning of January 21, 1776. It may be of some interest to examine it.

On the day of his appointment as colonel, January 12, Peter Muhlenberg made his last recorded appearance at the Convention. On that day he made a report for the committee which had been appointed to consider a petition from Joseph Bowman. Muhlenberg is not again referred to in the minutes of the Convention. There can be little doubt that, on receiving his military commission, he hurried back over the mountains to the Valley and set about the work for which he was soon to be famous: the enlisting, equipping, and training of troops for the field. By January 23 his recruiting was well under way.

On that day we find a certain Benjamin Wilson writing angrily to "Peter Muehlinburg" to say that he would not accept appointment as lieutenant under Captain Langdon, as, according to Mr. Swaine, the Colonel desired him to do. Wilson had raised twenty-five men who would serve as *regulars* under his own command. But, said Wilson, "I Purpose to Decline Serving as a Minuite Man."[1]

The letter is important not for anything it tells us about Benjamin Wilson, but for the help it gives us in dating Peter's sermon. Evidently by January 23 the recruiting was well advanced. This is indication that Peter had not waited at Williamsburg for the adjournment of the Convention on January 20. Woodstock is more than two hundred and fifty miles northwest of Williamsburg, and it would take the better part of a week, hard riding, to make the journey. If Peter left Williamsburg on Saturday, January 13, we might expect to find him home at Woodstock by Friday or Saturday, the nineteenth or twentieth, which would be soon enough to allow for the recruiting proposals which disturbed Mr. Wilson.

It is unlikely that Peter delayed his farewell sermon beyond the first Sunday after his return, since a prime object of his message was to get recruits. All versions agree that after the sermon he enrolled large numbers of his congregation.

The story has been told many times, each teller adding what embellishments he thought fitting. Though all versions agree that Peter threw off his gown (if you doubt it, go to the Library of the Lutheran Theological Seminary at Mt. Airy and see the gown for yourself), there is no agreement on such questions as whether the Colonel wore his uniform in the pulpit, where and at what time he removed the gown, and what precisely were the words he used.

Dr. James Thacher, from whose *Military Journal* the story seems to stem, picked it up apparently at a dinner party at West Point, November 3, 1778, when General Muhlenberg entertained forty-one officers of his brigade. Thacher says that on the day following his farewell sermon, the Colonel "marched at the head of his regiment to join the army." Since the regiment marched for Suffolk on Thursday, March 21, this would date the sermon Wednesday, March 20, which, from all other evidence, is absurd. Thacher is not to be relied on, but here is the story as he launched it:

> General Muhlenberg was a minister of a parish in Virginia, but participating in the spirit of the times, exchanged his clerical profession for that of a soldier. Having in his pulpit inculcated the principles of liberty and the cause of his country, he found no difficulty in enlisting a regiment of soldiers, and he was appointed their commander. He entered his pulpit with his sword and cockade, preached his farewell sermon, and the next day marched at the head of his regiment to join the army. . . .[2]

In the hierarchy of the story's priesthood, Thacher is first, but next is Peter's great-nephew, Henry A. Muhlenberg, whose *Life of Major-General Peter Muhlenberg of the Revolutionary Army* (1849) gives us the rendering on which most other versions are based. According to this well-filled-out account, Colonel Peter Muhlenberg

> ascended the pulpit, his tall form arrayed in full uniform, over which his gown, the symbol of his holy calling, was thrown. . . . After recapitulating, in words that aroused the coldest, the story of their sufferings and their wrongs, and telling them of the sacred character of the struggle in which he had unsheathed his sword, and for which he had left the altar he had vowed to serve, he said "that, in the language of holy writ, there was a time for all things, a time to preach and a time to pray, but those times had passed away"; and in a voice that re-echoed through the church like a trumpet-blast, "that there was a time to fight, and that time had now come!"
>
> The sermon finished, he pronounced the benediction. . . . Deliberately putting off the gown, which had thus far covered his martial figure, he

stood before them a girded warrior; and descending from the pulpit, ordered the drums at the church-door to beat for recruits.[3]

J. T. Headley, in *The Chaplains and Clergy of the Revolution,* tells us that the Colonel first closed the service before stepping "into the vestry-room," and there, "laying aside his gown, put on his colonel's uniform."[4]

But disagreements over the details of the incident need not disturb us. Some such dramatic gesture, in "the spirit of '76," was undoubtedly made by Peter late in January—in time for the news to travel to Frederick in New York, and for Frederick's comments on it to be relayed, through Philadelphia, to Woodstock before the beginning of March.

Frederick's letter, like Peter's sermon, was surprising. It was a brotherly letter, in the sense that it expressed the natal right of the one brother to deflate the other's egotism.

At Woodstock the sermon had been an electric success. Two or three hundred (estimates vary) men of the congregation are said to have enlisted that day. Posterity continues to praise the "Fighting Parson." But in Philadelphia and New York the news was received, at least by Peter's brothers, with distaste and no little exasperation. Peter had done it again. It was Lübeck, 1766, all over again.

From New York Frederick wrote a frank letter to Henry Ernest in Philadelphia, expressing regret, not for Peter's politics or patriotism, but for his confusion of mind (so Frederick considered it) in trying to blend the clergyman with the soldier. Frederick was not a pacifist. He respected the soldier's calling as he respected the pastor's. But pastor and soldier in one—that was a contradiction Frederick would not accept. The man, he thought, who tried to be both, must be false to one or the other.

Henry Ernest forwarded Frederick's letter to Peter. When the Colonel read it, he let himself go. With Patrick Henry's phrases still ringing in his ears, he wrote Frederick a letter (probably to be assigned to the date March 2, 1776) denouncing him as a "Tory." In a passion of resentment and suspicion, he proposed fire and sword as the only remedies for the sins of New York—the breeding ground, as he seemed to think, of the Tory maggots infesting Frederick's brain.

It was not Frederick's habit to lose his temper. He could be angry, and he was very angry now. But he had a reflective and powerful mind which lifted him above his emotions and which now enabled him to apply the salve of wit to Peter's wounds.

The letter he wrote to Peter (in German) covers many pages. That Peter's previous letter to him (in English) has been lost is no great matter, since Frederick in his letter quoted long passages from Peter's to point his own replies.

We print fragments of the two letters together, to show colonel and parson in a duel of quills.

PETER. I have not received a Line from you since I saw you last in Philada. & if Daddy did not sometimes give me some information of you, I would not know there was such a Person in the World, however though you thus neglect I would not retaliate—

FREDERICK. . . . No wonder if a man holding two important jobs forgets things at times. . . . Didn't I write to you from Philadelphia when our Poll made such a fool of herself and ran off with the drummer?

PETER. Thus far I had wrote, when I recd. Brother Henrys Letter from you to him, wherein you made some exceeding sensible Observations on my Conduct in the present alarming Crisis, from what those Observations flowed, I'm at a Loss to coniecture.

You say as a Clergyman nothing can excuse my Conduct, this excellent Doctrine is certainly a Production of that excellent City N. Y. which must be purged with Fire, before ever it is cleaned from Toryism; may there be none to pity it.—

FREDERICK. *Purged with Fire—Toryism* . . . I am convinced the majority here are as strong for the American cause as the Virginians, if not stronger. . . .

None to pity it Good God! . . . Brother, brother, the rough soldier peeps out from behind the black hat— . . . That is contrary to the teaching of Jesus, which you formerly preached.

None to pity it . . . Heathenish.

PETER. I am a Clergyman it is true, but I am a Member of Society as well as the poorest Layman, & my Liberty is as dear to me as to any Man, shall I then sit still & enjoy myself at Home when the best Blood of the Continent is spilling? Heaven forbid it.

FREDERICK. *Verba, praeterea nihil* [Words, words, words].

PETER. . . . Seriously Brother, I am afraid you have imbibed bad Principles in N. Y.—

FREDERICK. How do you make that out? Because I think it wrong for you to be both preacher and soldier in one? Bad logic. . . . You do not know me—I believe I have always been, and still am, as firm in our American cause as you are, even though I am not a colonel marching to the field.

PETER. But even if you was on the opposite Side of the Question you MUST allow that I have in this last Step acted for the best. You know that from the Beginning of these Troubles, I have been compelled by Causes to you unknown to have a Hand in public Affairs. I have been Chairman to the Committee & Delegate for this County from the first, do you think then if America should be conquered I should be safe, on the contrary, & would you not sooner fight like a man than die the Death of a dog?"

FREDERICK. . . . Why must I admit it? Listen: Because from the beginning you have been the Committee Chairman and Delegate . . . You would have acted for the best if you had kept out of this business from the beginning.

You was impelled by causes to me unknown— . . . I think a needless self-love and ambition, a desire to appear the big man . . . were the secret causes. . . . The Convention could have got along whether you were a delegate or not.

Die the Death of a Dog . . . [Here Frederick quoted some verses in German, the gist of which was this: Whoever dies with Christ's image in his heart *dies well.*]

PETER. I am called by my country in its defence—the cause is iust and noble—were I a Bishop, even a Lutheran one I should obey without Hesitation, and so far I am from thinking that I act wrong, I am convinced it is my Duty so to do & Duty I owe to God & my Country.—

FREDERICK. Sophistries. . . .

O Tempora o mores.

I must make a few more comments before I close.

You hope to find an Asylum among the Savages. No brother, if England wins, & I am still in N. York—I'll make you sexton and then you can sing this little song: *Sic transit gloria mundi.*

Deign to write to a Colonel. Yes—I can so far condescend as to write to a colonel . . .

I must hasten to a close—I see I have written a gigantic letter—I now give you my thoughts in brief—I think you are wrong in trying to be both soldier and preacher together. Be either one or the other. No man can serve two masters. I have long had some doubts of my own. . . . I recognize well my unfitness as a preacher. . . . I incline to think a preacher can with good conscience resign his office and step into another calling. You think a man can be both preacher and colonel at the same time. How different are our ways of thinking! . . . If anything I have said in this letter has offended you, look at it this way—as the text is, so is the sermon—your letter attacking me with the godforsaken name of Tory was just too much—but . . . rest assured I shall always think of you in my prayers. . . .

Most truly

Your Brother F M.[5]

If the letter shows turmoil in Frederick's mind, it was not, as the concluding paragraph makes clear, because of any uncertainty about taking sides in the Revolution. It was rather that Frederick was unsure of his call to the Christian ministry. Henry Melchior came to admit to himself, though unwillingly, that his son Peter took to soldiering like a fish to water. It was his natural element. It was also in Henry Melchior's stars to learn that his son Frederick took to the "high life" of politics like a bird to the air.

But at this time, in 1776, Frederick's famous oyster suppers for the sustenance of congressmen lay far in the future. For the moment, Frederick was engrossed with the humbler problems of a man trying to find food for his family on the edge of a volcano.

We have already seen that in 1775 Frederick had had to send Cathy and the children away to escape the bombardment of New York by a British warship. Cathy soon returned to her husband. But in January 1776 the old anxieties returned. It now seemed certain that the British would soon attack New York in force. If they did, they would take it. General Lee had reported that it could not be successfully defended against an enemy commanding the sea.

Cathy was expecting another baby. Prudent friends advised her to flee, while there was time, to Philadelphia. Again Frederick had to make a decision. If Cathy stayed, she would be virtually interned. If he stayed with her, he might fare badly. His opinions were too well known in New York.

Accordingly Frederick came with his wife and their two small children to his parents' home in Philadelphia, arriving there on February 10. Though he himself returned at once to New York, his mind was made up. When the British came, he would leave. There could be no question.

Henry Melchior in Philadelphia was also making decisions. In 1775 his mood had been one of passive resignation. He saw the Revolution as a weapon used by God to punish *two* rebellious peoples.

"God, who rules over all things," he had written in June 1775, "is first using the motherland as a rod for America; then when the divine purpose is achieved and the rod is worn out, it will be cast away."[6]

But early in 1776 he came to see that there was more in the Revolution than God's punishment for sin. There was a principle of growth in all this fermentation. Tom Paine helped him to see it. Henry Melchior read *Common Sense* in a German translation, and was so impressed with it that he sent a copy to Emanuel Schultze at Tulpehocken.

Tom Paine was no metaphysician. He dealt with principles, it is true, but actively rather than profoundly. He put them to work. He transformed ideas into slogans, into appeals for action. And he equated them with common sense. A great propagandist, he gave, in lightning flashes, glimpses of vast horizons, and at the same time made clear as day to his readers the first step forward they must take.

> The cause of America is, in great measure, the cause of all mankind . . . the design and end of government, viz., freedom and security. . . .
>
> O ye that love mankind! Ye that dare oppose not only the tyranny but the tyrant, stand forth! Every spot of the old world is overrun with oppression. Freedom hath been hunted round the globe. Asia and Africa have long expelled her. Europe regards her like a stranger, and England hath given her warning to depart. O receive the fugitive, and prepare in time an asylum for mankind.

Henry Melchior was overwhelmed. This wild, free country—could it be that its very freedom, despite the froth on the surface, was a good thing in itself, or at least held promise of good for the future?

He sent a copy of the pamphlet to his favorite son-in-law, and with it he sent a letter. Considering the importance of what he wrote in it, we should remember that he spoke more freely to Emanuel Schultze than to other members of the family. He wrote to him without reservation. What he said on this occasion, puts his convictions beyond dispute:

"The young people are right in fighting for their God-given native liberty."[7]

He was, of course, speaking of others, of the young, native product. For himself, there was still the intolerable anguish of a divided loyalty: loyalty to his adopted country and the young people in it who were fighting for the rights of mankind; and loyalty to the King to whom he had given his oath of allegiance.

Later in the spring, Frederick visited his family in Philadelphia. On his return to New York, May 20, finding feverish preparations for defense under way, with troops stationed close to the city, he wrote to say that Cathy and the children must certainly not think of coming north again.

He did not wait for the Battle of Long Island and the British landing at Kip's Bay. On the approach of the first squadron bringing Howe and his troops from Boston, he left New York for good. He arrived in Philadelphia "bringing such household goods with him as he was able to take from the city."[8] An unmarried ministerial candidate named Crelle was left behind to attend to the New York congregation, but it needed little looking after. Most of the congregation, including all the women and children, had fled.

It was on the memorable July 2, the day on which Congress arrived at the decision to declare the independence of the thirteen colonies, that Frederick arrived with his furniture in Philadelphia. It was no triumphal entry. His promising career in the ministry had come to an end. His experience during the next few years, supplying pulpits here and there, fluttering from country church to country church, confirmed a distaste for the work of the clergy, and deepened the suspicion, which we have already seen expressed in the letter to Peter, that he had missed his calling.

If July 2 was a dull day in Philadelphia, July 4 was its twin. On the day Jefferson's final draft of the Declaration of Independence was accepted by the Continental Congress, there were no firecrackers and there was no oratory.

To Henry Melchior Muhlenberg, a prey to divided loyalties, it seemed evident that the rose of Liberty had thorns. He wrote in his Journal:

> July 4. Today the Continental Congress openly declared the united provinces of North America to be free and *independent* states. This has caused some thoughtful and far-seeing *melancholici* to be down in the mouth; on the other hand, it has caused some sanguine *miopes* to exult and shout with joy. *In fine videbitur cuius toni* [The end will show who played the right tune].

Four days later came the public reading of the Declaration.

"July 8. Today the united North American provinces were proclaimed *independent* from the *state* house. Psalm 127:1." ("Except the Lord build the house, they labour in vain that build it: except the Lord keep the city, the watchman waketh but in vain.")

There was no fanfare. Charles Biddle, who was present at the reading (and who afterward mistakenly dated it "the memorable 4th of July, 1776"), said: "I was in the Old State-House yard when the Declaration of Independence was read. There were very few respectable people present."[9]

Mistress Deborah Logan, who heard it from her father's garden, wrote of it: "I distinctly heard the words of that instrument read to the people . . . the first audience of the Declaration was neither very numerous nor composed of the most respectable class of citizens."[10]

It was not a time for cheering. The Declaration of Independence was a reminder to thoughtful people that the Goddess of Freedom, however glamourous she may seem when viewed from afar on the mountaintop to which poets consign her, looks stern enough when she comes down to reveal her face in the market place—and asks from her admirers not compliments but sacrifices.

The ending of the struggle over "Dependence and Independence," as Henry Melchior expressed it, brought his own conscientious scruples to a head. Whatever his sympathies for the American cause, and they were deep, he could not follow the Continental Congress without breaking his oath of allegiance to King George. Yet, unless he accepted the authority of the new republic, he could no longer live safely in Pennsylvania, where his heart was. The dilemma was profoundly disturbing.

His first thought was for escape. The entry in his Journal immediately following that of July 8 is this: "July 11. Inasmuch as Pastor Kuntze's strength is largely restored and my presence on the property is very necessary, I hired a wagon and moved to Providence with my sick wife and very young daughter [ten-year-old Sally]—to remain there until a better solution presents itself."

Writing of the same journey a few months later, he said: "Robbed of my former protection, old and cast aside, unwilling to change my oath of allegiance nor yet to be a sacrifice to *Anarchie* at the hands of the angry mob; I retired . . . to a little country place of 7 acres . . . intended for poor superannuated Lutheran preachers or poor widows, in the hope of having here a quiet, retired life. . . ."[11]

It was not a sudden resolve that took him back to the Trappe. As early as December 1775, foreseeing, as he wrote, "that the flames of war will spread farther over the united North American provinces during the coming year," and noting the example of the "clucking hen," which, though "only an irrational little creature, instinctively seeks some spot in which she might find shelter for her young ones," he resolved to flee to Providence.

He regretted that he had sold his farm, but, happening upon an advertisement in an English newspaper of a place in Providence (which, as he noted, was "neither too near the city nor too near the Indian frontier" for safety), he made up his mind to buy it. With a little financial maneuvering, getting an advance of £100 from David Schaeffer (on behalf of Schaeffer's son-in-law, Frederick Muhlenberg, who might also in time find it a convenient refuge), £120 from his wife out of a legacy she had received from Conrad Weiser, and putting a mortgage on the property to cover the remainder, he bought the place. In March 1776 he visited it and admired the residence: "a large two-story dwelling, built of massive stones," with eight rooms—four on each floor, together with a smaller stone workshop, "two draw-wells, and a large stone barn with stables." It needed repairs, and these he attended to at once. Thirty-eight windowpanes were put in, the rooms and hallways were whitewashed, and the cellar was cleaned. Two hundred fruit trees were pruned. Firewood was chopped and split. The house was ready.

Anna Maria wanted to leave Philadelphia. She had been sure, ever since her return from Ebenezer, that the city was bad for her paroxysms. She had written to Betsy, April 11, 1775, to say that she wished "papa" had taken a place in the country.

But the move, when it came, was a wrench to them both: the separation from city friends of fifteen years' standing, and the physical discomfort of another "flitting." Henry Melchior noted that this last moving (for him, as it turned out, the final one) was his eighteenth change of residence since he had come to America.

The day her parents moved to the Trappe, Peggy Kuntze wrote to her sister Betsy in Tulpehocken. It is a sad little letter, written bravely in English (a language the spelling of which she had not mastered), full of true feeling. It reminds us of the sacrifices men and women all around her were now being called upon to make in the name of freedom. We are going to like Peggy. She is all gold.

July the 11 [1776]

Dear Sister
I only [write] to let you know that whe are all well dady a[nd] mamy a[nd] Sally went up to the trap this morning to stay a cupple weeks . . . our Millishe are all a going towards Newyork Yesterdad too campanays went to day 3 campeneys the Yagers are most all gone next Sunday whe Shall have very few men in our Church, it looks very Mornfull to See wemen Some with 4 or 5 Children Some redy to lay in Some Sick and the men must go or be taken to gail or tard a[nd] fetheard . . . all my neabors are gone you may think how hard it Seemed to day there was matter of 50 took there leafe of us and to so many more not one came without tears in his eyes maby they never will come back. . . . my love to all

Peggy

Just now
Peter dick taks
his leafe I cant rite more[12]

For a time the quiet at Providence brought back Henry Melchior's health and his courage. He fortified himself in the belief that the young people were right in fighting for their liberties by recalling the story of Rehoboam, I Kings 12:

3 . . . And Jeroboam and all the congregation of Israel came, and spake unto Rehoboam, saying,
4 Thy father made our yoke grievous: now therefore make thou the grievous service of thy father, and his heavy yoke which he put upon us, lighter, and we will serve thee.
5 And he said unto them, Depart yet for three days, then come again to me. And the people departed.
6 And king Rehoboam consulted with the old men, that stood before Solomon his father while he yet lived, and said, How do ye advise that I may answer this people?
7 And they spake unto him, saying, if thou wilt be a servant unto this people this day, and wilt serve them, and answer them, and speak good words to them, then they will be thy servants for ever.
8 But he forsook the counsel of the old men, which they had given him, and consulted with the young men that were grown up with him, and which stood before him: . . .
10 And the young men that were grown up with him spake unto him, saying, Thus shalt thou speak unto this people that spake unto thee saying, Thy father made our yoke heavy, but make thou it lighter unto us; thus shalt thou say unto them, My little finger shall be thicker than my father's loins.
11 And now whereas my father did lade you with a heavy yoke, I will

add to your yoke: my father hath chastised you with whips, but I will chastise you with scorpions. . . .

16 So when all Israel saw that the king hearkened not unto them, the people answered the king, saying, What portion have we in David? neither have we inheritance in the son of Jesse: to your tents, O Israel: now see to thine own house, David. So Israel departed unto their tents. . . .

19 So Israel rebelled against the house of David unto this day.

There was variable news from Colonel Peter in the South. On March 21 his regiment, the men uniformed with hunting shirts and leggings, had marched for Suffolk. A few days later we find Peter (if we look into his account book) paying £3 "for a fish net,"[13] which may suggest that the campaign at this time was not too absorbing. Mr. Swaine, now Peter's adjutant, kept Daddy Muhlenberg pretty well informed of what was going on; though his letters, receipt of which is recorded in Henry Melchior's Journals, have unfortunately (because what Swaine wrote always had spice in it) not been preserved.

Daddy Muhlenberg may have heard about the fish net. In a letter of May 26 to Betsy and Emanuel Schultze, he wrote caustically, "Our Sons of Freedom have not yet accomplished any heroic deeds."[14]

But the Pastor spoke too soon. It was only the day after he had dropped this unflattering remark that General Lee ordered Peter and his regiment to a post where they were to win reputation if not glory. Peter, it is to be observed, was a bold but safe commander who won high commendation by every action in which he was engaged. But publicity, which is the better part of glory, he never sought; and he was content to let those with better press agents reap the fame.

The British planned an attack on Charleston. So well had Peter Muhlenberg equipped and trained the men of his four-months-old regiment that General Lee spotted it for the action.

"It was the strength and good condition of the regiment," wrote Lee, who had from that time on the highest opinion of Muhlenberg, ranking him with Schuyler, Sullivan, Wayne, Greene, and Knox, "that induced me to order it out of its own province in preference to any other."[15]

The Eighth Virginia reached Charleston on June 23, in time to get into the hot action of June 28. Its arrival, as Lee said, "made us very strong."

The action began with a British attack on Fort Moultrie, on Sullivan's Island. Muhlenberg's regiment was sent to reinforce Colonel Thompson's, which was trying to prevent the enemy from getting onto the island behind Fort Moultrie and thus attacking it from the rear. The British were repulsed by a vigorous and brilliant defense.

General Lee, in his report on this important engagement (which ended all serious British attempts in the South for two and a half years), after praising the garrison of Fort Moultrie and complimenting Colonel Thompson, wrote, "I know not which corps I have the greatest reason to be pleased with, Muhlenberg's Virginians or the North Carolina Troops; they are both equally alert, zealous, and spirited."[16]

Alert, zealous, and *spirited* are good words for a soldier. They serve to remind us that Muhlenberg, though known as a good disciplinarian and recruiting officer, proved himself to be much more than that at Brandywine, Germantown, Portsmouth, and Yorktown.

But the months that followed the American success at Charleston were not months of victory. Peter's regiment was sent south to Savannah with an expedition intended to destroy the enemy post on St. Mary's River and overawe the Florida Indians with a show of force. It accomplished neither objective. It destroyed only the health and morale of its own officers and men. The troops had been sent off too hastily, without proper equipment, proper supplies, or a proper medical chest. They spent nearly two months in Savannah, during the most sickly season of the year. The experience was particularly hard on men from the Shenandoah Valley, accustomed to the mountain air of Virginia. The regiment went to pieces. Major Helfenstein was taken ill and died soon after returning to the north. Peter Muhlenberg contracted a disease of the liver that was to bother him, on and off, for the remainder of the war, and finally carry him off at the age of sixty-one.

When Peter, back in Virginia, wrote to his father, December 20, 1776, about the campaign he and Mr. Swaine had made together, he had no cheerful news to tell. Indeed, there seemed to be no cheerful news from any quarter. The British had won the Battle of Long

Island, had easily taken New York, had captured Fort Washington, and had hunted and harried the beaten American army, now reduced to a pitiful three thousand men, across New Jersey to the Delaware. Despondency was everywhere. Even George Washington was not immune to it.

"In a word," he wrote to his brother, "if every nerve is not strained to recruit the new army with all possible expedition, I think the game is pretty nearly up."[17]

At the Trappe, Henry Melchior and Anna Maria had the evidences of the war before their eyes. "Wagons filled with household goods," wrote the Pastor on Friday, December 13, "men, women, and children fleeing from Philadelphia went by all day."

News came that on December 12, in a tavern at Baskinridge, near Bedminster where the elder Muhlenberg and his sons had often preached, General Lee had been captured by British cavalrymen. The General surrendered himself politely, in order to save, as he said, the inn in which he was found from being burned. It is suspected he had given himself up to save the humiliation of being involved in the impending collapse of the American cause.

"In short," wrote Henry Melchior, "it is said, to the joy of many and the terror of many more, that the British armies will eat their Christmas dinner in Philadelphia. . . ."

The final blow seemed to fall when it was rumored that General Washington himself had been killed.

"Weel," said a Scotsman in the American army, "I'm glad to hear it, for he was too gude a mon to be hanged."[18]

CHAPTER XV

BRANDYWINE

Despite the news Frederick sent his father of the Battle of Princeton ("the Americans seem to have won," wrote Henry Melchior in his Journal), the year 1777 opened with foreboding. It is true, General Howe had not eaten "his Christmas dinner as a guest of the rich Quakers, etc. in Philadelphia," as rumor said he had promised to do; but to the worried Pastor in New Providence the situation seemed dismal enough, especially with refugees pouring into the parsonage in such numbers. On January 2 he noted that during the past night he had had thirty souls in his "hospital"—most of them children, who entertained their elders "with concerts made up of semitones."

What was one to think? The victories of Trenton and Princeton might have refreshed the spirit of the Americans, but they had not changed the military situation. They had only made the British more cautious. The enemy had now entrenched himself near Brunswick, and was in a position to make what sorties he liked. Meantime the colonial economy was slowly disintegrating.

"Depressing prospects!" he wrote. "The provinces are being ruined, high prices prevail, and impoverishment is growing apace."[1]

Howe would have been pleased to see these lines, for this was precisely the effect he intended to produce. He aimed not so much at a smashing military victory as at the exercise of judicious pressure, in order to let the Americans see for themselves that it was to the material advantage of the colonies to work with the mother country and to continue to gear their policies, economic as well as political, with hers.

If Henry Melchior at times appears to us bewildered, it is not because he was in any doubt where his sympathies lay. There was irony, but no confusion about issues, in his professed inability to decide which was right, England or America: whether England, as he put it, had the right to make serfs of the Americans, or whether the Americans had not a better right to defend their God-given liberties.

His neutral principles forbidding him to cheer for either side, he took a seeming pleasure in condemning both. It is to be noted, however, that the burden of his wrath lay heaviest on the mother country.

"It is true," he wrote, January 4, 1777, "America needs and deserves God's rod of correction and punishment. Yet it is to be regretted that England has so degenerated that the Lord God finds it a fit agent to serve as disciplinarian and executioner over its own daughter. In former times, when a criminal was found guilty and sentenced to death by the court here, neither the chief justice nor the *sheriff* wished to carry out the sentence, and so they usually hired a scoundrel to do it who himself deserved to be put to death."[2]

Fears for Philadelphia mounted. In March a friend from the city said that a huge British army was being assembled from all sides to give the American cause the *coup de grâce*. In April the Pastor heard that a captured British spy from New York had, before his execution, revealed that he had been sent "to secure the most skillful pilots who were to pilot the British battleships up the Delaware to Philadelphia."

In the midst of all these causes for uneasiness and depression, there came to Henry Melchior sad news from England. It was word of the death, on March 20, of Court Preacher Ziegenhagen. Henry Melchior's world was breaking up—the Old World as well as the New.

Muhlenberg was not alone in his apprehensions. The colonies as a whole took no sanguine view of American affairs. It seemed for a time not unlikely that the war might bog down in the sheer apathy of discouraged housewives and tradesmen.

But there was Tom Paine, building morale with *The American Crisis*. And there was Washington. To those actually in the field under Washington's leadership, even the shadow of disaster seemed a spur to greater courage and energy. Out of the apparently unending defeats of the New York and New Jersey campaigns, Washington had suddenly wrested the victories of Trenton and Princeton. It could be done again, and his men knew he would do it.

But first there must be more soldiers. Trenton and Princeton had been mere tactical successes. They had not seriously impaired the growing British strength. To stave off defeat and persuade America's possible European allies that aid to the colonies was not what today's slang calls "Operation Rathole," it was necessary to build a new army.

Colonel Muhlenberg, who in the spring of 1776 had raised and trained his regiment with such speed and firmness that General Lee had pronounced it the most complete regiment of the whole continent as well as "the best armed, clothed, and equipped for immediate service,"[3] was accordingly, by resolution of Congress, instructed to bring his now much depleted regiment back to full strength and to send on each company to Washington's camp as soon as its ranks were filled.

On the twenty-first of February, Muhlenberg was advanced to the rank of brigadier general. On the twenty-third, still unaware of his promotion, he wrote to Washington reporting the want of officers for recruiting, and proposing his adjutant, "Mr. Swaine," as a "good officer" to raise a company.[4] Mr. Swaine rode with this message 218 miles in five days to the Trappe, where he spent a day with the family, and then went on to Washington's camp at Morristown.

Washington sent Swaine back with a captain's commission for himself and an earnest entreaty to Brigadier General Muhlenberg to hasten recruiting.

"Much, very much indeed, depends upon our being reinforced immediately," wrote George Johnston, Washington's aide-de-camp. He concluded, "His Excelly expects to see you here in a few days; there being at present not a sufficient Number of Gen[l]. Officers with the Army."[5]

When Mr. Swaine left the Trappe on his way back to Virginia with a batch of letters, a quantity of money, and a "young, wild horse" cavorting under him, Henry Melchior viewed his departure with an anxiety that was mixed with amusement. Mr. Swaine, it appears, was "not an experienced rider," and his horse, apprised of this situation, had a very evident mind to throw him.

Pastor Muhlenberg noted demurely in his Journal, "Unless the

Lord affords him special protection, it is a question whether he will reach home, two hundred miles from here, without an accident."[6]

Mr. Swaine went home to Virginia by way of Tulpehocken, where he had a long letter to deliver from Daddy Muhlenberg to the Schultzes. Two days later, Henry Melchior was inspired to write again to the Schultzes, this time with pressing inquiries about the bearer of his earlier letter.

"We are rather worried about Swaine," he said, "and would like to know whether, when, and in what condition he reached you? He has a small, wild and unbroken horse, and he is still an inexperienced rider. . . . When he mounted here, the horse bounded into the air backwards, forwards, and sideways and tried every trick to throw him off, so I am afraid he had a perilous journey, unless the Lord took him under His special protection."[7]

Mr. Swaine reached Virginia safely with his letters, money, and good news; and when next we hear of him, on May 16, he is posted in General Orders as Brigade Major to Brigadier General Muhlenberg.

Peter Muhlenberg remained in Virginia long enough to bring order into the Virginia Line, which, having for some time been without a brigadier because of the death of General Mercer and the withdrawal of General Lewis, had fallen into confusion. Peter paid a flying visit to Washington's camp at Morristown early in April. On the thirteenth he was formally assigned the First, Fifth, Ninth, and Thirteenth Regiments of the Virginia Line (the Eighth was added later) to make up his brigade, with instructions to get them ready at once "to take the Field." He returned to Virginia on this duty.

At the Trappe there was much movement and uneasiness. British warships having been sighted, April 13, at the mouth of the Delaware, Henry Melchior ordered a freight wagon to bring Henry Ernest's household things up from Philadelphia. On the seventeenth Henry Ernest's parents-in-law, the Halls, came to Providence, occupying there a small house belonging to the Pastor and beside the one he himself occupied. On the eighteenth Mr. Kucher and David Schaeffer, with their wives and children, stopped on their way into the country for safety, which they hoped to find at the distant village of Lebanon on Quittapahilla Creek. On the nineteenth Major Swaine and Polly, with Chaplain Streit, turned up from Virginia.

In Philadelphia, Peggy, whose husband was remaining in the city to look after the Lutheran congregations of St. Michael's and Zion (with help for the time being from Henry Ernest), wrote another letter to her sister Betsy in Tulpehocken. It gives so excellent a picture not only of the spirited Peggy herself but also of Philadelphia before the occupation, that it must be presented in full.

The top of the letter is scribbled over with shopping notes, intended, one may suppose, to show what inflation meant to a city housewife.

April 24

Tea 31 sch a pound Coffe 4.6 a p
Chocalate 4 sch black Shugar 2 sch
lofe Shugar 5.6 a pound

Deer Sister,

this Morning i received your letter and the butter I dont know now wether you Sent me the butter for a present or wether you bought it for me because you did not Send the priss of it

2 weeks ago i had a man to thake the wool cards up but I beleife he got presst he never came for the things I bought 2 pair but very dear there are none to be had for love nor money it Just happend that very day Mr Marsteller brought your letter I bought 6 pair to go to New-garmintown So I kept 2 pair they cost 25 schil a pair by the half a dosen a good friend of mine got them now I Shold [be] very much oblidge to you if you wold get me butter for one pairs and Some of Mr Spykers or Som other Clean person duch Cheese. I have eat them all of Mis Spyker or 30 pound of butter and the rest of money for Cheese try your best

the town is prety much in uprore the People move fast out of town I do intend to Stay only make hast and Send Cheese and butter before the regulars come I think it tis better for us to live in town than for daddy for he declairs if whe move he will come doun he says he is old but i am afraid he wold fair bad because Peter is Genral So whe must Stay I hope god almighty will help us thrieve he can thake kear of us as well in toun as in the contry

if you cold Send the butter and Cheese to daddy then he wold Send it here or when Kuchers waggons Coms to town for Shaffers you might Send it only be quick about it for fear the English wold be here before i get it maby this may be the last letter you get of me I hope you will thake good kear of my Chessts if you must Fly thake them along for all my riches are at your house in the hary trunck be quick about what you do for me little betsy has not had the Smallpox yet maby She will get them Soon they are all about our neaberhood all old friends are well

I have a very big family Mistris Zetwitz and 3 Children and a neguere boy So you may think I have work anuf or i wold write more and then i have no oppertunity up to your house If this Shold be the last letter you get from me before our City gets destroyed I hope that whe Shall See one another again but if not I hope to See you in another world Farewell god bless you and all your Family remember my love to Mr. schultz and all other Freinds

dont let no appertunity pass without writing and if only you write your name then i can write back again

P S mind the woolcards cost 25 sch a pair the 2 pare Come to 2.10 if they are to dear Send them back [or?] keep them

I remain your Sister Peggy
them that i gave you only cost 5.6 last year[8]

The high cost of living in a time of revolution was abundantly attested in Henry Melchior Muhlenberg's Journal. On May 5 the Pastor noted that the Lutherans of Reading would have been glad to have Frederick as their preacher, but the price of necessaries in that town, to which many well-to-do Philadelphia folk had fled, made it impossible for him to live there.

Which reminded him, he said, of the time King George of England, on a journey to Hanover, was driven by storm onto the coast of Holland. He with his escort stayed for the night at the hut of a peasant, who gave them supper. For five eggs and a little pumpernickel the man charged 120 guldens.

"Are eggs so rare here?" asked His Majesty with a laugh.

"No," replied his host, "but kings are."

The signs of disaster for Philadelphia grew rapidly more ominous. At twilight on May 11 Henry Melchior's neighbors saw the unusual sight of large numbers of "ravens and crows crying and fighting." Muhlenberg, who was neutral about many superstitions, said that one should not ascribe significance to the cries of birds, but that, nevertheless, one might reasonably conclude that "wheresoever the carcass is, there will the eagles be gathered together."

Frederick Muhlenberg packed three freight wagons, and left on

May 13 for New Hanover, some nine or ten miles farther back in the country. With him in a stage wagon went his wife, three children, the children's maid, and Polly. Polly had been for some time living in Virginia with Peter's wife, Hannah; but she could not exist without Mr. Swaine, and so, when Major Swaine found himself in Washington's camp, Polly posted north to be in his vicinity. Which, thought Daddy Muhlenberg, was mere foolishness. To leave Virginia for Pennsylvania at such a time as this was but "fleeing from a drizzle into a downpour" or "from Goshen to the desert."[9]

It was on May 16 that Henry Melchior drove in a chaise to Philadelphia to see Henry Ernest, who was ill with a swollen neck and face, and by so doing unleashed a pack of rumors. Some innocent words, as he learned a few days later, which he had dropped about his son's stiff neck, had been twisted into a report that his son had been hanged for treasonable correspondence with General Howe.[10] Old Muhlenberg himself, said the rumormongers, had been taken to the city for a dose of the same medicine. The rumor spread widely, to the grief of his friends and the delight of his enemies.

Peter during these last few weeks had been organizing his brigade at Morristown, where Washington's army, carefully drawn up behind entrenchments in a strong position on the heights, was watching to see which way the British cat was going to jump. Muhlenberg's brigade and Weedon's, both composed of Virginia troops, were put under the command of Major General Greene.

Months passed, filled with skillful maneuvering between the opposing armies in northern New Jersey, during which Peter Muhlenberg's brigade saw some spirited skirmishing. But the real campaign did not begin until late in July. Then Washington, learning that Howe had finally put to sea with his army, took his own troops south to Chester, Pennsylvania, to be ready for Howe when, and wherever, he landed.

The progress of the Pennsylvania campaign is clearly mirrored in Henry Melchior's Journal, for his home at the Trappe was constantly visited by Major Swaine or General Peter. On July 29 (the day Peter's brigade reached Coryell's Ferry, now New Hope, on the Delaware), the Pastor observed that the American command was bewildered by Howe's tactics and at a loss to divine his intentions. The British fleet was "still cruising about with its troop transports," being sighted now and again, only to disappear off to sea again, leaving the "American politici" (as well as General Washington himself) at a loss as to the British objective. The American army was kept on the move, and the men suffered much from the heat. Pennsylvania's state militiamen were called to arms.

The Pastor reported on the thirtieth the "frightful news" that the British fleet, with 160 transports, had reached the Capes of the Delaware.[11]

Peter was in Philadelphia, and Frederick, Mr. Swaine, and Polly went off to meet him there. The militia were pouring through the Trappe, headed for the city.

"What one used to hear in the country at this season of the year," wrote Henry Melchior, "was the music of the swish of flails in three-quarter time, but now one hears drums, fifes, and war cries instead."[12]

Still no one knew what the British were up to. At a Board of General Officers held at Neshaminy, August 21, it was concluded that Howe must have gone south to Charleston. General Muhlenberg advised, accordingly, that the army should move immediately toward the Hudson in order to meet the threat from General Burgoyne in the north.[13]

The strain of all the marching and countermarching in this extreme heat, of attending to his duties in camp, which included providing straw and rum for those on the sick list, and of keeping an eye, too, on his lovesick wife—all this was too much for good-natured, easy-going Major Swaine. He grew slack in his work and was court-martialed. At Headquarters "near the Cross Roads," on August 22, he was reprimanded in General Orders for "repeated neglect of duty,"[14] and he withdrew from the service. He turned up next day at the parsonage in Providence.

It was sad for Mr. Swaine, not because he was sensitive to reproof, nor because the disgrace, such as it was, seriously interrupted his conviviality in camp (he was all the time riding back to visit his old friends and pick up the latest camp news), but because he missed taking part in the grand parade of the American army as it passed through Philadelphia, August 24, 1777. Mr. Swaine, in uniform, would have been good for public morale.

General Muhlenberg's brigade of some two thousand well-equipped and well-disciplined troops had been chosen by Washington as the vanguard of the procession, one of the prime purposes of the show being to strengthen the loyalty of wavering citizens by the spectacle of American power and polish.

Washington's General Orders, with instructions for the march, do special honor to Muhlenberg's brigade. After a few small units which were to lead the procession, the order of march was to be as follows:

> One hundred yards in rear of the pioneers, a regiment from Muhlenberg's brigade; and close in the rear of that regiment, all Muhlenberg's Field Artillery; then his brigade, followed by Weedon's, Woodford's, and Scott's, in order, with all their field artillery . . . ; Lincoln's and Lord Stirling's divisions following . . .
>
> The whole is to march by subdivisions at half distance, the ranks and files at the most convenient distance for marching. Which is to be exactly observed in passing thro' the City, and great attention given by the officers to see that the men carry their arms well, and are made to appear as decent as circumstances will admit. . . .
>
> The drums and fifes of each brigade are to be collected in the centre of it, and a time for the quick step played, but with such moderation, that the men may step to it with ease; and without *dancing* along or totally disregarding the music, as too often has been the case. The men are to be excused from carrying their Camp Kettles tomorrow. . . .[15]

The irrepressible Mr. Swaine was not the man to brood or to harbor a grievance. By August 25 he had recovered his poise sufficiently to ride off to Philadelphia, and we find him frequently thereafter riding between the Trappe and the camp, carrying someone's message or just going for a chat and to pick up the news.

August 25 was a busy day for the Howe brothers as well as for Mr. Swaine. That was the day, as Henry Melchior heard, that the British fleet, composed of some three hundred vessels, put in at the Head of Elk and proceeded to land the troops.

The invasion of Pennsylvania had begun. Henry Melchior hid his Journals and sent his best clothes for safety to the Schultzes at Tulpehocken.

George Washington was at his best during the next few weeks. He had small hopes of winning any major engagement. But, having a wavering public opinion to lead as well as an army, and knowing the temper of his people, he was resolved to give no appearance of avoiding battle. It was safer to be beaten than not to fight.

Sir William Howe, too, was at his best. It was his policy to give the impression of unhurried, irresistible power—the backbone of law and order. He, like Washington, had always the general public in his mind. He meant to coax the Revolution to collapse. His purpose was as much to convince the American citizen of the hopelessness—and worthlessness—of the struggle, as it was to occupy towns or defeat the enemy in scattered battles.

Howe's prime objective, therefore, appears to have been, not the capture of Philadelphia, but either the annihilation of Washington's army or the cutting it off from its base of supplies at Reading and so separating Pennsylvania from the southern colonies.[16]

Washington, for his part, had small hope of saving Philadelphia. But he wished to accomplish four things:

1. Teach Howe (and the citizens of Pennsylvania) that the American army was not afraid of British regulars.
2. Escape annihilation in the process of demonstrating this.
3. Save his supplies.
4. Preserve his liberty of movement and his communications with the other colonies.

In the outcome, Howe, though his soldiership was brilliant, got only the city. Washington gained all his objectives.

On September 10 Peter Muhlenberg, who for the past few weeks had been dashing about "now at the Swamp [New Hanover], now at the Trapp, now in camp or in Philadelphia," took position with his brigade in Greene's division at Chad's Ford on Brandywine Creek, covering the approaches to the city.

Greene's division, assisted by Wayne's brigade, was in the center of the army, facing the ford. The divisions of Sullivan, Stirling, and Stevens were strung out along the creek to cover the fords as far north as the Forks of the Brandywine. Armstrong and the Pennsylvania militia held the fords to the south, on Greene's left.

Howe's position was at Kennett Square, a few miles to the west of Chad's Ford.

The English took the initiative and fought a daring, brilliant, and successful battle. At daybreak Knyphausen's Hessians, assisted by a couple of English brigades, advanced to Chad's Ford.

"About sunrise," wrote an American volunteer who went through the battle, "a small body of the enemy appeared opposite Chad's Ford and began a heavy cannonade upon our lines, which was returned with equal vigor."[17] Infantry attacks were launched, to be met by the American General Maxwell's light troops on "the meadows of the Brandywine." In one of these engagements, Lieutenant Peter Weiser, a cousin of General Muhlenberg, was shot through the body and left to be captured by the enemy.[18]

These British thrusts at Chad's Ford were, however, intended to do no more than "amuse" their opponents while the battle was being decided in another quarter. General Cornwallis in a daring but well-executed movement took the larger part of the British army north, making a circuit of seventeen miles, and crossed the Brandywine above the Forks at Jeffries' Ford. Washington's intelligence service faltered, and Cornwallis approached without interference. If it had not been for Squire Cheney, the Quaker, who saw the British troops coming through the woods, and galloped his horse across the fields to give warning, the American army might have been annihilated. As it was, it was a near thing. Cheney's news was at first discounted, and the British had time to get into position behind Sullivan and draw up in line of battle on Osborne Hill behind Birmingham Meeting.

Once certain of the new British plan of battle, Washington moved swiftly. Wayne's brigade was instructed to hold Knyphausen at Chad's Ford. Sullivan, with Greene's division as a reserve, swung his three divisions round to face Cornwallis. In executing this maneuver, however, Sullivan's troops fell into some disorder, and, before they were able to take proper form, Cornwallis attacked them. A sharp fight followed, lasting nearly an hour; but in the end the Americans gave way.

Washington, meanwhile, had ordered Greene's division, composed of Muhlenberg's and Weedon's brigades, to leave Wayne at the Ford and go to the assistance of Sullivan. The men moved fast, covering the four miles, it is said, in three-quarters of an hour. At a spot already chosen by Washington for defense in just such an emergency, where the road from Birmingham Meeting to Dilworth passed through a defile flanked by woods on both sides, Greene's division was quickly posted. Weedon's brigade was drawn up in the defile, to provide a protecting point behind which the retreating troops might have time to rally, while Muhlenberg's brigade advanced to meet the enemy on the road.

". . . about half after five o'clock," continues the volunteer writing for the *Pennsylvania Evening Post,* "the attack began again, and lasted near one hour longer. . . ."

There was good fighting during that hour. Muhlenberg charged again and again. His brigade was outnumbered, for Cornwallis' main force was now directed against him. But the Virginians succeeded in breaking the momentum of the British advance, and held the enemy until the bulk of the American army escaped. Then Muhlenberg and Weedon retired in good order, helping to extricate Anthony Wayne, whose brigade had at last given way before the Hessians at Chad's Ford.

The approach of darkness saved the American army. Cornwallis' men had marched too far and fought too hard to risk a twilight engagement with disciplined troops like Muhlenberg's. The pursuit was not pressed.

The British paid high honor to Muhlenberg's and Weedon's brigades. "They exhibited a degree of firmness, order, and resolution," said an English writer in the *Annual Register,* "and preserved such a countenance in extremely sharp service, as would not have discredited veterans."[19]

The American army withdrew to Chester. It had been outmaneuvered and outfought. It had been driven from the field. But it had not been crushed. It still had resilience. It was to come back, three weeks later, at Germantown to demonstrate its unbroken spirit, and to corroborate Howe's judgment that the Revolution was not to be crushed by winning a few battles.

On the day after the Battle of the Brandywine, there appeared in the *Pennsylvania Evening Post* the fourth of Tom Paine's series of articles on *The American Crisis.* It served then as a morale-builder. It serves now to put this great battle in perspective.

> Those who expect to reap the blessings of freedom, must, like men, undergo the fatigue of supporting it. The event of yesterday is one of those kind of alarms which is just sufficient to rouse us to duty, without being of consequence enough to depress our fortitude. It is not a field of a few acres of ground, but a cause that we are defending, and whether we defeat the enemy in one battle, or by degrees, the consequence will be the same.

CHAPTER XVI

THE FALL OF PHILADELPHIA

On September 11, 1777, Henry Melchior Muhlenberg, in his parsonage at the Trappe, wrote these words in his Journal: "This morning we heard heavy and long continued cannonading some thirty miles away on Brandywine Crick. . . ."

A few hours later he added, "Now prepare thyself, Pennsylvania, to meet the Lord thy God!"

The Pastor was a badly frightened man, and he had cause to be. He knew that this was the battle for Philadelphia and that the Americans had lost it. He knew that he himself, as a leader of the Germans who formed so considerable a part of the population of Pennsylvania, would be watched by the British, especially since his son was a general in the American army, and since he himself had accepted the authority of the new republic. Once the British were in Philadelphia, they would have him within reach, for the Trappe was only twenty-seven miles away. He may have had a premonition of what he was soon enough to know with certainty, that some among the enemy were determined to get their hands on him and hang him as an "arch rebel."

His anxieties were not only for himself. There were many dependent on him. In the first place, there was that part of the general public which looked to him as a church leader for guidance in this time of political perplexity. There were also many refugees who had fled to the Pastor's house at the Trappe for protection, at least for a night or two, on their way to find safety with relatives or friends farther back in the country. In addition to all these were the grown-up members of his own family who, with careers interrupted and homes broken up in New York, Philadelphia, and Woodstock, had made the house at the Trappe their headquarters and relied on "Daddy Muhlenberg" for advice and security.

Before we embark on the story of the adventures war brought to the parsonage, we should stop for a moment to remind ourselves of the more or less permanent members of the household.

There was, first of all, Hannah, wife of "our general," as the family called Peter, and their child, Henry, not quite two years old.

Peter himself, of course, was with the army. But during the weeks before and after the Battle of the Brandywine the family never knew at what moment he might pop in on them, seeking a good bed for the night and exchanging news of the war for news of the family. After a time these visits became less frequent, and during the months the army was at Valley Forge, although Peter's brigade headquarters were only seven or eight miles away, he rarely communicated with his father—not from neglect but rather from solicitude. Peter knew the Tories held his father under suspicion. For the General to have been in constant communication with him would have subjected them both to great danger, because the house was almost certainly watched. Peter tried to get his father to move back into the country, but the old man, for reasons he thought good, declined to go. Peter settled the difficulty, in part at least, by himself avoiding the place, and meeting his father, as he did on occasion, at some distance from his home.

Though the elder Muhlenberg was proud of his son, a brigadier general at the age of thirty, he had not yet quite forgiven him for throwing off his ministerial gown on that memorable Sunday morning at Woodstock in January of '76. A churchman should not take up arms. The reconciliation of father and son, toward the end of the Valley Forge winter, at a rendezvous back in the country, is one of the beautiful incidents in the history of the Muhlenberg family; for there Henry Melchior was finally convinced that a revolution sanctioned by George Washington and supported by Brigadier General the Reverend Peter Muhlenberg and his friends could not be running counter to religion.

But we are looking too far ahead and must return to the anxious household at the Trappe on the day of the battle.

Frederick Augustus Muhlenberg was in the neighborhood with his family. So also was Henry Ernest. That is to say, at the time of Brandywine Henry was flitting back and forth between Philadelphia and the Trappe, unwilling to leave the city and at the same time fiercely determined not to work with the invader. When the British finally took possession of the city, he left it and stayed away—though he did not mind getting a copy of Linnaeus' *Philosophia Botanica* passed through the British lines[1] (with the help of his sister Peggy), and beginning with it his famous career in American botany.

Henry Ernest is a surprising character. Underneath the wise and kindly patience that was to make him a good pastor, a good college president, and a great botanist, lay a generous irascibility, untouched by anything vindictive or mean, which reminds us of his grandfather Conrad Weiser. Henry Ernest, though not as explosive as General Peter, could quickly grow hot in good causes.

Then there was the romantic Polly, who had shocked the family by her elopement; and of course her husband, Mr. Swaine.

Henry Melchior himself, the head of the family, was not at this time the dynamic figure the church histories have made familiar to us. The title by which he is best known, Patriarch of the Lutheran Church in America, conveys no impression of the toiling life of a saddlebag preacher which had been his for many years after his arrival in America, and which had at last so worn him down that now, at the age of sixty-six, he had little joy left in living.

But there was nothing sickly or feeble about his mind and will. To pursue the neutral course he had charted for himself through the troubled waters of the Revolution took resolution and nerve, both of which he had in abundance, and both of which were to be shown at their best during the months that followed Brandywine.

Chief among his anxieties in the fall of 1777 was the condition of his wife, Anna Maria. Though she was strong and buoyant on her good days (it was easy to see from which side of the family came the spirit and dash of Peter and Polly), Henry Melchior never knew when one of her epileptic paroxysms might seize her. He was always afraid of her falling into the fire. Excitement brought on the attacks, and the proximity of the parsonage to the theater of war was the worst thing possible for her. Yet she feared to leave home. She hated the thought of travel and of living among strangers.

Their youngest daughter Sally was, of course, always at hand to help. She was the only one of the children not yet married and with responsibilities of her own to attend to. But she was at this time only eleven years old, and not strong enough to take much of the burden off her mother.

Such was the household that listened to the guns of Brandywine, and knew that Washington's beaten army (the news traveled fast), with its ill-clad, ill-fed, and ill-disciplined troops, could afford them little protection against the cruelties of civil war.

The dreaded climax of the summer had now come. The enemy, in Henry Melchior's expressive phrase, were now "in the heart and bowels of Pennsylvania." They were about to take Philadelphia. The Pastor himself had long foreseen this event. As early as March of that year, in anticipation of Pennsylvania's becoming "the rubbish heap," as he called it, "of this wretched war," he had considered forsaking Pennsylvania, as Peter advised him to do, and taking a farm in Virginia near Peter's place in the Shenandoah Valley. Here he would find quiet, safety, and comfort. There was plenty to eat in Virginia. Here a man could still "fry his bacon in butter."

But he decided against it. It was not because he was ignorant of the dangers at the Trappe, but because he did not think it right to leave his flock, like a hireling, as he said, in time of danger. His flight would have a bad effect on local morale. Sticking to his post at Augustus Church in Providence was one way in which he could help his son's patriotic cause without breaking his own strict neutrality. Frederick, to whom he confided his problem, advised him to stay.

The decision, although made earnestly, was not irrevocable. When he first made it, the dangers were merely hypothetical. Later, when they materialized and took an unexpected and deadly form, he had to make up his mind over and over again, each time with increasing difficulty. The way of the neutral was almost too hard. Both sides threatened him—the one with tar and feathers, the other with a rope.

To understand the crisis when it came, and the strange methods the Pastor took to meet it, it is necessary for us to know something of the unceasing strain upon a sickly man of the military campaign now swirling past his doorstep, and the many incidental annoyances that accompanied it.

For a man who liked to have a book or a pen in his hand, and a quiet room to work in, there was pain as well as distraction in the noise and bustle of the crowds that now pressed into the eight-room parsonage, with a clatter of coming and going, cooking and washing and eating, the small children "muling and puking" in everybody's arms.

Movement was all about him. On Friday, September 12, the day after Brandywine, Mr. Swaine rode off to Philadelphia to see what was to be seen and hear what was to be heard. During the afternoon of the thirteenth, Mr. Swaine came back with his news, and in the evening Henry Ernest arrived from the city, accompanied by "his wife and child and maid, . . . his parents-in-law, Mr. and Mrs. Hall, and a manservant." Early on Sunday morning, the fourteenth, Frederick Augustus and Henry Ernest went back to Philadelphia to get out Frederick's parents-in-law, the Schaeffers. It was a "noisy Sabbath," as the Patriarch wrote in his Journal. There was no end to the riding by on the Philadelphia Road of "chaises, coaches, and freight wagons" filled with refugees.

Monday was no quieter. The air was filled with the sound of ammunition wagons toiling by up the road toward Bethlehem, in an effort to save the American ammunition magazine from capture. Washington had rightly surmised that this, as much as the capture of Philadelphia, was Howe's objective. Toward evening Frederick came back from the city with news that the American forces had left it. With Frederick was his mother-in-law and a wagon full of household goods. Eighteen persons slept that night in the house. Some moved on next morning to safer places, and Henry Melchior himself was urged to flee with his wife and daughters.

Across the river, he was told, the British army could be seen from Providence with the aid of a field glass. The American army was also approaching. In the vicinity of two maneuvering armies, law and order could not be expected to prevail. Greater than the danger from shot and shell was that from stragglers thrown off by both armies, and from the professional criminals who took advantage of these unquiet times to ply their trade.

"No place is safe," wrote Muhlenberg. "Where the two armies do not go, one finds thieves, robbers, and murderers . . ."[2]

On September 19, the American army crossed the Schuylkill River at Parker's Ford, the men wading up to their waists in swift water, and came four miles across country to the Philadelphia road, which they reached at Muhlenberg's house. During the night Washington himself passed through the Trappe. All night long the Muhlenbergs heard the rumble and clatter of men, horses, and guns moving past their door toward Swede's Ford (at Norristown), where Howe was expected to attempt a crossing. There was much knocking at the Muhlenberg door.

"At midnight," wrote the Pastor, "a regiment camped in the street in front of my house. Some vegetables and chickens were taken, and a man with a flint came to my chamber, demanded bread, etc."[3]

All next day Anna Maria and her daughters were busy making bread. Two large bakings were distributed among the soldiers as they came out of the huge outdoor bake-oven.

On Sunday the twenty-first, word sped through the village that the British army was in motion, headed for the ford near Providence, and would come out on the Great Road, as Washington's army had done, at Muhlenberg's house. The British had, in fact, made such a motion, and in consequence the American troops which had recently passed through Providence to watch the lower fords, turned back to check the new threat from above—and avoid being cut off from their supply base.

Again the Muhlenbergs were urged to fly. The place, it was said, was about to become a battlefield, and the house would be plundered and burned. The younger members of the family made up their minds to go, and began to pack. Their father was undecided. Perhaps his wife should go, despite the dangers of traveling in her condition; but he himself . . . While he was debating the matter, a sudden storm of rain sprang up and delayed the departure. When the storm ceased, plans were resumed. They would go at midnight when the moon was up. But at twelve o'clock they heard the rumble of fieldpieces moving up the road, announcing the vanguard of the returning American army. The road was blocked and the Pastor's family could not get through.

The remainder of the night was not for sleep. Soldiers stopped at the house and pounded on the door "as if they would break it." Fortunately one of their officers, German-speaking, came up and drove them away. Hour after hour, in the darkness, the troops tramped by.

By morning the road seemed to be clear. They hitched up a wagon, and a few of them (but neither the Pastor nor his sick wife) drove off. A mile up the road they were stopped at the American camp, which stretched across the road, and had to go back to try a detour.

Meanwhile Henry Ernest, who had remained behind with his father and mother, decided to make one last visit to the city (where he had property), and he disappeared in that direction. There was anxiety in the family when he did not reappear the next day.

In the campaign for the city, there had now come a sudden turn for the worse. Washington, who, it will be recalled, had a few days before crossed the Schuylkill to the city side, had marched and countermarched in order to watch the fords at which Howe might attempt to cross. But Howe had eluded him. Making a feint at the American flank higher up the river, Howe forced Washington to move his troops back up the road beyond the Trappe. Then Howe doubled back, crossed the river at the Fatland (near Valley Forge) and Swede's Ford at Norristown, and planted himself between the city and Washington's army.

"O poor Philadelphia!" wrote Henry Melchior in his Journal on Tuesday morning, September 23. "It is reported that the British army set out last night by moonlight and marched to Philadelphia."

We know now that by the twenty-fifth the British were actually in possession. From his orchestra seat in the parsonage, Pastor Muhlenberg had watched every move, and it must be admitted that Howe had put on a good show. But it was not the artistry of the performance that interested the Pastor. It was the tragedy of the outcome: the city cut off, and his children within it caught behind what seemed at the time to be an iron curtain.

This was the trap into which Henry Ernest had thrust himself when he made his last journey to the city; and this time Henry Ernest had trouble enough getting out. Tradition tells us he dressed himself up as an Indian—though why he should have made himself conspicuous by adopting this masquerade costume is something to wonder about. However that may be, he did finally get home by a roundabout way, and thereafter he devoted himself, till the end of the Valley Forge episode, to preaching and botanizing in the country.

During the days that followed, fresh visitors crowded into the parsonage. At breakfast on the morning of September 25, the Muhlenbergs entertained two generals, Lord Stirling and Anthony Wayne. That night a hard, cold rain settled down. The soldiers had no tents, and some of them crowded into Muhlenberg's barn. He did not begrudge them shelter, but it distressed him to find the next morning that the little hay he had stored for the cow's feed in winter had all been spoiled or carried away.

Thursday and Friday, September 25 and 26, the Great Road was again flooded with troops. The main American army passed a third time through Providence to take up a position nearer the city. When the army was gone, Muhlenberg looked about him and saw evidences of what Washington described in General Orders on that same Friday as "the base and Wicked practice of plundering the Inhabitants." Destruction was everywhere, as though the gardens, fields, and woods about the Trappe had actually been the scene of a battle. The place had, indeed, been swept by trampling armies. His three acres of buckwheat, which had promised him some fifty bushels for the winter's needs, had suffered like the field described in the Eightieth Psalm: "The boar out of the wood doth waste it, and the wild beast of the field doth devour it." Twenty horses and head of cattle had been turned loose in it. His ten acres of woodland were ruined.

And there seemed to be no end. Washington threatened death to plunderers, but the ravage continued. When the main army moved out, other troops, mostly militia, moved in. For a distance round their camp, the country looked as if a swarm of locusts had been over it. Fences were torn down, houses invaded.

Even Augustus Church was not spared. When the Pastor entered it on Saturday for the funeral of a deacon's child, he saw, as he said, "the abomination of desolation in the temple." The militia were in noisy possession. Straw and manure lay on the floor. Food was scattered on the altar. Someone was at the organ, and what the soldiers sang to his accompaniment was not for edification.

When the Pastor appeared, he was greeted with jeers. The officers joined in. Some of them called up to the organist, "Play a Hessian march."[4] When Muhlenburg presented himself before Colonel Dunlap and asked if this was the promised protection of civil and religious rights, the Colonel excused himself by saying that these were militia, made up of all sorts of nationalities, and could not be kept in proper discipline. There was no redress.

The parsonage itself was not molested. Other homes at the Trappe were less fortunate. The schoolmaster, with tears, complained that for days past he and his wife had not been permitted to warm themselves by their own hearth or to sleep in their own beds.[5]

On October 1, some of the regiments stationed at the Trappe marched off "with flying colors." The remainder of the troops followed them next day, all in the direction of the city. There followed an interval of quiet, but not for long. Rumor reached the parsonage during the night of October 3 (the eve of the Battle of Germantown) that Washington intended to attack the British outposts in the morning.

The night was a strangely disturbed one for the Muhlenbergs. At midnight there came a pounding at the door. Old fears returned. The American troops having left the vicinity, it was thought this might be a visit from the British dragoons. A light was lit, the door was opened, and the Pastor looked out. There was no one in sight. Nothing could be seen but two riderless horses.

Early in the morning the guns began sounding out Germantown way, and the family waited for news. They could not know at the time that General Greene's division (with Muhlenberg's brigade on the left), advancing on Germantown by the Lime Kiln Road, was the only unit in the American army that achieved its first objectives in that misty, mixed-up battle. It routed the enemy in fierce hand-to-hand encounter and got round behind his lines. But other parts of the battle went wrong for the Americans. There was little of that neat coördination that had made the dispositions on both sides at Brandywine a model for military historians. Greene's division, unsupported, had to fall back. It had some difficulty in extricating itself, and then joined the weary retreat toward the Skippack and the Perkiomen.

The family at the Trappe could not know, either, what surprising effect this lost battle was to have in Europe, where France, pondering the wisdom of supporting the new republic, saw in Washington's spirited attack on the Germantown lines so soon after his defeat at Brandywine, evidence of stamina in the American army sufficient to justify the risks of an alliance.

But news of a kind reached the Trappe soon enough. In the afternoon it was known that the troops which had marched away so bravely on Thursday were now streaming back without fanfare.

The next guns heard at the parsonage were salvos fired—endlessly, as it seemed—over the graves of American dead.

CHAPTER XVII

VALLEY FORGE

To all Pastor Muhlenberg's worries a new one was now added. Communications being cut off, no news came out of Philadelphia from Peggy. Not until October 23 did her father receive the German letter she had written on September 29.

Honored Papa and Mama,

I simply want to report that all of us here are well and that everything remains as it was. Thank God, so far not one hair has fallen from anyone's head, and our great fear of fire has been checked to a large extent by the very careful provisions of the military and civilian authorities. Mr. Kuntze is fair. He preached twice in Zion on each of the two Sundays he has been alone. We have heard of some disturbance caused by the troops in your house. Although we are still dubious about the report, we are nevertheless very anxious. We wish you could give us some news of your condition. I remain, with filial regard,

Margareta Kuntze[1]

The letter had come by way of the underground. "On the second page of the letter," her father noted in his Journal, "a good friend had written the following:

Very dear friends,

Yesterday I received this letter in the city unsealed, but did not read the contents. Your children are well, but little is heard from them. People only look at one another there, and even this suspiciously. Samuel Shoemaker is mayor. Mr. Duche was arrested but was released again. . . .

I should like to hear about you and your children. There is a rumor in the city that your house has been burned, or at least plundered and wrecked. So far, thank God, I have not suffered, nor have I lost anything. A letter handed to the Jew on the *hill,* where the two roads fork, will reach me. I commit all of you, together with myself and all mine, to the faithful leading of God, and remain,

With the affection and respect of old,

Manus Signum*

For Senior Mühlenberg in Provid[ence]

September 30, 77

P. S. I wonder if you know anything about my son.

* Mark of the writer's hand.

Thereafter, letters were interchanged constantly between Peggy and her father, thanks to the intermediary at Barren Hill—where the Ridge Road and the Germantown Turnpike meet.

For a time after the fall of Philadelphia the tension was eased and Pastor Muhlenberg filled his Journal with homely and more or less comfortable things: the rising cost of food (more homely, perhaps, than comfortable), a visit from General Peter with particulars of Burgoyne's defeat; grandchild Betsy's German measles; Peggy's difficulties in getting meat and butter; the visit of an Indian who had served as a volunteer for three years with the American army, and was now going home to the Forks of the Susquehanna for the hunting season.[2]

But there were less comfortable things, too: in particular, rumors of British raids being planned against the Trappe, the hostility to his person of some Hessian officers, and their determination to capture him as a Lutheran renegade and string him up.

When the Pastor heard in December that the American army had gone into winter quarters at Valley Forge, his fear burst out and he wrote in his Journal, "We live now in constant expectation of a raid from Philadelphia, because the American army has crossed the Schulkiel . . . and left the pass open."

The last words are unexpected: "left the pass open."[3] In writing thus, Muhlenberg may seem to have missed the point of Washington's strategy. We know that Valley Forge had been chosen for winter quarters precisely because a strong camp so close to the city locked the door on General Howe, denying him control of Pennsylvania's rich hinterland. The hardships of the men at Valley Forge, shivering in their huts, were not too high a price to pay for this advantage. General Peter Muhlenberg, when Washington asked his advice on the choice of winter quarters, thought first of the comfort of the men, and proposed a line extending from Reading through Allentown and Bethlehem to Easton, because in those towns sufficient housing would be available to keep the men warm. But Washington chose Valley Forge because there he could watch Howe more closely.

The camp at Valley Forge was only seven miles south of the Trappe, and lay between it and Howe in Philadelphia. Yet Muhlenberg was right when he said the pass was left open—open, that is, to a raid on the Trappe. Valley Forge was on the wrong side of the river. The way was now clear for the British Hussars.

General Peter was sure of that. His brigade held the most advanced lines in the camp, near Port Kennedy, and he knew every ford on this part of the river. But he was well aware that, should the British come out on a lightning raid, they could easily overrun the Trappe and get back out of reach before any effective force could cross the river to intercept them.

It is true, detachments could be, and were, constantly dispatched across the Schuylkill to "chastize the Torys,"[4] as Peter expressed it; and an occasional Tory was hanged—and left hanging, as he said, to be "an instructive lesson to others." But such punitive measures could be of little use against a determined enemy.

"Therefore Remember the Trapp," wrote Peter to his brother Frederick.

"I still wish Sincerely," continued Peter, "that Pappa & his Family were removd from the Trapp: for should he be taken & escape being Murdered by those Villains, Yet he would perhaps perish in the ruins of Philad.[a] [Peter was here thinking of an assault upon the city by 35,000 American troops, which, he said, were already marching in for that purpose.] I beg you would once more try to have him removd, spare no Costs & I will repay."[5]

Peter rode over from Valley Forge on the day after Christmas and did what he could to get his parents out and away to safety. He offered to take them under his own escort to Tulpehocken. His father was almost persuaded to go, but not Anna Maria. We can understand that she was unwilling to risk travel over winter roads and then, at journey's end, impose herself with her paroxysms on other homes. She would rather stay in her own home and take what God sent her there.

She would not go.

"It is difficult to know what to do," wrote her poor husband in his Journal.[6]

That night at two o'clock, Anna Maria was overtaken by the worst paroxysm she had suffered in three years. They thought she would surely die. Toward morning she recovered, but the question of flight had been settled. Anna Maria must stay where she was, and her husband would stay with her.

The days passed and no raiders came. Indeed, the country around them seemed settling down to quiet. On New Year's Day, old Andrew Stahl brought a letter from Peggy in Philadelphia,[7] written only three days before. Things looked better there, said Peggy. No soldiers had been quartered on them. Zion Church had been converted into a hospital, but worship services were still held in St. Michael's: three services each Sunday, one in the early morning for the Anspachers, and two services, morning and evening, for the regular congregation.

Another letter from Peggy came only two days later. It had been written on December 31, and wished them a Happy New Year.[8] Peggy said she could sometimes send out into the country for butter and meat. It was all very reassuring.

From what happened afterward, we may make some estimate of what passed at this time through the Pastor's mind. Perhaps the dangers had been exaggerated. Perhaps the stories of atrocities which Henry Melchior had heard and accepted as true, stories of the wanton burning of churches and the killing of ministers, had just been propaganda. Perhaps the British, whose freedom-fostering institutions he had formerly admired, had not changed so much and sunk so low as he had been led to believe. There were good, religious people, Lutherans no less, even among the Hessians, whom report had given such a bad name.

The high-spirited younger members of the family became positively gleeful about the situation. Letters penetrated the British lines easily enough. Why not they themselves? The girls especially went into ecstasies over the prospect. After all, there is such a thing as chivalry in war.

Polly and Cathy (the wife of Henry Ernest) conferred with a young lady then visiting them, Katy Graff of Second Street,[9] Philadelphia, who knew the ropes. Together they made their plans, with apparently some connivance from their menfolk. Horses were got ready, a neighbor was enlisted to go with them as an escort, and on the afternoon of Saturday, January 10, the three Rosalinds mounted and set out.

They did not take the Ridge Road to the city but the Germantown Road. The neighbor accompanied them to Hickory Town, within about four miles of Chestnut Hill, and there left them, returning with the horses. Who, if anyone, met them there and escorted them the rest of the way, we do not know. Perhaps it was "the Jew on the hill, where the two roads fork," which is within a mile or so of Hickory Town. At any rate, they continued their journey on foot. That was all the news the family had of them for several days.

Next morning at Providence it began to snow, and it continued snowing heavily all day. By night the snow was a foot deep. On Monday it lay so heavy on the roof that Pastor Muhlenberg engaged two neighbors, as he tells us, "to set fire in the chimneys to burn them out." On Tuesday afternoon Henry Ernest struggled through the snow from New Hanover with two horses to send on to Hickory Town to pick up his wife and Polly when they came out. The roads were dreadful. The family was beginning to get uneasy.

Then, unexpectedly, the same evening, the two girls turned up on foot, exhausted, struggling through the snow.[10] They had reason to hurry, for they brought charming news. The British were coming. The girls had learned in the city of a scheme on foot to capture old Muhlenberg and hang him. The Hessians especially, it seems, were incensed against him, and would string him up if they caught him.

There was no peace that night in the parsonage. What was to be done? Anna Maria would not leave home, and her husband would not leave Anna Maria. That was settled. But something had to be done, and quickly. Henry Melchior's life was at stake.

Then an idea came to him. It was suggested by a letter Polly had brought from the Kuntzes in Philadelphia—an open letter from David Grim, an old friend in New York. It was addressed to Frederick, Grim's former pastor, but it contained a message for his father. Grim had received, he said, Henry Melchior's letter for the Reverend Mr. William Pasche and had sent it on by the boat *for London.*[11]

Evidently David Grim had access to the British authorities. Why not, thought Muhlenberg, through Grim present his own case, that of an honest neutral, to the British, and let them decide *with full knowledge of the circumstances* whether it was honorable for them to bring his gray hairs to the grave. He sat down and wrote.[12]

It cannot be argued, let us say at once, that the method Henry Melchior used to save himself in this crisis was an altogether wise one. The points that could be made against it are too obvious to need even mention. But that his course was a brave one we can maintain.

He might have saved himself at any moment by saddling a horse and moving farther back into the country, where he had plenty of friends ready to receive him. But he would neither leave his wife nor take her away against her wishes. At the same time he felt a man has a duty, as well as a right, to save his life if he can do so without hurting anyone else; and to save not only his life but, in this case, also his reputation. If he were now to be miserably and ignominiously hanged—and this was the fate that seemed to confront him—"O what a wounded name . . . shall live behind me."

And so he wrote for British eyes a defense of himself. He began with a story an old Scotsman had told him about "the Jedbury jury." It seems the prisoner was hanged before the jury considered his case. But after the execution the jury sat to determine "whether the deceased was guilty or not guilty." Henry Melchior thought he had a right to be heard before the Hessians strung him up as a rebel.

He did not conceal his sympathy for those who were fighting for their liberties. You cannot change men's minds, he warned, by mechanical force.

"As the soldier said when the corporal drove him to church: 'You can push me in but I can still think what I like.' "

Despite these latent American sympathies, he insisted that the British ought to regard him as a good man, a true man, and loyal—*loyal to government.*

He had lived, he said, during the reigns of three Georges, and was doubly a subject of the English House of Hanover, having been born in the Electoral Principality of Hanover in 1711, and having been naturalized a British citizen after coming to America. His oath of allegiance had never been broken. He recognized that this last might be open to some question. How could he reconcile this profession of loyalty with his admitted acceptance of the authority of the government of the United States of America? The answer, he believed, was to be found in the Scriptures, Romans 13.1:

"Let every soul be subject unto the higher powers. For there is no power but of God: the powers that be are ordained of God.

"Let every soul be subject unto the higher powers." The pertinence of this text to a time of revolution is best understood if we turn to Luther's Bible, which Muhlenberg quoted. Luther's translation is much more explicit than the King James version about the meaning of "higher powers."

"Jedermann sei untertan der Obrigkeit, die Gewalt über ihn hat."

"Let every soul be subject unto *that* authority which has *power* over him"—power, as Muhlenberg understood it, to guard and protect the subject.

He had kept his allegiance to King George as long as he could: that is to say, as long as the King exercised actual sovereignty over him, with the power to guard and protect. But when, in the summer of 1776, the United States declared their independence and Pennsylvania set up a new constitution for herself, the power to protect was transferred from the old government to the new. It was useless to think otherwise. For, as he said, the tongue of the strongest speaker cannot reach so far as a sword or bayonet in the hands of an angry man fighting for what he believes to be his freedom.

We must admit that there was nothing new in the argument. It is as old as civil war, which has a very ancient, if not a very honorable, lineage. In literature it finds striking expression in Shakespeare's *Richard II*, where the Duke of York, who remained a loyal supporter of King Richard until all power had departed from that unwise monarch, turned to support *the principle of order* now embodied in the new king, Henry IV.

There was no trace in the letter of Thomas Jefferson's political idealism. There are no words about responsible government or the rights of man. Admittedly Muhlenberg's approach to the problems involved was conservative and pragmatic. But it was neither superficial nor dishonorable. And when we remember his circumstances, especially the condition of his wife, we must admire him for seeking safety, like the stiff-necked Lutheran he was, not in flight but in exegesis.

It was a bold letter to send through the American underground. But these were times, he felt, that demanded boldness. He was quite well aware of the risks he ran. He held the letter for some days before dispatching it, by Mr. Nagel, to his daughter in Philadelphia for her to send on to New York. Even then he was not satisfied. After waiting another week, he sent Peggy a postscript, urging caution. He wrote it discreetly in Latin. If Peggy could not read it, he knew her scholarly husband could.

"*Mariti tui dilectissimi,*" he began: "I want your dear husband's best judgment on the letter to Dav. Grim. If he thinks it will have a good effect, send it, if not, conceal it, I beg and entreat, lest your poor Dad light upon Scylla in trying to avoid Charybdis."[13]

No word came from Peggy that she had received the letter, and tension at the parsonage mounted. On February 18, Tory raiders were reported to have been, the night before, within five or six miles of the house. A few days later the Pastor noted in his Journal: "We received the dreadful news that the British light cavalry were near and would visit us tonight. I had nine feeble women and four children under the roof. I was alone and all perplexed, I had recourse in silence to Jesus Christ."[14]

The raiders did not come. At four o'clock in the morning, when it was reasonable to suppose that the horsemen were galloping back to reach the safety of their own lines before daylight, he went to bed and got some rest.

It was the same on other nights. Again and again warning came that this time the Hessians would really get him. But they never came. The British, for whatever reason, did not molest him. It is possible that the Grim letter did get through to the British authorities—in Philadelphia, if not in New York or London—and that they, recognizing the integrity of Pastor Muhlenberg's apologia, saw to it that he should be given the protection he needed.

That he had enemies in Philadelphia, there can be no question. One in particular, a German named Verner, working for the British and keeper of the jail, appears to have been a stupid, loud-talking, vindictive person who boasted of what he would do to "old Muhlenberg" when he got hold of him. Several times he is said to have made preparations to go out himself on a raid to get the Parson. But nothing ever came of these arrangements. Perhaps Verner's schemes were motivated by nothing more substantial than wind and rhetoric. Or perhaps they were thwarted by secret orders from some high officer who wished to protect the good old Lutheran pastor from Hessian vengeance. General Howe's conciliatory policy and his dislike of Hessian methods are well known. Whatever the explanation, this we do know: "Daddy" Muhlenberg stayed at Providence and the British stayed away.

By degrees the tension relaxed. Spring came and hopes rose high for the relief of Philadelphia. At the Trappe one evening occurred a pleasant little interlude.

The childhood of Anna Maria had been a happy one. Now, in her illness, anything pleased her that brought back those golden days. It was, therefore, a delight to her to hear the sound of Indian voices when, on the evening of May 13, a party of Oneida Indians from the great Six Nations in the north, camped close to the Muhlenbergs for the night.[15] It reminded her of the days when Indians by the hundreds camped in her father's orchard under Eagle Peak.

Most of the good people at the Trappe were rather fearful when they found "savages" in their neighborhood. But they had no cause for alarm. The chief of the party forbade the white inhabitants to give his warriors brandy, and the Indians' own customs were gentle enough. Indeed, Henry Melchior's description of them has an idyllic touch.

Their young people, he tells us, shot birds and squirrels with bows and arrows, and prepared and ate them by the fire. He went on to tell of hearing from one of them the "Jo-hah," or sound of approbation, the exquisite cadences in which Conrad Weiser had taken such delight whenever he heard them rise and fall at Indian treaties in Philadelphia or Onondaga.[16]

"One of them came to us and asked for milk," wrote the Pastor, "and because my wife can still understand a word here and there of their speech, relating to food, he was greatly delighted, took the milk and bread, and expressed his joy in their musical way. The poetry of it I could not understand."

Next morning the Indians departed for the American camp at Valley Forge.

They arrived just in time to get into a hot action. Peter Muhlenberg, who had an affection for his grandfather's Six Nations Indians and was proud of what a band of them now accomplished almost under his eyes, rode over to the Trappe a few days later to tell his mother and father how well these Iroquois had served the American cause.[17]

On Wednesday, May 20, Pastor Muhlenberg heard three cannon shots fired in the camp at Valley Forge, and the sounding of the drums. He did not know at the time that the camp had been alerted because of the sudden disaster which seemed about to overwhelm

Lafayette across the river—a disaster these same Oneida Indians played a dramatic role in averting. The story is worth telling.

On May 18, 1778, General Washington wrote to the President of Congress: "A valuable detachment under the command of the Marquis de Lafayette, marched this morning, which is intended to move between the Delaware and the Schuylkill, for restraining the enemy's parties and procuring intelligence and to act as circumstances may require."

To the young Lafayette, high-spirited, and ambitious, Washington spoke a word of fatherly warning. "Your detachment is a very valuable one," he said. "Any accident happening to it would be a severe blow to this army."

At Swede's Ford Lafayette crossed the Schuylkill River with a very considerable body of infantry (some twenty-two hundred Continentals), a few horse, and about seventy Indians who had just come to the American camp. He moved down the Ridge Road toward the city, and took up position at Barren Hill—"where the two roads fork."

Sir William Howe shared Washington's opinion that an accident to Lafayette and his detachment would be a severe blow to the American army. He accordingly threw out two columns in a pincer movement to entrap him. The maneuver, as at Brandywine, was executed with speed and great skill. Lafayette suddenly found himself all but surrounded by greatly superior forces. It was then that Muhlenberg at the Trappe heard the cannon and the drums sounding at Valley Forge.

The remainder of the story is best told as Henry Melchior received it a few days later from his son, General John Peter Muhlenberg. This is how it appears in the Journal for May 23, 1778:

> At noon came our eldest son J. P. and a few other officers with their servants from the American camp, for a short visit with us. We learned from them the particulars of the action that took place last Wednesday, May 20. The better part of the English army had quietly moved out of Philadelphia on the night of May 19. One column directed its march west-northwest toward the Barren Hill Church, where a French General with 2 thousand and several hundred men, besides 70 Indians belonging to the American army, were posted as an Observation Corps. The other English column took its way out of the city to the east through Frankfurt on the New York Road, and then turned northwest, so that the two

columns should meet and catch the Observation Corps between them and cut it off on this side of the Schulkiel. The main American camp was on the other side of the Schulkiel about 7 or 8 miles from the Barren Hill Church. The two English columns had made a wide circle and cut off retreat for the American Corps over the bridge to the main camp. But the French General retired with his Corps to a little-used ford in the Schulkiel River [Matson's Ford, Conshohocken], and though it was breast deep, the men got through safely to the camp. The Indians were the last to cross, and were surrounded by the English Light Horse in a little wood. But they retired behind the trees as their way is and made their usual horrible war-cry, which threw horses and riders into disorder and put them to flight, when the Indians shot a few cavalrymen and picked up their cloaks.

Lafayette, many years later, told another version of the story, making it a laughable encounter between fifty Indians and fifty horsemen who scared each other almost to death and ran for their lives in opposite directions.[18] Peter's version was contemporary and may be trusted.

At the Trappe, rumor still had a thousand tongues, but the tune was changing. It was the British, not the Muhlenbergs, who were on the defensive. Rumor came to the parsonage that Zion Church, which the British had used as a hospital, had been evacuated. It was rumored that the enemy had taken fresh water on board their transports, that they were moving guns down to the Delaware, that they were destroying equipment they could not carry away with them, and that they had burned their salt.

On June 17 and 18, flying reports reached the parsonage that the enemy had crossed the Delaware, that the American army was in motion, and that General Peter's brigade was on its way to Philadelphia.

Then, on the morning of the nineteenth, they heard the sound of guns once more from the direction of the city. They did not know for certain what it meant. Perhaps Peter was again in battle. Or could it be the sound of rejoicing? The Pastor cited in his Journal for that day Exodus 32, 17 and 18.

> And when Joshua heard the noise of the people as they shouted, he said unto Moses, There is a noise of war in the camp.
>
> And he said, It is not the voice of them that shout for mastery, neither is it the voice of them that cry for being overcome: but the noise of them that sing do I hear.

Mr. Swaine, assiduous as always in collecting news, and Frederick, who was not at all behind him in curiosity on this occasion, posted off to the city to find out what the guns meant.

Meanwhile the Pastor waited. That the boys did not come back the next day was as great a satisfaction to him as the tardiness of a dove had once been to another patriarch of old. On Sunday the twenty-first, when the Pastor returned from service in Augustus Church, he found the boys returned with certain news that Philadelphia was free. What they had heard on Friday was a *feu de joie* fired by the American artillery regiment on first entering the city.

The children had more news yet. The German jailer in Philadelphia had been arrested for abusing his prisoners.

"This Mr. Verner," wrote Mr. Swaine a few days later to his brother-in-law Schultze at Tulpehocken, "was very Inveterate again Daddy Muhlenberg he said if no person else would hang him, he would, he is now in irons in the Provost Guard, expect the State will turn upon the lad For we have heard he had been try'd and Condemn'd to be hang'd, a Just reward For such villans—"[19]

But justice, however satisfying to the moral sense, was not the final goal of Mr. Swaine's desires. A cold and platonic avowal of the blind lady's attractions, unaccompanied by ceremonies of fellowship, was abhorrent to Mr. Swaine's convivial soul. In a word, he wished to celebrate. He accordingly asked Pastor Schultze to open the tavern (dispatching a key for that purpose) and get out his best clothes.

"The weather being exceeding warm," he wrote, "I have been Oblidg'd to send for my trunk, to get summer Cloaths, and more Especially as the tyrants has left PhiladA (people like to put on their best bib & tucker). . . ."

But before the gentleman from Cork begins his celebrations, it will be well for us to draw the curtain.

FRANCIS SWAINE

CHAPTER XVIII

ALTAR, SWORD, AND PEN

Emanuel Schultze sent Mr. Swaine his best clothes. Polly went down to the city with Frederick's wife, and came back ill, having walked part of the way and, as her father said, having drunk cold water while overheated.[1] Henry Melchior himself would have gone to the city at once, had it not been for a lack of clean linen, he having sent his shirts in an old trunk to the Widow Weiser's at Tulpehocken for safekeeping during the occupation. He sent word for them now to be returned, as also the Journals, which, too, he had sent into the country to get them out of the reach of the Hessians, who read German.

He did at length go to the city, July 10, and described the sad scenes he saw on the way and in Philadelphia itself: in particular St. Peter's Church at Barren Hill, its chancel, altar, seats, doors, and window shutters torn out and burned, the windowpanes broken, and the empty space between the four walls filled with dung, for the cavalry had used the building to stall their horses. In Philadelphia, those who cared to worship with him in Zion Church on Sunday, July 12, had to bring their own chairs and stools to sit on.

On this visit he had the pleasure of seeing his friends again, especially old Henry Keppele, who had just returned to his Philadelphia house from Lancaster, where he had lived during the British occupation.

It was on this same visit, a few days later, that Henry Melchior suffered a very serious injury to his ears. During the afternoon of Sunday, July 26, he attended the funeral of a young artilleryman. A regiment was there with fife and drum.

"At the close of the prayer," as Henry Melchior described the incident in his Journal, "the soldiers fired three volleys over the grave. I stood with the left side turned to the graveyard wall and the soldiers fired on my right side; the report hit the wall with a shattering rebound and injured my hearing on both sides."

He was left with a roaring in his ears as if he were standing beside a waterfall or a mill.

From that time on his head was full of strange noises. When he talked, his voice sounded to him as if he were speaking in an empty barrel. When he heard the organ play, the sound crashed over his head as if there were nothing but reed-stops and tremolo-stops. The cry of children hurt him like the sound of a nail scraped on glass. A never-ending roaring and whistling in his ears made him dizzy.[2]

After the two armies, Washington's and Clinton's, had made contact in New Jersey, before the Battle of Monmouth was fought, delirious rumors spread about the country, rumors which Mr. Swaine, who collected them, was in no mood to discount.

General Knyphausen was killed, he wrote excitedly to Schultze. ". . . their is bets in the City, of six to one, that Harry Clinton is burgoyn'd, before six days—the Lord of his infinite Mercy Grant it—"[3]

The truth was less exciting to his brother-in-law Peter, who had a closer view of the chase across New Jersey and who saw the Battle of Monmouth, on June 28, from the inside. We know now (from the outside) something of the bungling that occurred on that day, which saw the breaking of General Lee and the escape of Harry Clinton with his enormous, and vulnerable, baggage train.

An enthusiastic writer, Henry A. Muhlenberg, great-nephew of "our general," tells of the gallantry with which Muhlenberg's brigade fought on this occasion, and how Peter Muhlenberg himself "displayed the same skill and impetuous ardour which so highly distinguished him at Brandywine and Germantown."[4] But military skill and bravery are evidenced not solely in moments of impetuous ardor. The good soldier is one who can "take it" as well as "dish it out." On this day Peter Muhlenberg's heroism consisted in standing still and keeping his head, despite the blazing heat of the sun and the excitement of the battle raging near him.

We are fortunate in having a description of the engagement from his own pen, in one of his very few battle letters that have been preserved. It was written to Pastor Schultze at Tulpehocken.

Camp at White plains July 28th 1778.

Revd Sir. Dear Brother.

Your favor of the first instant by Thoms Keen came safe to hand, & it gives me great Satisfaction to hear, that Yourself and Family are in good Health,—I have not wrote you before, since We left our Camp at Valley Forge, but it really did not proceed from neglect as You seem to hint in your Letter, but from want of time and Opportunity, for I Assure You that from the time we left Valley Forge untill we Arivd at Brunswick, I did not get my Clothes of for one Night, & now we are just got to a Camp where I believe we shall remain for some time so that I really embrace the first Opportunity of writing to You, & at the same time to Congratulate You on the happy Change of our Affairs since We left Pensylvania, You can now Sit in Your Study without being pester'd with the noise of Cannon and being disturbed with the Melancholy News of the Militias being routed, and 150 killd & taken out of 73—I hope by this time You have given over all Thoughts of fleeing to the Mountains in Company with Mr Handell, & sit Contented on the Banks of Tulpehocken—I should be very happy were it in my power to give You some Agreeable News, but we have none of Consequence at present, & the particulars of the Battle of Monmouth You have had over and over again however I shall only tell You, it was tho' a Glorious day, very distressing times, We fought in a Sandy Barren, on one of the hottest days ever known in this part of the World, and where neither Money Authority, or favor could procure a drink of Water many brave fellows expired before our faces who might perhaps have been preservd with a drink; but even here we had greatly the Advantage of the Enemy, for as the Proverb says, it is an ill Wind that blows nobody good—for our Soldiers, at least the greatest part, were thinly clad—and the Clothes they had on, had airholes in plenty so that they receivd the Benefit of every Breeze, while the Brittish Grenadiers with their Uniforms Packs &c. sank beneath the Weight,—I had little Share of the Action, I comanded the two first Virginia Brigades, in the Second Line or Corps de Reserve, it was indeed a disagreeable post to me, as we were Oblig'd to Stand within Sight of the Enemy, where they Cannonaded us Severely, while we Stood patiently without returning the Compliment, waiting when we should be Ordered to Attack, however they saved us the trouble by running away before it came to our turn, I lost two fine Officers by their Cannon, Major Dickinson & Captn Fauntleroy, who was killd very near me . . .

You Complain my dear Sir, that my Wife has neglected to write to You, I Assure You I am in the same predicament, I have receivd but one Letter from her since she left You, & that was imediately on her Arrival in Virginia, since that I have not heard a Word of her ——— to proceed to my former Stile it is time to Conclude, for my Subject is exhausted, & I shall only add, by way of preventing erratas in the Settling of our Corresponding Accounts, that You now are in debt to me one Letter, & that for the future I cannot agree to take Letter for Letter, unless You please to Lengthen Yours a little—My Compliments to Mr Handell & Family, & other Friends in Your precincts my love to Your Spouse & little Family

I remain Dear Sir
Your Affectionate and hble Servt
P: Muhlenberg

P.S. White Plains is exactly
15 Mile from Kings bridge[5]

Peter went on up to the state of New York, and we soon find him writing from West Point, which was, for a time, his headquarters. On September 16, in response to Washington's request to his officers for advice on winter quarters for the army, Peter Muhlenberg, although he expressed his hesitation about giving an opinion since he was not too familiar with that northern part of the country, made some sound observations which show his understanding of the general strategical problems with which Washington was confronted:

. . . as it is impossible to Guard the whole Continent, We ought to keep particularly in View two Grand Objects, The Posts in the Highlands, & the French Fleet; to answer this purpose, and at the same time to cover as well as possible the Neighbouring States the Army ought to be in such a position that the whole might be able to Join in three or four days if it should be found necessary—The Main Body of the Army might be near Fishkill, a very Secure Post, which the Enemy cannot come at, but by marching thro' Mountains allmost inaccessible, when in the least opposed—Three or four Brigades Advanced three days March on the Boston Road, to be in readiness to act in conjunction with General Sullivan and the Militia, to Counteract any designs the Enemy might have upon the French Fleet . . . Some Brigades in the Jersey who would serve as a Cover not only to the State but to the Highland Posts—A strong Garrison at Westpoint . . . In this Situation I presume We might be able to Frustrate any designs the Enemy may have, upon either the Fleet or the Highland Posts, and at the same time be in the best Situation possible to provide For the Army— . . . no time should be lost in providing Materials for raising temporary Barracks to cover the Soldiery during the Winter, & to keep them as Compact as the Situation of Affairs will permit—Your Excellency will please to remember that last Winter, many inconveniences might have been prevented, and our Winter Quarters rendered mor Comfortable, if we could have begun upon them before the Severity of the Winter came on—[6]

It turned out that Washington's disposition of the troops followed the general outlines Muhlenberg had proposed. Army headquarters were established at Middlebrook (now Bound Brook), and the troops were disposed in cantonments in a semicircle round Clinton in New York: Middlebrook, Elizabeth, Ramapo, West Point, Fishkill, and Danbury, Connecticut.

Some of the few glimpses we have of Peter Muhlenberg's social life while in the army come from the pen of an army surgeon, Dr. James Thacher of the First Virginians. When Major General Putnam was ordered to Hartford to replace General Gates, who had gone to Boston to take command of the Eastern District, Washington gave Peter Muhlenberg temporary command of Putnam's division. On assuming this position at West Point, General Muhlenberg gave a banquet in Putnam's honor.

"The guests," wrote Thacher, "consisted of forty-one respectable officers, and our tables were furnished with fourteen different dishes, arranged in fashionable style. After dinner Major General Putnam was requested to preside, and he displayed no less urbanity at the head of the table, than bravery at the head of his division. A number of toasts were pronounced, accompanied with humorous and merry songs. In the evening we were cheered with military music and dancing, which continued till a late hour in the night. General Muhlenberg was a minister of a parish in Virginia . . ."[7] Here Thacher launches into the story of Peter Muhlenberg's sword in the pulpit (see page 118), which suggests that he may have first heard the story himself during the anecdotal part of the evening's entertainment.

The gallantry of Peter Muhlenberg's Virginians was not to be dashed by the discomforts of winter cantonments. Dr. Thacher has left us a vivid picture in his *Military Journal* of the grand ball held at General Muhlenberg's quarters on New Year's Day, 1779, at Middlebrook, to which place he had moved his unit a few weeks earlier.

The officers, wrote Thacher, were "introduced to a number of ladies assembled to unite with the gentlemen in the ball-room; a very elegant supper was provided, and not one of the company was permitted to retire until three o'clock in the morning. Thus have the gallant Virginians commenced the new year."[8]

As far as external hostilities were concerned, it was a peaceful enough season at Middlebrook; but Peter Muhlenberg had troubles of his own that kept him perpetually on edge. He was always susceptible to his environment, and the restless ambitions of his fellow officers infected him with extreme jealousy concerning his rank. An old sore rankled. It was one of many disputes that bedeviled the army, especially since George Washington's arrangement of his officers was subject to Congressional interference.

When Mr. Swaine visited Peter in camp, he found the General on the point of resigning. The trouble stemmed from a dispute about rank with Brigadier General Woodford. Woodford and Muhlenberg had been colonels together, the former being Muhlenberg's senior. But Woodford had resigned his commission (in another dispute about rank) and had left the service. Peter Muhlenberg, now senior colonel of the Virginia Line, was in February 1777 appointed brigadier general. At the same time Woodford, reëntering the service, was also made brigadier general. The question was whether Woodford should now outrank Muhlenberg, as he had done when they were colonels together. Muhlenberg's friends contended that Woodford's resignation, and his absence from the service while Muhlenberg saw two hard campaigns in the South, carried with it a loss of seniority. The army and Congress agreed, for a time, that it did. Peter Muhlenberg was accordingly acknowledged to be the senior brigadier of the Virginia Line, and was so ranked throughout the campaign of 1777. But in March 1778 General Woodford obtained a special resolve of Congress in his favor, reinstating him in his seniority and thus causing him to outrank General Muhlenberg.

Muhlenberg offered his resignation. On Washington's request, however, he consented to postpone his withdrawal in view of the situation at Valley Forge, where general officers were greatly needed, and in view, also, of the impending campaign. But the action of Congress rankled in his mind. It seemed to cast reflections upon him, and he feared lest his fellow officers interpret it as demotion for some fault.

He wrote to John Adams in Congress, declining to accept a rank below Woodford's, unless, as he said, it could be done in a manner that would give no reason for anyone to think he had been "superseded for Misconduct."

The affair was finally settled on December 29, 1779, when, on recommendation from the Board of War, Congress passed a resolution stating that, in their action of March 1778, when they had instructed Washington to call in the commissions of Generals Muhlenberg and Woodford and issue new ones ranking Woodford ahead of Muhlenberg, "the arrangement made therein was founded upon principles not affecting the personal characters or comparative merits of these officers."

Muhlenberg showed his good sense in dropping the issue. A few months later General Woodford was captured at Charleston and soon after died. Peter Muhlenberg again became senior officer of the Virginia Line.

While Peter was worrying about his rank, he was worrying also about his finances. He wrote to Patrick Henry about getting a share of the western lands it was proposed to open to settlement. Patrick Henry was thinking of a tract "about the Falls of Ohio."

"God forbid," wrote Henry in reply, "that the Defenders and Saviours of America should want any of the good Things she possesses. You may rest assured, I shall exert my self to procure you some good Land. I will represent the whole Case to the next Assembly. . . ."[9]

He added, however, a word of caution: "Let me take the liberty just to hint, that I think a Resignation now, might defeat a Claim, which otherwise I trust will be approved by every one."

Governor Henry addressed a communication, dated October 14, to the Virginia Assembly on Peter's behalf.

Peter had other causes for worry, particularly the circumstances in which Hannah, his wife, now found herself. Mr. Swaine had returned from a visit to Virginia with the report that she was "in a deplorable condition": quite alone, without a maid, and expecting a baby.

Peter had already appealed to Washington for leave of absence, but Washington had had to reply that the state of the service still required General Muhlenberg's presence with the army.

"From the tenor of your letter," wrote the Commander in Chief, "I am pleased to find that you are determined to wait untill the service will admit of your absence with convenience and you may be assured that whenever that is the Case I shall give my consent to your visiting your family and Friends."[10]

As we have seen illustrated in the Lübeck episode, Peter had enormous patience. He dammed up his feelings and allowed them to accumulate great pressure before they exploded. But, when an explosion was finally touched off, it was the more violent. Now, worried about his lands, his rank, his wife, he was working up again to a shattering outbreak.

Fortunately, he wrote in time to his father, whose advice, if Peter did not always follow it, he at least respected. On this occasion the elder Muhlenberg presented counsel so judicious that he reduced the pressure and so saved George Washington from what might have been an unpleasant interview with the veteran of Lübeck.

A husband and father, said Henry Melchior,[11] has undoubtedly responsibilities to his wife and family. At the same time, if he holds a public position, he has duties which belong to his office. Since a man cannot divide himself and be in two distant places at the same time, it is necessary for him to weigh circumstances, subordinate the lesser to the greater need, and value more highly the good of the public than any private interest of his own. Thousands of children are born into the world without the benefit of their father's presence. One has only to think of merchants, sailors, soldiers, ambassadors, preachers, and the like.

It is well, of course, if a husband can be at home for the blessed event, but husbands should nevertheless remember that the really pressing need at such a time is a good midwife. It is not midwives, however, that are going to beat the British. In war what is needed is soldiers, men with training and a heart for the job. It is apparent, therefore, that at this juncture neither a resignation nor a leave of absence is what the country needs of Brigadier General Muhlenberg.

The Pastor at the Trappe went on to suggest some practical measures to meet Hannah's difficulties: the immediate assistance of friends and neighbors at Woodstock; afterward, when Hannah's strength had been restored, perhaps a visit to the Trappe, where the old folks would welcome her to share with them the house, garden, and cows.

As it turned out, just one week before Henry Melchior wrote this letter, Hannah had already given birth to a son, Charles Frederick, at Woodstock.

Although Pennsylvania was now relieved from the hottest blasts of war, the air was still warm enough over the Trappe. The militia continued their depredations. Henry Melchior, therefore, provided himself with a good watchdog. There were many unpleasant incidents. One evening in November 1778 a drunken soldier came to the house, flourishing a pistol. He demanded powder to charge it with, because, as he said, he wanted to shoot a prisoner—a "deserter" —who refused to follow him. Henry Melchior reminded him that powder and bullets were not in a preacher's armory, and got rid of him.[12]

During the winter, sad news came from the South. In December the British had landed a large force and seized Savannah.

"What will happen," wrote the Pastor, "to poor Eben-Ezer?"

He learned later that on January 2, 1779, Ebenezer, to which the American forces had retired in hope of receiving aid in time from the Carolinas, had been captured.[13]

Pastor Rabenhorst, he learned further, had died, and the unspeakable Triebner had profited both by his death and by the British invasion. Muhlenberg wondered what had happened to Rabenhorst's widow, whose home was in the disputed ground between Ebenezer and Savannah. The news from the South sent Anna Maria into such a paroxysm that her husband thought she could not recover.

Chaplain Streit, writing from Charleston,[14] informed him that Mr. Treutlen, who had been one of Pastor Rabenhorst's strongest supporters and who had, since the Declaration of Independence, been elected Governor of Georgia, had told him during the summer how Triebner had taken possession of the disputed church when the British came, and had set about absolving the church members of their allegiance to the United States. But he had been so impertinent to the British officers that they turned him out and converted his church into a hospital.

Ebenezer was much on Pastor Muhlenberg's mind. In October news came to the Trappe that a small French force had landed near Savannah, joined with Major General Lincoln, and driven the British (after they had burned their stores) out of Ebenezer. Muhlenberg was glad of the victory, but fearful of the cost.

"Poor Ebenezer," he wrote; "the flames will have consumed her."[15]

Further news came that neither siege nor assault had been able to expel the British from Savannah ("where scarcely one stone can now stand upon another"); that Count Pulaski had been killed in the assault and Count d'Estaing wounded; that the American army had withdrawn to Ebenezer and thence to the Carolinas; and that the French troops had embarked and sailed away.

"O poor Eben Ezer!" ran the Muhlenberg refrain.

At home, both Henry Ernest and Frederick were very restless. Henry was back in Philadelphia, working under the brilliant, oversensitive, hypochondriacal Kuntze. Henry found the situation trying. It was becoming apparent that he, like his brother Peter, was working up to an explosion.

For the time being, however, he found solace in the study of botany. There was plenty of time for it. Indeed, if his father is to be believed, he had too much spare time. A member of Henry Ernest's congregation once told the elder Muhlenberg that his son could put a sermon together in half an hour.[16] What was he to do with the remaining six days and odd hours of the week?

The soul of the great Linnaeus (who departed this life in 1778, and is said to have left his mantle, at least in America, with Henry Ernest Muhlenberg) might have provided the answer. Failing that, it will be found recorded in Henry Ernest's "Botanical Tagebuch."[17] The entry for November 20, 1778, shows that he was already planning the systematic pursuit of what was in the eighteenth century the most aristocratic of all the sciences.

"How shall I best proceed with the study of plants?" wrote Henry Ernest, who followed, and improved upon, his father's orderliness of mind. "It is winter and there is little to do. In winter I must observe which plants keep their foliage. . . . In spring I must go out and keep a chronology of the trees, how they come out, of the flowers, how they gradually unfold. . . . I must particularly observe the blossoms and fruit."

He then jotted down in the "Tagebuch" a list of items to be examined:

1. Flowers—stamens—pistils—corolla—calyx;
2. Seeds—fruit;
3. Roots—stalk—leaves;
4. Uses.

So much the better if I could make a herbarium . . . I would plant the most important in a garden. A good friend who had knowledge and inclination would certainly be a help. (Mr. Young three miles from here.)

Take equipment on excursions—an inkstand with quill and paper—and a case, to carry the flowers uninjured. If possible a microscope. Besides the case, a few sheets of paper bound together, to lay the plants in and carry them.[18]

So successful was he in following his plan, and in the botanical writings that soon began to come out of it, that before seven years had passed he was elected to membership in the American Philosophical Society. By that time he had begun an attempt to organize botany on a national scale.

In the year 1779 Frederick, growing dissatisfied with the care and feeding of a brood of country churches, began seriously to think of throwing off his gown and finding a profession better suited to his temperament. The squabbles in New Hanover, the confusion in Reading, and the fermentations that seemed to agitate every little country congregation he had to do with, wearied him beyond his patience. His father, too, had been sickened by confusions, but he had never thought of quitting. From the day he had accepted the call to America, he had had a single-minded devotion to his clerical work. Frederick had not. He had not been called to the field in any such dramatic way as had his father at Halle, nor had his determination been stiffened by such a challenge as had met his father on arrival in Pennsylvania. Frederick had grown quietly into religion and (dared he admit it, even to himself?) he had been pushed, though gently, into the pulpit. For him, under the shadow of his father and in the firm church organization his father had built up, there was no great chance for the exercise of pioneer initiative. For Frederick, church work simply meant routine. He wanted relief, a career of his own, such as his brothers had: Peter with his sword and Henry Ernest with his inkstand and microscope.

Frederick found, too, that the mounting cost of living was too much for a saddlebag preacher.

"A man with a riding horse," his father noted, "can not get through a single day and night on less than 2 or 3 £. A horse that used to be worth from £15 to £20, now costs from 100 to £ 150";[19] and think what saddle, bridle, horseshoes, and clothing mean in terms of money to a man who has a wife and family to look after.

"The poor boy's clothes," said Henry Melchior of his son, "were so worn out, that he had to get a new coat and vest, which cost him £ 40, and then people think a good pastor must live on faith and never complain of . . . want."[20]

Pastor Kuntze in Philadelphia was disturbed by rumors that assailed his ears about Frederick, and he wrote to the Trappe to say that he hoped his father-in-law would never give consent to Frederick's throwing up the ministry to enter business. If Frederick said he could not live by the church, continued Kuntze, it only meant he could not get rich in it.[21]

Following Kuntze's warning, there was an exchange of letters between Henry Melchior and Frederick.

But the temptations to which Frederick was at this time exposed were even more shocking than his devout father and scholarly brother-in-law had imagined. When the facts finally burst upon them, they found that Frederick, under the influence of his wife's family, the Schaeffers, had entered the "Machiavellian" field of politics.

On Monday, February 15, Mr. Swaine rode to the Trappe in company with John Schaeffer, Frederick's brother-in-law. They were on their way to New Hanover to get Frederick and take him to the city for an interview with the Governor. Frederick, as it happened, was at that time away on a visit to Lebanon. But Mr. Swaine and John Schaeffer, stopping off at the Trappe, told the good Pastor what was in the air. The Pennsylvania Assembly proposed to nominate Frederick as one of Pennsylvania's three new delegates to the Continental Congress.

Henry Melchior was heartbroken at the news. It reminded him of the sad end of his old Southern friend, Mr. Treutlen, in Ebenezer. Mr. Treutlen had formerly been a schoolmaster under "dear brother Boltzius." He later became a merchant, then a justice of the peace, afterward a member of the Assembly, on the coming of the Revolution a colonel, next a member of the Council, and finally His Excellency the Governor of Georgia.

And now, since the coming of the British, where was he? "With wife and children in sackcloth and ashes!"[22]

When he learned that his son was going into Congress, Henry Melchior was driven, as he noted that evening in his Journal, to the sixth petition in the Lord's Prayer: "Lead us not into temptation."[23]

But Frederick, despite his father's prayers, went on with his new course. It may be that he was led by a wiser hand than that which administered the sacraments in Augustus Church.

Daniel Hiester wrote from the Assembly, on February 28, to inform Frederick that he had been nominated "by the Majority of the House," that his election was now a certainty, and that on Tuesday next (when the election was to be held) he hoped to have the honor of congratulating him.

"Pleasing as the Thoughts are to me of seeing a Friend and Acquaintance of mine in Congress," he said; "they are the more so, as they will set our Friends in Newyork to rights, and will save them the Concern, how you might get into that City by the Influence of your Reble General."[24]

When the ballots were counted on March 2, it was found, as expected, that Frederick Muhlenberg had been elected to serve in place of Edward Biddle, who had dropped out. Next day Frederick took his seat in the Continental Congress—"the Rump Parliament," as Henry Melchior called it when he recorded the news in his Journal:

> O Father in Heaven, save us from temptation . . . ! Frederick Muhlenberg has not sought this dangerous service, but has been drawn into it by well-meaning intermediaries with their sinful motives. . . . If I should be called on to answer for this, I should reply in some such fashion as John IX, 21: He is of age; ask him: he shall speak for himself.[25]

Anna Maria was no happier than her husband over Frederick's backsliding into Congress. She wrote mournfully, and breathlessly, March 26, to Betsy at Tulpehocken:

> Last week Frederick went to the city god knows what it will come to or how it will turn out I had rather have seen him in the Swamp [i.e., Falckner's Swamp, or New Hanover] than this way in Philadelphia The example of David occurs to me as long as he looked after the asses of his brothers he had no trouble and was able to rend lions but when he came before the great lords of this world he had to play music and often came into mortal danger and had to hide himself you will have heard that he has been elected a member of Congress our people want papa to go back to the city and then Mr. Kuntze would go to the country but I hope and wish nothing comes of it for I have had enough of the city. everything is terribly dear here but not half so dear as in the city. thank

god we have had much kindness from all our friends and our . . . gardens and cows have been such a help to us that thank god we have suffered no want though everything is so dear.[26]

Anna Maria hired a man to take a cow and calf down to the city, to be delivered on Second Street at the door of David Schaeffer,[27] Frederick's father-in-law, with whom the new Congressman was staying. It would help Frederick keep down the high cost of congressional living. And she saw to it that nothing *did* come of the proposed interchange between city and country with the Kuntzes. It was not what Henry Melchior wanted, either. He was glad enough, this time, that Anna Maria would not go.

Frederick's entrance to politics in March had been through special appointment by the Assembly to fill out Edward Biddle's term in the Continental Congress. In the fall he entered the Pennsylvania Assembly through popular election.

October 12 at the polls was the climax of a stormy campaign, in which much fury had been expended against Tories and well-to-do Republicans. It ended in a complete victory for the radicals. It was on this radical wave that Frederick came in. The Assembly again elected him unanimously a delegate to the Continental Congress. He feared, however, that it was less for himself than for his connections. A Junto in the Assembly, as he wrote to his father, were afraid that if they dropped him (as they did two of his colleagues) their hold on the German vote would be lessened. This was a blow to his pride, and he thought of resigning. But he reconsidered and stuck to his post.

The radicals, who came to realize that Frederick Muhlenberg had a mind of his own and that they could not hold him, were soon vituperating him. But he remained a dominant force in Pennsylvania politics till the end of his life, and did much to modulate the more strident tunes of the early revolutionary years and give Pennsylvania's democracy stability.

Many high honors came to him. More would have come to him if he had not died at the age of fifty-one. At his death William Duane observed that his passing had relieved political tension in Pennsylvania by removing one of the chief contenders for the governorship of the state.

CHAPTER XIX

"WE ARE ALL WELL, THANK GOD"

Since this is to be a family chapter, with little in it of the big world outside, it is appropriate to begin with a bit of family tradition. A story is still told in Muhlenberg circles about Henry Ernest and the blacksmith.[1]

Henry Ernest, who lived the last thirty-five years of his life in Lancaster, Pennsylvania, was a very strong man. He was said, indeed, to be the strongest man in his locality. A local blacksmith, jealous of his own reputation for strength of arm, determined to challenge him. He sought out the parson and found him standing on the steps of his house. The blacksmith looked up and thus addressed him:

"Some people say you're the strongest man around here."

Henry Ernest reached down from where he was standing, seized the man with one arm, lifted him up, and planted him down beside him.

"Very well," said the blacksmith, "you are."

There was no discussion.

From his father, Henry Ernest had learned the maxim *festina lente,* hasten slowly, and he applied it with astonishing success to his botanical studies. But in his younger days it must be admitted that he was no less strong in his rages than in his biceps. The year 1779, when Henry Ernest was twenty-six, saw him at the peak of his emotional form.

There can be no question that Henry Ernest, who was something of an athlete (in his middle years he frequently made the journey from Lancaster to Philadelphia and back on foot), was an uncongenial teammate for the deeply spiritual but nervously fragile Christopher Kuntze. Henry Ernest had not wanted the appointment as third pastor in Philadelphia. He had, however, been overpersuaded by his mother, and had accepted the position. Now that he had it, he was unsettled.

He was a man of passionate loyalties and passionate dislikes. Such a loyalty he felt for his father, such a dislike he developed toward Christopher Kuntze. To explain this we must look back to the year 1776.

When Henry Melchior that summer left Philadelphia for the Trappe, he retained his official position as rector, although the work of the congregations was attended to by his son Henry and his son-in-law Kuntze. On the coming of the British, Henry Ernest fled, leaving Kuntze alone to keep watch over the flock.

After the British left and the work of St. Michael's and Zion came back to normal, some members of the vestry felt that the elder Muhlenberg, having virtually severed his connection with the two churches by leaving the city, should be dropped from the rectorship and that Christopher Kuntze should be elected in his place. To this, there was much opposition. Kuntze, however, thinking (mistakenly) that Henry Melchior approved the change, said nothing against it. Henry Ernest, on the other hand, made himself into a furious partisan for his father, and in no time a first-class confusion was in progress.

When the vestry did finally drop Henry Melchior and appoint Kuntze to the rectorship, Henry Ernest "blew up." To his "*zärtlich geliebter Papa*" he wrote an immediate report of the action,[2] and followed it up a few days later with an attack on Kuntze, who, said Henry Ernest, had made no objection to the move, "because his salary depended on the Corporation."[3] Kuntze, it is true, had said he would accept the rectorship only on condition Papa approved. But the election had now taken place, and Kuntze's appointment had not been made contingent on the former rector's consent.

It was the end for Henry Ernest in Philadelphia.

"No matter what happens now," he said, "I will stick to my purpose and go to the Swamp."

"*Festina lente,*" wrote his father, advising against the change. But Henry Melchior was not very sanguine about the result. In his Journal he noted sadly that "these controversies increase my deafness and the humming and dizziness in my head."[4]

"It seems," he noted a few days later, "as if my labors in America were to end in strife as they began 36 years ago."[5]

Henry Ernest resigned on April 5, 1779. A few days later his father was driven to Philadelphia (horseback riding was now more than he could bear), and he formally resigned the rectorship. He preached his farewell sermon in Zion, on a text found in Sirach (Ecclesiasticus) 7.40: "In what thou doest, remember thine end."

The quarrel sputtered on. Threats were made against Kuntze, who, whatever Henry Ernest may have thought, was innocent of any greed or jealousy. Kuntze was so distressed by the row that he contemplated returning to Europe as soon as his wife, Peggy, was safely delivered of her child. He stayed on, however, for a few years in Philadelphia and then went to New York as pastor of Christ Church, preaching, writing, serving as professor of Oriental Languages at Columbia University (without, however, enrolling any students or receiving any salary), and being sworn in as interpreter for the Federal Congress when it sat in New York.

Henry Ernest took his leave of Philadelphia in dramatic fashion. On Sunday, April 25, he faced the congregation from before the altar, and read a blistering statement. He had formerly hoped, he said, to live and die with them; but, in 1777, to avoid falling into the hands of what he called "pitiless traitors and tyrants," he had been obliged to leave them; now again he must leave them, partly for his health's sake (he had a cough), partly because of disgust at the abuse to which the name Muhlenberg had been put, and partly in order to "stop the mouths of slanderers." He would pass over the details, "that our shame be not known in Gath and Ascalon."

In conclusion he pronounced a benediction that had teeth in it: "Grow in the knowledge and grace of Christ–. Live in peace and brotherly love– . . . God bless you and me. Farewell!"[6]

Henry Ernest accepted a call to New Hanover (the Swamp). It was only nine or ten miles from the Trappe, and its woods, creeks, and marshes offered better opportunities for botany than did the streets of Philadelphia.

Aside from the fracas in St. Michael's and Zion, the spring and summer of 1779 was a comparatively happy, if not a very quiet, time for Henry Melchior and Anna Maria. After the storm and the whirlwind, Peter, Frederick, and Henry Ernest were settling down, each into the career for which he was best fitted: the army, politics, and the church—the latter edifice with broad windows opening on to the fields of botany.

The parsonage at Providence was always full of friends and relatives coming and going. It remained as surely the hub of the Muhlenberg family as Augustus Church was the center of Lutheranism in America.

Old Mrs. Weiser (Conrad Weiser's Ann Eve), who was now living at Reading, sent word she would like to visit her daughter Anna Maria at the Trappe, if she could find a way down. One day in June, on the Pastor's returning home from a visit to Philadelphia, he found "the Widow Weiser" at the parsonage. The ubiquitous Mr. Swaine had brought her down.

What memories Anna Maria and her mother revived during that visit we can only guess at. But we may be sure they talked about Conrad Weiser. Though her father had been dead almost nineteen years, Anna Maria (born January 13, 1725) could remember him very well in his prime. In 1737 she had been an alert twelve-year-old, keen to hear him talk about the adventures he had had that spring on his journey as Pennsylvania's ambassador, through woods waist-deep in snow, through flood and famine, to the distant Indian capital of Onondaga (Syracuse), where he delivered a peace belt of white wampum to the forty-nine *royaners* of the Six United Nations assembled in council under the Tree of Peace and beside the Fire That Never Dies. She had been eighteen years old when, again at Onondaga, Conrad Weiser had taken Virginia's hatchet "out of the head of the Six Nations." At Tulpehocken she had often seen her father's orchard filled with Indians—council chiefs and war chiefs, with their entourage, on the way to "brighten the chain of friendship" with Brother Onas (Penn's people) in Philadelphia.

These Indians had tried to keep out of the white man's quarrel but, as one of their chiefs had said long since, "You can't live in the woods and stay neutral." Some of the United Nations had sided with the British; others, notably the Oneidas and part of the Tuscaroras, had sided with the colonies. There had been some Indian raids against the border. General Sullivan had been sent north to destroy the Iroquois towns along the Ambassadors' Road which Conrad Weiser had trodden. Word came to the Trappe that the American army had reached Onondaga and burned it, destroying the corn and killing or capturing over forty Onondagas[7]—the People of the Mountains, Keepers of the Council Fire.

However well justified the expedition may have been by the necessities of Washington's strategy at this juncture, the news from the north could not but be sad for Anna Maria and her mother.

The members of the Muhlenberg family were as busy in exchanging presents as they were in exchanging visits. Over the roads between the Trappe, Tulpehocken, Reading, New Hanover, and Philadelphia, there was a constant circulation of mufflers, oysters, cheese, brown sugar, butter, books, chocolate, cows, horses, Bohea tea, and sugar candy (for Polly). On April 29, 1779, Sally at the Trappe thanked Betsy Schultze at Tulpehocken for the nuts.[8] Peggy had a craving for Dutch cheese, which Betsy was best able to supply. Mama, with aid from Sally, was always knitting stockings for the grandchildren. On November 12, 1779, Henry Melchior records receiving from his son Frederick's wife "1½ Bottel *mit* Snuff." At Augustus Church the present pastor, the Reverend W. Russell Zimmerman, will show you the meerschaum pipe which a certain Mr. Swaine is said to have presented to Henry Melchior Muhlenberg.

Let us hear from Peggy:

To
Missr Elisabeth Shultz
at
Tolpehoken

May Witsunday

Dear Sister
whe are all well thank god hoping you are the Same
there are 2 pair of Stokings here for Mr. schultz but I don't think it Suits to send them with Mr. Wagman Send for them as Soon as possible I paid 6 dollers a pair for weving that maks 4 lb 10 S I Shold be very glad if you wold beg Mis Spyker or any Cleanly body for a few pound of duch Cheese give any Prise. Cant you Send me Some, O it is too warm I forgot myselfe
My love to Mr. schultz
If you are leing in i give you joy

Peggy[9]

Betsy Schultze's "lying in" came to an end on July 8, 1779, when a son was born, John Peter Gabriel. This was the day that his namesake, Brigadier General John Peter Gabriel Muhlenberg, received orders from Washington to take up position on the morrow in the Forest of Dean—ready to move up to cover Anthony Wayne at Stony Point.

Peggy herself was not far behind Betsy. A daughter was born to her September 6, and baptized Anna Christina.

Not to be behind the others, Mary Catharine, Henry Ernest's wife, gave birth on October 26 to a daughter, Susan Elisabeth.

There was bad news from Tulpehocken. Peter Weiser had died. During the spring of 1778 he had spent three days at the Trappe, on his way home, and they all knew his story. He had enlisted early in the war, and at the time of Brandywine he was a first lieutenant in the First Pennsylvania Rifles, commanded by Colonel Chambers. Sent out with a detachment under Captain Wilson to attack the Hessian Jägers, who were attempting to cross the creek, he had been shot through the body, a musket ball entering the right side of the chest, passing through the right lobe of the lung, and coming out below on the left side.[10] He was captured by the British, taken to Philadelphia, where he received the best attention from both English and German surgeons. But the wound remained open, discharging pus. Peter was accordingly allowed to go home on parole. He reached the Trappe in a fever.[11] Henry Melchior talked to him about his soul, and sent for Captain Conrad Weiser, Peter's brother, to take him home. Captain Conrad came down post haste with a cart and drove his brother back to Tulpehocken. Before the end came, Peter was advanced to the rank of captain. On September 11, 1779, the second anniversary of the Battle of Brandywine, Henry Melchior Muhlenberg received news that his nephew, Captain Peter Weiser, had died of his wounds.

The campaign in the "Highlands of York" had meanwhile been getting under way. It will be remembered that during the winter Washington had thrown a semicircle of forces around the British in New York. West Point had been made the center of a system of forts, now rapidly being strengthened, which was to guard the vital communications between New England and the middle and southern states. Howe in Pennsylvania had failed to break the chain of communications between the Northern and southern states, and Burgoyne had failed to break the chain between the eastern and middle states; but the British still hoped, by seizing the forts and ferries on the Hudson, to "divide and conquer." In May they made a start by capturing Stony Point, which commanded the important Hudson crossing of King's Ferry. By means of this, West Point, key position a few miles farther up the river, was threatened.

Peter Muhlenberg's brigade was sent to cover West Point. On June 15, from a post in the "Highlands of York," Peter wrote to his father, giving a succinct account of the situation: "The campaign seems to open fast. The Engl. have Possession of Kings Ferry and are strongly fortifying. We lay about eight Miles from them, in order to prevent an Attack on our Fort at West Point, which covers the Communication between the Southern and Eastern States and is a Post of the utmost Importance to us–"[12]

Anthony Wayne's subsequent recapture of Stony Point (which he held for only a few hours), while not of any great military significance, had some psychological value in stiffening the spirit of the colonies, and its story still makes an appeal.

Peter Muhlenberg's contribution to Wayne's success has received little attention, because his detachment (three hundred strong) took no part in the actual fighting. It was a covering force, designed primarily to protect Wayne from pursuit should he be defeated–as Muhlenberg and Weedon had done for Sullivan at the Battle of Brandywine.

A week before the engagement, in order to give the enemy no hint of what was coming, Washington moved Muhlenberg's force into position at the Forest of Dean, in the mountains a few miles north of Stony Point, to be ready to move when the time was ripe. Final orders came from Washington on the afternoon of July 15. Muhlenberg was to move "about midnight," as secretly as possible, traveling "perfectly light," with "one day's provision," and to be prepared to act as Wayne's situation should make necessary.[13]

Wayne tells us that, when the attack began, soon after midnight, he had drawn Muhlenberg's three hundred men into his rear, where they took post on the opposite side of the marsh flanking the post, "in readiness either to support me, or cover a retreat in case of accident. . . ."[14]

As it turned out Wayne's bayonet charge (not a man fired a shot) was entirely successful, and he captured the garrison without too much difficulty. It was a neat operation, and Congress struck a medal in his honor.

The position, however, was found to be untenable, and Washington withdrew the American forces after twenty-four hours. Clinton regained possession on the nineteenth. Muhlenberg's forces were again posted at the Forest of Dean, ready to oppose Clinton if he should attempt to move in strength from King's Ferry.

When dispute arose afterward about disposal of the booty (which was to be distributed among those who had taken part in the attack), Washington had to remind the officers of Muhlenberg's detachment that it "was intended as a covering party in Case of Accident and to give countenance to the Assailants rather than as a body of *support,* to give serious aid in the attack."[15]

The printed account of the affair, which Frederick forwarded to his father at the Trappe, made no mention of General Muhlenberg.

Less than two weeks after Stony Point, Mr. Swaine won his most signal victory of the war. On July 28 he was appointed, by the President and Council of Pennsylvania, Clothier to the State of Pennsylvania, and he wrote at once to Daddy Muhlenberg to tell him so.

The Pastor licked his lips at memories of Europe and the courtly old tradition which made French the universal language of epistolary address and gave even eminence its final touch of distinction. What grace Mr. Swaine's name now would give to the back of a letter—in Europe! He entered the address lovingly in his Journal of July 29, 1779:

"A monsieur Francois Swaine Marchand Drapier pour l'Etat du Pennsylvanique a Philadelphia."

The war made but slight impression on the Muhlenberg family for the rest of the summer. Even Peter in the Highlands had little to do. Clinton decided to leave West Point alone for the time. Other plans were in the air.

There was a certain Benedict Arnold ("of approved valor," like another Benedict, but not, like Shakespeare's creation, "of confirmed honesty"), who found the Sons of Freedom growing tedious. A few months after the Stony Point action, Arnold received command at West Point. But by that time Muhlenberg had left the Highlands and was back in Virginia. Of Arnold, later. He did not directly cross

Peter Muhlenberg's path until New Year's Day, 1781. We shall meet him then.

It did not take a British invasion to provide anxiety and excitement at the Trappe. Anna Maria by her illness kept the family always on edge. She bravely but obstinately insisted upon continuing her normal activities about the place as if nothing were the matter. Her seizures were apt to come upon her at the most alarming moments, while she was working beside the spring in the washhouse, tending pots over the fire, or holding a baby on her knee.

At ten o'clock on the morning of November 4, 1779, a blaze burst out in the washhouse, started through the drying of flax by the fire. Neighbors came in and put it out, but the excitement had been too much for Anna Maria. Next day her husband noted in his Journal that her mind was deranged. She came to herself after a time, but it was a sad warning to her husband and all the household.

November 16 was another trying day, but a more cheerful one, and one for which Anna Maria was entirely competent. For one thing, Henry Ernest and his parents-in-law, the Schaeffers, turned up on their way from New Hanover to Philadelphia, and Anna Maria provided them with what her husband calls "a patriarchal meal." Those who have enjoyed Pennsylvania Dutch hospitality, with its "seven sweets and seven sours" and all the rest of its profusion, will understand the Pastor's use of the word "patriarchal."

More important, this was the day on which Polly gave birth to her first child, a son—"after almost five years," as her father observed in his Journal.

When, early in the morning, Polly was "seized with birth pains," her husband, Mr. Swaine (*Marchand Drapier*, etc.) being at that time absent in Philadelphia attending to the duties of his office, the Muhlenbergs, especially Anna Maria, turned to and made the necessary arrangements. A midwife was sent for, and a neighborwoman came in to help. The child was safely delivered between eight and nine o'clock in the morning.

Henry Melchior all this time was in a dither. He had to entertain a visitor, Mr. Hartwick, whose Confusion at Rhinebeck he had looked into in 1750, and who now chose the wrong time to be voluble.

"I would have been glad to assist her with counsel and medicine," wrote Pastor Muhlenberg of Polly, "but Mr. Hartwig kept holding me with some new scheme he had thought up, since he has no feeling for anyone but himself and has no heirs."

And so little George Washington Swaine entered the world without his grandfather's advice. In the Journal of November 24, when Henry Melchior tells of the baptism of the child (the grandparents being the sponsors), he records only the name "George." Perhaps the "Washington" was omitted for security reasons.

Sunday, December 9, had been proclaimed by Congress a day, as Henry Melchior expressed it, of *Buss-Bet-und-Dankfest*—repentance, prayer, and thanksgiving. The good Pastor did not expect to find many people at church, because, in the first place, the weather was bad; in the second, too many of his neighbors were "dissatisfied with the military situation"; and, in the third, the Plain Sects pretended "too delicate a conscience to approve of such a man-made ordinance."[16] He was the more pleased, therefore, on arriving at Augustus Church, to find a good congregation awaiting him. Perhaps the world was better than its complaining voices might seem to indicate. Or perhaps (but these are not the Pastor's thoughts) it was the better for its open complaints. Freedom to murmur is one of the healthy purgatives of democracy.

The Christmas of 1779 was a happy time for the Muhlenbergs at the Trappe. The three boys were all close at hand. Peter and Frederick came up from Philadelphia to spend the holiday with their parents at the Trappe and with Henry Ernest at New Hanover. For a Christmas gift, Peter gave his father a pair of trousers and a neckcloth—the more welcome in that they were made of the now nearly unprocurable English cloth. While he could not himself cut the figure of a general in them, the Pastor observed, they would at least serve to clothe his nakedness.

Mr. Shep of Philadelphia sent him seven bottles of wine, for which the Pastor gave thanks in the words of Barzillai: "How long have I to live, that I should be fed with precious Dainties, having no refined taste of what I eat or drink, nor can I hear the harmonious Voice of Singing Men and Women?" Yet, he added, I shall "take now and then a small portion of it for a weak Stomach and spare the Rest for poor and sick fellow-Christians. . . ."

He wrote a letter to Their Worthinesses, the Directors at Halle, and sent it (presumably through diplomatic channels which were accessible to his son, a congressman) to Benjamin Franklin in Paris for forwarding. Though Frederick and Peter, as he said to his old friend Keppele, had allowed themselves "to be drawn up into the political heavens, where, in the ordinary course of nature, they must fall again, unless God in his mercy work a miracle," it was no doubt pleasant to him to find that Frederick's involvement with the great ones of this world served (like Joseph's) to smooth his father's path.

The letter was addressed "To His Excellency Dr. Franklin, Minister Plenipotentiary of the U. S. of North America at the Court of Versailles."

Here is the letter itself,[17] written in a style commensurate with Franklin's dignity.

May it please Your Excellency:

Your Excellency's most humble Servants, the united German Lutheran Ministers in the American States should not perturbate the extensive political Circles in Your most weighty Station for the Interest of the Indep: States, if we could avoid it. Being called, sent and supported into these parts of the Globe by the Reverend Directores and Professors of the Orphan House and College of His Sacred Prussian Majesty's Dominions at Halle in Saxony and permitted to keep up a Correspondence with the said Reverend Gentlemen concerning religious Matters, but left destitute to get any Letter home, we trust therefore in Your Excellency's approved innate Philanthropy, Magnanimity and condescending Kindness, that you will be pleased, if possible, to recommend the enclosed Letter to His Prussian Majesty's most Excellent Ambassador, or to His Honble Secretary, to be conveyed in their Packet to Berlin, from thence it will safe come home. But if not suitable that Way, to send the Letter to the Post-Office. By granting this our most humble Request, Your Excellency's Petitioners shall in Duty be bound to continue in fervent Prayers.

H: Mb: Sen: Min:

Dec: 25th 1779

CHAPTER XX

"I ENTREAT"

The British, probing along the Atlantic coast in search of a weak spot, selected the southern theater with an eye to the ultimate "breaking up of Virginia." They took Savannah in December 1778, and, from that base, in December 1779 Clinton moved north against Charleston with a good-sized fleet and an army of more than eight thousand regulars.

To support General Lincoln, who had with him to defend Charleston only fourteen hundred Continentals and a thousand militia, Washington sent down to him all the Virginia and North Carolina Continentals in his army. It was now of the utmost importance to raise fresh troops in Virginia in order to supply the southern theater with reinforcements or, if Virginia itself should be threatened, to defend that state. General Peter Muhlenberg was assigned to the task.

There were many difficulties in the way: the absence of even a skeleton army in Virginia; the lack of money with which to pay the troops; the lack of an effective conscription law; the jealousies between the civil and military authorities. The circumstances under which Muhlenberg received his instructions provided, perhaps, the greatest difficulty of them all.

From his headquarters at Morristown in New Jersey, General Muhlenberg had started for Woodstock on the long delayed leave of absence. But he did not get far. He was held up by bad weather in Philadelphia. Heavy snow, which at one time lay three feet deep, made the roads impassable, and, after the snow, rain so swelled the creeks that they were unfordable. While waiting in the city, he received instructions from the Board of War (apparently without the knowledge of the Commander in Chief) to proceed at once to Virginia and take charge of recruiting there.

War Office Febr^{y} 24th 1780

Sir

The board are of opinion that You should proceed to Virginia & there wait the orders of the Commander in Chief. In the mean time you will be pleasd to employ yourself in collecting the recruits & Drafts in proper places. You will co-operate with the Government of the State, in any measures necessary for this Service, & inform the board from time to time of the progress of the business & of the supplies necessary, to enable the troops to proceed wheresoever directed[1]

On the same day Muhlenberg communicated with General Washington.

Philadelphia Febr^{y} 24th 1780

Sir Enclosed I have the honor to transmit Your Excellency a copy of the Instructions I have receivd from the board of War; to Morrow I set out for Virginia, & shall be happy to receive Your Excellencys Orders at Fredericksburg, or Williamsburg– . . .

P: Muhlenberg[2]

It was an anomalous position in which General Muhlenberg now found himself. He was under three masters: the Board of War, General Washington, and Thomas Jefferson (Governor of Virginia). It is a tribute to his skill and patience (and to theirs) that the difficulties of conflicting jurisdictions did not immediately wreck the whole undertaking.

On his way south, the General reached the Trappe on February 26, where he was held up for nearly two weeks, waiting for the floods to subside. While there, he saw the wild pigeons pass, February 29,[3] on their journey north; and on March 4 seventy horsemen of Colonel Armand's Independent Cavalry Corps came by on their way south to Charleston.[4] In the afternoon a noncommissioned officer came to the parsonage door asking for accommodations overnight for horse and man; but house and stall were already taken up by General Peter and his entourage. Armand's cavalry had to find lodging elsewhere.

Peter got off at last with his cavalcade, March 10. Riding on horseback were the General, his Brigade Major, their two servants, and Henry Metzger of Pottsgrove. In the stage wagon were his wife Hannah, the two children, and a Negress. A neighbor, Mr. Diehl, had lent his son to drive them as far as Pottsgrove. From there Henry Metzger was to take them on to Virginia.[5]

The roads were still bad, and it took Peter Muhlenberg the better part of a month to reach his destination. He lost two horses on the way, for one of which he had paid six thousand dollars.

While Peter was thus being held up by wind, snow, ice, and flood, Henry Melchior at the Trappe was warned in a dream one Sunday night by his "guardian spirit" of a dreadful commotion in the Philadelphia congregation. Peter, to whom he related his dream at breakfast next morning, talked him out of it, which was the easier to do since, as his father said, he did not believe in dreams indiscriminately.

The truth about the affair in Philadelphia was, however, as painful as any nightmare could make it. The charge was there being circulated that "the old fox" at Providence was trying to drive Pastor Kuntze out so that he could force his own sons in. Peggy was weeping her eyes out, and Kuntze, hurt that anyone could think him intending to act against his father-in-law, had practically decided to go back to Germany. Anna Maria gave way under the strain and was seized with convulsion after convulsion.

The burden of wartime economy and a dislocated, overflowing household fell heavily on Anna Maria. It was difficult to get, and impossible to keep, a servant maid. Thirteen-year-old Sally did what she could to help, but she was "not strong enough to take charge of the housekeeping." The strain proved too much for her mother. One day in the springhouse (which contained the bake-oven), while stirring up the fire she had an attack and "fell to the ground between the bake-oven and a deep spring." Polly and Mr. Swaine found her and carried her into the house.[6]

Henry Ernest, who had been eager for months to leave the Swamp and take his family to Lancaster, at last had his wishes fulfilled. On March 4 he set out on the difficult journey, by very bad roads, over hill and dale, across flooded streams, through swamps and stony places, to the town of his dreams—which, however, he did not reach until March 9. The rest of his family (which he had for the time being left with the Schultzes at Tulpehocken, where Peter found them on his way to Virginia) he brought to Lancaster on the seventeenth.

In Lancaster he found his pastoral work invigorating, preaching, visiting, and conducting young people's classes. He had a flair for young people's work. He managed to find time for other work, too, for which his father felt in duty bound to reprimand him. Modern textual criticism of the Bible interested him, and also the collecting, classifying, and naming (where the specimens proved to be new) of plants in the vicinity of Lancaster. Between 1780 and 1791, within a radius of three miles, he collected nearly eleven hundred different species.

But on botany and textual criticism Henry Melchior Muhlenberg looked with no sympathetic eye.

Tending the sheep and lambs which Jesus Christ has bought with his blood, he wrote, April 3, 1780, "will give you infinitely more blessing and reward than all this research into hidden variants and the plants of Linnaeus."[7]

Though Henry Ernest loved his father and took pleasure in obeying him, he had, like his brothers, a mind of his own. He stuck to his church and tended his lambs, but he never closed his eyes to the flowers at his feet.

To return to the campaign in the South. It was known from the beginning that General Muhlenberg's recruiting commission in Virginia was crucial to America's success in the war. Washington called it "very interesting," which in his restrained style meant "of the last importance." Urgency is written into the letters that passed between them. Indeed, all who understood the situation experienced the same feeling of urgency, coupled with powerlessness, which is one of the characteristics of nightmares.

When Muhlenberg arrived in Virginia, already Clinton from the land and Arbuthnot from the sea had set about the siege of Charleston. Muhlenberg presented himself before Jefferson to ask his advice, and received a most dubious account of the state of the forces in Virginia. On April 10, the day the British first demanded the surrender of the city, Governor Jefferson put down in writing, at Muhlenberg's request, the recruiting prospects.

"There are some drafted Soldiers in different parts of the Country," wrote the Governor, "but they are so few, so dispersed, & enlisted for so short a time that we have not thought them worth the expence of gathering up."[8]

There were two state regiments still in Virginia, but, the terms of a large part of the men having expired, they had been given furloughs till May 1 by their officers, who hoped that by that time money enough might have accumulated in the treasury to reënlist them. Voluntary enlistment, noted Jefferson, was, under certain restrictions, permitted by law. But that was all. "Consent of the governed" stood like a lion in the path of any effective military law.

But so pressing was the danger to the southward that no time was to be lost in attempting, by whatever means were available, to build regiments up to strength. Reinforcements were to be dispatched in driblets, company by company.

"As the Recruits and Drafts come in," wrote Washington, "You will have them formed into Companies immediately . . . and whenever they amount to 50 strong they are to march and join the troops of the State to the Southward."[9]

Washington suggested further that deserters (of which there were large numbers in the state) should be induced to return by promises of pardon, and that the old soldiers who were now on furlough should be collected—though where, "in the present deranged situation of our Treasury," the necessary money for this ingathering was to come from, he frankly did not know. Possibly "the Honorable the Board of War," on whose instructions Peter had undertaken his recruiting duties, might find a solution.

Peter had little good to report to his Commander in Chief when he wrote on May 8[10] to say that without money in the treasury little could be expected from the drafts. He did, however, say that he was about to send the First and Second Virginia Regiments on to Charleston, each having been recruited up to a strength approaching 350. According to the latest authentic accounts, he added, Charleston was still safe.

Charleston fell on May 12. It was "the greatest disaster," writes Francis Vinton Greene, "sustained by the American army during the war."[11]

Muhlenberg hastened to Petersburg to support Colonel Bluford, who had been sent south with newly raised reinforcements for the city. At Petersburg he learned that all was over. Bluford's Third Virginia Regiment had been caught by Tarleton's cavalry at Waxhaws and wiped out. Virginia was wide open to the enemy.

The next few months were among the worst in America's history, and the best in Peter Muhlenberg's career. It was no longer a matter of recruiting and sending off driblets of reinforcements. He had to raise, officer, train, and equip an army, not merely to save Virginia, but also to prevent the collapse of the whole American line, even that part of it which held posts in the north. Everything had been risked to save Charleston. The Highland fortress line itself, devoid of both men and provisions, was now exposed to the enemy.

Quickly the State of Virginia, its Assembly prodded by impending disaster, passed the necessary laws. Drafts began to pour in. A corps of officers was built up. Training on a large scale was organized. Everywhere men rose to the emergency.

But where were the munitions? Muhlenberg reported to Washington, June 19, that the first draft of twenty-five hundred men was nearly ready and would march in a week; five thousand more would be raised immediately; but there were not more than four thousand arms available.

The Fourth of July, 1780, did not dawn glorious in Virginia. When, on that day, General Gates left Fredericksburg, where Muhlenberg was then stationed, for the South, Peter gave him a gloomy memorandum of the military situation in Virginia. At Chesterfield, where the men were being assembled, there were few tents and scarcely any other military stores of the kind necessary to fit men for the field. The hospital there was almost totally unprovided. It had only two surgeons. The powder magazine at Richmond, which was said to contain forty tons of gunpowder, was but a small wooden building and not even provided with a guard for its protection.[12]

In his report on that same Fourth of July to General Washington, Peter observed, "A British fleet is at present in our bay."[13] Its strength and destination were, when he wrote, unknown to him.

Washington's reply to Muhlenberg's news was a masterpiece of restrained excitement. The Generalissimo (as Henry Melchior liked to call him) knew that, once again as in the summer of 1776, the game was nearly up.

"I have now only to entreat," wrote Washington to Muhlenberg, July 18, 1780, "that You will use every posible exertion to collect and form the Drafts and to have them disciplined. I entreat this; I expect it of all the Officers. They will remember that the forming of a New Army or at least of a whole State line and fitting it for the Field, devolves in a great measure upon them, and as it shall act, so in a degree will be their reputation. They have a glorious opportunity to signalize themselves, and I doubt not they will avail themselves of the occasion. The crisis is a most interesting One, and on your and their exertions, and the discipline and bravery of the Troops, great and early events much depend. . . ."[14]

To Governor Jefferson, Washington wrote in the same vein. "I have entreated Genl Muhlenberg," he said, ". . . to use every possible exertion to collect and discipline the Men. . . ."[15]

Back in Pennsylvania the Glorious Fourth seems to have passed off rather better, at least in the Muhlenberg circle. On that day, at the Commencement Exercises of the University of Pennsylvania, two members of the family, Henry Ernest Muhlenberg and Christopher Kuntze, received from the Trustees the honorary degree of Master of Arts.

When Henry Melchior read about it in the English newspaper, he shook his head and grasped his quill pen to enter his disapproval. Matthew 23.8: "But be not ye called Rabbi: for one is your Master, even Christ; and all ye are brethren."

One does not find, he wrote, the letters A. M. or Th. D. in the Gospels. Rather, "Paul, a *servant* of Jesus Christ, John, a *servant* of Christ, Peter, an *apostle* of Jesus Christ . . . and what good is *onomatopoeia* for the Kingdom of Jesus Christ? . . . All flesh is grass. I Peter 1:24-25, Matt. 9:37-38 . . ."[16]

But Frederick, high in the Great World ("now in the Hurle burle," wrote his father, "till his waxen wings are melted"),[17] member of the Continental Congress, chairman of the medical committee which directed the army hospital service, did not take the pomp of academic circumstance too seriously. He prepared a burlesque poem for the occasion:

> *Gratulatio poetica in honorem celeberrimi doctissimi et praeclarissimi Dom. H. H. Artium Magistri quem d. 4 Jul. 1780 Universitas Pensilvaniens honoris causa Magistrum creavit Autoritate antea praedicta a vivis illis praeclarissimis qui praesidium habent et quos vulgo vocamus* Trustees of the University of the State of Pensilv.[18]

These "Gratulatory verses in honor of the celebrated, learned, and illustrious Henry Muhlenberg, A. M." (signed "*Knittelmacher* [Doggerel Maker] Poet Licentiate and Laureate, A. M.") were composed in the monstrous, limping hexameters (with a sprinkling of pentameters and septenaries) of which he had exuberant command,

and were annotated with great fullness—in the taste, as he said, of these enlightened times when people like the notes better than the text.

It is perhaps fortunate for the reader that the best line in the poem, with which our printing of the text shall here commence, is also the last one:

Potz Welten! dreymal hoch—du bist Magister worden.

Frederick wrote to his brother-in-law Emanuel Schultze, suggesting that Henry Ernest might write a dissertation on the question whether they could raise an army of Masters in Europe—and so get his Doctorate from the University.[19]

Perhaps Frederick's high spirits were a defense against the gloom that pervaded the nation's capital, Philadelphia, and that seemed to be spreading over the whole country. Everywhere inflation and taxes formed the basis of conversation. Henry Melchior himself was touched with the prevailing pessimism. What the country now lacked, he observed ironically, was two commodities, freedom and salt.[20]

His mood was not relieved by the news from upcountry. In January Peter visited his grandmother, the "Widow Weiser," and found her destitute.[21] Her two eldest sons, who had looked after her so well, had died, and the care of her had been left to Sammie and Benjamin Weiser. But Sammie and Benjamin had careers of their own to make in the Sunbury region, and their mother at Reading was, for the time being, overlooked. Her house in Reading was now falling to pieces. She, who had entertained governors and Indian sachems in the days when her husband was honored by the Iroquois with the name *Tarachiawagon*, Holder of the Heavens, now could not find a dry corner in her shack when it rained. She had to dispose of furniture and clothing to pay the taxes.

Henry Melchior, on receiving Peter's report, at once sent up to her money and food: chocolate, brown sugar, salt, coffee, tea, allspice, and a "sweet orange." Later in the year he paid her a visit and found the house in dreadful decay. He could not sleep at night because of the crawling things that infested it.

Henry Melchior, Anna Maria, and Sally made the trip to Reading together, and went on farther to visit their friends in the Tulpehocken

Valley. It was noticed that during the three weeks they were away Anna Maria, being among the scenes she remembered so happily from her childhood, had no seizures.

They visited the old Weiser homestead near Womelsdorf late in the afternoon of August 2.[22] A little company of friends gathered about them; and there, at the foot of Eagle Peak, they sang and prayed together as in the old days when Henry Melchior had first visited the Weisers and fallen in love with Anna Maria over the hymns.

They went on a few miles to visit the Schultzes, who lived beside Christ Church, where Anna Maria and Henry Melchior had been married. They visited the massive stone structure of the new Tulpehocken Reformed Church, built in 1772, and saw the place where the old wooden church had stood when Henry Melchior had preached in it thirty-seven years before.

They left Betsy and her husband on the fifteenth of August and started home, stopping at the Weiser homestead for lunch.

The heat was frightening. They decided to escape it on the way home from Reading by traveling at night, by moonlight. In Reading they had difficulty in finding a conveyance. It was wartime, and they had to take what they could get—which turned out to be a small, uncomfortable wagon with an old "Low Dutch" driver at the reins.

This person provided the only amusement of the night's journey. He was from Shamokin (Sunbury), having fled that settlement (which was situated on the Wyoming Path) in fear of Indian attack. It was this experience, seemingly, that had left him with a nagging fever from which he could find no relief, when the attacks came upon him, except in the form of liquid medicament. His constitution having, in the course of time, become inured to this prescription, it required considerable dosage to produce any amelioration of his condition.

They left Reading at nine o'clock. It was soon apparent that it was not to be a romantic drive. The road was rough, the moon did not come out, and the driver did not know the way. Anna Maria and Henry Melchior were old and brittle. Sally was nursing a swollen foot. Every time the wagon hit a stone or a rut, they were thrown about and barked their shins. By one o'clock the driver was overcome by one of his recurrent attacks, which came upon him as they passed a house, before the door of which sat an old woman, trying to cool herself in the night air. They stopped, but found she had nothing with which to assuage the driver's torment but a drink of cold water. The horses, however, were refreshed with some hay, and the Muhlenbergs enjoyed a few minutes of relief from the jolting.

They drove on till daybreak, at which time they reached the "shield of the White Horse," an hostelry which afforded medicine for the driver in the form of rum, to the tune of eight dollars—not, however, so handsome a ration as those who have never experienced inflation might suppose. Four miles beyond the White Horse they arrived at Pottstown and stopped for breakfast. From that point they did a good deal of the remaining nine miles on foot, to help the horses. At noon they reached home safe if not sound. Sally's foot was much inflamed, and the two old people felt as if they had emerged from a torture chamber. They put the horses into a green meadow. As for the driver, they poured into his "Low Dutch stomach" such medicament as it seemed to require, and let him sleep it off for a space of some thirteen or fourteen hours.

Two days later, Anna Maria's attacks returned. While she was sitting by the door with Polly's baby on her lap, she was suddenly overcome. Her husband heard the baby scream, and ran out to find his wife lying on the stone pavement. He picked up the child, unhurt, and called for Sally to come and help him. It required all their strength to carry Anna Maria into the house and get her to bed.[23] The happy memories that had brought back her health had forsaken her.

Meanwhile Congress in Philadelphia, again without consulting Washington, had given General Gates command of the southern army. Gates hurried to North Carolina, joined De Kalb, who commanded a force of some two thousand men detached from the army in the north, and ordered an immediate march against the British post at Camden. He was joined by over a thousand North Carolina militia and some small units, including Armand's light horse.

At Camden, on August 16, General Gates' army was destroyed. De Kalb was killed. The militia fled and Armand's cavalry fled with them. They hurtled back with such momentum that they smashed the Maryland Brigade behind them, and with them they carried

General Gates so far to the rear that he was not heard from again for several days.

When news of this catastrophe arrived in Pennsylvania, Henry Melchior's faith faltered. For a time he had been assured, in the fact that the American army had survived so many disasters, that a mightier hand than theirs was upholding them. Now he was no longer sure. Perhaps he had wrongly interpreted the signs. It might be that the Almighty intended only to chastise the American people. "Generally the consequences," he wrote, "of this excessive freedom to be bold is slavery and humiliation."[24]

Peter, meanwhile, was not reading signs in the sky. He was too busy with his present task, which was to save Virginia.

> I do not ask to see
> The distant scene—one step enough for me.

Soldiers in plenty, but no weapons—that was the tenor of his letters as he worked with furious earnestness to keep the Virginia Line from falling apart.

"The New Levies of the lower Counties are nearly collected," he wrote to Washington, September 29, "and are forming into Battalions but we are totally destitute of every Article necessary to equipp them for the Field—"[25]

He belabored the Governor of Virginia, the Council, and the Commissary of Stores for equipment for his men. "There is a total want of everything necessary to fit them for the Field," he wrote.[26]

His troops were without tents, teams, blankets, camp kettles. "In what manner they are to be equipped for the Field," he wrote a few weeks later, "is at present a mystery to me."[27]

General Gates wrote urging him to send on all available troops without waiting for equipment: ". . . hunting shirts, over-alls, and shoes will be sufficient."[28]

But there were hardly any shoes. There was not even leather to make shoes. Nevertheless, taking Gates at his word, Muhlenberg kept a stream of men flowing south without waiting for their equipment.

Washington continued to urge him on, but wrote without confidence in any prospect of getting clothes or arms, especially since the help in this kind which had been expected from France had failed to arrive.

Gates was bitter. He wrote to Muhlenberg that the troops being sent to him, "with neither clothes, blankets, arms, nor accoutrements," were a naked rabble that only increased the distress of his present army.[29]

Distress was not confined to the Army of the South. At the Trappe, no less than in Virginia, clothing was difficult to procure. Henry Melchior, making preparation for a journey, was constrained to note in his Journal, "If there is any small way in which I have something in common with the sainted Dr. Luther, it must be sought in the incident on his journey to Worms when he lacked breeches. . . ."[30]

Out in the country, people were openly murmuring against the government. When Frederick said he was getting tired of the Great World and was thinking of going back to preach in the Swamp, his father told him that it was too late. Frederick had been in Congress, and people at the Swamp were suspicious of anyone connected with that body.[31]

Was the family going to pieces? "Poor Peter and Frederick" lay heavily on their father's mind. "Frederick's act is near an end."[32] And Peter? "The fortunes of war are fluctuating." Only a miracle could now uphold him and his army. Kuntze was unhappy in Philadelphia and wanted a change. Henry Ernest, in his father's estimation, was dabbling too much in botany.

Then there was Mr. Swaine. Undoubtedly, another miracle was needed here. For the second time Mr. Swaine had been dropped from public office. Henry Melchior reminded his daughter Polly of this when he wrote to her, July 24, to awaken her and her husband. Swaine had failed twice in public business, formerly as brigade major and now as state clothier. He had also failed twice in private business, once at the Swamp and again in Philadelphia. Swaine had taxes to pay like everybody else. Since he was now out of public office, he would have to join the militia or pay a heavy fine—which latter course he could not take because he had no money. Mr. Swaine, the Pastor had heard, was thinking of taking up shopkeeping. But these were precarious times for a shopkeeper.

In his distress, Henry Melchior confessed to his favorite son,

Henry Ernest, that he prayed God to make his children an example, not of His judgment, but of His mercy.[33]

"You should therefore," he wrote to Polly, "Bel[oved] Ch[ild] loose no day, hour or Minute to consider your present Situation and to ask Counsel of wise and prudent People, who have Understanding in oeconomical Affairs and Love for the Wellfare of their Neighbours.—

"P.S. Ephes. 4, 28. Let him labour with his hands . . . Proverbs 24, 33, 34. Yet a little Sleep, a little Slumber, a little Folding of the Hands to sleep: So shall thy Poverty come as one that travelleth, and thy want as an armed Man."[34]

For the Muhlenbergs, as for America in general, this was their darkest hour.

All at once the sky cleared. Henry Melchior's church work took his mind off the state of the nation and of the family. On Wednesday, October 4, Mr. Swaine brought Christopher Kuntze and Peggy with their little girl to the Trappe, where Kuntze was to attend a meeting of the Synod. A number of other ministers stayed at the parsonage. Polly, Peggy, and Sally turned to and did the cooking, under the superintendence of their mother. They prepared another patriarchal repast for the evangels, who were thirteen in number and had great success. Much business was attended to: the ordination of a Mr. Ernst, an appeal from the Swamp for Mr. Voigt as their preacher, and the case of Mr. Lehman, who had left his Reading charge without first notifying his church council. On Friday Mr. Swaine escorted Peggy and her family safely back across the rain-swollen Perkiomen and Skippack creeks on their way to Philadelphia.

Frederick was getting along all right after all. On October 10 an election for the Pennsylvania Assembly was held, in which the "Yellow Whigs" (radicals or "Constitutionalists," who wished to preserve the radical constitution of 1776) were soundly defeated, and Frederick's more moderate Republicans were swept in. Frederick received 869 votes—only one below Samuel Morris, who received 870, and 220 above Robert Morris, who received 649.[35]

Frederick next day, in a disconnected, chatty letter (written in the House, amid the noise of a spirited congressional debate) addressed to his "little brother" Henry, made it apparent that he was no longer dissatisfied with his world. It was in general the fact, he said, that "true public spirit and Virtue" were declining. But "our brave soldiers" were an exception. Peter down in Virginia, the "commanding officer of the state," had had a hard time getting equipment for his army; but his difficulties were now over. Pennsylvania was supplying him. Benedict Arnold had escaped, it was true, but André had been hanged—and we should get Arnold yet (a prophecy the fulfillment of which was a task soon to be entrusted to "our General," as we shall see). As for himself, Frederick said, he found a political career to be expensive, but if he was really needed in the Assembly (and the German-speaking part of the electorate had recently demonstrated that he was), he was content.

"I am here not my own master, and must be satisfied to serve where my fellow-citizens want me."[36]

Skies were clearing for Peter Muhlenberg, too. On October 22 it was known in Richmond that a British fleet of some sixty sail had appeared in Chesapeake Bay. Landings had been made near Portsmouth at the mouth of the James.

Virginia was invaded.

The day had come for which Peter Muhlenberg had been born. He hastened with what troops he could muster to confront General Leslie and try to confine him to the seaboard.

"Doubt of whatever kind," said Goethe, "can be ended by Action alone."

The tragic interlude was over. The war was now only waiting to be won.

CHAPTER XXI

BENEDICT ARNOLD

When Leslie landed his three thousand troops at Portsmouth, General Muhlenberg, in the language of the newspapers his father read with pride, stepped into the breach.

Official Virginia, however, was not very sanguine about the result. Jefferson wrote, October 22, to say that the body of troops then being collected would be "lamentably inadequate" if the enemy were in any force.[1]

There were plenty of generals on hand: Muhlenberg and Weedon of the Line, Nelson and Stevens of the Militia. But there were few men for them to lead, and there was not enough equipment even for those few. The draftees were coming in rapidly enough, but they were not trained, and there was no sufficient corps of officers to train them.

Governor Jefferson, much given to "likelihoods of hope," nevertheless formed a scheme (successful later at Yorktown when the tools were ready) to trap Leslie's force at Portsmouth by bringing in a French fleet to close the mouth of the bay while Muhlenberg's forces attacked Leslie's army from the land.

General Muhlenberg wrote a cheerful enough letter to General Gates,[2] telling him of the steps he had taken with his eight hundred regulars to confront Leslie, and with what rapidity the militia were coming in to reinforce them. But it was not fear of Muhlenberg's forces that prevented General Leslie from overrunning the state. It was the receipt of urgent instructions from Cornwallis, who had retreated after the King's Mountain action, to come south by sea to his assistance.

Muhlenberg's task during the past year had been to recruit and dispatch troops from Virginia to the South. When Virginia herself was invaded, it was found that the troops remaining in the state lacked firearms, clothes, food, means of transportation, and officers. They had to live off the country—"from hand to mouth," as Peter Muhlenberg said—and they did not live well. Major General Steuben, when he saw them, pronounced them "naked and as ill armed as possible."

There can be no doubt that Muhlenberg was not dissatisfied when the enemy were seen to be reëmbarking (soon after a vessel had been observed to arrive at Portsmouth from Charleston), leaving behind them a number of escaped Negroes as well as some new vessels they had been building—these latter unfinished and undestroyed.

The British left Portsmouth on the sixteenth of November. The ships hung about in Hampton Roads for a few days, waiting for a good wind. On the evening of the eighteenth Peter Muhlenberg reported hearing signal guns fired (it was too foggy to see anything), and supposed it to mean that the enemy were preparing "to seek their fortune elsewhere."[3] On the twenty-sixth he was able to inform Steuben that "the enemy have entirely left our bay, and are gone to sea"—some said to New York, but he himself thought (rightly, as it turned out) to Cape Fear.[4]

Baron Steuben, inured though he supposedly had become to pioneer conditions through his winter at Valley Forge, was shocked at what he found in Virginia, where the doctrinaire Thomas Jefferson sat in the governor's chair, and where General Muhlenberg was expected to conduct a campaign without men, horses, cooking utensils, or anything to shoot at the enemy.

When Steuben, shortly after taking command at Richmond, December 3, of all Continental forces in Virginia, instructed Muhlenberg to send eight hundred recruits to Petersburg, to be dispatched thence to reinforce Greene in the South, he was amazed at the sequel.

". . . the Men under general Muhlenberg," he wrote, "I found in a most Destrist Situation so intirely Destitute of Cloathing that it was impossible to get them to march."[5]

It was not merely a problem of dispatching troops to strengthen distant armies that confronted Muhlenberg. It was a problem of keeping them alive where they were. The worst provided, Muhlenberg moved up to Chesterfield Court House, because it was a "healthy spot" where there were barracks to shelter them.

For some time after Leslie's departure, Muhlenberg busied himself with the details of this new emergency, which reminds one of nothing so much as the spectacle of a run-down orphan asylum. But it was evident to a man of Baron Steuben's acumen that General Muhlenberg's special gifts as a fighter and disciplinarian were thrown away on this kind of military housewifery. He reported to General Greene, December 15, that "General Muhlenburgh's Services are not Essentially Necessary here,"[6] and asked whether he should not send him down with the next detachment for the South. In the meantime he gave Muhlenberg a short leave of absence, to go over the mountains and visit his family at Woodstock.

At home Peter found plenty of news (if what his father put into his Journal was transcribed into letters for his son) about the Muhlenbergs in Pennsylvania. Henry Melchior had heard of God's judgment at King's Mountain. An eclipse of the sun had been seen on October 27. The Honorable Frederick Augustus Muhlenberg, Esq., member of the Pennsylvania Assembly from the City of Philadelphia, had on November 3 been elected Speaker. Mr. Swaine was thinking of going back to his old store at New Hanover. Christian Schrack (son of the Schrack whose tavern was reputed to have given the name *Trap* to the vicinity) had died. The Widow Weiser, now living at Tulpehocken with her son Peter, was paralyzed on one side and going blind. Henry Melchior himself had written his will. He had visited Philadelphia and preached in St. Michael's. He had apprehended being overcome by dizziness in the high pulpit, but with God's help he had been able to preach for three-quarters of an hour. Old friends at the Trappe had brought him a pleasing gift of pudding broth for a New Year's present.

The state of Virginia received for her New Year's gift something less homely than pudding broth, but quite as hot. On January 1, 1781, General Benedict Arnold reached Jamestown with a force of sixteen hundred men and orders to break up the American base in Virginia. He sailed up the James River to Westover, marched his men overland to Richmond, which he reached on January 5 without the loss of a man, spent the night there, burned a few buildings, and returned to Westover.

Of the two hundred militia assembled to defend the capital on Arnold's approach, only one hundred were armed and none of them were ready. Steuben gave orders to harass the enemy's approach; but the orders were promptly disobeyed, and the militia marched off.

For the moment, Virginia was knocked into the ropes.

Governor Jefferson, who never failed for words, was more than voluble in his report to Washington about this new infamy on the part of what he called "the parricide Arnold."[7]

Baron Steuben sent a special express rider over the mountains to Woodstock for General Muhlenberg.

When the express arrived, Peter Muhlenberg, who had had just three happy days with his family, again sprang into the breach. He called out the militia, and before the next evening, was over the mountains and in Fredericksburg, where, according to his instructions, he was to remain since it was thought the enemy had designs on that area. More expresses came from Steuben, the instructions changing as the situation cleared. Muhlenberg was to come down with all speed to Williamsburg, bringing his militia with him. Brigadier General Weedon, with local militia, could attend to the defense of Fredericksburg.

Arnold landed at Portsmouth on January 19. The troops to oppose him were put under Muhlenberg's command on January 25.

Virginia's purpose was to confine Arnold to the seaboard. Virginia had seen enough of him (rumor said that Governor Jefferson's view had been from under a bed). Arnold's purpose was to hold the best of Virginia's troops before him, so that no reinforcements could be sent to Greene in the South. Both purposes, Arnold's and Virginia's, were achieved.

The presence of Benedict Arnold in Virginia had a curious effect upon the people. The story of his treason was everywhere known, and he was hated as few men have ever been hated. But he was also feared. The depth of their hate for him gave Americans, as they believed, a measure of his hate for them; and his abilities were only too well known. He had done good service in Canada, brilliant service at Saratoga. Now, after the hanging of André, he was reported to have threatened to deal the Americans such a blow as would shake the continent.

General Muhlenberg arranged his forces. To the east, behind Arnold, General Gregory was moving up to cut him off from Princess Anne County. To the south was the Dismal Swamp, all but impassable. To the north, across the James River, was General Nelson with his militia. To the west were various detachments: General Lawson at Smithfield with some five hundred infantry (nine hundred on paper) and a few horses; Colonel Parker with the Suffolk militia at Reddick's Mills; General Muhlenberg himself, with eight hundred infantry and Armand's cavalry, in reserve at Cabin Point. It looked very neat.

But as always in Virginia, Muhlenberg was handicapped by lack of equipment. From Cabin Point he wrote urgently to Steuben for wagons, tents, axes (to erect huts in place of tents), medicine, physicians, "and a few regulars to serve as Artillery Men, as the frequent changes we are obliged to make with the Militia render them totally unfit for that business."[8] He wrote to Greene, February 20, to say that he had nearly two thousand men, but among the whole lot were only "three hundred bayonets and two brass six pounders!"

But Thomas Jefferson from his governor's chair, hot with wrath at the thought of Arnold's treachery at West Point and of his own humiliation at Richmond, was dreaming of revenge. He wrote to Muhlenberg proposing rewards for the capture of "the greatest of all traitors."

Jefferson's spirit, as here shown, warms the heart. But the letter contains some surprises. It must be remembered, as we read it, that the man who drafted the Declaration of Independence was not only an idealist but also a good hater. It is to be doubted if the proposals he advanced and the special service to which he would have assigned Muhlenberg's men "from the Western side of the mountains," appealed to the cooler judgment of the general-in-the-field.

The letter is here given in its original form, as the rough draft appears in Jefferson's Letter Book at the Library of Congress. Such corrections as were intended only to improve the style, are not here indicated. But the extended passages through which Jefferson later drew his pen, as revealing thoughts which he decided were not suitable for the Governor to put his name to, are printed in full, enclosed in brackets. These passages were not discreditable, though they were injudicious. Earlier editors have ignored them. But they afford too rich a disclosure of Jefferson's youthful feelings, and of the connotations already attaching to Arnold's name, to be disregarded.

Richmond Jan. 31 1781.

Sir

Acquainted as you are with the treasons of Arnold, I need say nothing for your information, or to give you a proper sentiment of them. you will readily suppose that it is above all things desireable to drag him from those under whose wing he is now sheltered. on his march to and from this place I am certain it might have been done with facility by men of enterprise & firmness. I think it may still be done though perhaps not quite so easily. having peculiar confidence in the men from the Western side of the mountains, I meant as soon as they should come down to get the enterprise proposed to a chosen number of them, such whose courage & whose fidelity would be above all doubt. your perfect knowlege of those men personally, and my confidence in your discretion, induce me to ask you to pick from among them proper characters, in such number as you think best, to reveal to them our desire, & engage them [to] undertake to seize and bring off this greatest of all traitors. whether this may be best effected by their going in as friends & awaiting their opportunity, or otherwise is left to themselves. the smaller the number the better; so they be sufficient to manage him. every necessary caution must be used on their part, to prevent a discovery of their design by the enemy, as should they be taken, the laws of war will justify against them the most rigorous sentence. I will undertake if they are successful in bringing him off alive, that they shall receive five thousand guineas reward among them, and to men formed for such an enterprise it must be a great incitement to know that their names will be recorded with glory in history with those of Vanwert, Paulding & Williams. [I shall be sorry to suppose that any circumstances may put it out of their power to bring him off alive after they shall have taken him, & of course oblige them to put him to death. should this happen however and America be deprived of the satisfaction of seeing him exhibited as a public spectacle of infamy & of vengeance, I must give my approbation to their putting him to death. I do this considering him as a deserter from the American army, who has incurred the pain of death by his desertion, which we have a right to inflict on him and against which he cannot be protected by any act of our enemies. I distinguish him from an honourable enemy, who, in his station would never be considered by me as a justifiable object of such an enterprise. in the event of his death however I must reduce the reward proposed to 2000 guineas, in proportion as our satisfaction would be reduced.] The inclosed order from Baron Steuben will authorise you to call for & to dispose of any force you may think necessary to place in readiness for covering the enterprise & securing the retreat of the party.

mr Newton the bearer of this, & to whom it's contents are communicated in confidence, will provide men of trust to go as guides. these may be associated in the enterprise or not as you please; but let that point be previously settled that no difficulties may arise as to the parties entitled to participate of the reward. you know how necessary profound secrecy is in this business, even if it be not undertaken.[9]

It has been questioned whether the letter was actually intended for General Muhlenberg. No address accompanies it in the Jefferson Letter Book. It has been suggested that the letter may have been meant for the eyes of Brigadier General George Rogers Clark. That is hardly likely, however, since Jefferson had already commissioned Clark to his western expedition, and he was already on his way. The reference to "the men from the Western side of the mountains" is almost certainly to the militia Muhlenberg had brought from Shenandoah County.

If it be questioned whether the Governor would have been likely to select the Reverend Brigadier General Muhlenberg for this kind of melodrama, it may be replied that Thomas Jefferson was not too good a judge of men, and that he was, at that moment, in an unusually excitable mood. Besides, while we do not have Peter Muhlenberg's written acknowledgment of Jefferson's letter, we do have record of his attempting, two weeks later, to do (though in his own more soldierlike way) what Jefferson had proposed: to capture Benedict Arnold.

He prepared an ambuscade and tried to draw Arnold into it.

Muhlenberg approached Portsmouth with six hundred of Colonel Matthews' riflemen, five hundred of Colonel Dick's musketry, and some of Colonel Armand's and Major Nelson's cavalry. At one o'clock on the morning of February 18, he advanced the whole force to within a mile and a half of the town, and placed the riflemen and musketry in concealment.

General Arnold's forces in Portsmouth were at this time much depleted, Colonel Simcoe being out in force on a raid. It was reported by General Gregory afterward[10] that only three hundred men were in Portsmouth at the time Muhlenberg's trap was laid. It was perhaps this hopeless inferiority in numbers that saved Arnold: he was too weak to risk a man outside his works.

This was the bait prepared for him: the cavalry were sent to surprise a picket, well within sight of the British works.

"The Pickett," reported Muhlenberg, "consisting of a Serg^{t} Corporal & 12 were taken without firing a Shott . . . a Waggon & eight Horses were likewise brought off," all without the loss of a man to the attackers.[11]

But Arnold refused to be drawn.

"We have waited for Mr Arnold within one mile & a half of the Town for three Hours," wrote Muhlenberg to Steuben, "but as he shews no inclination to turn out we shall this Evening return to Col^{o} Matthews Camp—" "not caring," as he said in another letter to General Greene, "to risk an action in the night with my riflemen."[12]

If the demonstration had failed in its main objective, which was to lure the British out and capture their general, it had at least been a great success as a morale builder.

Muhlenberg followed up his first report, written to Steuben on the day of the action, with another the next day:

> Yesterday I did myself the Honor to inform You that I was in the Enemies Lines, that we had cut off their Pickett consisting of a Serg^{t} Corporal & 12: & killed two Yagers— The troops are all returned without the loss of a Man, & I am making preparations to encamp on Shoulders Hill Sixteen Miles on this Side of Portsmouth, I have a Sufficient Number of Men to fight them any where, & shall confine them close to their works— we waited for them Yesterday three Hours, but they would not Suffer a Man to come out of their works, a Deserter came out this Morning who informs me that they are in the utmost consternation—[13]

The English were perhaps less worried in Portsmouth than the deserter had seemed to indicate. Colonel Simcoe, in his *Military Journal*, says that Portsmouth was a good "entrenched camp," with an excellent redoubt at Norfolk on the Elizabeth River, as well as several others which could wear down any force likely to be brought against it for direct assault; and that "the regular siege of the whole, or any single work, would take up more time than any French squadron could venture to employ before it."[14]

Simcoe's estimate of the situation at Portsmouth was well justified in the event. But the Americans were all for action, and twice plans were made to assault the town. If they could not smoke the fox out, they could destroy his hole. Both plans were predicated on the assumption that the small forces Muhlenberg could bring against the town would be supported from the sea side by a French squadron. The strategy that did finally work at Yorktown in October, when Washington was convinced that the quarry was worth risking the whole war on, was attempted in February and March with somewhat ludicrous inefficiency.

On January 26 Richard Henry Lee had written to a friend in Congress to say that, if they had but the assistance of one French ship of the line and two frigates, "the militia now in arms are sufficient to smother these invaders in a moment."[15] This "plan," which savored more of rhetoric than military science, was sent to Admiral des Touches at Newport, who, supposing it to have been weighed (as it had not been) by the proper military authorities, dispatched De Tilly with one ship of the line and two frigates as requested.

When news came to Jefferson and Steuben that a French squadron was in the Chesapeake, preparations were launched at once for the assault on Portsmouth. Muhlenberg advanced with a thousand men to within eleven miles of Arnold's camp. General Nelson across the James River, and General Weedon at Fredericksburg were notified to be ready to march at any moment to assist him. General Gregory was ordered to assemble all the forces in his power on the east side of the Dismal Swamp, with expresses in constant touch with Muhlenberg on the west side. Steuben sent a staff officer to arrange details.

But De Tilly, when he arrived and looked the situation over, was not amused. He had no troops of his own and, quickly learning that the Americans had little equipment for an assault (he could scarcely be impressed by such items as Muhlenberg's three hundred bayonets and two brass six pounders), he informed the American commander that he had no instructions to remain in the Bay, and would sail "the moment the wind would permit him."

"The departure of the French Vessells," wrote Steuben to the Continental Congress, February 23, "has destroyed all hope of Success in an attempt on Portsmouth."[16]

There was further cause for anxiety. Steuben's face was turned toward Arnold, but out of the corner of his eye he caught glimpses of storm clouds approaching from the south.

"Lord Cornwallis," he wrote in the same letter to Congress, "is in Virginia but has not yet crossed the Dan River. General Greene is near him, on this side The Dan—"[17]

The defection of De Tilly had seemed a blow to Virginia, but hope springs eternal, and in a few days the political barometer had risen again. News came that a large French fleet was headed for the Chesapeake, and that this time Washington himself was interested. He was sending reinforcements to Virginia under Lafayette.

Steuben's plans were ready by the first of March. He sent word to that effect in a dispatch to Washington. It is probably only a coincidence, but it is a curious one, that on that day something happened to bring the machine to a shuddering stop. Time was lost in investigating the cause of the trouble; and, when the machine was once more set in motion, it had lost its old, familiar, confident hum.

General Steuben had recently become aware of the fact that the enemy's espionage was all too active. Some treachery, he feared, was in the air. The proximity of Benedict Arnold did nothing to allay the suspicion. Observing that men carrying flags of truce from Arnold's camp were being allowed to penetrate far into the country, and in a very leisurely manner, he resolved to put a stop to this traffic. He instructed Muhlenberg, March 2, to forbid all officers at outposts to receive any further flags of truce. The flags were to be sent back, and there was to be no further intercourse with the enemy.[18]

On the same day, March 2, the Gregory scandal broke. Colonel Parker, who had been sent with a detachment of three hundred men to the Great Bridge, wrote in haste to say that his men had captured a gunboat containing the papers of Captain Stevenson, who had commanded at the Bridge.

One of these papers was most disturbing. It was a letter written by Captain Stevenson and addressed to General Gregory:[19]

G. G.,—

Your well-formed plan of delivering those people now under your command into the hands of the British General at Portsmouth gives me much pleasure. Your next I hope will mention the place of ambuscade, and the manner you wish to fall into my hands, &c. &c., and I am

Dear Gregory,

Yours with esteem.

1st March, 1781

General Gregory, who was present when these papers were discovered, denied having had any correspondence with the enemy. But Colonel Parker was deeply suspicious, especially when he found that the guards which General Gregory had furnished for that night were very ill provided, many of them being "without a cartridge box, and some without a single cartridge."[20]

Muhlenberg was puzzled. At the moment he was fully convinced that some treason was hatching and that Gregory was a party to it. At the same time some of the evidence was shaky. The lack of cartridges did not, perhaps, seem as suspicious to Muhlenberg as it had seemed to Colonel Parker. It was only a few days after this incident that Muhlenberg said of his own forces, "I hope nobody will be surprized if on the Enemys coming out I take myself out of his reach"—because of a lack of cartridges.[21]

But, whatever hesitations Muhlenberg may have felt, the scandal was already known, and his force in consequence was in danger of breaking up. Gregory's officers, in particular, were so disturbed that Muhlenberg found they "would disperse," as he reported to Steuben, if Gregory were not removed. He thought that Gregory should "give up his command," at least until the matter was cleared up.[22]

Steuben at Williamsburg replied, in French, with a manly and chivalrous letter:

Williamsb[g] 7 March

Genl Muhlenberg

J'ai recue Vos deux lettres du 4 de Mars. Quoiqu'un peut frappé du contenue de la premiere, je suspende mon jugement et je serai faché de faire tort a un Galanthomme,

J'approuve cependent entierement Votre Arrangement; . . ."*[23]

Lieutenant Colonel Simcoe of the Queen's Rangers (who abominated Arnold and his kind; it was said that at Portsmouth the British kept Arnold under surveillance) wrote to Muhlenberg to say that Gregory was quite innocent.[24] Captain Stevenson had written the letter as a joke, to pass the time (under the shadow of Benedict Arnold). At first the incident, when the Rangers heard of it, "served

* "I have received your two letters of the fourth of March. Although rather startled by the contents of the first, I suspend judgment and I should be sorry to wrong a gallant man,

Nevertheless I approve entirely of your action in the matter; . . ."

for laughter," as Simcoe wrote in his *Military Journal,* "but when it was understood that Gen. Gregory was put in arrest, Capt. Stevenson's humanity was alarmed, and . . . letters . . . passed between Lt. Col. Simcoe and Col. Parker, who had taken the boat: they prevented all further bad consequences."[25]

Not entirely. The incident left behind it an uneasy feeling among Muhlenberg's officers.

"I cannot be sufficiently on my guard," wrote Colonel Parker, "being surrounded by enemies."[26]

Plans went ahead for the combined land and sea attack on Arnold's camp. Military reinforcements for Muhlenberg were ordered by Governor Jefferson: 164 men from Chesterfield County, 187 from Dinwiddie, and so on.

To Granville Smith the Governor wrote: "A very great and important [demand] has arisen for 130 Waggon Horses & 50 Saddle Horses. The Call is as immediate as it is important. . . . These Horses must be delivered at General Muhlenburg's Head quarter's by Half dozens as fast as they are procured & at farthest by the 20th instant."[27]

Arms and ammunition were sent by General Steuben.

Jefferson, all enthusiasm, arranged for a line of expresses between Muhlenberg's headquarters and Richmond, crossing the James River at Hood's.

"I think that a successful attempt on the present Army in Portsmouth will prevent our enemies from ever trusting another in Chesapeake. . . . I shall be glad to hear from you frequently. . . ."[28]

The eager young Marquis de Lafayette arrived with reinforcements. He visited Muhlenberg's camp, and on March 19, the two commanders went with some three hundred men to have a look at the enemy.

". . . we drove in the Picketts," wrote Muhlenberg, "killd 9, took some & wounded several, but were prevented from viewing the works, by want of Cartridges, which renderd it imprudent to risk any thing like a General Action."[29]

When, on March 20, Muhlenberg at his "Camp near Sleepy Hole" received intelligence of the arrival of a fleet in the Bay, anxiety tugged at the heels of his elation. It was known not only that Des Touches had left Newport with a good French fleet on March 8, but also that an English fleet under Arbuthnot was off the coast, shepherding transports filled with reinforcements from New York for the South.

By the twenty-third it was known that the ships were English. Arbuthnot had met the French near the Capes on March 16, and the combat, into which each fleet had put eight ships of the line, had been severe. Both sides had been badly mauled. But the English had the inside track, and, in the end, the French returned to Newport while the English escorted their transports into Portsmouth.

Lafayette, whose instructions from Washington had been to march his force back "as soon as we lose the naval superiority in this quarter," prepared to leave.

Steuben wrote to Muhlenberg to say that it was necessary "to suspend, tho' not to give over, our intended Expedition."[30]

CHAPTER XXII

THE TIDEWATER CAMPAIGN

The blow to Peter's spirits occasioned by this last turn of affairs was not lessened by the news from the family in Pennsylvania. He was able to keep in touch with them through his brother, Frederick, Speaker of the Pennsylvania Assembly, who had access to the official channels of communication. At Richmond, Colonel Muter, Commissioner of the War Office, permitted Peter to send his letters by government express rider, who, at a pinch, could do the journey from Richmond to Philadelphia in less than three days.

The news from the Trappe was this: On Friday, February 2, his mother had had an accident in the kitchen.

Her husband was never quite sure exactly how it had happened. At first he said she had fallen, when the paroxysm came on her, face down into a pot of boiling water in which she was cooking beets.[1] Later he said that in falling she had struck the pot with her left arm and so poured the contents over herself.[2]

The first he knew about it was the sight of her standing at the door, "trembling, shivering and wet." Her "left hand, breast, shoulder, right arm, neck, and half her face" were horribly scalded.

He called the children, and they got her into bed. When she recovered consciousness, the pain seemed unendurable, and there began a long fight for life. At first they were without a doctor's help. There was no physician at the Trappe, and the neighbor whom they had sent at once for an English doctor seven miles away was unable to get across the flooded Perkiomen Creek to call him.

Anna Maria could not lie down. The pressure was too dreadful. She could not sleep. Her only comfort was that, having recently been reading of the tortures of the early Christian martyrs, she knew that her suffering was no greater than they had borne.

Polly was the heroine of this emergency. She never left her mother.

Anna Maria would allow no one else to touch her. Before any doctor came, Polly made up poultices of potatoes and sweet oil and applied them gently. But the pains grew worse. On the second day the English physician arrived, gave the patient an opiate (not strong enough, however, to put her to sleep), and prescribed poultices of white bread cooked in milk and linseed oil. During that day the burned throat swelled until they feared it would shut and she would be suffocated. Mercifully the swelling was relieved a little before evening.

Day after day and night after night, Polly dressed and bandaged the suppurating wounds. Various doctors came, some of them from considerable distances. Henry Melchior noted the figures down: Dr. Morgan, 12 miles; Dr. Martin, 27 miles; Dr. Heimberger, 12 miles. But they could do very little to help. It was only Polly who could bandage the patient so as to give her relief. Polly had some snatches of sleep while others watched, but when the time came for bandaging, Polly was wakened.

Neighbors came in, and each pressed her own remedy on the patient. The house was soon filled with all kinds of salves. Peggy and Frederick sent up from Philadelphia quantities of linen rags for bandages.

After a week, Anna Maria had her first wink of sleep. On Thursday night she slept for two hours. But on Saturday a new and terrifying danger threatened. The paroxysms, which had been quiescent for a time, came on her again. They tore the half-healed wounds open. Truly she might say in her agony, "I die daily."

On Wednesday, February 14, after nearly two weeks of the strain of nursing, Polly collapsed.[3] It had seemed at first that she had nothing but a bad cold. But her nerves were worn out. A frantic toothache so swelled her cheeks that both eyes were sealed shut. For some days she was helpless. Old Mrs. Sattler was engaged as a nurse, but she was not competent for the bandaging. A maid was hired to help Sally attend to the cows and do the rough housework. A day laborer came to split wood. A warm fire was needed, night and day, for the patient.

Poor Anna Maria, whose mind was foggy with pain, was tortured by a waking dream. She saw the whole house in a litter. The rooms were filled with straw and hay. Henry Melchior, who had no Peter at hand now to talk him out of it, thought he recognized the dream as a portent of another British invasion of Pennsylvania.

By Sunday, Polly was somewhat better. Her eyes were open again and she could get back to the bandaging. There was a minor emergency when it was found that the supply of candles was giving out. They had to keep candles burning in Anna Maria's room all night. Frederick, however, was appealed to in time, and he sent up a quantity from the city.

By the twenty-second of February, Polly was wholly recovered, and they let Mrs. Sattler go. But Anna Maria was still too ill to leave her bed. As late as March 13, nearly six weeks after the accident, Henry Melchior reported to the Schultzes that, though the hand and arm were healed, the burns on the breast, chin, neck, cheeks, and ears were still raw and suppurating and had to be bandaged both morning and evening. She was able, however, to be out of bed for a couple of hours a day. The danger seemed to be past.

In the southern theater of war, Cornwallis defeated Greene at Guilford, March 15. Before Portsmouth, General Muhlenberg found the situation becoming desperate. For Arnold's relief, Arbuthnot had brought two thousand reinforcements, under General Phillips, who now superseded Arnold in command. Greene was much disappointed over the failure before Portsmouth. If the attack had been successful, it would have released troops, clothing, and equipment for his own assistance against Cornwallis. "Most of my men are naked for want of Overalls," he wrote. It is true, Cornwallis' victories were being bought at a price dangerously high for an army operating so far from its base; but the strain was severe also on the American forces. Greene feared the southern states might be put out of business before Cornwallis had time to bleed to death. If Steuben and Muhlenberg could not contain the British at Portsmouth, what would prevent the British there from joining forces with Cornwallis and so ending the campaign in the South with another disaster for the Americans?

On April 1, General Muhlenberg reported to Baron Steuben that he suspected the enemy of a design to come out of Portsmouth and attempt to make a junction with Cornwallis.[4] Muhlenberg drew in Colonel Parker's forces, the men marching through the Dismal Swamp on logs to avoid being cut off. The same day he wrote to

Governor Jefferson to say that the term of most of the militia from Augusta, Rockingham, Rockbridge, Sussex, and Brunswick was about to expire, and that if these troops were not immediately replaced, his force would not be "adequate to do what they were intended."[5] On the eighth he informed Steuben that his army was breaking up. The men were discharging themselves. That morning a hundred had deserted from one regiment alone. He was unable to persuade those of the militia whose term would expire on the tenth to continue their service, "so that I shall be left with about 700 Men." He was, in the face of this bleak prospect, sending the military stores upcountry for safety. He saw nothing now to prevent the enemy, as he said, from "breaking me up, if I continue in their reach."

Five days later he wrote from the "Camp at Broad Water" to say that he had now removed to that place all the stores which had been collected for the attack on Portsmouth, and that he had barely five hundred men with him. A few other detachments were scattered over the country between him and the British camp.[6] Next day he wrote to say that he thought the stores should be moved still farther back, but that he was short of wagons.[7] Jefferson the same day bewailed the fact that the militia had not come in, and that General Muhlenberg would "probably continue some Time too weak to oppose the Enemy."[8]

To Washington, Steuben reported that Muhlenberg had seven hundred militia with which to oppose Phillips' three thousand regulars, that the militia were deserting every day, and that Muhlenberg's pitiful little army was short of such necessaries as arms, ammunition, powder, horses for the cavalry, swords, and cartridge boxes. ". . . if the Enemy have any intention to penetrate the Country the opposition we can make will avail little."[9]

By April 16 the British, as feared, had come out, and the chase was on. Not Arnold, but Muhlenberg, was now the hunted.

Jefferson ordered out the militia of seven counties, but they could hardly be in the field before May 1—another two weeks. Muhlenberg now had firearms in plenty, the deserting militia having left behind what weapons they had. But the arms were found to be useless, ruined by exposure, since the men who carried them had been without tents. Most of the military stores had been removed to temporary safety, but the cannon were still to be brought off, and this Muhlenberg feared would be difficult to do, at such a distance and with such poor facilities as he had for transportation. He was much depressed.

". . . while I had a respectable force," he wrote to Davies from Camp Broadwater Bridge, April 17, "& could keep the Enemy at Bay I was perfectly content—now after three Months exertions to render the Men fit for Action, all my plans are at once laid in the Dust, by their dismission & the few I have remaining convincd of our Weakness I am afraid will hardly suffer the Enemy to get within a Mile of them, however fight they must for they cannot retreat over the Bridge, where I have my Artillery placd, without my permission & there is no other safe retreat but that way—"[10]

The British, meanwhile, had embarked at Portsmouth in a fleet of flat-bottomed boats and were ascending the James River. General Muhlenberg sent out cavalry to observe their motions, and kept Baron Steuben informed by means of express riders. He wrote to say he was moving fast "in order to keep ahead of the Fleet."[11] On the nineteenth, learning that the enemy was passing Pagan Creek, he broke camp at Broadwater about four o'clock in the afternoon and moved thirteen miles to Wellsbridge, where he camped for the night.[12] Next day he went on to Cabin Point.

"I shall endeavor to keep pace with them," he reported.[13]

Steuben, good soldier, kept closely in touch with his Brigadier, encouraging him during the chase and approving the dispositions he was making in face of the enemy. ". . . you must govern your movements," he wrote, "so as to prevent their reaching Petersburg before you."[14]

Steuben appointed "Blands Ordinary," just outside Petersburg, as a rendezvous for the new militia. He directed Muhlenberg to make for that place. Steuben said he hoped to meet him there on the twenty-third.

When, on the twenty-fourth, Phillips passed Westover, entered the mouth of the Appomattox River, and late in the afternoon landed his men at City Point, Peter Muhlenberg was waiting for him.

Steuben had no intention of making a back-to-the-wall stand of it. "I have not yet learnt," he said, "how to beat regular troops with one third of their number of militia."[15]

Retreat was accordingly prepared. But Steuben was not going to ask Muhlenberg to walk tamely off without making a pass or two at his opponent. Such a defection would have been bad for public morale. He accordingly instructed his general-in-the-field to put on a good show at the head of the Pocahontas Bridge.

Muhlenberg's Battle of Petersburg (Steuben was careful to give him the honors) was fought on April 25, the same day that Greene was beaten again, this time at Hobkirk's Hill. Cornwallis had slipped past, and was on his way north to join General Phillips.

Petersburg was not one of the great battles of the war. But it was well fought. Neither Colonel Simcoe nor Governor Jefferson has done it justice: Simcoe (who did not have to lead militia) when he said that "the disposition of the enemy was not such as marked any ability in those who made it,"[16] nor Jefferson (sitting in Richmond) when he said that the British ran like sheep.[17]

The Americans took up a position at Blandford, a mile or two east of Petersburg, with the Pocahontas Bridge on their left.

Peter Muhlenberg sent his brother Frederick, next day, a very good description of the action:

> Yesterday, about one o'clock, p.m., the enemy approached the town in two columns, and were met by our light infantry about a mile from the town, where the skirmish commenced, and every inch of ground to the bridge was warmly disputed. The dispute was very hot at the bridge for some time; but at length they cannonaded us so severely, that we broke up the bridge and retreated in the greatest regularity, after maintaining the fight for nearly two hours. I have the pleasure to assure you that the militia behaved with a spirit and resolution which would have done honour to veterans.[18]

After this engagement at Pocahontas Bridge, Major General Steuben, well pleased with the little demonstration (which had done what it had been intended to do: show, without imperiling their inevitable retreat, that the Virginians had fight in them), was all courtesy to friend and foe. To General Phillips, who had written on the day after the battle to insist on a point of military etiquette (the immediate return of General Phillips' aide-de-camp's batman, who had been taken prisoner), he replied in neat fashion: "If I was difficient in not sending him in the same day he was taken, yourself have been happy enough to find my excuse—A Retreat before three times my number, commanded by Gen. Phillips, certainly demanded all my attention."[19]

In General Orders, Steuben complimented the officers who had been in charge of the troops on the ground. He begged "General Muhlenberg to accept his very particular thanks for his gallantry and good disposition."[20]

In a dispatch to Congress, he commended Muhlenberg's dispositions in the field as well as his personal gallantry. The praises he gave the rank and file were a further compliment to Muhlenberg, who "possessed the rare faculty of making *soldiers* out of *militia*."[21]

Steuben was resolved that Muhlenberg should be the hero of the Tidewater Campaign. He wrote in the same fashion to General Greene as he had written to Congress. "Your report of the good conduct of General Muhlenberg," replied Greene, "and the troops under his command, affords me great pleasure. . . ."[22]

Ten days later Henry Melchior Muhlenberg received a report from Virginia which he noted in his Journal with some pride: "that on April 25, a[nno] c[urrente] Generals Philips and Arnold captured Petersburg, Virginia with 3,000 picked British troops; an American brigadier with 1,000 militia offered brave resistance but had to give way to the Superior forces with heavy guns."[23]

"We fight, get beat, rise, and fight again," said General Nathaniel Greene.

His words are a presage of what was to happen when Cornwallis and Muhlenberg came together. They are also a reminder that the God of Battles is not always on the side of the big battalions, but those with the stoutest heart and longest wind.

CHAPTER XXIII

YORKTOWN, REDOUBT 10

The progress of the Virginia Campaign up to this point has been told in some detail in order to show the trust in which Peter Muhlenberg was held by Washington and Steuben, and the fidelity as well as the efficiency with which he carried out his tasks. He was not, of course, responsible for the general strategy. That was determined at headquarters in Richmond. He was, however, responsible for the disposition of the troops in the field, and he led them in action. He had to work against almost incredible obstacles, but he never lost heart and he made his command respected by the enemy. He held Arnold. He eluded Phillips. And, as we shall see in this chapter, he played a major part in finally pinning down and capturing Cornwallis.

Leaving Petersburg in the hands of the enemy on the afternoon of April 25, Muhlenberg crossed the Pocahontas Bridge and brought his militia safely and without pursuit to Richmond. There, on April 29, Lafayette arrived, with reinforcements from the north. Muhlenberg found himself in command (under Major General Lafayette, who now superseded Steuben) of about a thousand Continental light infantry—"the flower of Washington's army."

It was a good weapon. The veteran of Brandywine and Germantown, Monmouth, the Highlands, Portsmouth, and Petersburg, wielded it with delight for the rest of the summer.

On May 13 General Phillips died, and for a few days Muhlenberg found himself pitted again against Arnold. But when, at Petersburg on May 20, Arnold joined forces with Cornwallis, the latter took charge of the British forces in Virginia for the remainder of the campaign.

In the attempt to bring down Cornwallis, Lafayette used Muhlenberg's light infantry as the fangs of his army, and a brave, snappy chase "our general" made of it. Cornwallis, though now hampered by indecision in high places across the sea and by conflicting instructions from London and New York, was a magnificent fighter. He made the best of a deteriorating situation. In a stand-up fight he could still whip his enemies, and they knew it.

"I hope the Marquis will be successful in Virginia," wrote General Greene to Washington, June 22, 1781. "What I mean by success is to avoid a capital misfortune."[1]

If the Americans were not prepared to take Cornwallis' main punch, he, on the other hand, could not forever stand Lafayette's shower of stabbing blows. The Marquis hoped to tire His Lordship out. The latter wrote that he found the American forces very enterprising. What could they be else with Lafayette, Muhlenberg, and Anthony Wayne in the line?

There was constant movement. On June 18, Muhlenberg, thrown a little too far forward, was snapped at by Tarleton in one of the lightning movements of his daredevil cavalry. But Anthony Wayne, recently arrived with reinforcements from Pennsylvania, gave Muhlenberg such quick support that Tarleton's legion veered off for other adventures.

When Cornwallis, who had been thrusting about skillfully enough though without accomplishing anything decisive in the Richmond area, decided to move east toward the sea, Muhlenberg was at his heels and the Pennsylvanians were close behind. On the James River chase Wayne supported Muhlenberg as formerly Muhlenberg had supported Wayne at Stony Point.

General Muhlenberg was confident and eager to make contact with the enemy. Even "Mad Anthony" was startled and a little uneasy at Muhlenberg's provocativeness and daring.

"To strike Cornwallis," wrote Wayne, "would be a desirable Object, provided it could be done with effect, but to commit the troops too much without being properly supported may be attended with disagreeable consequences.

"Your own good Judgment will therefore be the best Criterion to determine by. I shall endeavor to be in time to give you effectual support provided you can by any means halt them."[2]

Peter Muhlenberg made no slip as he followed Cornwallis to the sea. It was Wayne who overreached himself, and Muhlenberg who saved him, on July 6, at Greenspring.

Mad Anthony fell into a trap. Cornwallis allowed it to appear that he had taken the bulk of his forces across the James River. Lafayette, believing that he had to deal only with a British covering force, pushed forward, General Wayne on this occasion providing the advance. Soon Wayne discovered that he had taken on the whole British army, and that his retreat was being cut off. It was the right hook to the jaw they had all dreaded.

Muhlenberg, hearing the unexpected volume of gunfire, knew Wayne was in trouble, and, without waiting for orders, rushed up in time to extricate him. Wayne came out badly mauled. He had lost a seventh of his brigade.

However enterprising and valiant Muhlenberg's pursuit, Cornwallis' retreat was not motivated by fear of his enemy. He had received instructions from Clinton in New York to embark as many men as he could for the northern theater. Clinton feared to be caught in a combined land and sea attack on New York, General Washington and Admiral de Grasse providing the pincers. Cornwallis, accordingly, crossed to the south bank of the James River and marched to Portsmouth. Later dispatches from Clinton instructed Cornwallis to prepare a military base sufficient to support a British fleet, which was soon to be expected in Chesapeake Bay. Cornwallis then took his troops to Yorktown, which his engineers had selected as the best place for this purpose.

General Washington, meanwhile, had been studying the situation, with an eye on Europe as well as America, in hope of springing the greatest surprise of the war. He now feinted just such an attack as Clinton feared. Henry Melchior Muhlenberg noted in his Journal for July 6 (the day Peter was engaged so hotly near Jamestown) that Washington was about to besiege New York. Cunningly Washington maneuvered his army into position for a sudden dash to the south, where Cornwallis was to be trapped with aid from the fleet France was lending for this operation.

Secrecy was vital. The time element was important. Washington and De Grasse had to reach Yorktown before the British (whose armies and navies were still superior to anything the Americans could bring together) got wind of the plan. Washington's purpose could not, therefore, be disclosed to too many people. Especially was it dangerous to put his plans into dispatches which were to be carried by express riders to his southern commanders through country exposed to Tarleton's Rangers.

At the same time it was essential to encourage these same commanders to stand firm and hold Cornwallis immobile while the trap was being built round him. Washington wrote letters to Greene, Wayne, and Lafayette, adapting his style to the temperament and situation of each, and expressing veiled hints of what was taking form.

To Greene (whose situation for many months had been one of sheer misery), he spoke of honor and of reinforcements. He added a hint of important movements to come.

"A particular Reason which cannot at this Time be communicated induces me to request that you will be pleased to give me the earliest and most minute Information of every Event that takes Place with you—"[3]

To Wayne he spoke of action. He congratulated him on the affair at Greenspring.

"I think," he added, "the Account which Lord Cornwallis will be obliged to render of the State of Southern Affairs will not be very pleasing to the Ministerial Eyes and Ears. . . . I am in hopes that Virginia will be soon . . . so far relieved as to permit you to march to the Succour of General Greene. . . ."[4]

To Lafayette—young, ardent, affectionate, yet very much the man of the world—he wrote an intimate letter giving broader hints of his plans than he had done to any of the others, and paying him the compliment of entrusting to him the responsibility of communicating these hints to General Greene in the South.

"I am convinced that your desire to be with the Army arises principally from a wish to be actively useful— You will not therefore regret your stay in Virginia. . . ."[5]

Washington let Lafayette know he was thinking of giving up the siege of New York and endeavoring to expel the enemy totally from the southern states.

"The difficulty of doing this," continued Washington, "does not so much depend upon obtaining a force capable of effecting it, as upon the mode of collecting that force to the proper point."

If the young generals in Virginia, Lafayette, Wayne, and Muhlenberg, had been eager before, these hints of some great and perhaps final stroke impending gave them tenfold more energy and optimism. Anthony Wayne, when it became known that De Grasse with a large fleet had arrived in Chesapeake Bay, wrote exultantly, "His Lordship has not a retreat unless desperation may induce him to attempt to hop to Carolina by land."[6]

This last was not thought to be fantastic. Already Washington, on August 15, had written urging Lafayette "to prevent if possible the Retreat of Cornwallis towards Carolina."[7] To General Muhlenberg was assigned the task of making the trap tight in that quarter. He was sent across the James River, not to try to stop Cornwallis by a stand-up fight, but to raise the militia and, by a "scorched earth" policy, to impede his advance while a force was collected from all sides to prevent his crossing the Roanoke River, the boats on which were meanwhile to be destroyed.

Muhlenberg was over the water in no time. His activities south of the James River are described in a letter dated "Cabbin Point August 29th 1781" and addressed to Brigadier General Jones:

Dear Genl

The Marquis has recd certain intelligence that Lord Cornwallis means to penetrate with his Army from York to So Carolina by Land, to avoid being blocked up by the French West India Fleet which is now on the Coast— The Marquis directs me to give you this information and request you immediately to collect every Boat and Canoe on Roanoke below Halifax and have them either brought there or destroyed— Those brought to Halifax must be kept under a Guard, that they may be either removed or destroyed as circumstances may render necessary— You will be pleased to use the same precautions in Meherrin River— I am just arrived at this place in order to collect the Militia on the South side of James River & shall as soon as the Enemy begin their movements endeavour to throw as many obstacles in their way as possible—by destroying Bridges Mills, provisions &c. as soon as I am able to ascertain their route I shall give you immediate notice, retreat before them and endeavour to form a junction with you on Roanoke— Should the Enemy have sent armed Boats or establish Magazines in any place in North Carolina (particularly Newbern) The Marquis requests you will endeavour to destroy them—

"I have my dear Sir just given you a sketch of our plan, The main army is now moving towards James River, but will not cross untill his Lordship moves, but I make no doubt, if your Militia and those from this Place turn out well, we shall be able to keep his Lordship at Bay at Roanoke untill our main Army can get up– I shall be happy to hear from you as soon as possible– I shall give you immediate notice if the Enemy move

I have the Honor to be
&c
P. Muhlenberg B.G.[8]

On August 31, Washington (having edged his troops as far south as he could with any plausibility under the pretext of a movement to Sandy Hook to coöperate with a French fleet there) dropped all concealment and ordered his troops to march with speed for the Head of Elk.

In his Journal for that day Henry Melchior wrote: "Had a visit from a friend from Reading who was returning from Philadelphia. He said that His Excellency General Washington and His Excellency le Comte de Rochambeau were on the march south with 7,000 men and that His Excellency Comte de Grasse was hourly expected in Chesapeake Bay with the French fleet."

Washington had need to hurry. De Grasse had written to say that he was bringing twenty-nine vessels to the Chesapeake, with three regiments of a thousand men each, one hundred artillerymen, field pieces, mortars, and siege cannon. But he said explicitly that he would leave again on *October 15*. The date is to be remembered.

"In boldness of conception and celerity of execution," writes Francis Vinton Greene in *The Revolutionary War and the Military Policy of the United States*, "this march to Virginia was comparable with Napoleon's famous campaign of 1805, when he suddenly abandoned the camp which he had formed at Boulogne for the invasion of England and marched to the Danube . . . but the effect on the world's history of Ulm and Austerlitz was a . . . fraction of the results which flowed from Yorktown."[9]

Washington predicated the success of his plan on the assumption that the French could maintain control of the sea, at least of Chesapeake Bay, until October 15. But it was touch and go. When De Grasse sailed north from the West Indies, he was pursued by Admiral Hood, who, however, lost De Grasse, passed the Chesapeake, and went on to join the main British fleet at New York. This fleet, under Graves, at once came down to Chesapeake Bay. De Grasse met it off Cape Henry on September 5.

The battle that ensued was inconclusive. There were heavy losses on both sides. For some time the fleets continued to maneuver about each other. But this time it was the French who had the inside track. After four days the British found themselves obliged to go back to New York for repairs. The French had control of the Chesapeake. Further reinforcements, especially in siege artillery, were brought in by a squadron under De Barras.

The lines were closing about Yorktown. General Muhlenberg moved his forces back to the north side of the James River. He was getting ready for the kill.

"I have upon the lines General Mughlenburg," wrote Lafayette (whose pen balked at German names), on September 8, "with one thousand Men four hundred of whom are Virginia Regulars and one hundred Dragoons . . . we may add one hundred Hussards . . ."[10]

When on September 14 Washington and De Rochambeau arrived in Williamsburg, there was rejoicing everywhere. "Strong toasts," as Henry Melchior reports, were drunk in Philadelphia. Jefferson at Monticello, to which place he had retired after resigning the governorship on June 1, wrote to Edmund Randolph, "I think it is impossible Lord Cornwallis should escape."[11]

But there were anxious voices, too. Henry Melchior records them. Mr. Swaine, just back from Virginia, gave but a gloomy picture of conditions in that state. The Tidewater Campaign had proved to be quite as exhausting to the inhabitants as it had been to the invaders.

The northern states were apprehensive. Washington, risking everything on getting Cornwallis, had left the North dangerously unprotected. Clinton in New York had over sixteen thousand men. Heath had to hold the Highlands against him (if he should strike) with less than three thousand.

In Pennsylvania fears of a new invasion mounted to panic. Mr. Swaine went down to Philadelphia to see about bringing Peggy and her children out for safety into the country.

But Washington knew what he was doing. He knew how weary his people were. He knew of the talk among country folk, of the impoverishment of the homes. He knew that "without a great victory the Revolution would die of exhaustion."[12] He knew, besides, that this particular victory (if he could win it) might end the war. He was not unaware of what was going on behind the scenes in England.

At Yorktown Washington's machine was moving with beautiful

efficiency. Cornwallis remained motionless within his lines. Muhlenberg captured so many of Tarleton's Rangers that the legion had to rest.

From "Burwells Mill," September 23, Muhlenberg wrote to inform Washington that the scouting parties he kept out continuously, sometimes within sight of the enemy's pickets, had discovered no sign of any enemy movement. The number of the enemy's boats was "much diminished"; "but whether they attempted to get out the Night before last," he said, "or whether the Enemy have sunk them in the Channel I cannot yet find out; a large Smoke was seen Yesterday Morning below York, which has occasioned a report that the Enemy have burnt some of their shipping."[13]

When the army advanced, September 28, to siege lines before York, the French were given the left wing and the Americans the right. Washington's "Order of Battle"[14] is of some importance for an understanding of what follows.

Head Quarters, Willimsburgh,
Thursday, September 27, 1781

Till circumstances shall render a change of disposition Necessary, the following will be the order of Battle for the Army, the American Troops composing the right Wing will be formed into two lines, the Continental Forces in the front line, consisting of the following devision and in the following order viz. Muhlenberghs and Hazens Brigades to form The Division on the right under the Command of the Marquis de la Fayette, Waynes and the Maryland Brigade, the Division of the centre for the present to be commanded by Baron de Steuben, Daytons and Clintons Brigades, that on the Left. The senior Continental Officer will Command the Right Wing and his Excellency Count Rochambeau the Left Wing of which he will be pleased to make his own disposition. . . .

The whole Army will march by the right in one Column at 5 o Clock tomorrow Morning precisely. . . .

General Muhlenberghs Brigade of Infantry with the Artillery attached to it, preceded by Colonel Lewises Corps of Rifle men and the light Dragoons will form the advanced guard. . . .

The siege was formally opened on September 28. Muhlenberg was up in front, enjoying himself. From the "Camp before York," on October 2, he wrote a good letter to his old friend, Taverner Beale,[15] who had been with him on the Committee of Safety and Correspondence for Dunmore County in 1774.

Peter Muhlenberg had come a long way since then: Charleston, Georgia, Brandywine, Germantown, the Highlands, Stony Point; and now, back in Virginia, he had for a year past hunted, or been hunted by, Leslie, Arnold, Phillips, Cornwallis. But the game was nearing an end. He now commanded an advanced corps before York. He was only waiting for the signal to give Cornwallis the *coup de grâce.*

The letter is packed with enthusiasm and anticipation—anticipation of good things to come both for his country and for himself. He was a soldier, and did not despise honor for well-earned service.

The sights and sounds of the siege he found both "interesting and entertaining." He does not enumerate them all, but we know something of what it was he saw and heard. There were the French ships in the York River, the camp around and behind him, the line of trenches then being prepared within nine hundred yards of the enemy, and the enemy's twin redoubts. These, most of all, must have held his attention, for it was well known that these must be taken by assault before the siege could be brought to a successful conclusion. They stood three hundred yards in advance of the enemy's principal works. From these redoubts the British were now able to enfilade any trenches which might be advanced toward their lines. On the other hand, once these redoubts were taken, we could enfilade the enemy's works and the British would no longer be able to defend themselves. They were the keys to Yorktown.

". . . the cannon are roaring continually," wrote Peter Muhlenberg to Taverner Beale, "and in about four days more we shall have 120 cannon and 20 mortars playing upon them; in short by the 13th I hope Lord Cornwallis and his army will be in our possession."

A good part of the letter must be quoted, not only to show Peter Muhlenberg's exhilaration at this moment, and the grounds of it, but also to prepare for the dénouement.

> When I returned [from the expedition designed to prevent Cornwallis from escaping across the James River] I was ordered to the command on the Lines with 400 Regulars and 400 Riflemen and 1400 Militia. There I remained until we marched to this place. During the time I was in the Lines we took about twenty of Tarleton's men and confined him so closely to the town, that he was compelled to give over dashing. The Commander in Chief expressed his entire approbation of my conduct and in terms that

flattered my ambition. The army is at present arranged in the following manner. The first Brigade of Light infantry, with the Riflemen and Cavalry on the right—Commanded by Gen. Muhlenberg. The 2 Brigade of Light Infantry by Gen'l Hazen. The Pennsylvania Line and Gaskin's Regiment by Wayne. Marylanders next by G'l Gist. Jersey, New York and Rhode Island next by Gen'l Clinton. The French Army comprise the left wing. In our March from Williamsburg to this place I had the advance with my Brigade, the Cavalry and Riflemen. As I know it will give you pleasure I shall just tell you that there never was more Harmony subsisted in any Corps than in mine at present and that I am established in the Command, not only by the Order of the Commander in Chief, but with the best wishes and congratulations of every officer in it. . . .

Yours Affectionately,
P. Muhlenberg.[15]

The siege works crept closer. Communication trenches were rapidly opened. The first parallel was run October 6. On the ninth, fifty-two pieces of siege artillery were in place and at work. The second parallel was run on the eleventh, within three hundred yards of the enemy's works. There remained only Redoubt 10 and its mate between Washington's army and victory.

On the thirteenth Brigadier General Muhlenberg's brigade, with Hazen's, was assigned to "mount in the trenches."

But on the fourteenth the brigades of Muhlenberg and Hazen, which constituted Lafayette's division, were left free for other duty. On that day the second parallel was completed. Batteries were turned against "the abattis and salient angles" of the British redoubts. It was the eve, also, of the day appointed by De Grasse for his departure. But he had been persuaded to wait until this very interesting action had been completed.

The French were to assault the redoubt on the British right, the Americans, that on the British left. This latter was Redoubt 10, overlooking the river. To its capture Lafayette's division had been assigned. Muhlenberg, commanding a column of light infantry, composed of his own and Hazen's brigades, was to be the general-in-the-field.

Redoubt 10 was destined to be America's symbol of victory; its capture, the prime laurel of the Virginia Campaign and of the war.

Final dispositions were made. Late in the afternoon, from the

American and French camps, rockets rose into the air. That was the signal.

At this point the picture becomes blurred. At the very moment our photographic apparatus was pointed at General Peter Muhlenberg to catch him in the assault on Redoubt 10, something ran between him and the camera.

When the print was developed, in acid, there appeared, not Muhlenberg, but . . .

CHAPTER XXIV

ALEXANDER HAMILTON

. . . "Alexander Hamilton, storming the redoubt at Yorktown":[1] one of the imperishable memories of the American people.

"As soon as the shell of the Americans reached its zenith," writes John C. Hamilton in his *History of the Republic of the United States of America,* "that from the French battery ascended. Hamilton then gave the order to advance and push forward. Placing one foot on the shoulder of a soldier who knelt for that purpose, he sprang over the abatis upon the parapet, stood on it a moment with three of his men, encouraged the others to follow, and jumped into the ditch."

After the engagement, Lieutenant Colonel Hamilton presented a report to Lafayette, who sent it, with a covering report, to Washington. The Commander in Chief, in turn, sent both reports to Congress. They were printed in full in the newspapers. In some, Hamilton's report was specially featured.[2]

Hamilton to Lafayette[3]

Sir

I have the honor to render you an account of the corps under my command in your attack of last night, upon the redoubt on the left of the enemy's lines.

Agreeable to your orders we advanced in two columns with unloaded arms—the right composed of Lt Col Gimat's battalion and my own commanded by Major Fish—the left of a detachment commanded by Lt Col Laurens, destined to take the enemy in reverse, and intercept their retreat. The column on the right was preceded by a van guard of twenty men led by Lt Mansfield—and a detachment of sappers and miners commanded by Capt Gilliland for the purpose of removing obstructions. . . .

Lieut. col. Gimat's battalion, which formed the van of the right attack, and which fell under my immediate observation, encouraged by the decisive and animated example of their leader, advanced with an ardour and resolution superior to every obstacle. . . .

There was a happy coincidence of movements . . . Permit me to have the satisfaction of expressing our obligations to colonel Armand. . . . Enclosed is a return of the prisoners. . . .

I have the honor to be
with the warmest affe[ction and]
attachment
Sir
Y^r most Obe[dient and]
humble S[ervant]
A Hamil[ton]
Lt Col

Camp before York Town
October 15. 1781
Major General
The Marquis De la Fayette

Lafayette to Washington[4]

Camp before York
16th Octob^r 1781.

My dear General.

Your Excellency having personally seen our dispositions, I shall only give an account of what passed in the execution.

Colonel Gimat's batallion led the van, and was followed by that of Colonel Hamilton's, who commanded the whole advanced corps, at the same time a party of eighty men under Col. Lawrens turned the redoubt. I beg leave to refer your Excellency to the report I have received from Col. Hamilton, whose well known talents and gallantry were on this occasion most conspicuous and serviceable. Our obligations to him, to Col. Gimat, to Col. Lawrens, and to each and all the officers and men are above expression. Not one gun was fired; and the ardor of the troops did not give time for the sappers to derange the abattis; and, owing to the conduct of the commanders, and bravery of the men, the redoubt was stormed with an uncommon rapidity.

Colonel Barbers batallion which was the first in the supporting column being detached to the aid of the advance arrived at the moment they were getting over the works, and executed their orders with the utmost alacrity. The Colonel was slightly wounded. The rest of the column under Gen Hazen–General Muhlenberg and Col Vose [A pen was drawn through the last five words, and Muhlenberg's name was inserted before Hazen's, so that the amended passage read: "The rest of the column under Gen Mühlenberg and Hazen"] advanced with admirable firmness and discipline. Col Vose's batallion displayed to the left, a part of the division successively dressing by him, whilest a kind of second line was forming columns in the rear. It adds greatly to the character of the troops, that under the fire of the enemy, they displayed and took their ranks with perfect silence and order.

Give me leave particularly to mention Major Barber, division inspec[tor,] who distinguished himself, and received a wound by a cannon ball.

In making the arrangements for the support of the works we had reduced, I was happy to find Gen: Wayne, and the Pennsylvanians so situated, as to have given us in case of need the most effectual support.

I have the honor to be with the most perfect respect your Excellency's

Most obed^{t} s

Lafayette

His Excellency
Gen: Washington

Where was Muhlenberg during the attack? Lafayette's report provides the answer: He was senior commander in the field, in charge of the column that took the redoubt. Of that column, only a detachment, the assaulting party, was commanded by Hamilton. Yet Lafayette's report mentioned Muhlenberg so casually that the public has never even associated his name with the action.

Goodhearted, freedom-serving Lafayette, whom we all love and to whom the highest honor is due, had nevertheless the weaknesses of an amiable disposition and an aristocratic upbringing under the *ancien régime.* Impulsive and generous in sharing honors with a friend, his free, careless manner of attending to official business offended many an officer who served under him. Of these Captain Olney will serve as an example. Olney, seriously wounded on October 14, was offended because Lafayette, in complimenting the Light Division, cited the captain "only after mentioning a subordinate."[5]

The part Hamilton played in the action at Redoubt 10 was conspicuous and gallant. He deserves high praise for his conduct. But the question in our mind is not whether he deserved to be commended. It is how an officer who had not seen more than a few days service in the Virginia Campaign should, when it came to the distribution of honors, have picked the plum.

When we have answered that question, we shall, I think, have found an answer to another: Why did Muhlenberg after Yorktown disappear from view? The army saw nothing more of him for months. Even his family in Pennsylvania could get no news of him.

Let us go back to gather up some threads which will enable us to weave an answer to all these questions at once.

On September 30, 1781, Lafayette wrote a charming letter to "my dear General" (Washington): "Owing to your partiality and friendship for me, I have during the Campaign acted the Most Agreable part— I commanded the Army in Virginia, I was opposed to Lord

Cornwallis, and the troops you entrusted to me had the greatest share in the fatiguing movements that will end in the ruin of the ennemy in this quarter."[6]

But now, the Marquis finds, it is no longer so pleasant. From being commander of the army in Virginia, he has become only one of General Lincoln's officers (Lincoln commanded the right wing at Yorktown), "with nothing almost to say even in the Light Division." In short, he wants "the command of the Right Wing in this siege," and he adds that this is of "the Highest importance to me."

It was of the highest importance to America that Washington should keep the good will of the French, especially of De Grasse, whose stay in these parts was a limited one. He had set as his deadline, October 15. Lafayette served as a liaison officer between Washington and De Grasse.

Lafayette did not receive command of the right wing. That remained under the senior officer, Lincoln. But Lafayette did, nevertheless, receive the honors of the siege. To his division was assigned the task of taking Redoubt 10.

Lafayette had a young friend in the army, a youth of about his own age, Alexander Hamilton. Hamilton had seen warm service at the beginning of the war—New York, Trenton, and Monmouth—but for three years past he had been one of Washington's aides at headquarters and his confidential secretary.

Lafayette and Hamilton were both young, impressionable, and ambitious. They understood each other.

"Come here, my dear friend," Lafayette had written, May 23, 1781, "and command our artillery in Virginia. I want your advice and exertions."[7]

Hamilton had recently taken the occasion of a small rebuke offered him by Washington to throw up his secretaryship and leave his chief. On the thirty-first of July, Lieutenant Colonel Hamilton was assigned a battalion under Colonel Scammel. He came down in September to take part in the siege of Yorktown, in Hazen's brigade. He watched the situation closely, seeking the moment when his country's cause might best be used to serve his own.

De Grasse was persuaded to overstay his time, "at least to the end of the present operation."

The siege proceeded regularly and smoothly. The French kept control of Chesapeake Bay. The trenches were advanced, the batteries trained. The end was inevitable. The taking of the last redoubts was a foregone conclusion. Their capture was to be no more than the last nail in the coffin. Cornwallis already knew that he was beaten. As a test of strength, the assault on Redoubt 10 was negligible. When it was taken, few on either side were killed, and few of the enemy (despite large reports afterwards circulated) were captured. They retired to their inner lines.

The importance of the affair, as Washington had seen in advance, was as a symbol. This final action would be the means of throwing the spotlight on the heroes of the Virginia Campaign.

The Commander in Chief, therefore, saw to it that the honors should go to those who had fought the long campaign. Colonel Barber of Muhlenberg's brigade was appointed to lead the storming party.

The publicity value of the post was not unknown to so astute an adventurer as Alexander Hamilton. He wanted to wave his sword on the last British parapet for all coming generations of Americans to see.

At this point in the narrative we hand over to John C. Hamilton again:

> Hamilton now saw the opportunity he had so long, so eagerly hoped, of signalizing himself by some act of distinguished prowess. He was on the point of losing it. The fourteenth of October was his tour of duty, but from a supposed precedence due to those of the light infantry who had made the Virginia campaign, Washington had determined to give the assault to Colonel Barber. The moment Hamilton was apprised of this, he left Major Fish, proceeded to the general's quarters, and remonstrated with him, claiming the right of making the attack, as the officer on duty. His appeal prevailed, and he returned in the highest spirits, exclaiming to Fish, "We have it, we have it."[8]

"Hamilton, always true to the feelings of honor and independence,"[9] as Henry Lee says of his hero's conduct at this moment.

The arrangements were changed, the signal was given, the assault was launched. In nine minutes from the passing of the abatis, the redoubt was taken. But there was some sharp skirmishing during those nine minutes. Muhlenberg, seeing some signs of hesitation, sent up Colonel Barber's regiment, which "arrived at the moment the advance was getting over the works."

Just what happened at this point is in some dispute. Major Isaac Heydt, one of General Muhlenberg's aides, said afterward that Muhlenberg himself came up with Barber's men, went over the parapet with Hamilton's van, "and in person led the storming party."[10]

The rest of the column, Hazen's Brigade and the remaining regiment (Colonel Vose's) in Muhlenberg's, then moved up and occupied the redoubt.

It would be pleasant if we could end here, but the story goes on. In his report to Lafayette next day, Hamilton spoke of "the corps under my command in your attack of last night."[11] Between *my* corps and *your* attack, Muhlenberg was squeezed out. Hamilton could refer to himself afterward as "the officer who was to command the attack on a British redoubt in the course of the siege of Yorktown." The public forgot Muhlenberg altogether.

But let us give Brigadier General Muhlenberg his due. He was unquestionably in command (under Lafayette) of the operation against Redoubt 10. Major Heydt, his aide-de-camp, so understood it. Captain John Pryor also, writing from Yorktown the day after the battle, so understood it:

"Whilst writing the Letter that incloses this last Evening, three attacks were made on some of the most advanc'd of the Enemy's works by the Marquis de Lafayette, Baron de Viomenil M.G. & Genl: Muhlenberg . . ."[12]

Evidently Pryor did not know that Muhlenberg was acting under Lafayette. He only knew that Muhlenberg was on the ground, in actual command, and he ranked him with the French commander who took the other redoubt.

Henry A. Muhlenberg, in the life of his great-uncle, *Major-General Peter Muhlenberg*, presents further evidence. He quotes an article which appeared in the *Aurora* (edited by Duane) some time after Alexander Hamilton's death:

Among the Germans, the man most celebrated was General Peter Muhlenberg, who had distinguished revolutionary services to be proud of, but who has been the last ever to name, and the most reluctant to hear them spoken of. General Muhlenberg, now in the advance of life, with the resolution of a lion when in danger, and with a highly cultivated mind, displays the simplicity of one unacquainted with human affairs, and unsuspecting of human infirmities. This man it was, who, at the memorable siege of Yorktown, achieved that laurel, with which a certain orator at New York wished to ornament the tomb of a man, of whom, being dead, we shall speak not irreverently.[13]

Jared Sparks has also a word to say. Replying to Henry A. Muhlenberg, who had written asking for an opinion on his interpretation of the Yorktown incident, the great biographer said this: "It appears to me that you have presented the right view of the affair at Yorktown. In fact it is confirmed by Lafayette's letter. Gen. Muhlenberg commanded the division of troops called out on the occasion, & Hamilton led the assaulting party."[14]

It is useless to ask why Muhlenberg did not write the report. Perhaps because he thought it was unnecessary. Perhaps because he was not asked to write it. Hamilton wanted the publicity.

It may have been that Peter Muhlenberg was too ill to write it. Henry A. Muhlenberg says that the General was wounded in the action.[15] Evidence for the wound is not strong, but it is known that at the time of the engagement he was suffering from a fever, which, once the siege was over, took him to Williamsburg and then home on furlough.[16]

As far as the glory-thirsty Hamilton was concerned, Peter Muhlenberg said nothing—unless his long silence be interpreted as having the effect of speech. He went over the mountains to Woodstock and disappeared from the public eye for many months. He never spoke. He took no action. He had greater patience than Aaron Burr.

For Alexander Hamilton, Yorktown had been a good publicity stunt, and he was very well pleased with it. He had reason to be, for some time.

We shall, however, meet him again in the Muhlenberg story. We shall meet him on Saturday, December 15, 1792. On that day Congressman Frederick Augustus Muhlenberg, accompanied by James Monroe, broke the Reynolds affair over his head.

CHAPTER XXV

"OUR GENERAL"

On October 19 General Lincoln received Cornwallis' surrender. The password for the day was *Independence.*

The news was not long in reaching Philadelphia. An express rider arrived with it a little after three o'clock on the morning of October 22.

"A watchman of this City," reported the *Freeman's Journal* in its issue of Wednesday, October 24, "after having conducted the express rider to the door of his excellency the president of Congress, on Monday morning last, the honest old German continued the duties of his function, calling out, 'Basht dree o'glock, und Gorn-wal-lis isht da-ken!' "

Two days later, when Washington's aide, Tench Tilghman, arrived with the same news, Congress went to Zion Church to return thanks to the Lord, as Frederick Muhlenberg wrote, "for this singular mark of interposition in our favor."[1]

Peter Muhlenberg in Virginia was too ill to savor the triumph. He had been running a temperature for some days, and, now that the military strain was removed, he retired to Williamsburg for rest and medical attention.

From Williamsburg on October 23 he wrote a letter to George Washington:

Sir

A few days ago, I received permission from Major General The Marquis de la Fayette to retire to this place for the recovery of my health; A Constant & violent fever I have had for Ten days past, has not only reduced me very much, but I am afraid if it continues much longer will put it out of my power to remove for some time,—I would therefore request Your Excellencys permission to go over the Mountains, as I have at present an Opportunity to make use of a Carriage going that way—

Your Excellency will please to remember that I had obtaind permission to visit my Family in the Spring of 79. but was prevented by General Woodfords remaining longer in Virg[a] then was expected—in Nov[r] 79. I obtained Your Excellencys permission again but was Stopd in Philad[a] By the Board of War, when The Virg[a] Line was Ordered to Charlestown—Since that I obtained permission From Baron Steuben to go home for a time, but had been there only three days, when I was recalld by Express at the time when Arnold invaded the State.

I have the Honor to be
with the greatest Respect
Your Excellencys
Most Obed[t] & hbl[e] Serv[t].
P: Muhlenberg[2]

The letter is endorsed on the back, "his request granted."

Peter Muhlenberg returned slowly across the mountains to Woodstock. We hear no more of him for many months. His brother Frederick and the rest of the family up in Pennsylvania wondered why no news came. They could only suppose that he had gone with reinforcements to General Greene.

"Since the arrival of the Fr[ench] fleet," wrote Frederick to Henry Ernest, "I have neither seen nor heard anything more from him than appears in the newspaper."[3]

General Washington went back to Philadelphia, where Frederick Muhlenberg, as Speaker of the Pennsylvania Assembly, waited on him to deliver an address of congratulations.

While Peter was at Woodstock, recuperating, the army in Virginia went to pieces. Desertions were wholesale—of officers as well as of men. There was no coördination between civilian and military authorities. No reinforcements were sent to General Greene.

To Greene, the breakup in Virginia was a disaster. He knew how precarious his situation was should the British continue the war. He wrote an appeal, dated December 27, 1781, to General Muhlenberg:

I have not had a line from you for a long time. The late success in Virginia and the new arrangements there leave me at a loss how or when to address myself upon matters which concern the line of your state.

Capt Ragsdale by whom this will be delivered you comes on the most pressing emergency to solicit aid from Virginia for the Support of our Army. The Enemy are in dayly expectation of very large reinforcements from New York and Ireland which will make them so very formidable as to leave us little or no hopes of holding any footing in this Country without speedy reinforcements. I beg you therefore if you have this business in charge to forward us every man fit for Duty. . . . Every thing depends upon speedy reinforcements.[4]

Though Peter was still weak from pleuritic fever, Greene's appeal moved him to try to get back into harness. He wrote, February 1, to Brigadier General Hand, Adjutant General, to say that, being now somewhat recovered, he awaited Washington's orders "when and where to take the field."[5]

The orders, when they came, were to remain in Virginia and superintend the recruiting service: most of the recruits to be forwarded to General Greene, the remainder to be sent to Fort Pitt.[6]

As a military power, all that gallant Virginia needed was General Muhlenberg again to build her an army.

This he now proceeded to do. With the same efficiency as in 1780, he made Virginia the blood bank for the southern forces. But his success in recruiting, training, and equipping troops for Greene's reinforcement need not detain us. The war, in fact, was over. No fresh military movements occurred after Yorktown. The capture of Redoubt 10 had written *finis* to the Revolutionary War.

Lord North resigned March 20, 1782. On July 11 the British evacuated Savannah. The ingenious Mr. Triebner, after collecting the Ebenezer church bonds and gathering into his pockets the savings of some of the widows in his congregation, fled for his life. On December 14, the British evacuated Charleston.

Preliminaries of peace were signed January 20, 1783. When news of this reached America, peace was proclaimed by the Commander in Chief. That was on April 19.

The final Treaty of Peace was signed at Paris on September 5, 1783. On the thirtieth of the same month, Brigadier General Muhlenberg was promoted to the rank of Major General. He retired from the service on November 3.

He retired also from the church. At Woodstock his congregation wanted him to return, but he declined.

"It would never do," he said, "to mount the parson after the soldier."[7]

He decided to try his fortunes once more in "the land of his mother." Wife, children, Negro servant, household furniture, horses, drivers, a freight wagon, and a stage wagon—Major General Muhlenberg headed this column and prepared to invade Pennsylvania.

In the month of November 1783, "our general" descended in force on Lancaster and saw Henry Ernest's new baby, Henry Augustus Philip (who was in time to become the first minister of the United States to Austria). At Tulpehocken he and his cavalcade visited Betsy and Emanuel Schultze and their growing brood of children: Anna Maria Margaretta, Henry L., John Andrew Melchior (aged eight), Frederick Augustus (six), John Peter Gabriel (three), Catharine G. (eighteen months), and Christiana Salome (six months).

Passing through Reading, they picked up Mr. Swaine, who was there on a visit, and took him along with them to the Trappe, the General and Mr. Swaine in the vanguard.

Never was seen such a family reunion.

First of all, there was Peter's meeting with his parents. They were living alone now, since Sally's marriage. Henry Melchior's first intimation of the approach of the soldier prodigal was on Friday, November 21, when a Mr. Zehring of Virginia stopped to tell the Pastor that his son was on his way with all his family.

Next day a freight wagon stopped at the parsonage and unloaded a quantity of Peter's household goods. Later the same evening the General himself rode up with Mr. Swaine. The Pastor's Journal omits details of the greetings. Some things are too intimate even for the eyes of posterity.

The following evening Hannah, the General's lady, tired and cold in the late November air, drove up in the stage wagon with her children and the Negro boy.

The really big family reunion came a few days later. Peter had gone down alone to the city (Hannah stayed behind for a washing day) on Wednesday, December 3, and came back on Saturday with Frederick—and the never-to-be-missed Mr. Swaine. That same evening Polly and Sally came in from New Hanover, Sally with her nine-months-old baby, Henry Muhlenberg Richards, in her arms.

Sunday was a terrible day for the Pastor. He loved to have his children and grandchildren around him, talking about old times or laying plans for new, but the noise of the invasion was almost too much for him. It made his ears crackle and his head swim, and he grew worried about himself.

There was no service in Augustus Church that day, and the private devotions held in the house were much interrupted by the "shrieking and clatter of the little children," as the Pastor wrote in his Journal, continuing: "and when brothers and sisters have not seen one another for a while and come together, they have much to tell one another, much to say and much to complain about in connection with their sinful circumstances, and they 'see with *the tongue*' as my little grandson said, and Solomon out of his own experience said: Eccles. 1.2 ['Vanity of vanities, saith the Preacher, vanity of vanities; all is vanity.'] But that is not anything new under the sun, for Job found it necessary to offer burnt offerings for his children's sake Job 1.4-5."

> And his sons went and feasted in their houses, every one his day; and sent and called for their three sisters to eat and drink with them.
> And it was so, when the days of their feasting were gone about, that Job sent and sanctified them, and rose up early in the morning, and offered burnt offerings according to the number of them all: for Job said, It may be that my sons have sinned, and cursed God in their hearts. Thus did Job continually.

There was plenty of news for them all to pour into Peter's ears.

Mr. Swaine and Polly had got an establishment in New Hanover, where Mr. Swaine conducted a small retail business over the counter. In short, they had a store. Sally had married a widower, Matthias Reichard or Richards. Mr. Richards was a very fine fellow, Frederick said: he had a house of his own, as well as his own furniture, cattle, and plantation.[8] The marriage had been held at Mr. Swaine's residence in New Hanover, May 8, 1782. Daddy Muhlenberg had performed the ceremony.

Peter's brother-in-law Kuntze had, on the Fourth of July, 1783, received from the University of Pennsylvania an honorary degree, Doctor of Theology—along with George Washington, who was made a *Doctor Juris.*

But the biggest news was about Frederick. If his father was now less active, Frederick was keeping the Muhlenberg name high in Pennsylvania. He was thick in what his father called the "hurle burle" of politics. Henry Melchior was only waiting for his "waxen wings to melt"; but Frederick somehow managed to keep aloft, although the Radicals who had first pushed him forward regretted their former enthusiasm for one who now allied himself with the more moderate and conservative Republicans. Ten days before Cornwallis surrendered, Frederick had been reëlected to the Assembly and (after a sharp fight) reëlected also as speaker.

In 1782 the election had been hot with personalities, and Speaker Muhlenberg came in for his share of printed attack.

"The Son of Saul," writing in the *Freeman's Journal* of November 13, 1782, attacked him for "being so clever in 1780 as to attend the meetings of both the contending parties," to pledge himself to both, "to preside at both," and to put his name on both tickets. The Son of Saul seemed to write more in sorrow than in anger. "When you turned your back so suddenly upon your constitutional friends, who first raised you from a private station, and, without provocation, all at once became a furious persecutor of them . . . still I forebore." But not forever. "I wish you great folks," he burst out, "who are scrambling for offices would contrive some way of climbing into your seats, without treading on your neighbours."[9]

The same *Freeman's Journal* declared that the Speaker sprang from obscurity and would return to it again. In E. Oswald's *Independent Gazetteer; or, the Chronicle of Freedom,* for October 26, 1782, a writer demanded, "where in the name of fortune did the late Speaker of the Assembly spring from?"

But the question was a trick of irony, aimed at the enemies of Frederick Muhlenberg and designed as a defense of the Muhlenberg name. The writer wished to know whether the obscurity sprang from the Speaker's having been a former member of Congress, or brother of a general in the American army, or son of "a learned and reverend gentleman," or from having "travelled in Europe, and finished his studies in the Universities there."

Frederick was again elected to the Assembly by the city of Philadelphia, and again elected speaker. His father wrote gloomily to Henry Ernest about Frederick's prospects. He could not live and support his large and growing family on a government salary, especially since he now had to "keep up with the gentry." These reflections drove Henry Melchior to nightmares. He dreamed one night of Frederick sitting on a stool, dressed in rags. All at once he fell and lay in a heap. His father was powerless to help him.

When he awoke, Henry Melchior, who believed dreams reflect

not past but coming events, thought it sad that Frederick should have hidden his talent "in the political dungheap."[10]

Frederick had some doubts of his own. The city was ruining his health, and he had bought a house at the Trappe, close to his father's, where his wife kept a small store and to which he retired for week ends whenever he could. Henry Ernest from Lancaster advised him, if he must be a merchant, to sell books and medicines from Halle. Frederick was strongly tempted to give up politics, but the people of Pennsylvania had another mind and would not let him.

Besides, he had convictions. He believed, along with many other responsible citizens, that there must be a revision of the Pennsylvania Constitution of 1776—to complete, as he said, "the Triumph of Reason Justice & Good Order amongst us!"[11]

Framed in the heat of the Revolution, the Constitution of '76 had been designed to put power into the hands of "the people" and keep it there. It was found, on cool appraisal, to put power into the hands of a radical minority and keep it *there.*

There was only one way, according to the Constitution itself, by which it could be changed: through the recommendation of the Council of Censors. This august body, which was to meet every seven years to determine whether the Constitution needed changing, was heavily weighted in favor of the sparsely settled western counties, which were radical. Yet this Council alone had authority to call a convention for the purpose of changing the Constitution by legal process.

The most bitter political struggle in Pennsylvania, from 1776 to 1790, was over this question of revising the Constitution; and for that reason control of the Council of Censors, which alone had the right to propose any changes, became the goal of the fighters.

On October 14, 1783, after a wild election marked by much expenditure of "Toryphobia" (the chief propaganda weapon used by the Radicals), the Republicans or Anti-Constitutionalists emerged victorious. Both Republicans and Radicals had sent their best battalions into the fight for the Council of Censors. Frederick Muhlenberg was elected a Censor, on the Republican ticket, for the city of Philadelphia. The Republicans won a majority in this body, but not the two-thirds majority necessary (according to the Constitution) for calling a convention.

But a majority of three was sufficient to enable the Republicans to elect a Republican chairman. On November 13, 1783, Frederick Muhlenberg was elected President of the Council of Censors.

"*Armer Wurm!*" was his father's comment, when Frederick broke the news to him on Saturday at the Trappe: "Poor Worm! Your fall is near."[12]

But Frederick's neighbors at the Trappe were not disturbed. On that same Saturday, November 15, a township meeting was held at which Frederick Muhlenberg was elected justice of the peace.

Two nights later Frederick's store was robbed. Money and the best of his goods were stolen. It was not suspected that the Radicals were responsible for the crime. It looked more like the work of the Doane gang.

One of the war's worst offshots—about which Henry Melchior had often complained—had been the gangs of robbers that infested the countryside. The state of Pennsylvania had recently taken steps to put a stop to their depredations. A proclamation against them, bearing the signature of the Speaker of the Assembly, Frederick Muhlenberg, had been printed and posted.

A party of militia, hunting down a band of robbers who called themselves the "Royal Refugees," caught one of the gang, Joseph Doane by name, and clapped him into a Philadelphia jail. A second party of militia came on the brothers Moses and Levy Doane, with their cousin Abraham Doane, in an empty house at the mouth of Tohiccon Creek. Moses was shot and killed; the others fled and escaped. Beside Moses' body was found a paper containing the following screed:

These May inform Any That It May Concarn that If Joseph Done prisnor Now in philadelphia Is not Released And Acquitted Immediately That We Will put Mulinburgh to Death In ten Days Without fail; and take another of your head Man and An other till Wee have taken ten for Every Refugee you put to Death Wee Will put ten to Death and for Every person you put In Jail on Our Accounts If you hang them Wee will hang five and Burn ten houses and Barns and We Will shew you Other Sort of Diversion than you have Ever Been Acquainted With yet for We Are Not your Subjects Neither Will Wee Ever Bee But If you Will Release Joseph done And Acquit him Interely then We Will Release Mulinburgh Directly Without harm As Soon as We know for Certain that Done Is Released But If you Dont think proper to Release him then

Abide By the Consequence; for All you Can do Is to hang him And If you Do Wee Will follow your Example to your Confusion So you and Us for It

[Signed] The Royal Refugees your Sworn Enemies

N.B. We perhaps May give him Liberty to Write his Sentiments and We Shall Endeavour to Convey It to Where he thinks proper

If you Dont know I Can Inform you that your governor Is As proper A person to Apply to On This Account As Any you Can Imploy

If you Make any Search We Will put our prisoner to Death at the first Appearance of Danger

To Mulinburghs friends if he has Any[13]

"They'll have to catch me before they hang me," wrote Frederick Muhlenberg to Emanuel Schultze. "But see how it is when one is a person of consequence!"[14]

The Chief Justice of Pennsylvania saw to it that the Speaker should not go unprotected. When on Saturday, September 6, Frederick came home to the Trappe, he had quite an escort: a sheriff specially detailed to be his bodyguard, and three colonels who had volunteered to accompany him.[15] On Monday morning his escort took him safely back to duty in the city.

Levy and Abraham Doane were still at large. A few years later, two good horses were stolen from Frederick's stable at the Trappe. But the law soon caught up with the Doanes. The case of "Respublica v. Levi Doan" came before the Supreme Court (for the robbery of a Mr. Lawrence King) on June 16, 1788.[16] Levy's brother Abraham was no more fortunate. In September 1788 the two Royal Refugees, Levy and Abraham Doane of Bucks County, were hanged by the neck until they were dead.[17]

CHAPTER XXVI

OHIO PARADISE

After the siege of Troy, when Ulysses returned to Ithaca, he felt it good to get home but difficult to stay there. It is a feeling familiar to all army veterans, and General Muhlenberg was not immune to it. After the close of the Revolutionary War, he was restless for movement. A man who had hunted such royal game as Sir William Howe, Sir Harry Clinton, Benedict Arnold, and Lord Cornwallis, could hardly be expected to sit at home by the fire.

Like many another restless man in the generations that were to come after him, he turned his face toward the West.

The West, though the term at that time connoted no such vast distances as it does today, had nevertheless names to conjure with, names that stirred men's minds with bewildering and alluring associations: the Allegheny Mountains, the Monongahela, Pittsburgh, Scioto, Muskingum, Chillicothe, the Falls of the Ohio.

The *Ohio—la Belle Rivière* of the French—was then in America of all words the key to romance, suggesting the beauty of strange countries, the mystery of the unknown, and a dash of fear: fear of the wilderness, fear of painted savages and scalping knives. Yet it had more homely connotations, too, which explorers, Indian traders, and pioneer homesteaders had made familiar. It was the land of *hope*. There were fortunes to be made in its forests, its farm lands, and its rivers. The Boones and the Lincolns were lured by it, and ready to risk their lives on its development. Thomas Jefferson, philosopher, turned his eyes toward it to expand the bounds of human knowledge.

Peter Muhlenberg had to go. Not all the warnings of his father and mother, the tears of his wife, Hannah, and of his sister Polly, not even the affectionate dissuasions of Polly's husband, Mr. Swaine, could alter his decision. *Peter would go.*

The hopes of Virginia went with him. The government of that state wanted his report on the wealth long dreamed of, now seemingly within reach: boundless lands which the Revolutionary War veterans should begin to develop, lands stretching into the distance beyond the Falls of the Ohio—gateway to the great Northwest, Virginia's not-yet-surrendered Manifest Destiny.

In the National Archives at Washington, D. C., there is preserved among the Virginia Bounty Land Warrants, one dated March 13, 1783, for the survey of 11,662⅔ acres of land "due unto the said Peter Muhlenburgh, In consideration of his services for seven years, as a Brigadier General in the Virginia Continental Line." It is underscored, "To be laid in Six Surveys five of two thousand Acres each & One of One thousand Six Hundred Sixty Six & two third Acres
P. Muhlenberg."[1]

On July 7, 1783, Peter wrote to his brother Frederick to say that he had a "Patent for twelve thousand acres of land at Sciota 160 miles beyond Fort Pitsburg."[2]

He wished to see these lands, with a thought to settling on them. At the same time the Assembly of Virginia appointed him to locate the lands for the officers and men of the Virginia Line—lands set aside on the western bounds of the state. The center from which preliminary surveys were to be made was the Falls of the Ohio—Louisville.

The winter of 1783-84 was the worst old Pastor Muhlenberg could remember, and the early spring was no better. But Peter Muhlenberg was resolved to make an early start. His mother and father were distressed. The winter still held tight, the roads were in shocking condition, the rivers were full of ice, and Peter had not yet fully recovered his strength after his long illness. But Peter was not to be frightened. On Sunday, February 22, accompanied by his brother Frederick and a Negro servant, he left his father's house and set out on his journey to Louisville. The leave-taking was too much for Anna Maria. That night she had three heavy paroxysms.

Peter went first to New Hanover, where he put up for a day or two, and said good-bye to Frederick, who returned to the Trappe. Peter puttered around at Swaine's, getting a horse, a portmanteau, and other necessaries. By Tuesday he was ready to start off again.

Mr. Swaine, an affectionate soul, was all upset. He had done his best to dissuade his brother-in-law from risking his life in the wilderness, but in vain. Peter had a will of iron. The British had not stopped him at Yorktown. Now forests, mountains, vast rivers, and savages—nothing should stop him from reaching the Falls of the Ohio.

Polly broke down. The parting scene was so affecting that Mr. Swaine (who had an eye for drama as well as a heart for sentiment) dashed down a description of it for the eyes of his brother-in-law, the "Rev^d^. M^r^. Emanuel Schultz" of Tulpehocken:

> . . . Excuse my scrall & diction, I'm all in frustration this Morning, the Genl is setting out upon a perilous Journey, and God knows if we shall ever see him again—do use Your influence with him, to go no further than Fort Pitt, there he can get people to transact his business, he has no occasion to go—his Circumstances are very good, and he can go into trade, besides his health is very much impair'd, in short the Journey which he intends to *make* requires the Constitution of an Indian—
>
> Mrs Swaine Joins me in Love to you Mrs Schultz and the Children—
>
> God bless you
>
> Yours Affectionately
>
> Francis Swaine
>
> P.S.
>
> Mrs Swaine is bawling and I am listening to her Notes— She bore it nobly 'till he turn'd his back—and then ——— that Affection which we all bear to him Overcame her—[3]

From Peter's Journal[4] and letters, from a letter of Frederick's after talking with the returned wanderer from the Ohio,[5] and from the notes Henry Ernest put into his Botanical Journal about the Ohio's wonders in flora and fauna,[6] we have a pretty good idea of where, when, and how the General traveled.

He had a good horse to ride, as far as Fort Pitt, and a blind but dependable horse to carry his baggage. Nevertheless, the journey over the mountains was slow and exhausting. The snow lay two feet deep over much of the way, and in places was so badly drifted that Peter had to break new roads through the woods. He spent a little time with the Schultzes at Tulpehocken, and at Colonel Kucher's near Lebanon, ten miles from the Schultzes.

From Harris's Ferry he crossed the Susquehanna River on the ice, and went on to Carlisle, where he arrived in time to join the large company of people who, as Peter says somewhat dubiously, were "liberal in applauding" the tragedy of *Douglas* as presented by "some young students at law."[7]

From Carlisle the road (which, for much of its course, followed an old Indian path) took them to the head of Conodogwinet Creek, through Path Valley to Burnt Cabins, thence to Fort Littleton, the Juniata, "Slyding Mountain" (today's Sideling Hill), and Bedford.

At Bedford he was glad to be "incog." His name was on men's tongues as they talked in their cups.

> I had flattered myself [wrote the General] that, as we were going toward the frontiers, we should soon be out of the latitude of politics; but even here two men cannot drink half a gill of whiskey without discussing a point in politics, to the great improvement and edification of the bystanders. Especially so to me, while I stand by incog. and hear the name of Muhlenberg made use of, sometimes in one way and sometimes in another; for were I known, I believe no one would have the hardiesse to mention that name with disrespect, and look at me, for I have at present the perfect resemblance of Robinson Crusoe: four belts around me, two brace of pistols, a sword and rifle slung, besides my pouch and tobacco-pipe, which is not a small one. Add to this the blackness of my face, which occasions the inhabitants to take me for a travelling Spaniard, and I am sure that my appearance alone ought to protect me from both politics and insult.[8]

The "Fortitude and Perseverance of old Soldiers" brought Muhlenberg and his companion, Captain Paské, who had joined him near Carlisle, at last to Fort Pitt on the afternoon of March 10. But there they were stuck for three weeks. The ice was driving fast on the Monongahela and not even broken up in the Allegheny. It was not until March 31 that Peter, having given his blind horse away, brought the other one on board the flat-bottomed boat named the *Muhlenberg* in his honor, which was to bear him the rest of the way to the Falls of the Ohio.

The *Muhlenberg* carried some 22,000 weight of flour and 1,500 weight of bacon, besides other goods that brought the total cargo to some 35,000 pounds. In addition there were nine horses and fifteen men. There were three boats, with some forty men all told, that set out together from Fort Pitt, to be joined next day by two more boats "with families going to the Falls." It was a respectable flotilla: the *Muhlenberg*, the *Lewis*, the *Ellis*, the *Dowdon*, and the

Carpenter's Mistake. We can only regret that the General did not record for posterity the story that lay behind the last name.

They left Fort Pitt with a bang, giving the fort a salute from thirteen cannon (they were sufficiently armed against the savages) and receiving one of twenty-two in reply. A few hours sailing brought them past Logstown, where Peter's grandfather, Conrad Weiser, in 1748 had held his treaty with the Ohio Indians, and past Fort M'Intosh at the mouth of the Beaver.

Near sunset the current swept the *Muhlenberg* against the point of an island, and stuck it fast for the night. This was Indian country, and there was fear among the passengers lest the Indians attack them and loot the boat. But the hero of Brandywine was not now to be daunted. He took command and set watches, each man taking the guard in turn.

The General felt no such elation, however, during his watch, as had been his when confronted by Cornwallis in Virginia. The lonely river behind him, the dark forest hanging oppressively over and around him—this was the mysterious and fatal Ohio the thought of which had caused Polly to shed mortuary tears on his behalf. He confessed to depression at "the noise of the wild fowl, the screaming of loons, the whooping of owls, and the howling of wolves, which continued around us all night."[9] "It was no happy place," as the old bard of *Beowulf* sang.

But the morning saw them safely off and on their way again, laughing, no doubt, at last night's fears, and at the *Carpenter's Mistake,* which soon joined them. They passed Fort Wheeling. Its sturdy history of defense against a force of British and Indians—who made a cannon of wood in the forest and fired it at the garrison until the gun, not the fort, blew up—entitled it to a better fate than that now observed to have befallen it. Captain Zane, the only inhabitant of the neighborhood, was busying himself taking the fort to pieces to serve him for firewood.

By the time they passed Muskingum on April 2, their fresh meat was running out, and they had to run ashore every day thereafter to shoot turkey, ducks, pigeons, deer, and buffalo to keep the ships' larders full. Peter, a born hunter, noted that the land was "delightfully Stockt" with game—at least within four or five miles of the river.

"I did not care to venture further," he said, "for fear of losing my Scalp."[10]

He was a born fisherman, too, with a fisherman's rod and repertoire.

"The fish caught in the Ohio," he wrote, "are large. . . . The catfish weigh from five to one hundred and forty weight"[11]—all depending, may we suppose, on the art of the narrator.

Frederick, in sending a report to Henry Ernest on this part of Peter's travels, compromised at "from 60 to 70 lb."[12]

Henry Ernest himself, more exact if not more gullible, recorded: "*Catfish* the largest 141 common 73."[13]

Peter's party encountered innumerable species of birds, according to Henry Ernest's report, including pheasant duck and black duck, two kinds of geese, swans, and pelicans. As a man of science, Henry was much interested in the skeleton they had found on a height. "I believe it is a *hippopotamus,*" he wrote.[14]

They saw the Great Button Tree, and some ancient Indian forts, one of which was capable, so it was said, of containing 10,000 men.

The party reached Louisville, the Falls of the Ohio, on April 11, and saluted the fort with three cannon—to announce, as Frederick put it, the arrival of a Big Chief, John Peter Gabriel.

The town smacked strongly of the frontier, consisting as it did of a fort, "a court-house, a jail, and seven huts." But the country around it was attractive.

"From the prospects of the lands in the vicinity of this town," wrote Peter, "and its situation, it promises fair to become a place of great importance."[15]

To Frederick he called it "Paradise."[16]

The first business to be attended to was the drawing of lots for priority of location. All in all, Peter had 30,000 acres to look after, his own and the acres of his friends. This task accomplished, he wrote to Baron Steuben, Governor Benjamin Harrison, Patrick Henry, Esq., and others who had commissioned him to look after their lands for them.

He explained what had been done, and *what could not be done.* The lands could not be safely or honestly surveyed. They were not Virginia's to survey. The Indians who owned them would not allow it. It is to be recalled that two years later, in 1786, Abraham Lincoln, the President's grandfather, was killed by Indians within fifteen miles of Louisville.

"I was much surprised on my arrival here to find," wrote Peter from the Falls to Baron Steuben, April 23, "that nothing had been attempted by Government to conciliate the affection of the Indians— They seem anxious to brighten the chain of former Friendship, but are allmost weary of being kept so long in Suspense."[17]

After Peter's return, he told Frederick much that he had not put in his Journal, especially about the Indians around the Falls. As Frederick reported it, it provides the cream of the narrative.

While Peter was at Louisville, three Indian deputies visited him, in particular Cornstalk, a chief of the Shawnees. They expressed alarm at "finding so many Warriors assembling here," in preparation, as the Indians feared, for some mischief against them. Cornstalk wondered why the Big Men at Annapolis had so long delayed arranging for a treaty with the Indians. Many moons, he said, had passed since the Americans had made peace with the Man beyond the Great Water, but still no treaty of peace had been made with the Indians.

These latter supposed it must be the intention of the Long Knives (Virginia) to seize their lands. As for that, there were two ways to go about it: either to take the lands by force, or to buy them. If they chose the first way, there would be broken heads; if they chose the second, the price would be high.

"But in the end," as Frederick reports, "he gave advice that would do honor to an old Roman Senator or perhaps even a Censor." Frederick, it will be remembered, was at this time president of Pennsylvania's Council of Censors.

> He said he knew a way of avoiding these alternatives. Send your young warriors, he said, to our nations, and let them fetch our young squaws, and then our young warriors will come and fetch your young squaws, and soon everything will be Big Knife.— Cornstalk brought messages from the old warriors—of the above tenor, and also from the old squaws, the latter proposed, that if a war broke out, Big Knife should leave them and their corn in peace, and fight only with their warriors. The young squaws too sent a message and a belt [of wampum]—the purport: they much desired to see the time when they might nurse the young warriors of the Big Knife with the milk from their breasts—it is well expressed in figurative language.[18]

Peter wanted to stay at the Falls, but a conversation he had with the delegates of the Shawnees, who were at that time the most powerful Indian nation in this part of the continent, made him feel that it was "absolutely necessary," as he said, "to wait on Congress to give them some information relative to the settlements on the western waters, and to hasten, if possible, the treaty with the Indians."[19]

He hurried back, following an Indian path through the wilderness.[20] Frederick reports that for two hundred miles his brother saw neither house nor cabin.[21] There were no serious adventures on the way, though the sight of bleached human bones by the wayside reminded him that this had been Indian country.

Henry Melchior Muhlenberg was rejoiced on June 25 to open the parsonage door to receive his son Peter once more, returned, with his Negro servant, safe and sound.

"He went away sick and he comes back well," wrote the Pastor in his Journal. "God the Lord had heard my poor prayer."[22]

Peter talked rapturously of the West. "I mean to become a resident of the western waters,"[23] he said in a letter to Congress.

He caught Frederick up in the same enthusiasm. In another year, thought Frederick, he would take his family and go West: "and then good night Pennsylvania unhappy Pennsylvania that is so badly torn by factions—good night Politics Parties deviltry and cunning—"[24]

A wave of western fever struck the whole family. It caught Sally and Mr. Richards. They would go, too. And Mr. Swaine with Mrs. Swaine—they were all going with Peter to the Ohio.

But it was not to be. The gates of Paradise were barred. Later in the summer, when the bubbles of his effervescence had subsided, Peter Muhlenberg presented Congress with a sober account of the Indian situation at the Falls and beyond. Samuel Hardy, chairman of the Committee of the States, sent it on to Governor Harrison of Virginia, with a covering letter:

Congress previous to their Adjournment appointed Commissioners, gave the necessary instructions and made other arrangements requisite on their part for forming a General Treaty of Peace with the Indians as far Southward as the Cherokees.

But if persons under grants from Virginia are permitted to enter upon and settle the Lands Westward of the Ohio before the Treaty is compleat and a line of property ascertained between the Indians' *Villages and hunting Grounds* and the United States, it seems impossible to avoid an immediate War with those People. . . .

The Committee of the States therefore rely that effectual steps will be immediately taken by the State of Virginia to prevent any settlements being made on Lands not clearly within the former line of property between the State of Virginia and the Indians. . . .[25]

"The Indians," wrote Peter Muhlenberg to Baron Steuben, "shew many signs of discontent, & can not bear the Thought of our Settling on the West side of Ohio, where the most valuable part of our Military land lies. . . ."[26]

Frederick, too, decided to stay in Pennsylvania. His Radical enemies threatened to have him tarred and feathered; but he played out the "farce," as he called it, until the battle with the boys of the back counties was finally won and a new constitution was adopted in Pennsylvania, which restored stability to the state and enabled it to march down the road to prosperity.

CHAPTER XXVII

"CANDIDATUS MORTIS"

There were giants on the earth in those days, and the Muhlenbergs were at home with them. This we must realize when we find the Marquis de Lafayette writing from Paris to ask George Washington to get their friend Peter Muhlenberg to prepare an Indian vocabulary for the Empress of Russia—Catherine the Great.[1]

Henry Melchior Muhlenberg, in his country parsonage at the Trappe, was pleased—but by no means overwhelmed—to receive from his old friend Dr. Wrangel, former pastor at Wicaco, now Court Preacher in Sweden, a letter describing the honors that had come to him since his departure from America.

"I suppose you have heard," wrote Wrangel, "that after my return I have been called to bear the Testimony of the ever Blessed Saviour before a Court and the Great of this World. Instead of riding on horse back, I have been obliged to drive in stately Coaches . . . I keep my Station at Court as great Almoner and Captain to the most Honble Order of Seraphim. . . ."[2]

Henry Melchior shook his old sheep-dog's head. To Wrangel's request for news he had no Order of Seraphim to write about—though he might have said much about Major General Peter Muhlenberg and the Order of the Cincinnati. The news he did send was not all parochial. He told about the Revolution; his own efforts to be neutral; his move, during the "fermentation," from Philadelphia to Providence; the academic revolution whereby "the Presb. politico-Christiani" had driven out Provost Smith, and established in place of the College of Philadelphia the University of Pennsylvania, which proceeded to call his son-in-law, Pastor Kuntze, to the chair of Oriental Languages and German, and which gave George Washington and Henry Melchior Muhlenberg honorary degrees—though, as for himself, he professed to have no more aptitude for the D.D.

"than a donkey has to play the organ." The letters D.D. after his name, he said, could mean no more than *Demutiger Diener*—Humble Servant.

To this letter he signed himself, "H. Mbg. Candidatus Mortis."[3]

Weak in his limbs, hard of hearing, distracted by a buzzing in his ears and a swimming in his head, the Pastor nevertheless managed to keep an interest in the world about him, especially that part of it in which his children were active.

When Christopher Kuntze, weakened in health (not so much by his labors as by the jealousies, vendettas, and almost maniacal spirit of division which persisted in his congregation, especially after Henry Ernest's stormy withdrawal), determined to accept a call to a church in New York, Daddy Muhlenberg was ready with advice. When, in July 1784, the Kuntzes all came up to say good-bye at the Trappe, there was much fluttering about. Polly and Sally came down from New Hanover to see Peggy, and Mr. Kuntze rode off into the country to say good-bye to the Schultzes.

It was a bad time for Henry Melchior, who was attacked by trembling and dizziness, and thought he was going to have a stroke.

"We are not likely to see one another again in this world," he said sadly at the leave-taking.[4]

In St. Michael's and Zion, Kuntze's departure was sufficient to start another confusion. Who was to take Kuntze's place? It must assuredly be someone who could heal the congregation's wounds. Here was the place for the patient, hard-working, generous, and utterly devoted Emanuel Schultze (Betsy's husband) of Tulpehocken. The Philadelphia congregation invited him, and Henry Melchior urged him to accept.

Poor Emanuel Schultze was already too deeply rooted to find it easy to decide. He loved his various country charges. The effort to minister to their needs had worn down his strength, but he loved them as a mother loves her children. And he feared the peculiar responsibilities of a city church. He determined to decline, on grounds of health.[5] The duties, he said, would be too much for his constitution. Besides, he thought privately what a rats' nest the Philadelphia congregation hid within its bosom.

Henry Melchior was disappointed at this decision, and wrote to implore him not to decline. "I beg you, not to turn the call down in the first heat. For God's sake, I beg you."[6]

Frederick sent his brother-in-law, Bernard Schaeffer, with a letter urging Schultze to accept. "God's hand is in it," he said.[7]

When Emanuel Schultze left Tulpehocken, on his way to Philadelphia to talk with the officials of the congregation, he was fully determined to decline their invitation. But before he reached the city, he having meanwhile stopped at the Trappe, something had happened to make him change his mind. God had given him the *Wink*—the sign—he said to the elders; and so, if the congregation was content to put up with his infirmities, he would—unless something unexpected happened—come to them in the month of November.[8]

But between August and November the unexpected did happen. Perhaps Pastor Schultze, or Henry Melchior, had mistaken the *Wink*. Both Emanuel Schultze and Betsy, his wife, were struck down with the *Hitzigen Fieber*—the Hot Fever. Emanuel Schultze's condition was aggravated by an attack of melancholia. The illness was critical and long. The Muhlenberg family held their breath.

Late in September, Henry Ernest came over from Lancaster to Tulpehocken, botanizing on the way, to administer communion to Emanuel. He also prescribed medicine and offered advice. As a medical practitioner, Henry Ernest was, though of the newer generation, in some matters far behind his father. He recommended to his fever-wasted brother-in-law that he should cover himself up more closely and keep his windows shut. When Henry Melchior heard of this, he could not forbear, in a letter to Peter who was then visiting at Tulpehocken, deprecating the old *Deutsche Mode* of keeping fever patients "smothered under heavy covers" and shutting them up in oven-hot rooms without a breath of fresh air.

"The best doctors say a mouthful of fresh air," he wrote, "does a patient more good than a spoonful of medicine."[9]

Month after month Emanuel Schultze's illness dragged on, through the fall, winter, and spring, accompanied by fever, lightheadedness, and toothache—for which latter Henry Melchior prescribed "Blisters."[10] There seemed to be no end. The burden upon Betsy, who had recovered for a time, was somewhat eased by sending the boys Henry and John Andrew (governor-to-be) to board with Polly and enjoy the advantages of being taught English by Mr. Swaine. Who could teach them better? Mr. Swaine's pen had the best flourish in all Pennsylvania, and his tongue the liveliest flow of English idiom.

But, even with this relief, the strain of watching her husband waste away was too much for Betsy Schultze. In the spring of 1785 she had a relapse of the Hot Fever, and the doctor who attended her said she would die.

Life, however, was strong in the Muhlenberg women, and she recovered. So did her husband. But the question of leaving Tulpehocken was settled. Conscientiously, Emanuel Schultze explained to the Philadelphia elders that his long illness had so weakened his body, depressed his spirits, and impaired his memory, that he could no longer think of attempting to serve them. They must look elsewhere.[11]

Then was the voice of Confusion raised in the Philadelphia congregation. It was the Muhlenbergs, so the tongues wagged, who were to blame! If only the Muhlenbergs were out of the way, the waters would not be so muddied.[12]

Worry pressed hard on old Henry Melchior's head. Being now, in his retirement, out of the actual battle line, such unpleasantnesses as the new Confusion brought to his ears were no longer problems to be solved by aggressive action, but perplexities to be brooded over. His old brain was in a whirl, and it grew tired. Besides the St. Michael's and Zion affair, there were so many things to oppress him: his wife's *passio hysterica,* his own debility, the troubles of his seven children and his swarm of grandchildren, the Kuntzes in New York, poor Ebenezer—

"*Ach Gott!*" he cried, "a heavy stone lies upon me, who will lift it off me?"[13]

And then there was science. That Gargantua was already rearing its head in Henry Melchior's century. Progress, as we in this mechanical age understand it, oppressed the good Pastor. Franklin's experiments and the newfangled notions of the American Philosophical Society appalled him.

"Our American Philosophers," he wrote, July 26, 1784, "are now very busy trying to bring balloons and flying machines to perfection."[14]

He was not impressed by the attempt at Philadelphia to send up a balloon filled with hot air. This last was an ingenious contraption: a balloon of silk, filled with air heated by the fire in a stove tended by a man. Unfortunately, in taking off, the balloon hit a wall, the man jumped out, the stove upset, the fire spilled out, and the balloon, half a mile up in the air, burst into flames.

Such attempts to conquer heaven with silk and hot air seemed to the Pastor both impious and silly. It behooved all creatures to remain in the element appointed them by an all-wise Creator: "birds in the air, fish in the water, and cattle and men on the earth."[15] Besides, *cui bono?* What sustenance had the air to offer man?

Of his three sons, now that the achievement of Independence had drawn Peter's rebel neck out of the halter, Frederick gave him the most concern. Frederick himself had cause enough to worry. His finances were getting tangled, and the political situation was deteriorating. The Republicans, after a short period of triumph, were losing ground. Frederick was disillusioned and disgusted. The calling of a convention to amend the Constitution of 1776 seemed farther off than ever.

He wrote to Henry Ernest, June 28, 1784:

> The blind passion and mad party spirit of the common crowd, who, after all, cannot judge for themselves, are so strong and bitter that they would rather put up with three times as many defects of the constitution than with a convention. But is this not a real aristocracy, when a few leaders of the party, by untiring effort manage to withhold from the people, of whom their power is derived, the people's own power? Do they not betray a ridiculous fear that in a convention, based upon equal representation of the people (for such does not exist in Council), the people might alter the Constitution? But the rascals know well enough, if the intelligent people were properly and equitably represented in the convention, that a change would be the consequence and they be unhorsed. . . ."

For a moment, in discussing the principle of representation, he dropped into English. But soon he returned to the tongue he more commonly used when writing to the family. We continue in translation:

> But what am I about? I just thought I was arguing with an Englishman in Lancaster—and I confess on the subject of politics English comes easier to me than German—and here I almost fall into a passion about my countrymen when I think of their dreadful credulity, envy, lack of sense,

and hence their foolish peasant conceit. . . . If I had looked more to my own interest than to theirs, had I danced to their stupid whistling without consulting my judgment and my conscience, I might be a fugleman among them. . . .

Whether we are going to make a new code? I do not think so. They have now the majority. . . .

Eheu! risum teneatis—in brief, the whole thing is a farce, costs the State five thousand or six thousand dollars, keeps the people in a ferment, and is not worth a farthing. I am ashamed to be a member, and if it might not be said, you forsook the vessel in the storm or you are afraid to weather it out, I would have resigned long ere this; perhaps I shall do so yet, for I can neither before God nor the world answer for thus wasting my precious time, robbing the State, and doing only mischief. The fellows from the back counties now hope to stay here till next October, to draw their 17/6, and to return home with well-filled purse; some of them will get at the end of the session more money than they ever had in their life. In short, dear brother, I am losing patience and draw a deep sigh at the corrupt political condition of our State. . . . I am afraid there will be some sorry scenes in Pennsylvania before we learn to govern ourselves. . . .

The letter, however, closes on a more intimate and hopeful note. "But see here, young fellow [*Aber höre Junge*]: I hear your wife is expecting again—how come? [*wie komt das?*] & why were we not officially notified—I would have you know that I am your elder brother. *Vale cum uxore . . . Vale cum tuis*[16]

F."

His own wife was "expecting," too, and she won the race. On Christmas Eve a son, John Peter David, was born to the Frederick Muhlenbergs at the Trappe. Henry Melchior records the event in his Journal: "Now they have 3 sons and 4 daughters."

In the October elections, as Frederick feared, the boys from the back counties swept in to victory. But Frederick had been preparing for just such a rainy day. He had a house, it will be remembered, at the Trappe, and his store there was doing well. In 1784, on the erection of the new county of Montgomery, he was appointed Recorder of Deeds—"Registrator of Wills and Testaments," as his father wrote it in his Journal.[17] On September 28, 1784, he presided, as Justice of the Peace (i.e., judge), at the first court held in the county.

The year 1785 opened auspiciously for Henry Melchior who, though he sometimes found it painful, nevertheless loved to have the noise of the family about him. During the Christmas and New Year season, members of the family were buzzing about the neighborhood in all directions. Peter was at the Trappe with Hannah. There was not enough snow for good sleighing, but Mr. Richards brought a sleigh with two horses down from the Swamp to take "*die Frau Generalin*" and her Negro servant upcountry on the festive runners. Later Peter and Richards and Mr. Swaine went off to see the Schultzes at Tulpehocken. Frederick came back after a visit to New Hanover, bringing a cotton cap from Polly as a New Year's present to her father. Not long after, Polly herself turned up with more presents for the parsonage: five pounds of butter and two candle-snuffers. On the same day "Our General" and his consort came in, as well as Sally, Mr. Richards, and their children.

It was on the twenty-first of this same month of January that Henry Ernest, already known throughout the world of science for his accomplishments in botany, brought another honor to the family. He was elected a member of the American Philosophical Society, along with James Madison and Joseph Priestley.[18]

And it was on this same Friday that Peggy Kuntze in New York wrote one of her brave English letters to Betsy at Tulpehocken.

Newyork Jan the 21
1785

Dear Sister
I hope Mr Shultz and you are quiet well again i was very Sorry to here you both laid Sick at one time but you must think it was the will of the lord his Name be Praised that he Spaired your lives for Sake of your Children You was not forgot in our dayly prayers and are not forget yet

i Shold a wrote long ago to you but i thought you wold have been in Philadelphia before now

i hope you may like to live better in Philadephia then i have these few years past i am Very well Satisfied here & how good it is for a minnister to live alone our income is Smaller than in Phi but what is that if you live without fals Poeple aside of you

a man that is fare to your face and fals behind your back is nothing but a DEVIL

Whe are all well and if you move to Phil in Spring i Shall See you if not i Stay in newyork and you Come to See us Mr Kunze and i remember our kind love to Mr Shultz and you and Children

i remain your Sister
Peggy Kunze[19]

Peter was at this time much interested in the Society of the Cincinnati. He had in May 1783 been elected to preside over the officers of the Virginia Line when they assembed at Fredericksburg before the army disbanded. Popular opposition, meanwhile, had all but killed it. It was said that the order, through its rule of primogeniture, carried within it the seed of a new military aristocracy. From Berkeley, Virginia, on March 27, 1785, General Muhlenberg wrote to General Gates to say that he had been talking with a number of members in Virginia who thought the Society was likely to fall through in that state unless strong efforts were made to revive it. They proposed that a meeting be called at Fredericksburg, and were most solicitous that the President or the Vice-President should attend, "as many object to the gentleman who presided last at Fredericksburg."[20]

Henry Melchior Muhlenberg was slowly mellowing into the Patriarch of the Lutheran Church in America. He was superintending at this time the compilation of a new hymnbook, the *Erbauliche Lieder-Sammlung,* which appeared in 1786—the first hymnbook published by the Ministerium he had founded. He grew milder as he grew reminiscent. The early battles he had fought in Pennsylvania's Holy War now troubled him less. He surveyed his past life with humility, not a little humor, and much satisfaction.

A beautiful letter of his, written March 23, 1785, has been preserved in the great Muhlenberg collection at Mt. Airy. In it the Patriarch offers advice to Henry Ernest, in the guise of some fatherly reminiscence.

> *Oratio, Meditatio et Tentatio faciunt Theologum* [Preaching, Pondering and Practice make the Divine] said B[rother] Lutherus. The sainted Arnd says: "Christ the Lord has many servants but few followers." . . . I too have been only a servant and no true follower. The blessed 24th Count Reus once said: "our Lord Jesus, the head shepherd needs not only under-shepherds, but also sheep-dogs, which must by their barking round up the sheep and goats on the pasture into one flock." . . . I myself have barked these forty years past in America and have brought some little flocks together. . . .[21]

The elections of 1785 brought another Muhlenberg recruit into politics. Peter was elected by Montgomery County to be their representative on Pennsylvania's Supreme Executive Council for a three-year term. The parties were just about evenly divided, but the political trend was definitely back to the middle of the road. Benjamin Franklin, just returned from France, was elected President of the State.

Looking back over his life from "this side the border-line of Eternity," Henry Melchior wrote a long letter, dated September 6, 1785, to his old friends, Eike and Westphal, in Germany.[22] He acknowledged with sadness the news they had sent him of the death of his youngest sister and of his brother Christopher's loss of his sight. Standing, as he said, on the banks of the Jordan, waiting for a merciful crossing, he gave a report on his children—evincing more pride in his sons than his admonitions to them might have led us to expect. Which is a reminder to us that the *real* Henry Melchior Muhlenberg was a better—that is to say, a warmer and more "human" —person than he makes himself out to be when writing or speaking for what in those days was considered to be edification.

The Revolution looms large in the narrative: Peter—chaplain, colonel, general; Frederick—refugee from New York, delegate to Congress, member of the Pennsylvania Assembly, Speaker, Censor, and finally Registrar of Last Wills and Testaments and Justice of the Peace for Montgomery County (Henry Melchior never lost his love of a good title); Henry Ernest—refugee from Philadelphia, now pastor in a large church at Lancaster (nothing said about his Linnaean indiscretions). The daughters came in for good mention: Elisabeth, married for nineteen years to Pastor Emanuel Schultze—eight children still living; Margaret, married to Pastor Christopher Kuntze of New York—four children living; Maria (Polly), married to "a protestant Irishman Francis Swaine," former major, now a storekeeper—one child; Salome, married to Matthias Reichard, saddler—two children. In all, "7 children and 29 grandchildren."

For the benefit of prospective immigrants, he ended on a note of warning. The Revolution was not over yet. Things were still all mixed up. His friends had better not think of coming to America until the "fermentation" had settled.

During the year 1786, it was principally Peter who kept the Muhlenberg name in the public mind. He attended meetings of the Supreme Executive Council and ran for the vice-presidency of Pennsylvania against Charles Biddle. He was beaten by three votes.

Henry Melchior, willing to forget the "vanity" of his boys' careers in consideration of the undoubted good they were accomplishing for their country, looked round him with satisfaction: Philadelphia, Lancaster, Tulpehocken, New Hanover, and New York—everywhere the family was doing well. Even Mr. Swaine managed to look prosperous. He was educating the Schultze boys and teaching John Andrew how to speak and write like a governor.

For the benefit of their father, the Reverend Emanuel Schultze of Tulpehocken, Mr. Swaine flourished a quill and indited an exuberant epistle:

Montgomery Octob^{r} 25th 1786

Dear Sir

By Mr Meyer I have the opportunity to ask how you and Family are, we have been inform'd that Mrs Schultze was unwell but now better, we are glad to here it, may she long continue in perfect health all the Connections here are well, especially Sally Richards, whom I'm inform'd you hear'd was sick— if eating a pound of protwersht is a sign of being indisposed then she certainly is— Andrew is well and beheaves well also— I keep him to his Writing and reading—and alternatly attending the Store in Conjunction with the big Boy and some of the family— When a snow falls sufficient to waft us along in a sleigh you certainly may expect to see us—when I expect you will have a quantum sufficit of Potatoes, & spear Rib with something on them. Mrs Swaine joins me in presenting our Love and best wishes to the Gauntza famülei—not forgiting our well-beloved Cousin Her Bridenbauch &c &c &c————————————

I am Dear Sir

Yours affectionately

Francis Swaine

And^{w} would have wrote a Letter but the time was to short—he therefore through his uncle Swaine, begs his Love and Dutiful respects may be presented to his Papa Mamma, Brothers & Sisters————————[23]

Of all the family, Henry Ernest was, in the eyes of his father, the most successful. He was by now well established in the "large and ancient town of Lancaster," as the Reverend Manasseh Cutler described it—"the best built inland town in America."[24] His church was flourishing. In one year, 1784, as he reported to his father, he had baptized 179, confirmed 72, and buried 48.

Some of his theological views might be a trifle on the broad side, but his main beliefs, as he listed them for his father in a letter of February 7, 1785, were essentially sound: One God; His revelation through the Scriptures and through Nature; the Fall of Man; the Redemption; the Divinity of Jesus of Nazareth; the Forgiveness of Sins; the Resurrection and Life Everlasting.[25]

There was something peculiarly winning about Henry Ernest. The boy defended even his botanical vanities in such terms as seemed to rid them of their secular taint. It was to his botanizing excursions, in the woods and through the fields about Lancaster, that Henry Ernest attributed his present good health—and something more. He told his father in the February 7 letter that, when he walked alone under the open sky, his spirits never failed to be lifted, nor his thoughts to be deepened with the consciousness of the Creator's presence.

> And I have felt
> A presence that disturbs me with the joy
> Of elevated thoughts; a sense sublime
> Of something far more deeply interfused,
> Whose dwelling is the light of setting suns
> And the round ocean and the living air.

In the history of the Muhlenberg family, 1787 was Henry Ernest's year. That was the year in which the dream of the German-speaking inhabitants of Pennsylvania to establish a college of their own took form, and Henry Ernest Muhlenberg, the popular Lancaster pastor and internationally known botanist, was made the first Principal of Franklin College.

It was, of course, to be expected that when Henry Melchior first heard of his son's prospects he should be perturbed. It was his fear that Henry Ernest might go the way of his two other sons, the soldier and the politician, and add a college president to the Hubbub of Vanity Fair. It is only to be regretted that he did not live long enough to see his fears belied.

The charter of the college was granted March 10, 1787. The Muhlenbergs figured prominently among the trustees: the Reverend Dr. Henry Ernest Muhlenberg, Peter Muhlenberg, Esquire, and the Reverend Christopher Emanuel Schultze. Benjamin Franklin, after whom the college was named, though he was not able to attend the laying of the foundation stone at Lancaster on June 6, gave a generous donation of £200 to the institution—by far the largest contribution made by any of the original subscribers.

If 1787 was Henry Ernest's year, June 6 was his day. The address he then delivered was afterward printed by order of the Trustees:

Eine Rede—
An
Address
Delivered the 6th of June 1787
at
the Dedication of the German High
School or Franklin College
in Lancaster
by
Gotthilf Hen. Mühlenberg,
Principal of the College and Pastor of
Holy Trinity Church of that place[26]

It was reported in the Philadelphia press that "The Principal, who . . . is a man of extensive learning and great liberality of sentiment, and who is universally beloved, delivered a judicious and elegant sermon in the German language."[27]

The Fathers at Halle approved. "I am especially pleased that this *Colledge* is called a German High School," wrote Fabricius.[28]

There were, of course, hard times in sight for the young institution. "We have agreed," wrote Principal Muhlenberg, to begin instructing students in the "Brewhouse."[29]

But with a son of the Patriarch Muhlenberg and a brother of the hero of Brandywine at the head, the institution could hardly fail. Foundations were laid solidly for the later distinguished career of the Franklin and Marshall College of a later generation.

Fabricius and the Directors at Halle, in their letter of congratulations, December 1, 1787,[30] sent their "respectful love" to Henry Ernest's "dear father," but the greeting was not received in this world. Henry Melchior Muhlenberg had uttered his last sigh on October 7.

His health had for many years been failing—ever since 1760, as he believed. He tells us with some exactness the circumstances under which he first became afflicted with his complaint and the means he employed for its cure, though he is vague enough about the diagnosis. It all began at the funeral of Conrad Weiser.

. . . on a journey to Jersey in March 1760, I caught cold in my back when I became wet. When this condition persisted stubbornly, the physicians recommended that plasters of Spanish fly be applied in the month of July. A plaster had hardly been applied when the news came unexpectedly of my father-in-law's death, and I was obliged to attend the funeral. In this hot season I spent three days traveling up and back without having opportunity to take care of the plaster and a mortification resulted. Although this was later healed, ever since that time I have had to be bled several times a year.[31]

Among the various ailments that afflicted him during his last years, dropsy had shown its premonitory symptoms some years earlier. Having studied medicine at Halle and distributed Halle medicines all through his American career, he watched his own symptoms with interest. He knew when the end approached.

Polly and Sally from New Hanover and Betsy from Tulpehocken went together to the Trappe to see him.

". . . he is very Sick," wrote Betsy to her husband. "I do believe he will not get over he has the gravl and the fevor he wold be very glad to see you once more . . . will you pleas to send daddy a glass of Saltz tingtur he hops it will do him good so pleas to write to daddy he cant Stand alone I told him you wold write . . ."[32]

When the Reverend John L. Voigt (whose offer of marriage Betsy Muhlenberg had declined more than twenty years before) came in to see him on September 29, and congratulated his old friend on his apparent improvement in health, Muhlenberg shook his head and said that "they were not likely to meet again in this world."[33]

He recited some lines from Boehme's hymn:

> A heavy road before me lies
> Up to the heavenly paradise.

Next day the expected symptoms developed, and it became known that he could not live. For a week he suffered intense pain, without sleep. His mind remained clear and his senses acute. Strangely, near the end his hearing returned.

He sat up till the last. Even on the night of his death, he would not go to bed until it was time for the last good night. His strong sense of order, his insistence on keeping times appointed, remained with him to the end.

"He expected to die at midnight," writes William J. Mann, "and inquired whether it were not yet twelve o'clock. At his request two of his children took him to bed."[34]

There he recited part of Paul Gerhart's hymn:

Haste, Lord, to end our sorrow . . .

He died between twelve and one o'clock on Sunday morning, October 7, 1787, at the age of seventy-six.

The funeral was held on October 10. Prayer was offered at the house by Dr. Helmuth, who had succeeded Kuntze in Philadelphia.

So many people came for the service in Augustus Church that they could not all be gathered indoors, and the funeral address had to be delivered "under the open sky"—where Muhlenberg himself had preached at Providence on January 16, 1743.

Mr. Voigt spoke on Psalm 15.1-2:

> Lord, who shall abide in thy tabernacle? who shall dwell in thy holy hill?
> He that walketh uprightly, and worketh righteousness, and speaketh the truth in his heart.

The woods were less dense than they had been in 1743. But there was still an echo.

CHAPTER XXVIII

MR. SPEAKER

There was something clean-cut and decisive about the American Revolution. There was bitterness while it was in progress and wreckage after it was over; but it did not leave behind it, as most revolutions do, a sputtering train of counterrevolutions and civil wars.

The success of American arms had been surprising. Still more surprising was the rapid settling down afterward—the speed and sureness with which reconstruction followed the dislocations of civil war. This was due to many causes, among others, these: the wisdom of the framers of the Federal Constitution, and the steadiness of the men who first administered it.

What America needed after 1787 was a few quiet years to enable the Constitution to find itself, and to give the public time to develop the habit of accepting it, of taking it for granted. Men were needed who could serve in Congress as checks on the extravagances of such leaders as Hamilton and Jefferson.

The two Muhlenbergs were political balance wheels. They both felt the need of a strong central government, and at the same time they recognized the rights of man. They believed in Jeffersonian democracy—with such qualifications as came natural to good Lutherans brought up with a wholesome heed of Original Sin.

The Muhlenbergs in politics were not crusaders. At the same time they had no phobias. They were plain good men, who took each day as it came, passed judgment on policies as they arose, and by their sane common sense and wholesomeness of outlook provided the stabilizing influence the country needed.

Neither Peter nor Frederick was a member of the Constitutional Convention. In such a gathering of political philosophers, they were not fitted to make their best contribution. Their part was called for a little later when, the general principles on which the American government was to rest having been determined, it became a matter of prime importance, first, to convince the public of the soundness of these principles, and second, to put them into operation.

When the great debates in the State House in Philadelphia were ended, and on Monday, September 17, 1787, as Washington noted in his diary, "the Constitution received the unanimous vote of 11 States and Colonel Hamilton's from New York," the practical work of securing ratification, state by state, still remained to be done.

Both Peter and Frederick in Pennsylvania exerted themselves for ratification. The election of delegates to the ratifying convention gave the Federalists a great majority. When the Pennsylvania convention for ratification assembled in November, Frederick was elected president. The Constitution was adopted, December 12, by a vote of 46 to 23;[1] and on December 15 "Frederick Augustus Muhlenberg, President of the Convention of Pennsylvania," in a letter to the President of Congress, transmitted Pennsylvania's ratification of the Constitution.[2]

In the absence of any letters from Mr. Swaine on the subject, Charles Biddle's *Autobiography* may be resorted to for a colorful picture of the celebration held on July 4, 1788, in honor of the new Constitution. It seemed as if the Glorious (but backward-looking) Fourth were destined to give way to the More Glorious (because forward-looking) Seventeenth.

> There was a grand Federal procession [wrote Biddle] in which all classes of citizens joined. In the front there were twelve axemen, dressed in white frocks; second, the First City Troops; third, the Cap of Liberty, carried by John Nixon, Esquire; . . . tenth, Richard Bache, as a herald, proclaiming a "New Era;" eleventh, *General Muhlenberg carrying a blue flag with "Seventeenth of September, 1787," in silver letters;* twelfth, a band of excellent music; . . . boatbuilders, sailmakers, . . . merchants and traders . . . Cordwainers, coachpainters, cabinet and chairmakers, brickmakers, house, ship, and sign painters, porters, clock and watchmakers . . . bricklayers, tailors, instrument makers, turners, windsor chairmakers . . . distillers, tobacconists . . . sugar refiners . . . engravers . . . plasterers . . . Supreme Executive Council . . . justices of the Court of Common Pleas, and the magistrates . . . constables . . . watchmen . . . gentlemen of the bar . . . clergy . . . physicians . . . eighty-seventh, students of the university; eighty-eighth, County Troops, brought up the rear.[3]

Meanwhile, in the fall of 1787, Peter Muhlenberg had been elected Vice-President of Pennsylvania, in which capacity it was that he carried the flag of the future in the great constitutional procession described by Biddle.

Since the President of Pennsylvania, Benjamin Franklin, was in declining health, much of his official duties fell upon Peter Muhlenberg. It is Muhlenberg's signature we find upon state documents relating to the Erie Triangle, the Hessian Fly, and the unhappy Wyoming controversy—which, springing from an original injustice to the Indians, was now finding a solution (as Conrad Weiser had foretold) through the blood and sweat of white men.

At the first election under the Constitution, November 26, 1788, both Frederick and Peter Muhlenberg were chosen for the national House of Representatives, Frederick receiving the highest number of votes given to any candidate from Pennsylvania.[4] The brothers ran on opposite tickets, but they both had the same end in view. Frederick, a true Federalist in his support of the Constitution, was resolved at all costs to defend the rights of man. Peter, a true Antifederalist in his support of the rights of man, was resolved at all costs to defend the Constitution.

Early in March, 1789, Peter and Frederick left Philadelphia together and traveled to New York, where they arrived on the morning of March 4, and took up residence with Peggy and the Kuntzes in Chatham Row.

We today look back with reverence on those fortune-favored persons who had a part in the beginnings of the great legislative body which now sits on Capitol Hill and draws to its halls the political business of half the world. But it must be confessed that Peter and Frederick Muhlenberg did not look round them with awe. There was no Statue of Liberty in the harbor to remind them of the significance of the experiment in democratic government they were about to launch, and the circumstances under which Congress assembled were dull, dismal, and inauspicious.

For one thing, the reconstructed Old City Hall (on Wall Street, at the head of Broad), which under the new name Federal Hall was to serve as the home of Congress was, as Frederick wrote, March 5, to Dr. Benjamin Rush, "not nearly finished."

Charles Pierre L'Enfant, a French engineer who had served as an officer in the Revolutionary army, was responsible for the remodeling. It was he who later made the plans for the city of Washington, D. C.

"The Building," wrote Frederick, "is really elegant & well designed —for a Trap—but I still hope, however well contrived we shall find Room to get out of it."[5]

Another inauspicious circumstance was the lack of a quorum on March 4. "Of the Senate 8, & of the Representatives 13 Members appeared," wrote Frederick on March 5. Day after day the Muhlenbergs waited for business to begin, but the quorum was like the sea serpent, a thing heard of but never seen.

"By the last Account from Albany no Senators had been appointed —some think none will be—"[6]

It seemed as if the Constitution might be stillborn after all. Even by the eighteenth of March, Peter found little immediate prospect of "making a house." But the numbers were at least sufficient for a lobby.

"The subject most canvassed," wrote Peter to Benjamin Rush, "is the permanent Seat of Congress"[7]—a subject that was to engross the best brains of New York, Philadelphia, the Falls of the Delaware, Lancaster, and Georgetown for months to come until at last the happy solution was hit upon of fixing the temporary seat at Philadelphia and the permanent seat on the Potomac.

There was another subject that touched Frederick more closely.

"My friends here," he wrote to Rush, "who indeed entertain a much better Opinion of my Abilities than I deserve think of me as a Candidate for the Speakers Chair. . . . the Thought of it makes me tremble. . . ."[8]

The period of waiting in the anteroom, so to speak, during Congress's difficult birth, filled Peter with foreboding. He wrote to Benjamin Rush:

Newyork April 2d 1789.

Dear Sir

I am honored with Your favor of the 21st of March, and should have acknowledg'd it sooner had any thing worthy of Comunication offered; but until yesterday, we have been laying on our Oars; and were unable to proceed to business, for want of a sufficient Number of Members to form a House— That four Weeks should elapse, from the time appointed for the first Meeting of Congress without doing any Thing, does not Augur much in our favor; The great Loss the United States will unavoidably sustain, thro' this neglect, as well as other considerations, occasioned a great clamor not only among the Citizens, but with many of the Members present—yesterday a bare Majority of the Members attended, and took their Seats— The House imediately proceeded to the choice of Their Speaker and elected Fred. A. Muhlenberg—[9]

Henry Wynkoop, in a letter to Dr. Reading Beattie, observed that, although "the competitor of Mr. Mughlenberg was Col. Trumbul from Connecticut, a gentleman well known for his singular Merrit & Respectability," the majority which "preponderated . . . in favour of Mr. Mughlenberg was very considerable."[10]

The Speaker was "conducted to his chair," as we read in the *Debates . . . in the Congress of the U. S.* "from whence he made acknowledgments to the House for so distinguished an honor."[11]

The election of Frederick Muhlenberg was not simply a compliment to the Pennsylvania Germans. His personal qualities fitted him for the post. He was a middle-of-the-road man, friendly, yet detached in his judgments, honest, scrupulous, fair—a man debaters and lawmakers could instinctively trust.

The inauguration of George Washington as President, on April 30, at last brought color into the congressional scene, and with it the dignity and the sense of significance that had hitherto been so sadly missing.

On the balcony of Federal Hall, standing before a great multitude, Washington took the oath of office. Then, withdrawing to the Senate Chamber, he delivered his First Inaugural Address.

He spoke of "the great constitutional charter" under which they were assembled, and of the principles which should inspire them:

that as, on one side, no local prejudices or attachments, no separate views nor party animosities, will misdirect the comprehensive and equal eye which ought to watch over this great assemblage of communities and interests—so, on another, that the foundations of our national policy will be laid in the pure and immutable principles of private morality; and the preeminence of a free government be exemplified by all the attributes which can win the affections of its citizens and command the respect of the world.

I dwell on this prospect with every satisfaction which an ardent love for my country can inspire; since . . . the preservation of the sacred fire of liberty, and the destiny of the republican model of government, are

FREDERICK AUGUSTUS CONRAD MUHLENBERG

justly considered as deeply, perhaps as finally staked, on the experiment intrusted to the hands of the American people.

After the address, as the *Pennsylvania Packet* of May 4 reports, "His Excellency accompanied by the Vice President, the Speaker of the House of Representatives and both Houses of Congress went to St. Paul's Chapel where divine Service was performed by Right Reverend Dr. Provost, Bishop of the Episcopal Church in this State and Chaplain in Congress."

In the evening, there was "a very ingenious and splendid show of Fireworks."

Before the inauguration there had been much discussion about the form of address that should be attached to the President's office, and much fur flew over the question whether the incumbent should be called Excellency, Highness, or what not. There is a story that Peter Muhlenberg displeased Washington himself with his outspoken scorn of such fripperies.

At a dinner to which Washington had invited him, Peter Muhlenberg is said to have found himself seated beside the tall Henry Wynkoop and opposite the short and tubby John Adams. The question of the title coming up, Washington, so the story runs, expressed his approval of "High Mightiness," and asked Peter Muhlenberg what he thought of it.

"Why, General," replied Peter, "if we were certain that the office would always be held by men as large as yourself or my friend Mr. Wynkoop, it would be appropriate enough; but if by chance a president as small as my opposite neighbor should be elected, it would become ridiculous."[12]

Whatever doubt there may be about attributing to a dinner-table conversation the expression of these sentiments, there is no doubt at all that Peter entertained them. They are recorded in a letter of his to Benjamin Rush, dated April 20, 1789:

> . . . with the Titles proposed for the President I am still less pleased– from appearances I think "Highness," bids fair for a Majority– I should have no objection to apply it to our worthy Friend Weynkoop, but in this case it will not apply–in short–I wish for no titles, but such as are fairly derivd from the Constitution; and in this instance we might establish a precedent, and annex a title to the Presidency which would perhaps not apply, with the Successors of General Washington–[13]

There was long bickering over the matter, the members of the House, as Peter Muhlenberg reported, May 11, to Rush, thinking that there should be no title at all but plain "Mr.," and the Senate standing out for some such thing as "His elective Highness—President & Protector of the Rights & Liberties &c."

Frederick Muhlenberg dubbed his friend Senator Maclay "Your Highness of the Senate."[14]

But a certain disillusionment with Congress (an affliction, then as now, quite as prevalent among congressmen themselves as among the members of their constituencies) did not at all depress the high spirits of the Muhlenberg clan.

Peter found time to write a whimsical letter to his young niece of fifteen, who was enjoying the whirl of society in Philadelphia.

New York Sept[r] 10th 1789.

To you My Dear Maria, I confess myself under great obligations—To receive a letter from you wrote in Philadelphia—surrounded by Belles and Beaux—amidst all the bustle inspired by paying, & receiving visits—To receive a letter from you, at such a time, and under such circumstances, requires, & merits, my warmest thanks— But notwithstanding this fair outset I am not entirely pleasd with the beginning of your Letter, You set out with telling me; That tho' I have not the first place in Your Heart—why what a little Hypocrite you are; dont I know better! I presume that part, of your Letter was dictated by prudence and caution, lest the Speaker, or Cam̄en should find us out—but you need be under no apprehensions— I wont tell, indeed I wont—you may therefore in your next safely give me the first place in your Heart.— That you are pleasd with Philad[a] and its environs—is what I expected from a Lady of your discernment and taste, and therefore I am not surprised at the encomiums you bestow on Grays Ferry &c &c. Quite as little was I surprisd to read the Account you give of Madam Bohlen & Miss Lang

I knew poor Child, you would meet with great difficulties, in trying to keep them in order, all I dread, is that you will be carried away with the Stream, and returnd to us, quite changd so that when you return, it will be so difficult perhaps for me, to put in a Word as when Madam Bohlen was here— You know Dear Maria, that I am a little, tho' not much older than You are, & therefore I am entitled to give advice, and I presume You are old enough to refuse advice, if it does not happen to suit You—but Hey day, where am I running to— I absolutely forgot, you was under the care of Madam Bohlen—nevertheless I would advise you to Church on Sundays, unless you have a Cold—to read good Books, such as you usd to read at Home—to refrain from playing Cards—& Whip up Stopye that is to say if You choose, but if You will Play I desire there may be no kissing Mam̄a Oswald bears the temporary loss of Her Girls like a Heroine. I believe You need not hurry on that account. poor Cam̄en seems to fall away— I hope it may not prove that He is in a decline— We still meet at the old rendezvous; but Oh how changd—

I hope Miss Will is equally well pleasd with the trip to Philad[a] She gave me but one parting Kiss I think— The other she stands chargd with

I expect neither of You will enter into a combination to withdraw yourselves from the Allegiance, due to Your Friends, & NewYork, & to remain in Philad But if you do, pray let me in the Secret, & I will assist all I can.— Your Friends are all well but Mam̄a Oswald writes Herself— with my best wishes for Your Health & Happiness

I remain very sincerely
your Friend & humble Servant
P: Muhlenberg

If Miss Will should wish to have any Billetdoux delivered here, if she will enclose them to me she may depend on their being delivered with secrecy & dispatch—& she may pay me with Kisses for my trouble, when she returns—[15]

The Muhlenbergs were not so conspicuous in the Second Congress, which convened on October 24, 1791. Peter was defeated at the election on October 11 by Israel Jacobs, a Quaker; and Frederick, though a member, was not elected Speaker.

But their total record in Congress was remarkable. Frederick was a member of the House in the first four congresses, and Speaker in the First and Third. Peter was a member of the House in the First, Third, and Sixth Congress, and he was elected to the Senate in the Seventh Congress—though he resigned before it convened in regular session. Between the two of them, they kept a Muhlenberg almost continuously in Congress from 1789 to 1801. The schedule is as follows:

First Congress (March 4, 1789–March 3, 1791)
Frederick A. Muhlenberg, Speaker
Peter Muhlenberg

Second Congress (October 24, 1791–March 2, 1793)
Frederick A. Muhlenberg

Third Congress (December 2, 1793–March 3, 1795)
Frederick A. Muhlenberg, Speaker
Peter Muhlenberg

Fourth Congress (December 7, 1795–March 3, 1797)
Frederick A. Muhlenberg
Fifth Congress (May 15, 1797–March 3, 1799)
Sixth Congress (December 2, 1799–March 3, 1801)
Peter Muhlenberg
Seventh Congress
Peter Muhlenberg elected to the Senate; attended special session, March 4-5, 1801; resigned before the first regular session opened on December 7, 1801.

In one important particular, Peter Muhlenberg had a remarkable, indeed a perfect, record, and one which his more voluble brother could not emulate. He never made a speech in Congress. There is no record of one in all his career.

It was during his second term in Congress, in the year 1792, that Frederick Muhlenberg, without *malice prepense*, opened up the Reynolds affair, to the very great embarrassment of Alexander Hamilton on whose career it turned out to have been the most serious stain. It came about in this way.

A certain Mr. Clingman, clerk in Frederick's employment, found himself involved "in a prosecution," as Frederick expressed it, "commenced against James Reynolds, by the Comptroller of the Treasury."[16] Clingman applied to Frederick Muhlenberg for aid, and the latter visited him in prison. Since Clingman had formerly had a good record, and was now repentant and ready to make restitution, Muhlenberg consented to speak for him; and, accordingly, in company with Colonel Aaron Burr, called on Colonel Hamilton, Secretary of the Treasury, on Clingman's behalf. Hamilton was willing to do for the man all that was consistent with his own position.

But, while negotiations were going on, and Muhlenberg repeated his visits to the prison, Clingman hinted broadly that Reynolds, his partner in peculation, had information of the most serious public concern against Hamilton.

"I paid little or no attention to these hints," wrote Muhlenberg, December 13, 1792, "but when they were frequently repeated, and it was even added that Reynolds said he had it in his power to hang the Secretary of the Treasury, that he was deeply concerned in speculation, that he had frequently advanced money to him

(Reynolds), and other insinuations of an improper nature, it created considerable uneasiness on my mind, and I conceived it my duty to consult with some friends on the subject. Mr. Monroe and Mr. Venable were informed of it yesterday morning."[17]

Interviews with Mr. Reynolds in prison and Mrs. Reynolds in her home disclosed certain letters purportedly written by Hamilton to Reynolds. Armed with these, Muhlenberg, James Monroe, and Abraham Venable called on Colonel Hamilton, December 15, to ask for an explanation.

In a storm of anger and humiliation, Hamilton defended his public honor as a financier by telling the truth about his private life. Letters and money had been sent, as it appeared, not to Reynolds but to his wife, with whom Hamilton had been tricked into an intrigue. It was evident that the great Federalist had been caught in a dirty, old-fashioned frame-up.

Muhlenberg, Monroe, and Venable expressed themselves as satisfied. It was agreed that the matter should be dropped: that the papers should not, as originally planned, be laid before the President of the United States; and that, for the protection of Hamilton, the letters should not be returned to the Reynoldses. As far as Muhlenberg was concerned, that was the end of the matter. He had no hand in what followed.

Monroe took the letters and sent them, for supposed safekeeping, to "a respectable character" in Virginia. The latter, after four years, allowed them to be published at a crucial time, and forced on Alexander Hamilton a public confession of the blot on his private life, in order to protect his reputation as a patriot.

Hamilton's writing of the so-called "Reynolds Pamphlet" is a far cry from his storming of the redoubt at Yorktown. There is no evidence that the Muhlenbergs had anything whatever to do with the intrigue that induced publication of the pamphlet. But it is nevertheless an interesting fact that the injured party in the first case (Yorktown) was a brother of the accuser in the second. "The whirligig of time brings his revenges."

It is pleasant, after this unsavory episode, to turn to the homely correspondence of Polly and Mr. Swaine, who had more agreeable things on their minds than the smearing of a great, though unamiable, man.

We shall first present a letter from Polly to Betsy.

october the 26

dear Sister

I think you must get tired of my writing for Every week or tow I write and you ar to lasy to answer one letter I shold of rote by Ant But I was tu Bussy, I will tel you Mrs McCape arrivt She wants P. F and Swaine to set her up with a store in Numans toune only a fue-artickels such as sugar tea Coff Chock, pepper rume wine . . .

god nose had we only a nufe for our selfes I shold bee thank full in theas hard times I think, if she was to spin & sow Nit and such like She Cold make More by it than Store kepping I think. She walks tu slow and smoks to much to kepp shop you no if a Boddy smocks and shold happen to have pouder in the shop it wold bee very deangres But she says see dus not want it for Nothing she will pay Entres . . . Mammy gaves her love to Mr Shulth and your self & all the Children I am your evry lovg Sister Mary Swain.[18]

Late in the year 1792 Mr. Swaine sent a bill to Betsy Schultze on account of her children, who had been staying with him for schooling. The items included such things as Henry's share of firewood; paper, ribbons, soap, plated buckles, calico, mohair, plush, Persian, muslin, linen, velvet, nankeen, fustian, handkerchiefs, tea, hats, and coats; stockings for Peggy, shoes for Henry, and brushes and a jacket for Andrew.

With the bill he sent greetings and a flourish of family news:

. . . with my Store, Farm and Magistrates Office, I have enough to attend to. . . . You may tell Mr Shultze, that I do not take less than half a Guinea to Marry a Couple— Fredk August. Conrad & Hans Peter Gabriel are both in Congress— Fredk left here Yesterday for Home—Eliza Kuntze started for New York on Monday last—all friends are well here, except Mrs Swaine who has sore Eyes, which is the reason she dont Write to You by this Opportunity—[19]

Frederick Muhlenberg ran for governor on the Federalist ticket in 1793, against Thomas Mifflin, Pennsylvania's first governor, who was up for reëlection. Frederick was soundly defeated.

His most important contribution to American history came several years later, in connection with the Jay Treaty.

President Washington, in 1794, had named John Jay envoy extraordinary to negotiate a treaty intended to settle certain differences outstanding with England—in a word, to clean up the litter left by the Revolution. Jay signed such a treaty in London with Lord Grenville on November 19.

In America, ratification of Jay's Treaty by the Senate evoked a fury of Toryphobia, and mobs threatened violence to those who had supported it. Whether it should ever be put into effect became a public question. When a resolution was offered in the House of Representatives for the necessary appropriations, there was fierce opposition.

The House resolved itself into Committee of the Whole, Frederick Muhlenberg (no longer speaker) in the chair. There was a warm debate on the resolution, which was this: "That it is expedient to make the necessary appropriations for carrying the Treaty with Great Britain into effect."

At its conclusion, the House divided, forty-nine for and forty-nine against.

It remained for Frederick Muhlenberg, as chairman, to give the casting vote.

"The chairman, after some little hesitation," so runs the report in the *Gazette of the United States* on the following day, April 30, 1796, "said,

"He was not altogether satisfied with the form of the resolution: but as he supposed it would undergo further discussion when it came before the house and perhaps some modification of it might take place, he should give his vote in favor of it.

"The question was accordingly carried."

When it came before the House, May 2, it passed, fifty-one for, forty-eight against.[20]

It was a brave and patriotic action Frederick Muhlenberg had taken. For the sake of peace, which his country desperately needed, he had by his vote made the treaty with England effective. But, while the country as a whole was in favor of this action, the most vociferous elements in it were not, and they proceeded to go into a frenzy. Muhlenberg knew, when he cast the deciding vote, that he was risking his political career and perhaps even his life. Better that than risk the future of his country.

His fears were not groundless. The political bosses turned against him, and he was never again elected to Congress. Not only that, but on May 4, two days after the House had voted to implement the treaty, he was murderously assaulted and stabbed by his brother-in-law, Bernard Schaeffer.

The Schaeffer connection had long been an anxiety to Frederick Muhlenberg. His father-in-law, David Schaeffer of Second Street, Philadelphia, was a man of substance and respectability: a sugar merchant and a prominent official in the Lutheran Church. But two of David Schaeffer's sons, John and his younger brother Bernard, were of a different caliber. Bernard seems to have been a good church member but nervously unbalanced, while John apparently knew no more about his father's religion or the Augsburg Confession than was comprised in that part of it which pertains to Original Sin.

Attempting to make a fortune in France, during the summer of 1781, in a manner that seemed to the French authorities (and to Benjamin Franklin, whom John Schaeffer tried to impose on) to be quite beyond the permitted freedoms of American democracy, John Schaeffer was allowed for some time to cool his heels in the Grand Châtelet. All that the family knew for a long time was that he had gone to France and disappeared.[21] Returning after a few years to Pennsylvania, he plunged into excesses that made them all long for his further disappearance.

To Frederick, with a political career in the balance, the exploits of his wife's brother were an agony.

"I shall set off for the City in a Day or two," wrote Frederick to Emanuel Schultze, January 11, 1788, "as my unfortunate Brother in Law John has again fallen into dreadful Excesses, which I fear will end in Shame & perhaps disgraceful Death. My heart bleeds at the thought—& I feel all the Horrors of his Situation. He is now in Jail—his Trial for Life will come on in a few Days, and I dread the Issue. He has brought infamy & Disgrace on the Shaffer Family—which even spreads its baneful Effects on me—tho' no honest Man can or will blame me for the Faults of a wicked and undone Brother in Law.—"[22]

In the Supreme Court Records (Oyer and Terminer Docket, February 15, 1788), we find the jury's favorable verdict recorded: "that John Shaffer is not guilty of the felony & Rape."[23] But we find also in the same record the court's less favorable sentence: that John Schaeffer "discharge the costs of Prosecution" and give security himself in one thousand pounds and one or more other securities in five hundred pounds, "for his good behaviour." And it is noted also that he is freed on condition "that he keep the peace &c. for three years."

It is easy to understand how Bernard Schaeffer, possessing something of his brother's instability of temperament, should break under the pressure of popular excitement over the Jay Treaty and try to kill the man who had cast the deciding vote in its favor. Two days after this escapade, he stabbed Constable West in the act of arresting him.

During the December term of the Supreme Court, 1796, as the records of "Respublica v. Barnet Shafer" inform us, the said Bernard Schaeffer was charged with assault and battery on "F. Muhlenberg," and was, after trial, given a heavy sentence: to "be imprisoned one year from this day in the Gaol of the County of Philadelphia pay a fine of one hundred dollars to the Commonwealth give Security himself in one thousand dollars and one good Surety in five hundred dollars to the Common wealth for his good behaviour for Seven Years from this time pay the Costs of prosecution and be in the mean time committed to the Sheriffs Custody."[24]

Frederick recovered from his wound. But Bernard Schaeffer had the satisfaction of knowing that, after the term of the Fourth Congress had ended, Frederick Muhlenberg was never again elected.

The Jay Treaty, if Muhlenberg family tradition may be trusted, brought more than just honorable wounds to Frederick. It also brought him a daughter-in-law and a famous grandson.

The story, as this same grandson, Dr. William Augustus Muhlenberg (of St. Johnland, Long Island), used to tell it,[25] is to this effect: In 1795, while Frederick was still Speaker, his son Henry was courting Mary, daughter of William Sheaff, a well-known Philadelphia merchant. William Sheaff was a Federalist and strongly in favor of legislation to carry out the terms of the Jay Treaty. Disturbed at the strength of the opposition to such legislation in the House of Representatives, and realizing that, in the event of a tie, the fate of the country would rest with the Speaker's casting vote, he delivered Frederick Muhlenberg an ultimatum: "If you do not give us [the Federalists] your vote, your son shall not have my Polly."

Finding that Frederick's sentiments on the subject of the treaty were sound (as the final crisis a few months later gave opportunity to demonstrate), Sheaff consented to the marriage.

Dr. William Augustus Muhlenberg, whose very existence had thus been contingent upon Frederick Muhlenberg's proper attitude to the Jay Treaty, used to wind up the story with words which though they may contain a slight anachronism provide, nevertheless, the happiest of endings: "But the vote went the right way, peace was secured, and here I am."

As the years passed, Frederick grew very stout, and the politician tended to settle down quietly into the businessman and civil servant. On January 8, 1800, Governor McKean appointed him Receiver General of the Land Office of the Commonwealth of Pennsylvania, and he moved to Lancaster, where the state government was at that time.

Peter, on the other hand, never lost his activity. In 1797 he went west to explore his lands, as he said, on the Scioto. To his friend, Colonel W. Sargent in Cincinnati, he wrote, August 8, from "Chillicotha": "I find the best part of my lands are in the vicinity of this place—I am pleased with them and if I can persuade my Ribb to accompany me I am allmost inclined to become a Settler here."[26]

Peter still loved rod and gun better than books and politics. Into a letter addressed to his old Virginia companion, Taverner Beale, he packed all we need to know about him and his family at the turn of the century.

Montgomery, Feb'y 4th, 1799.

My dear Sir:

. . . You may easily conceive that not having heard from you for a considerable length of time, the sight of a letter from you would give me pleasure, but this pleasure is doubled when I read your description of Situation &c. Shadd—Rock—Pike—Trout—Deer—Cyder & Brandy—'tis very well. But have you somebody—or anybody to assist you in catching the fish—or tapping the Cyder! as to Deer, I remember you could hardly kill one in Shenanndoa when you were young, & spry, & therefore I conjecture they are in no great Danger from you at the present time. This accounts for your wishing to have me alongside of you. You know (though you would never own it) that I am a better marksman than you are, and as to fishing you never disputed the pre-eminence with me. Your plan therefore certainly is that I shall head the Hunting and Fishing Department and leave the Government of the Cellar to you.

What an idea! What an excellent Group in prospective! Can it be realized? I believe not—for I just now call to mind that the Pike in the Ohio are much larger than those with you—and tho' the pike in Jackson's River are larger than those in Perkiomen, still they are not so sweet.

But before I fill my paper let me say a word or two relative to Family affairs. I am not in the present Congress, but a Member of Congress Elect. Next October the time of Governor Mifflin expires, and a new Governor is to be chosen. I am strongly solicited by the Republican, as well as German party, to declare myself a Candidate. But I cannot get my own consent, and I would rather resign my seat in Congress, than step one inch further in the way of promotion. Perhaps I am growing old—perhaps my nerves are weak. But I think I can without a Spirit of Divination foresee troublesome times when "The Post of Honor is a private Station."

With regard to politics I shall say nothing—not that I am afraid anything should slip from my pen, that would subject me to the penalties of The Sedition Laws. But because it would require volumes to make only an abridgment. I shall only say the Old Tories are singing Hallelujah, and the old Proverb is fast verifying, Every Dog has his day.

I still live at the Trapp in the house my father lived when you were here. Mr. Swaine lives in the first house below me where Colo. Patton lived. He keeps store and is a Magistrate. He and his Wife are both very well. But they have had the misfortune to lose all their Children and no probability of retrieving the loss.

My family consists of my Wife and myself, Harry, Hetty, Peter, Mary Ann, and Frank.

Harry is still one of the Senior Lieutenants in the Corps of Artillery, and for the present stationed at West Point. Hetty has for six years past been, and still remains with her Grandmother in Philada. The other three are with me. As to my future prospects I have already hinted, that I am heartily tired of Politics. I have 10,000 acres of most excellent land on the Sciota. I have been there twice, & there I wish to spend the remainder of my days, only a few considerations prevent my moving this Spring. My mother is still living and protests. My mother in law is also living and as my wife is the only remaining child she has, she joins the protest agt the separation, tho' neither want my assistance, my mother in law particularly, as she has the whole estate in hand, and adds to it considerably every year. My wife joins in affectionate & respectful compliments to Mrs. Beale & the family.

I am, Dear Sir

Yours Sincerely
P. Muhlenberg[27]

Though Peter said he was tired of politics, his star was actually rising. He declined, in the spring of 1799, to be nominated for governor, but he was appointed to the committee which was to manage the Republican campaign for Thomas McKean whose success must be attributed in some measure to Peter's popularity with the electorate.

Someone in the public press called Peter Muhlenberg "the Moses of the German Israelites."

Mr. Swaine, meantime, in a smaller way, had been doing very nicely for himself. On October 12, 1798, he received a militia commission and became captain of a light infantry company attached to the First Regiment[28]—a position which he later (with some assistance from Major General Muhlenberg) nursed into a brigadier generalship. Swaine was also in the service of Montgomery County, being commissioned, January 6, 1800, Prothonotary of the Court of Common Pleas,[29] and Clerk of various courts: Quarter Sessions, the Orphans Court, and the Courts of Oyer and Terminer and Jail Delivery.

Of Frederick's quiet life in Lancaster, and the happy family relationships which he, now a grandfather, superintended, no more delightful picture could be given than that contained in a letter to his daughter Betsy, concerning Kit (his daughter Mary Catharine, who married John S. Hiester, the only son of Governor Joseph Hiester of Pennsylvania).

Lancaster June 7th 1800.

My dear Betsy
I am to tell you, as a very great Secret, that—but stop now before you read any more, and promise me that you will not tell anybody a Word of it—well I think I heard you say Yes pappy—with a Smile—well then, under this Belief I will tell you the very great Secret—why it is—it is—I have really almost forgot it my self———Let me see—it is—oh! I suppose you know it already—for young people you know must be tattling—and I remember once to have read a Book on that Subiect, & Dr Hurt who is sitting aside of me grunting, says young folks cannot keep a Secret—Aye the Secret—why it is nothing more nor less, than that Dr Hurt told the Girls to Day he was 59 Years old & he actually has lost one of his fore Teeth— Now there you have the Secret, but not the one I meant to tell you, for that is quite something else which— Now try & guess what it is—Oh! oh! if you know it, I need not tell you of it—but nevertheless as I see you want to know from me why then here it is

Our———Kit———is———shall I tell you? going———to ———visit Mrs Hopkinson—that is true too—but that an't it yet—what then you say?– Why stop– I'll tell you– She is going to be———be ——— I cant keep it any longer–she is going to be MARRIED–there you have it now, & law me!–what trouble I had before I could tell you– however from now you know it–and the time I believe is fixed somewhere the 25–26–or 27th of this Month–& therefore if you wish to be present–pray had you not better come up a Week or 10 Days sooner– perhaps both you and Peggy, because Mamy means to go to Town with them the Day after.– Now I have not time to say any thing more, but my Love to your Children, & best Compliments to the whole family———

Yours affectionately
F. A. M.[30]

Frederick's congressional career had virtually ended with the conclusion of the debate on the Jay Treaty. In the fall of 1796 he was heavily defeated when he ran for reëlection.

"The great victory obtained here over the united and combined forces of the British and Aristocrats," wrote John Beckley from Philadelphia to General Irvine, October 17, 1796, "gives us great confidence and is a presage of success in the choice of Electors; to throw out Muhlenberg, who gave the casting vote for the British treaty and elect Blair McClenachan in his room, who recommended to kick the treaty to hell . . ."[31] was sufficient, as he said, to show the vigor of Republicanism in Philadelphia.

Nevertheless, despite the ferocity of party rancor, Frederick Muhlenberg remained a power behind the scenes. To the end he was reckoned a strong contender for the governorship.

His death from apoplexy, which came on June 4, 1801, was looked upon as an event of public significance. It produced, if not an earthquake, at least a sharp subsidence in the political terrain.

"The death of F. A. Muhlenberg on the 4th inst.," wrote the politico William Duane to Thomas Jefferson, "has produced a change in the political prospects in this state. His conduct on the British treaty lost him the confidence of all the independent republicans; the opposite party had determined to run him for Governor. . . . There is no other character among the Germans of talents and standing equal to the deceased; his capacity as a German writer was admired, and there does not appear to be any one equal to him left."[32]

CHAPTER XXIX

MARCH ON THE CAPITAL

"I think I see an antifederal Monster growing," Frederick Muhlenberg had written to Richard Peters, June 18, 1789,[1] during the disillusioning first weeks of the First Congress.

Fear of this "antifederal Monster" lived on for many years, deepening in the minds of some till it became a phobia. In 1801, when Jefferson and Burr tied for the presidency, and Congress, upon whom the decision now devolved, cast thirty-five ballots without breaking the deadlock, the Antifederal monster walked again.

With this apparition stalked Rumor: reports of uprisings, threatened or accomplished, to save the nation or the Constitution from disaster. Major General Peter Muhlenberg stood by, prepared to march on the capital to save it from the mob.

Some details of this curious episode in our history have not hitherto been brought to light.

Let us begin with the election manifesto, signed by Peter Muhlenberg and others, April 9, 1799, on behalf of Thomas McKean for governor:

Friends and Fellow-Citizens

The present crisis in the political affairs of the United States demands the attention of every lover of his country; since the exertion of every power, which the Constitution reserves to the People, has obviously become indispensable to the preservation of the republican system, to the peace of the nation, and to the harmony of society. . . .

Recent events, however, have developed a more awful, and more fatal, source of calamity; and a question has been artfully presented to the public mind, whether the Republican system of our FEDERAL CONSTITUTION itself, ought in practice, to be preferred to a MONARCHY! If we review the conduct of men in power, we shall find that the honors and emoluments of Public Office, are only bestowed on the partizans of the Administration; and if we attend to the language of those partizans, we shall find, that the Constitution of the United States is pronounced to be inefficient, that the authority of individual States is held in contempt, that the sacred right of universal suffrage is arraigned, and that Republicanism itself is considered as an idle phantom! Is it not, then, a solemn duty, to take every Constitutional precaution for guarding the Paladium of Liberty from the violation of secret machinations, or open force? And what precaution can be more effectual, what more decent and orderly, than to give the State Governments the full and legitimate influence of a Republican representation?[2]

In the election of a president in February 1801, the fears expressed in the above election manifesto came to a crisis. That the crisis was resolved without bloodshed was a tribute both to Thomas Jefferson's constancy under threats of violence, and to the readiness of General Muhlenberg to put down insurrection.

February 11, 1801, saw the opening of one of the most exciting dramas in America's constitutional history.

When on that day the votes of the presidential electors were quoted, this was the tally:[3]

Thomas Jefferson	73
Aaron Burr	73
John Adams	65
Charles Cotesworth Pinckney	64
John Jay	1

The President of the Senate announced the state of the vote to both houses, and declared that, since Thomas Jefferson of Virginia and Aaron Burr of New York were equal, "it remained for the House of Representatives to determine the choice."[4]

The House proceeded to ballot, state by state. It was required by the Constitution that nine states should agree on the choice. On the first ballot, eight states were found to be for Jefferson, six for Burr, and two others were divided. Then began the great contest, a battle of nerves. Within the walls of Congress, members settled down to a long vigil.

The political maneuvering was not only skillful; it was deadly. Some of Burr's partisans were resolved to frighten the Republicans into doing one of three things: switch their votes in order to save the public peace, take some overt action that would give their opponents plausible excuse for a *coup d'état,* or make promises at the expense of their principles. Jefferson's partisans were resolved at all costs to stand firm and not compromise. They had good reason to believe that by no constitutional process could they be ultimately defeated, and that the public was with them against the use of any unconstitutional measures.

Ballot after ballot was cast at intervals of one hour, but there was no change in the tally: 8, 6, 2. Peter Muhlenberg voted for Jefferson every time. Nineteen ballots were taken on that day, the voting continuing until midnight. It started again at one o'clock the next morning, and, on that day, February 12, continued through the twenty-eighth ballot, Peter Muhlenberg still voting for Jefferson. The results were always the same: Jefferson 8, Burr 6, and 2 divided.

Within and without the walls of Congress, the excitement was intense. Visitors jammed the city. A correspondent of the Baltimore *American* wrote: "The hotels and lodging houses have been so much crowded that in the house where I lodge, fifty persons have slept on the floors, with no other covering than their great coats—no other underlay than their blankets."[5]

"It is ludicrous," said the Philadelphia *Gazette,* "to see some of them [the members of Congress] running with anxiety from the committee rooms, with their night-caps on. Numbers of them provided with pillows and blankets, and the contest would seem to be who has most strength of constitution, or is most able to bear fatigue. Many of the members lie down in their places determined like the heroes of old, (at least to *sleep* if not:) to *die at their posts.*"[6]

As the voting went on, the ranks in Congress remained steady, the leaders implacable. But, outside, the excitement was mounting to a frenzy. Fears were expressed wildly that not this one election was at stake, but the Constitution itself, and even the republican form of government.

The Philadelphia *Aurora* referred to a piece from the *Federalist* in which it was said that "Congress, in certain cases specified, have a power to declare what officer shall act as President, and the officer so appointed is to 'act *until a President shall be elected,*' without *limitation of time however long the period may be before his successor shall be elected.*"[7]

The government did in fact propose to pass a law declaring the election null and void, and appointing some public officer—possibly the Chief Justice—to the presidency.

On Monday, February 16, the *Aurora* published a letter from a correspondent in Washington:

A Bill was prepared on Friday last to be introduced in the Senate by Mr. Hillhouse for the election of a person by that body to the Presidential chair. . . . The principle was avowed by *Henry Lee* to several members of Congress, and it was treated as you may conceive with indignation. . . . *Luther Martin* has been preaching up the same subject to crowds in Georgetown and the public taverns of this place. . . . Harper has talked of landing a body of New England militia in Carolina, and attacking Virginia on the fourth, while another body penetrates through Pennsylvania to attack it on the north— . . . When three such characters as *Harry Lee, Luther Martin,* and *Goodloe Harper,* are leaders and counsellors—there can be no danger to the integrity of Republicanism or the Commonwealth—but the country must suffer in its character, when such excrementitious matter swims at top.[8]

Rumors, once started, grew like germs in a test tube. Some parts of the public were infected with panic—and with the blind valor that often goes with it. The politicos balloting implacably in Congress could no longer be sure that the cold war of nerves might not at any moment become a shooting war.

A report was circulated that the Republicans in Philadelphia had seized the public arms. It was believed in responsible circles that a body of citizens of Maryland and Virginia had compacted, in the event a president was appointed by congressional *fiat,* to march on Washington and murder the appointee.

Civil war seemed to be just around the corner.

From Philadelphia John Beckley wrote to Albert Gallatin in Washington:

Philadelphia 15th February 1801.

Dear Sir,

You will receive by the same Mail with this, a letter under cover to you, addressed to the Republican Reps of Pennsa in Congress. It is predicated on the information public & private, that a Rumour prevailed in Washington, that the Republicans here had seized the public Arms. The truth is, that several hundred stand of Arms and 18 peices of Cannon, heretofore in the hands of the Militia, have lately been taken by Fœderalists and *removed* into the public Arsenals of the U:S.— On this fact is the calumny founded. At no point of time that I can remember since 1776, has there prevailed so solemn, calm and deliberate a disposition in the public Mind, to await the awful issue of your present proceedings, accompanied with a firm, fixed, unalterable, and universal determination that when the faction of opposition to the Voice of their Country shall have reached that point at which opposition is a duty and obedience a crime, prompt, energetic and decisive Measures shall be taken. No earthly consideration can or will induce the submission to an Act of Usurpation. The day such an Act passes and receives the President's Sanction, is the first day of Revolution and Civil War in our Country, and irrevocable the doom of the Authors of the National Calamity, unless they can support their Usurpation by Superior force. I do not utter to you, my friend, a Solitary opinion, it is the Sentiment of every Man I see and Converse with, and it will be regarded as the first duty of the Republican Representatives in Such an Event, to solemnly protest against the Act appeal to their Constituants and the World and withdraw from Congress, and that this decision should not be delayed one moment, so as to afford them any countenance to their future Measures, Or by delay frustrate the immediate, proper & necessary Measures of the peoples opposition. I deprecate the Crisis, but however awful the Consequences, they cannot be less so to them, than to us, nor will I suppose it possible that there Exists one Republican Member, that, from a fear of the Consequences, will direlict the principles or abandon the ground of duty and Respect to the Voice of his Country, Especially when such a direlection will only induce a State of things possibly worse than any other Consequence he can fear— Fœderal threats can never Subvert Republican firmness, or if it can, there is in truth no such thing as the latter.

The call of the Senate on 4th March—the manner of that call—the refusal to accept Latimers resignation in Delaware—the movements of A: Hamilton in New York—his overtures to Col[o] Burr, disdainfully rejected by the latter—the appointment of John Marshall—the deceptive letters written by the federalists in Congress in favor of Jefferson—all conduce to prove a settled Conspiracy, in which J. Adams has consented to act a part— Quaere therefore, ought not the Republican Senators to consider previously to 4th March, the propriety of defeating, if they can, the assembling of a quorum, if that quorum cannot be formed without their aid? In the progress of the business before you, this idea can be weighed.

Can you furnish us with the individual Votes of the Members on the Ballot by States, with their Names? If M[r] Jefferson has 55 votes, will it be possible to pass an Usurpation Act thro' your house, and how will the proceeding accord, of a continued Ballot agreeable to the Constitution, and an appeal from that to a Legislative *Choice* or *creation* of a president? Besides can *any* legislative proceeding intervene without superseding and vitiating the ballot? Excuse my questions, perhaps they are already resolved & settled. If you can spare a Moment to drop a line as you progress, it will be acceptable. With best wishes, I am, dear Sir, truly yours,

John Beckley.[9]

As the Crisis approaches, will the Mail be safe to *our* letters?

The Republican press exhorted their people to remain calm and not allow themselves to be prodded into violence. Referring to the rumored seizure of arms in Philadelphia, a correspondent to the *Aurora,* writing from Washington, said: "Every moderate man should exert himself to prevent so improper a step and every thing violent. When constitutional means fail us, it will then be time enough to resort to extremities. Perhaps this extremity may be forced upon us, but we must not be the means of producing it.—we despair not of the commonwealth—Be of good cheer, we triumph with the people on our side."[10]

The *Aurora,* in its issue of February 16, printed part of a letter, dated February 13, "from a gentleman in Washington to the editor of the Baltimore American":

> I conjure you to use all means in your power to repress a spirit of anger —let the republicans wait patiently, till the 3d of March—if the spirit of faction shall then by its opposition to the voice of the majority of the people and the states, put the constitution afloat, God send them safe out of the storm they may raise. Let not our friends by any act whatever countenance any turbulence, the resources of the people are enough, and the authors of this agitation will find themselves consigned to an infamy which will haunt them to the grave.

"No," fulminated the *Aurora* in the same issue, "—the Republicans will be the last to have recourse to arms—but should the day arrive on which Jonathan Dayton prophesied, *the Constitution of the United States would be burned at the Point of the Bayonet,* we trust every Republican would be emulous of dying in the last ditch."

Still the balloting went on, hour by hour and day by day, the Republicans "determined to a man," as a Washington correspondent put it, "to hold out, and if necessary expire with the liberties of their country."[11]

Peter Muhlenberg voted doggedly with the others, though he had other things, too, on his mind. Friday, February 13, saw the twenty-ninth ballot taken, without change; Saturday, February 14, the thirty-third; Monday, February 16, the thirty-fourth: Jefferson, 8; Burr, 6; divided, 2.

Nerves were near the breaking point. Jefferson was threatened with assassination. It was reported that 70,000 Massachusetts militia were "ready to support an usurper."[12] It was difficult to rid oneself of the feeling of impending disaster. Jefferson's mind teemed with expedients for forestalling it or meeting it when it came. He wrote, February 15, to James Monroe:

> If they could have been permitted to pass a law for putting the government in the hands of an officer, they would certainly have prevented an election. But we thought it best one and all to declare openly and firmly, that the day such an act passed, the Middle States would arm, and that no such usurpation, even for a single day, should be submitted to. This first shook them; and they were completely alarmed at the resource for which we declared, to wit, a convention to reorganize the government and to amend it. The very word convention gives them the horrors, as in the present democratical spirit of America, they fear they should lose some of the favorite morsels of the constitution.[13]

The other part of Jefferson's plan is best described in the words of Henry A. Muhlenberg's *Life of Major-General Peter Muhlenberg of the Revolutionary Army*. The author was a son of Henry A. Muhlenberg, first minister of the United States to Austria and nephew to the General, who himself is said to have been the source of the following narrative:

> General Muhlenberg was selected as the head of the military force necessary, and the militia of Pennsylvania under his command were to march immediately upon the capital and depose the usurping government, whilst the states called a convention to amend the constitution. It would have been a fearful blow to the cause of self-government, and every American should thank heaven that so great a calamity was averted. But before condemning those engaged in the scheme, among whom were Jefferson, Madison, Monroe, M'Kean, and others of the purest patriots in the country, it would be well to inquire whether a quiet submission to so fatal a violation of the constitution, would not have been a greater blow to the liberties of the nation, than even a restoration of the constitution by force. At all events, no one can doubt that the actors were influenced by the purest motives, and by what they firmly believed to be the good of the country. The dangerous nature of the scheme probably prevented any part of it being committed to writing, the extract from Jefferson's letter being the only documentary evidence the writer has been able to find; the other facts above stated were related by General Muhlenberg himself to his nephew, shortly after their occurrence.[14]

February 17 saw the climax of the drama. The thirty-fifth ballot was taken. No change: 8, 6, 2. Then the thirty-sixth was cast—

". . . and upon examination thereof," as we read in the *Debates*

. . . *in the Congress of the U. S.*, "and the result being reported by the tellers to the Speaker, the Speaker declared to the House that the votes of ten States had been given for Thomas Jefferson, of Virginia, the votes of four States for Aaron Burr, of New York, and that the votes of two states had been given in blank; and that, consequently, Thomas Jefferson, of Virginia, had been agreeably to the constitution, elected President of the United States, for the term of four years, commencing on the fourth of March next."[15]

At twelve noon precisely "the election of Thomas Jefferson and Aaron Burr, was announced by the firing of cannon in the arsenal, by the artillery company commanded by Capt. Shaw."[16]

The editorial in the *Aurora* for February 20 pulled out all the stops in its organ of rhetoric: "The Revolution of 1776, is now, and for the *first* time arrived at its completion. Till now, the Republicans have indeed berated the slaves of monarchy in the field of battle, and driven the troops of the King of Great Britain from the shores of our country; but the secret enemies of the American revolution—her internal insidious indefatigable foes, have never till now been compleatly discomfited. . . . The reign of terror and corrupt government is at an end."

What had happened to break the deadlock?

Henry Augustus Muhlenberg, after he had written the passage quoted above from his *Life of Peter Muhlenberg*, sent a copy of it to one of the actors in the "Revolution of 1801." The reply written by that wise old Swiss gentleman and American patriot, Albert Gallatin, never before printed for reasons which the letter itself will explain, must be given in full, because it provides the best behind-the-scenes picture available of the days when Peter Muhlenberg was waiting for the signal to lead troops on Washington to save the Constitution.

To Henry A. Muhlenberg Esqr New York May 8. 1848.
Reading Pens^a

Dear Sir,

A severe cold which rendered me incapable of attending to any business, has prevented an earlier answer to your letter of the 12th of April.

Although I was at the time probably better acquainted with all the circumstances attending Mr. Jefferson's election than any other person, and I am now the only surviving witness, I could not without bestowing more time than I can spare, give a satisfactory account of that ancient transaction. A few observations must suffice.

The only cause of real apprehension was that Congress should adjourn without making a decision, but without usurping any powers. It was in order to provide against that contingency, that I prepared myself a plan which did meet with the approbation of our party. No appeal whatever to physical force was contemplated; nor did it contain a single particle of revolutionary spirit. In framing this plan, Mr. Jefferson had not been consulted; but it was communicated to him and he fully approved it.

But it was threatened by some persons of the Federal Party to provide by law, that if no election should take place, the Executive power should be placed in the hands of some public officer. This was considered as a revolutionary act of usurpation and would I believe have been put down by force if necessary. But there was not the slightest intention or suggestion to call a convention to re-organize the government and to amend the constitution. That such a measure floated in the mind of Mr. Jefferson is clear from his letters of Feb. 15th & 18th 1801 to Mr. Munroe and Mr. Madison. He may have wished for such measure, or thought that the Federalists might be frightened by the threat.

Although I was lodging in the same house with him, he never mentioned it to me, I did not hear it even suggested by any one. That Mr. Jefferson had ever thought of such plan was never known to me till after the publication of his correspondence; and I may aver that under no circumstances would that plan have been resorted to or approved by the Republican Party. Anti-Federalism had long been dead; and the Republicans were the most sincere and zealous supporters of the Constitution. It was that which constituted their real strength.

I always thought that the threatened attempt to make a President by law was impracticable. I do not believe that if a motion had been made to that effect, there would have been twenty votes for it in the House. It was only intended to frighten us; but it produced an excitement out of doors, in which some of our members participated. It was threatened, that if any man should be thus appointed President by law and accept the office, he would instantaneously be put to death. It was rumored, and though I did not know it from my own knowledge I believe it was true, that a number of men from Maryland and Virginia, amounting it was said to fifteen hundred (a number undoubtedly greatly exaggerated) had determined to repair to Washington on the 4th of March for the purpose of putting to death the usurping pretended President.

It was under these circumstances that it was deemed proper to communicate all the facts to Governor McKean, and to submit to him the propriety of having in readiness a body of militia, who might if necessary be in Washington on the 3rd of March, for the purpose not of promoting, but of preventing civil war and the shedding of a single drop of blood.

No person could be better trusted on such a delicate subject than Governor McKean. For he was energetic, patriotic, and at the same time a most steady, stern, and fearless supporter of law and order. It appears from your communication, that he must have consulted General Peter Muhlenberg on that subject. But subsequent circumstances which occurred about three weeks before the 4th of March rendered it altogether unnecessary to act upon the subject.

There was but one man whom I can positively assert to have been decidedly in favor of the attempt to make a President by law. This was General Henry Lee of Virginia, who as you know, was a desperate character and held in no public estimation. I fear from the general tenor of his conduct, that Mr. Griswold of Connecticut, in other respects a very worthy man, was so warm and infatuated a partisan, that he might have run the risk of a civil war, rather than see Mr. Jefferson elected. Some weak and inconsiderate members of the House might have voted for the measure; but I could not designate any one.

On the day on which we began balloting for President, we knew positively that Mr. Baer of Maryland was determined to cast his vote for Mr. Jefferson rather than that there should be no election; and his vote was sufficient to give us that of Maryland and decide the election. I was certain, from personal intercourse with him, that Mr. Morris of Vermont would do the same and thus give us also the vote of that State. There were others equally prepared but not known to us at the time. Still all those gentlemen, unwilling to break up their party, united in the attempt, by repeatedly voting for Mr. Burr, to frighten, or induce some of us, to vote for Mr. Burr rather than to have no election. This balloting was continued several days for another reason. The attempt was made to extort concessions and promises from Mr. Jefferson, as the conditions on which he might be elected. One of our friends, who was very erroneously and improperly afraid of a defection on the part of some of our members, undertook to act as an intermediary, and confounding his own opinions and wishes with those of Mr. Jefferson, reported the result in such a manner as gave subsequently occasion for very unfounded surmise.

It is due to the memory of James Bayard of Delaware to say that, although he was one of the principal and warmest leaders of the Federal Party, and had a personal dislike for Mr. Jefferson, it was he who took the lead and from pure patriotism directed all those movements of the sounder and wiser part of the Federal Party which terminated in the peaceable election of Mr. Jefferson.

Mr. Jefferson's letter to Mr. Munroe, dated Feb. 15th. 1801. at the very moment when the attempts were making to obtain promises from him, proves decisively that he made no concessions whatever. But both this letter, that to Mr. Madison of the 18th of Feb. and some other of preceding dates afford an instance of that credulity, so common to warm partisans, which makes them ascribe the worst motives and occasionally acts of which they are altogether guiltless, to their opponents. There was not the slightest foundation for suspecting the fidelity of the Post.

You may use such portions of this communication as you may think proper, for the purpose of correcting or modifying what, in your life of General Peter Muhlenberg, you have to say on that subject. But I pray you to consider this communication, so far as I am concerned, as entirely confidential. My name must not be mentioned as your authority. I have enough to encounter in that which I think it my duty to write, concerning the present or future state of the country; and I do not wish to be annoyed, in my old age, by discussions on past events, to which I attach indeed but little importance. When I am no more you may do what you please with my letter. Permit me to add that although I have not the pleasure of a personal acquaintance with you, there is, on my part, an hereditary friendship for all that bear the revered name of Muhlenberg.

Please to accept the assurance of my high consideration and regard, and believe me to be, Dear Sir,

Your faithful and obed^{t} Servant
Albert Gallatin

May 11th 1848
To Henry A. Muhlenberg Esqr
Reading
Penns^{a}[17]

CHAPTER XXX

THE PORT OF PHILADELPHIA

Peter Muhlenberg, stalwart of the Democratic Republican party, was elected senator on February 18, 1801—"Fifteen of the Democratic party," as a shocked commentator wrote, "joining the whole body of the federalists to do it."[1]

The *Aurora* regretted that a man who "deserves and receives the gratitude of his country" should have allowed himself to become the tool of "the aristocratic faction"[2] in eliminating his rival, Dr. Logan. Indeed, the *Aurora* was sure that, if the General had been present at Lancaster when the vote of the two houses of Pennsylvania's legislature was taken, and had seen that Federalist fellow travelers were voting for him, his "republican principles, and his nice sense of honor" would have caused him to decline the election.

General Muhlenberg, however, entered the Senate when it convened in special session on March 4; but he sat for only two days. The session ended on March 5, and, before the Senate convened again in December, General Muhlenberg had resigned. Dr. Logan was elected in his place.

In June he was appointed Supervisor of U. S. Customs in the District of Pennsylvania, and settled down to the life of a civil servant.

A few days after receiving news of this political plum, he resigned his militia commission. He had been major general of the Second Division, which was composed of the militia from the counties of Bucks and Montgomery.

His resignation created a vacuum and induced a current of promotions, on the crest of which Francis Swaine floated forward to become "Brigadier General of the First Brigade of the said Division."

Polly was now "the General's lady."

Anna Maria, who had for some time past been under Polly's roof at Norristown, did not live long to enjoy her daughter's distinction. She died on August 23, 1802, at the age of seventy-five, and was buried beside Henry Melchior at the Trappe.

One gravestone covers their remains:

HOC
MONUMENTUM SACRUM ESTO
MEMORIAE BEATI AC VENERABILIS
HENRICI MELCHIOR MUHLENBERG

QUALIS ET QUANTUS FUERIT
NON IGNORABUNT SINE LAPIDE
FUTURA SAECULA

Here
are also deposited the
Remains of
ANNA MARIA MUHLENBERG

Peter found office work trying.

". . . I have been very much under the weather since I came into this Office," he wrote to Albert Gallatin, September 23, 1802, "but I might have expected that so strict, & close a confinement, would not very well answer, for a Man, so little accustomed to a sedentary life, as I have been for many years past."[3]

The change which came to him on January 25, 1803, when he was appointed Collector of the Port in Philadelphia, brought no relaxation of the strain which sedentary life imposed upon him.

There were, of course, some interesting glimpses to be had, even in the office, of the active life he loved, and there was correspondence with people who figured in the "hurle burle" of politics. He had much to do with cases like that of "the Brig Friends"[4] from Jamaica, which was suspected to be a British privateer, or the American "Brig Betsy,"[5] bound for the West Indies with an astonishing number of guns on board, and an oversized crew.

With Thomas Jefferson, Peter Muhlenberg, as Collector of the Port, had much correspondence concerning consignments which had arrived for, and duties which were to be collected from, the President.

There were such items for Jefferson as these: "a Box containing Books,"[6] on board the ship *Harmony;* "Two Drums of Raisins";[7] "one butt of Sherry Wine"[8] on board the ship *Eliza;* five hundred bottles of Champagne and Burgundy;[9] and a "Barrell of Mississippi Water."[10]

Peter Muhlenberg, "as President of the Vine Company," wrote to Jefferson to solicit a subscription. But Thomas Jefferson, as President of the United States, declined—though "with friendly salutations and assurances of great esteem and affection."[11]

There was always, in that office, the glamour of far places, to which Peter Muhlenberg, explorer of lands on the Ohio and the Scioto, cannot have been insensible. There were letters from Jefferson with instructions to forward them by some convenient ship to Cadiz and Lisbon. There were such oddities as the arrival of "one chest of tea, in the ship Ganges (Murdoch, master), from Canton."[12]

Outside of office hours, there was romance of another kind. Peter had not forgotten the woods and rivers of his boyhood—especially the Perkiomen and the Schuylkill, where as a boy he had fished with such abandon that his father had feared for his soul. On June 17, 1806, he bought a property near Philadelphia on the banks of the Schuylkill at Passyunk. Even the repetitious language of the deed cannot wholly obliterate the glamor of this "Lot or Piece of Land's" situation:

> . . . Situate on the Westerly Side of a Road or Lane leading into Gray's Ferry Road . . . extending . . . to Low Water Mark of the River Schuylkill thence up the said River on the General Courses thereof to a Corner in Rambo's Rock . . . Containing Twenty One Acres and Fifty Nine Perches including . . . about Five Acres of Marsh.[13]

There was good fishing here, but Peter did not long enjoy it. Hannah was very ill. For two months Peter was up every night with her. She slowly wasted away, becoming so worn that he could hardly recognize her for the same person who had gone gaily with him to Virginia in 1772, and since then had made many a trip with him in the stage coach with the children and the Negro boy.

She died on the night of October 27-28, 1806. Her body was taken to the Trappe, where on Wednesday, October 29, she was buried beside Henry Melchior and Anna Maria.

Sacred to the memory of
ANN BARBARA
The late Consort of
Major General P. Muhlenberg

Peter himself was worn out with the long vigil during which he had seen "the love of his youth" slipping away from him. It was his last campaign; and, as after Yorktown, he came out of it exhausted and ill. The old liver affection, contracted during the Georgia campaign, returned to plague him. On July 18, 1807, he made his will.

Sad news came from New York, which we leave to General Swaine to communicate in a letter addressed to Pastor Schultze:

Norristown, July 28th 1807

My dear Sir

I have taken upon myself a painful duty, to communicate to you, the Death of our friend and brother the Reverend Doctor Kunze, he died on friday last about one o Clock p m—it appears from the letter I received that he was possessed of all his faculties, until about ten minutes before his departure from hence, gave his blessing to his Mourning consort & Children, & died like a true & faithful Servant of his God— Thus it is with us frail Mortals—my much esteemed friend & Brother—going one after the other, which of the family will be called next by the Almighty is to us unknown— Doctor Kunze was a faithful Servant in the Kingdom of the Lord and will no doubt receive his Reward in a better World, for the good Works he has done in this— May you my Venerable friend & Brother enjoy the happiness in this World which you are so well entitled to and when called from here may You enjoy everlasting bliss. Mrs Swaine joins me in Love & affection to You and Mrs Shultze and all the Children. With every Sentiment of respectful attachment

I remain Dear Sir
Yours affectionately
F Swaine

Revd Mr Emanuel Shultze
Genl Muhlenbergs health is as it has been for some weeks—he & Hetty was here and remained five days with us—[14]

Peter Muhlenberg did not recover. He left the port of Philadelphia on his sixty-first birthday, October 1, 1807.

A funeral service was held in Zion Church, Philadelphia, after which the procession moved out to the Trappe, where his body was buried beside his wife and his parents beside the north wall of Augustus Church.

Sacred to the Memory of
General PETER MUHLENBERG, Born
October 1st AD 1746 departed this Life
October 1st Anno Domini 1807, Aged 61 Years

He was Brave in the field, Faithful
in the Cabinet, Honorable in
all his transactions, a Sincere Friend
and an Honest Man

CHAPTER XXXI

THE AMERICAN LINNAEUS

The career of Henry Ernest Muhlenberg at Lancaster as preacher, teacher, college president, and botanist, was less spectacular than that of his brothers, and it has not been possible in the course of a narrative overshadowed by their achievements to convey any proper sense of its significance. It has, accordingly, been left to this chapter to attempt an appraisal.

It should be said at the outset that his work, though it did not "catch the eye and take the price," was quite as important to the youthful United States of America as his brothers' labors had been in bringing the giant into being.

His services to botany (then the Queen of the Sciences) were a symbol of something wider: the stimulus given by men of letters and of science to the intellectual growth of their country, without which, as Thomas Jefferson knew, all that had been won on the battlefield and at the council table would have been thrown away.

> . . . by the soul
> Only, the nations shall be great and free.

It will be recalled that, in 1780, he had accepted a call to Trinity Church in Lancaster. He continued to serve that pastorate until his death in 1815.

At Lancaster he was the center of a warm circle of friends.

"A country preacher," he once said to his son Henry Augustus of Reading, "who is independent and beloved by his congregation is a happy man."[1]

He liked to have young people around him. The college gave him ample opportunity for that form of pleasure. And, though he traveled little, he drew the world to his door. Botanists came from all over the United States and from abroad to visit him at Lancaster and see his garden and herbarium.

GOTTHILF HENRY ERNEST MUHLENBERG

His prime devotion, at least in the realm of botany, was to the study of plants in the vicinity of Lancaster, especially the grasses. From this central hub of research he branched out to collect information on all the plants of North America. In 1791 he wrote to Manasseh Cutler that he had collected more than 1,100 different plants within a radius of about three miles of Lancaster.[2] By 1811 he could inform Palisot de Beauvois in Paris that his herbarium contained more than 320 species of American grasses and reeds alone.[3] His *Catalogus Plantarum Americae Septentrionalis,* published in Lancaster in 1813, included some 3,670 species.

In each of his careers, as botanist, college teacher and president, and pastor, his influence was deep and pervasive; but it is on his work as a botanist that his fame rests most securely.

"The pious, the learned Muhlenberg is no more!" wrote Dr. William Barton in 1815. "With him has fallen one of the oldest, the strongest pillars of that extensive fabric his exertions contributed so largely to raise—the edifice of botanick science in America."[4]

His importance as a general influence, through his infectious enthusiasm, on the development of botanical research during its formative period in America has always been known.

"The advantage your Correspondence affords me has revived my almost dormant attachment to that Science,"[5] wrote Stephen Elliot to him in 1809. Today, thanks in great measure to the work of Dr. E. D. Merrill (e.g., his "Work and Publications of Henry Muhlenberg," *Bartonia,* October, 1949), we have come to recognize how extensive and valuable were his own particular contributions to botanical knowledge. Dr. Merrill notes, for instance, that in Muhlenberg's description of about 380 species and varieties of grasses and reeds contained in his posthumously published *Descriptio Uberior Graminum et Plantarum Calamariarum Americæ Septentrionalis* scores of names were originated by him.

There is no need to dilate on the qualities that made Henry Muhlenberg so attractive to so many people: the modesty, humor, generosity, sincerity, warmth, and communicativeness that went to make up his abundant personal charm. It is sufficient to say that he possessed two principal gifts that dominated his life: a talent for friendship and a genius for putting things in order. They are the secret of his success, and explain the lead taken by Pennsylvania, through his influence, in American botany during the early years of the nineteenth century.

His letters, as full in volume as in matter, are sufficient to explain the warmth of personal feeling that caused so many persons (women as well as men, for the "botanical ladies," such as Anna Rosina Gambold, formed a considerable part of Muhlenberg's circle of correspondents) to follow him in the pursuit of systematic botany; and his notebooks, journals, and book manuscripts, no less than twenty-one of which are preserved in the Library of the American Philosophical Society alone, all attest the zeal for planning, arranging, and tabulating that characterized his work.

His journals are packed with outlines of projects: tabulated lists of what to look for in plants, lists of "Persons recommended to me" (William Bartram, for example), lists of places to be visited on botanizing excursions. In his "Botanisches Tagebuch"[6] for 1784 we find this entry, presented here in translation from the German, which was the language he used in his private journals:

> The chief localities I intend to visit
> 1, My old places on Mosers place
> Lichty's—Webs, Gross—Ross—
> Dietrich
> 2, My favorite haunts on the
> Little Conestoga
> 3, Over Mill Creek
> 4, Urbans place—Wagners place etc. . . .
> 5, Burkhalters ferry
> 6, Toschs place—and the
> Susquehanna Island . . .

He kept his Botanical Journal current through the years. It must be admitted that there is little meditation or color in it. It is no *Walden*. But even in its barest entries, there is often disclosed something deeper in the author than the spirit of a mere cataloguer.

September 19, 1786: "This morning between 3-4 o'clock the most glorious view of the starry sky—*Sirius, Orion, Aldebaran, Capella, Procyon* and especially *Jupiter.*"

February 26, 1787: "The wild pigeons were heard for the first time . . .

March 1: "We heard the blue birds."

March 14: "An unusually lovely day and we gardened a little for the first time the frogs are croaking a lot."

March 15: "Lovely again. Poa annua is in bloom."

April 1 (Saturday): "Official duties keep me from going out but there would be all sorts of things to find—"

April 4: "The martins for the first time, very lovely weather."

December 6: "A walk with my children for black walnuts . . ."

Not only was he constantly writing down plans for his own private work, but he was also presenting plans to his friends and associates throughout the country for the organization of botany on a national scale. He hoped that the American Philosophical Society at Philadelphia would take a lead in the matter.

"I repeat my former wish," he said in a paper read before the Society, February 18, 1791, "that some of my learned countrymen would join in botanical researches, and send in their Floras, for perusal or publication, to your Society, so that by gathering the Floras of the different States, we may have a general Flora of the United-States, drawn from good and certain observations."

He wrote often in his private letters of what might be accomplished for botany in the United States "if Scientific Men would join Hands together."

Of professional jealousy he seems to have had none.

"By joining hands," he wrote to Dr. William Baldwin, November 4, 1811, "we may do something clever for Science. Mine, indeed, begin to get old and stiff,—but the heart still beats high, and wishes that others may do what was left undone. Away with all jealousy."[7]

William Baldwin praised him "for that unbounded liberality of sentiment, which he uniformly manifested towards his contemporaries: and which ought ever to distinguish the genuine Christian Philosopher, and Naturalist, from the narrow-minded despot in science, who would exalt his own fame even at the expense of those around him."[8]

Though he published little, and in what he did publish modestly refrained from drawing attention to his own contributions to botanical nomenclature (to the embarrassment of later taxonomists, who, like Dr. Merrill, have been constrained to undertake extensive research in order to discover just what names Muhlenberg did actually originate), nevertheless his fame is secure. Dr. Baldwin called him "the Linnaeus of our country," and the epithet "American Linnaeus" has stuck to him—not, indeed, because of any new system or method originated by him (he had little of Linnaeus' breadth of vision), but because he was the most indefatigable follower of the Linnaean sexual system of classification, and because of his immense personal influence on the development of botanical study in this country.

His herbarium was the best in the America of his day. Specimens from it, which he sent to correspondents all over America and Europe, contributed much to the successful work of leading botanists in both continents.

In return, due honors were paid to him. Torrey and Gray, Grisebach, Barratt, Acharius, Swartz, and Elliott named species after him. Schreber named a genus of grasses *Muhlenbergia*.

Frederick Pursh, in the Preface to his *Flora Americae Septentrionalis* (London, 1814), refers to Muhlenberg as "a gentleman whose industry and zeal for the science can only be surpassed by the accuracy and acuteness of his observations."

F. André Michaux, in the Introduction to his *North American Sylva* (Philadelphia, 1817), calls him "one of the most learned botanists America has hitherto produced, and who well deserves a distinguished rank among those who in Europe have applied themselves most successfully to this pleasing and attractive science."

In Dr. William P. C. Barton's *Florae Philadelphicae Prodromus* (Philadelphia, 1815) appears this tribute: "His merits, though chiefly confined to nomenclatural botany, were of the highest order. In giving information he was conscientious as truth itself, and his patience and industry in correcting the errours and confusion of botany, have scarce a parallel."

Chief among the many distinguished men of science who sought him out was Friedrich Heinrich Alexander, Baron von Humboldt, who, with his companion Aimé Bonpland, visited Lancaster on the way back from his famous journey to Central and South America. On the eve of his departure for Europe, Von Humboldt wrote from Philadelphia thanking Muhlenberg for his recent hospitality and acknowledging receipt of the grasses (some 160 specimens) which Muhlenberg had asked him to have checked against the names in Michaux's herbarium.

My dear and honored friend,
I use these last moments before my departure tomorrow, to express once more my heartfelt thanks to you for the great kindness which you showed me and my friends in Lancaster. Your grasses and your kind letter have come to hand and I promise to let you know Michaux's names for them. Bonpland commends himself to you with gratitude for your kind remembrance. Yesterday he had a delightful noon with your brother the worthy General. Remember me to the good Ellicott and Mr. William Barton. We saw the Hamilton garden with astonished delight.

Yours
most gratefully
Humboldt[9]

Philadelphia
the 27th June 1804.

Muhlenberg's own letters though confined for the most part to matters of strict science contain nevertheless snatches of comment—gentle but discriminating and sometimes humorous—on celebrities of the day. Here are a few of them:

"Men say Jefferson is a deist, and they anticipate great danger from this fact to the church of Christ. I know him only as a very tolerant and honorable man."[10]

". . . that excellent Botanist and Entomologist, Stephen Elliott, Esq. . . . indefatigable . . . communicative . . ."[11]

"Mr. Rafinesque was rather too quick in naming the plants, and may have been mistaken in some names. . . ."[12]

"Mr. Kin, a curious botanist at Philadelphia . . ."[13]

"Mr. Lyons and Mr. Kinn are both my Friends, the former knows more of the System, the latter is a practical Collector of Plants though he Spells exceedingly bad. Both make their Living by Botany, with me Botany is Recreation."[14]

To William Bartram he wrote, January 29, 1810: "Hardly a Day passes but I am in Spirit with You and wander with You Hand in Hand through Your Garden and on the Banks of Schulkil."[15]

In a letter of April 9, 1807, to John Vaughan he sends his best respects to Mrs. Merry, whom he calls "my Flora Britannica," and with them his "sincere wishes" for her "safe and pleasant Voyage to England."[16] His Flora Britannica was the wife of the British ambassador, and an enthusiastic botanist who had visited Lancaster with her husband, "collecting everything for England,"[17] as Henry Muhlenberg observed.

With Constantine Samuel Rafinesque (who tells us that in 1803 he took what he calls a "pedestrian excursion" to Lancaster "to see Muhlenberg," and on another visit the following year "perused his herbal and herborized with him") he carried on a particularly vigorous correspondence. They exchanged plants, and Rafinesque deferred to his knowledge in Muhlenberg's special field. "Knowing of your extensive knowledge of Grasses and Cryptogamick plants," wrote Rafinesque, "I always shall refer myself to you for them."[18] Rafinesque's letters to him betray that quick and pounding eagerness for "discoveries" which led him to so many undoubted triumphs and at the same time into so many errors—in sharpest contrast to the gentle and cautious assiduity of Muhlenberg, whose advice to botanists was "Hasten slowly."

CHAPTER XXXII

HENRY MUHLENBERG CLOSES HIS JOURNAL

After the death of Peter Muhlenberg in 1807, the shades closed fast on the rest of the family. Betsy, at Tulpehocken, died in 1808, and her husband, Emanuel Schultze, followed her in 1809. For Henry Ernest, afflicted with an illness not unlike his mother's, it was becoming a struggle to keep going. In September 1805, after one of these attacks while on a visit to the Swaine's at Norristown, he was reported to have died.

It was apparently one of the Schaeffers who reported "the very sudden Death of his Brother in law Mr Henry Muhlenberg."[1] The news was relayed by a Peter Wager to Adam Reigart in Lancaster:

> Mr M[uhlenberg] on Friday last went on A visit for A few days to his friends at Norris Town, accompanyd with his son, about 13 years old, and within A short distance of Norris Town, was attacked with one of his fits that you know he has been accustomed to, he fell out of the chair and Died this Morning between 3 & 4 Oclock, weather it was owing to the fall or not I have not been able to learn, but I expect that both of the disasters assisted in his death . . .[2]

But Henry Ernest was a fighter, and his labors for church, college, and botany were by no means over. Next spring he was writing eagerly to Dr. George Logan about the Lewis and Clark expedition. "Has Mr. Lewis ever sent any Seeds from the western Parts? I am extremely interested in his Fate and anxiously wish that the Rumour of his Misfortune was unfounded."[3]

In the same letter he praised Thomas Jefferson, who had organized the expedition. "With infinite Satisfaction I daily hear that the Gentleman I so long respected, Mr. Jefferson, the Friend of the People and of Sciences is indefatigable in preserving national Prosperity and Dignity, and enlarging the Boundaries of Science, especially natural History."

The winters were becoming hard on him. He was troubled with "rheumatism in the head."[4] But he still found means of pursuing his favorite science. "In Winter when all Excursions are forbidden," he wrote to his friend Zaccheus Collins, "I botanize behind the Stove and before I put the wood in the Stove I look over every Piece for Lichens or Mosses. I have found many of them which I never have seen in the woods of the neighborhood. Your wood comes often from a great Distance by Water and from the Jersey terra incognita–"[5]

He welcomed the sun in spring, the sound of birds arriving, and the sight of small growing things.

His Journal for April 8, 1807: "A lovely spring day though there was still some winter frost in the morning–blackbirds and martins and other birds are singing lustily. Snow still lies in the back parts."[6]

There was good news as well as bad from the family. His son Henry Augustus on June 7, 1818, married Rebecca Hiester. This was not the end but the beginning for him of one of the most beautiful of love stories.

His sister, Sally Richards, was now a great lady. Her husband, Matthew Richards ("the well-bred Christian Mechanico"[7] of Hanover, as Henry Melchior Muhlenberg had described him in 1785), was a member of Congress from 1807 to 1811. We find him dining, November 17, 1808, with President Jefferson;[8] on June 16, 1809, and December 21, 1810, with President Madison.[9] He was appointed a collector of revenue under Madison in 1812.

To the end, Henry Ernest's industry was amazing. His spirit was unbreakable. On January 24, 1814, he had a stroke. He lost his memory and the use of his tongue. After a few days he began to master articulation again, but his memory was harder to recover. He understood his loss and, determined to repair it, he started methodically to learn to read and write again and to pick up the threads of his botanical studies. It was late in life to be making a fresh start, but he was resolved

> To strive, to seek, to find, and not to yield.

The children took over his correspondence for a time, trying to keep their father's friendships alive until he himself should be well enough to resume them. Henry Augustus came over from Reading to look after his church work.

It was at this time that Thomas Jefferson ("the Friend of the People and of Sciences") wrote him a letter which is perhaps the best of all contemporary tributes to the Muhlenberg whose patriotism was most deeply rooted in the soil:

Monticello Mar. 16. 14.

Dear Sir

I thank you for your catalogue of North American plants. it is indeed very copious, and at the same time compendious in its form. I hardly know what you have left for your "Descriptio uberior." the discoveries of Gov[r] Lewis may perhaps furnish matter of value, if ever they can be brought forward. the mere journal of the voyage may be soon expected; but in what forwardness are the volumes of the botany, natural history, geography and meteorology of the journey, I am uninformed. your pamphlet came during a long absence from home, and was mislaid or this acknolegement should have been sooner made. with my wishes for the continuance and success of your useful labors I embrace with pleasure this first occasion of assuring you that I have had long and much gratification in observing the distinguished part you have borne in making known to the literary world the treasures of our own country and I tender to you the sentiments of my high respect and esteem

Th: Jefferson

The rev[d]
Henry Muhlenberg[10]

Stephen Elliott (whose interest in botany owed much to Dr. Muhlenberg) wrote to him from Charleston, April 7, 1814:

A letter which I received this afternoon from D[r] Baldwin gave me the first information I have received of your late illness. I cannot postpone the expression of my sincere regret at this great misfortune nor delay a moment to assure you of the deep interest I take in your welfare. I hope the prospects of returning health have been realised. Many persons after similar attacks have enjoyed years of tolerable ease and comfort and your temperate and active habits give your friends great reason to hope for your entire recovery.

"Dii tibi dent annos" has been my constant wish and shall be the wish of every American Botanist you have perhaps lived long enough for your own reputation but not for our benefit. Every day I feel and on every opportunity I express my personal obligations to you. We should look in vain on this continent at least for your Successor, for one, who to your profound knowledge should unite your liberal and communicative temper, who would acquire knowledge for its true and best purposes and would distribute it, like you, to all who required it.[11]

He won his battle. His strength came back, his memory returned, and in a few months he was picking up the threads of his correspondence.

He wrote, July 4, 1814, to Dr. Baldwin:

> . . . *Polymnia Tetragonotheca is the same with Tetragonotheca helianthoides,* Willd. and Persoon. . . . Mr. *Elliott* has not favored me with an answer to my last letter. Indeed, my former correspondents,—if I except my indefatigable Dr. *Baldwin,* and friend *Collins,*—seem to have forgotten me; and I am reckoned among the dead. My excursions are narrowed very much, and I am confined to my garden.[12]

In 1814 he was preparing addenda for a new edition of the *Catalogus,* but he found the labor exhausting. "My health is neither good, nor bad," he wrote to Dr. Baldwin in October; "but my friendship and gratitude unchangeable."[13]

In this year he sat for a portrait to Thomas Sully.

On May 11, 1815, he wrote what is, as far as we know, his last letter. It was full of news about plants and collectors: Persoon, Barton, Collins, Correa de Serra, Le Conte, etc., etc. But he was growing tired before he concluded.

"The official business," he wrote, "—which, near Whitsuntide, is rather too much on me,—hinders me from adding more.—May you preserve your health, and not forget your faithful friend. My best compliments to Mrs. Baldwin.

"Affectionately I remain your obedient and sincere friend,

Henry Muhlenberg."[14]

The last entry in his Botanical Journal was made on May 20, 1815: "Very raw from N W.—Trifolium . . ."[15]

He notes that he has received a letter from Le Conte, and, looking ahead, he lists four questions (here tabulated) to ask him.

He died, May 23, 1815.

His son, Dr. Frederick Augustus Muhlenberg, who had studied medicine under Benjamin Rush and had recently received his medical degree from the University of Pennsylvania, wrote letters to William Baldwin and Zaccheus Collins. I quote from the letter to Collins.

Lancaster May 24th 1815.

Dear Sir.

Melancholy is the duty which now devolves upon me, of informing you Sir, that your old correspondant, and true friend, my father is no more! On Tuesday morning at half after seven O Clock he was suddenly affected with symptoms of paralysis, which however soon disappeared, leaving an unimpaired intellect, but great physical debility. He remained in that state, until evening at half after eight o clock, when the paroxysm was repeated, and having a few minutes previous utter[ed] a prayer for his children, and for mankind in general, and recommending himself to the mercy of his great redeamor and judge, he expired in my arms. . . .

P. S. My father had just finished a letter to La Conte if you could give me instructions how to dispose of it, I shall be much indebted to you[16]

From Bermuda, Dr. Baldwin, not knowing that his old friend had gone on a long voyage of his own, wrote, May 30, "We reached this little spot in the great ocean on the 19th inst."[17]

When he received the news from Lancaster, Baldwin wrote to Frederick Augustus Muhlenberg:

"May the lovers of Botany, throughout the United States, do honor to his memory by walking in his footsteps! . . . the Linnaeus of our Country. . . ."[18]

EPILOGUE

Hardly more than a block from the center of Lancaster stands Trinity Church, handsome in its four-square strength, beautiful with its well-proportioned spire. In the graveyard behind it Henry Ernest Muhlenberg was buried beside his brother Frederick.

In the course of years changes have been made in the church grounds, and the graves of the Muhlenberg brothers have been moved to Woodward Cemetery on a near-by hill. But their large gravestones—prone like their father's and brother's under the walls of Augustus Church at Trappe—are still together:

Hier ruhen die Gebeine . . .
Here rest the Bones
of GOTTHILF HEINRICH MÜHLENBERG S.T.D.
. . .
Sacred
To the Memory of
FREDERICK AUGUSTUS MUHLENBERG
. . .

The days were closing in.

Golden lads and girls all must,
As chimney-sweepers, come to dust.

The Muhlenbergs, as their grandfather's Indians might have said, were returning to their mother, the earth.

Polly died in 1812. General Swaine, her husband, after having in the meantime espoused a rich widow of Easton, followed Polly in 1820.

Sally Richards died March 13, 1827; her husband, Matthias Richards, August 4, 1830.

Peggy died October 23, 1831; Frederick's wife, Catharine Schaeffer, in 1835; Henry Ernest's wife, Mary Catharine Hall, in 1841.

The story of Henry Melchior's immediate family has come to an end.

AUGUSTUS CHURCH

NOTES

ABBREVIATIONS USED

A.P.S.—American Philosophical Society, Philadelphia.
H.M.M.—Henry Melchior Muhlenberg.
H.S.P.—Historical Society of Pennsylvania, Philadelphia
L.C.—Library of Congress, Washington, D. C.
L.T.S.—Lutheran Theological Seminary.
Luth. Arch.—Lutheran Archives.
N.Y.H.S.—New York Historical Society, New York City.
P.M. of H.B.—*Pennsylvania Magazine of History and Biography.*

Much of the biographical material for the years 1711-76 is found in the two published volumes of the projected three-volume edition of Henry Melchior Muhlenberg's Journals, translated and edited by Dr. Theodore G. Tappert and Dr. John W. Doberstein (Philadelphia, 1942 and 1945). Where such materials are dated in the text and so may easily be traced in the Journals, no reference to that source is here made.

CHAPTER 5: THE LORD'S SHEEP DOG

1. H. M. Muhlenberg to Eike and Westphal, September 6, 1785: Lutheran Archives, Library of the Lutheran Theological Seminary, Mt. Airy.
2. *Journals of Henry Melchior Muhlenberg* (Phila., 1942), I, 158.
3. *Ibid.*, I, 101.
4. Letter from H.M.M. to a friend in Europe, September 6, 1753: H.M.M.'s Journal, 1751-52, reverse, pp. 149-83, Luth. Arch., Mt. Airy.
5. Israel Acrelius to H.M.M., September 18, 1750: H.M.M.'s Journal, 1748-51, reverse, pp. 22-27, Luth. Arch., Mt. Airy.
6. *Journals,* I, 105.
7. H.M.M. to C.R.H., January 9, 1752: H.M.M.'s Journal, 1751-52, pp. 57-71.

8. *Journals,* I, 157.
9. *Ibid.,* I, 154.
10. *Ibid.,* I, 211.
11. H.M.M.'s Journal, June 20, 1777, Dr. Tappert's MS. translation.
12. H.M.M. to his son, Henry Ernest, March 23, 1785: Luth. Arch., Mt. Airy.
13. *Journals,* I, 268.
14. *Ibid.,* I, 98.
15. *Ibid.*
16. Ernest T. Kretschmann, *The Old Trappe Church* (Phila., 1893), p. 8, n. 22.

CHAPTER 6: ANNA MARIA

1. *Hallesche Nachrichten,* I, 117; Dr. John Ludwig Schulze, *Reports of the United German Evangelical Lutheran Congregations,* I, 176-78; *Journals of Henry Melchior Muhlenberg* (Phila., 1942), I, 102.
2. *Journals,* I, 282.
3. *Ibid.,* I, 134.
4. William Germann, "Crisis in the Early Life of General Peter Muhlenberg," *Pennsylvania Magazine of History and Biography,* XXXVII, 458.
5. *Journals,* I, 577.
6. *Ibid.,* I, 104.
7. H.M.M. to Ziegenhagen and Francke, July 5, 1754: Halle Documents, Library L.T.S., Mt. Airy.
8. *Journals,* I, 117.
9. Halle Reports, p. 178. Quoted by Ernest T. Kretschmann, *The Old Trappe Church* (Phila., 1893), p. 17.
10. *Journals,* I, 180.
11. *Ibid.,* I, 234.

CHAPTER 7: SADDLEBAG PREACHER

1. H.M.M. to Boltzius, 1750 (?): H.M.M.'s Journal, 1748-51, reverse, pp. 1-15, Luth. Arch., Mt. Airy.
2. *Ibid.*
3. *Journals of Henry Melchior Muhlenberg* (Phila., 1942), I, 188.

4. *Ibid.*, I, 378-79.
5. *Ibid.*, I, 155.
6. *Ibid.*, I, 537.
7. *Ibid.*, I, 211.
8. *Ibid.*, I, 156.
9. *Ibid.*, I, 183.
10. *Ibid.*, I, 210.
11. *Ibid.*, I, 230.
12. François André Michaux, *Travels to the Westward of the Allegany Mountains* (London, 1805), p. 48.

CHAPTER 8: PETER AND THE CHRISTIAN DRUGGIST

Most of the documents used in this and the following chapter are reproduced in the Halle photostats, Library of Congress, and in William Germann, "Crisis in the Early Life of General Peter Muhlenberg," *P.M. of H.B.*, XXXVII.

CHAPTER 9: BROKEN MIRROR

The documents used in this chapter are as noted above.

CHAPTER 10: FEED MY SHEEP

1. Autograph Collection, Gotthilf Henry Ernest Muhlenberg, February 14, 1770, Historical Society of Pennsylvania.
2. Germann, "Crisis . . . ," *P.M. of H.B.*, XXXVII.
3. *Ibid.*
4. *Ibid.*
5. *Ibid.*; also *Journals of Henry Melchior Muhlenberg* (Phila., 1945), II, 459.
6. H.M.M.'s Journal, 1769-71, p. 143, Luth. Arch., Mt. Airy.
7. Germann, *op. cit.*
8. Minutes of Synod, October 25, 1770.
9. *Lutheran Church Review*, 1905. The original diary is in the possession of Trinity Lutheran Church, Reading.
10. Germann, *op. cit.*, p. 469.
11. *Ibid.*, p. 467.
12. H.M.M.'s Journal, 1769-71, p. 315; William J. Mann, *Life and Times of Henry Melchior Muhlenberg* (Phila., 1888), pp. 426-27.

13. "Journal of Rev. Peter Muhlenberg in London, 1772," *Lutheran Church Review,* IV, 294-300.

14. Peter Muhlenberg's Account Book: Frederick Nicolls Collection, 1531 Mineral Spring Road, Reading, Pa. A microfilm copy of this is in the Library of the American Philosophical Society, Philadelphia.

CHAPTER 11: BLESSED BE THOU, THE LAND OF MY MOTHER

1. "Diary of Frederick August Muhlenberg," *Lutheran Church Review,* 1905-06; translated by J. W. Early.

2. J. C. Kuntze to Emanuel Schultze, June 12, 1771: Frederick Nicolls Collection, Reading; microfilm copy in A.P.S.

3. Frederick Nicolls Collection, Reading; microfilm copy in A.P.S.

4. Undated letter to "Lieber Polly," probably written in January or February, 1772: Halle Photostats, L.C.

5. See reference to this episode in Frederick's letter to Peter, undated, but probably written in March, 1776: Trinity Lutheran Church, Reading; photostat in L.C.

CHAPTER 12: EBENEZER

The materials for this chapter are found in *Journals of Henry Melchior Muhlenberg* (Phila., 1945), II, pp. 556-688.

CHAPTER 13: "THIS UNNATURAL WAR"

1. H.M.M. to Richard Peters, December 6, 1756: MSS., Indian and Military Affairs of Pennsylvania, 1735-75, A.P.S.

2. *Journals of Henry Melchior Muhlenberg* (Phila., 1945), II, 304-05.

3. H.M.M.'s Journal, 1751-52, pp. 57-71: Luth. Arch., Mt. Airy.

4. *Ibid.,* October 22-23, 1784: Luth. Arch., Mt. Airy.

5. Edward W. Hocker, *The Fighting Parson of the American Revolution* (Phila., 1936), p. 60.

6. *American Archives,* Fourth Series, I, 418.

7. Henry A. Muhlenberg, *The Life of Major-General Peter Muhlenberg of the Revolutionary Army* (Phila., 1849).

8. *Ibid.*, p. 46.

9. March (?), 1776: Trinity Lutheran Church, Reading; cf. Theodore G. Tappert, "Henry Melchior Muhlenberg and the American Revolution," reprinted from *Church History,* Vol. XI, No. 4, December, 1942.

10. Fragment of a letter from H.M.M., September, 1775: Luth. Arch., Mt. Airy.

CHAPTER 14: "A TIME TO FIGHT"

1. Col. Benjamin Wilson to Peter Muhlenberg, January 23, 1776: Brumbaugh, "Revolutionary War Records" (Washington, D. C., 1936), Vol. I, Plate 13.

2. James Thacher, *Military Journal* (Boston, 1827), November 3, 1778, pp. 151-52.

3. Henry A. Muhlenberg, *Peter Muhlenberg* (Phila., 1849), pp. 52-53.

4. *Ibid.*, pp. 123-24.

5. Frederick M. to Peter M., March, 1776: at the end of Frederick M.'s diary, Trinity Lutheran Church, Reading, Pa.

6. *Journals of Henry Melchior Muhlenberg* (Phila., 1945), II, 701.

7. H.M.M. to Emanuel Schultze, March 7, 1776: Frederick Nicolls Collection, Reading; microfilm copy, A.P.S.

8. *Journals,* II, 721.

9. *Autobiography of Charles Biddle Vice-President of the Supreme Executive Council of Pennsylvania,* ed. James S. Biddle (Phila., 1883), p. 86.

10. *Ibid.*

11. H.M.M. to a friend, January 14, 1778: H.M.M.'s Journal, January 22, Rev. Karl Schild's transcript, Luth. Arch., Mt. Airy.

12. Frederick Nicolls Collection, Reading; microfilm in A.P.S.

13. Peter Muhlenberg's Account Book: *Ibid.*

14. Frederick Nicolls Collection, Reading; A.P.S. microfilm.

15. General Lee to Richard Peters, August 2, 1776: Henry A. Muhlenberg, *op. cit.*, p. 66.

16. *American Archives,* Fourth Series, VI, 1129.

17. Francis Vinton Greene, *The Revolutionary War and the Mili-*

tary Policy of the United States (N. Y., 1911), p. 61; Sparks, *Washington,* IV, 190.

18. *Autobiography of Charles Biddle,* p. 96.

CHAPTER 15: BRANDYWINE

1. H.M.M.'s Journal, January 17, 1777: Dr. Tappert's MS. translation, Luth. Arch., Mt. Airy.
2. H.M.M.'s Journal.
3. General Lee to Richard Peters, August 2, 1776: Henry A. Muhlenberg, *Peter Muhlenberg* (Phila., 1899), p. 65.
4. Correspondence of George Washington (Officers), L.C.
5. *Ibid.*
6. H.M.M.'s Journal, March 15, 1777: Dr. Tappert's MS. translation.
7. H.M.M. to Emanuel Schultze, March 17, 1777: Frederick Nicolls Collection, Reading; A.P.S. microfilm.
8. *Ibid.*
9. H.M.M.'s Journal, May 13, 1777.
10. *Ibid.*, May 22, 1777.
11. H.M.M. to his children, July 30, 1777: Luth. Arch., Mt. Airy.
12. Journal, August 13, 1777.
13. *P.M. of H.B.*, XVIII, 329.
14. *Writings of George Washington* (Wash., 1933), IX, 120.
15. *Ibid.*, pp. 125-26.
16. Dr. Henry Pleasants, "The Military Operations of General Sir William Howe in and around Philadelphia in 1777-78," paper read before the Pennsylvania Historical Junto, Washington, D. C., November 12, 1948.
17. *Pennsylvania Evening Post* (Phila.), September 20, 1777: H.S.P.
18. See Peter Weiser's testimony: Frederick Nicolls Collection, Reading; A.P.S. microfilm.
19. Quoted in Henry A. Muhlenberg, *Peter Muhlenberg,* p. 98.

CHAPTER 16: THE FALL OF PHILADELPHIA

1. H.M.M.'s Journal, May 2 and May 6, 1778: Dr. Tappert's MS. translation, Luth. Arch., Mt. Airy.
2. *Ibid.*, September 17.

3. *Ibid.*, September 19.
4. *Ibid.*, September 27.
5. *Ibid.*

CHAPTER 17: VALLEY FORGE

1. H.M.M.'s Journal, October 24: "The lines received last night were from my daughter, Margretha Kuntze, and read as follows . . .": Luth. Arch., Mt. Airy.
2. *Ibid.*, November 7, 1777.
3. *Ibid.*, December 22, 1777.
4. Peter M. to Frederick M., February (?), 1778: Frederick Nicolls Collection, Reading; A.P.S. microfilm.
5. *Ibid.*
6. H.M.M.'s Journal, December 26, 1777.
7. *Ibid.*, January 1, 1778.
8. *Ibid.*, January 3, 1778.
9. Frederick M. to Emanuel Schultze, January 13, 1778: Frederick Nicolls Collection, Reading; A.P.S. microfilm.
10. H.M.M.'s Journal, January 13, 1778.
11. *Ibid.*
12. H.M.M.'s letter to David Grim, dated January 14, 1778, is found in the Journal entry for January 22.
13. H.M.M.'s Journal, February 4, 1778.
14. *Ibid.*, February 25, 1778.
15. *Ibid.*, May 14, 1778. H.M.M. does not name the tribe, but the evidence that these were Oneida Indians is strong. Alone among the Six Nations, the Oneidas *as a nation* had espoused the cause of the colonies. It is true, a part of the Tuscaroras also helped the "Thirteen Fires" (the United States); but it is scarcely possible that the Indians who camped by Muhlenberg's on the evening of May 13 and talked with Anna Maria were Tuscaroras, since their speech would have been unintelligible to her. The speech of the Oneidas, on the other hand, was very similar to that of the Mohawks, which Anna Maria's father had spoken fluently and which he no doubt had taught to his children as he had taught it to the Moravian missionaries.
16. Cf. Paul Wallace, *Conrad Weiser: Friend of Colonist and Mohawk* (Phila., 1945), p. 68.

17. H.M.M.'s Journal, May 23, 1778.

18. *Mémoires . . . du Général Lafayette* (Paris, 1837), I, 47-48.

19. Francis Swaine to Emanuel Schultze, June 28, 1778: Frederick Nicolls Collection, Reading; A.P.S. microfilm.

CHAPTER 18: ALTAR, SWORD, AND PEN

1. H.M.M. to Emanuel Schultze, June 29, 1778: Frederick Nicolls Collection, Reading; A.P.S. microfilm.

2. H.M.M.'s Journal, July 26 and 27, 1778: Luth. Arch., Mt. Airy.

3. Francis Swaine to Emanuel Schultze, June 28, 1778: Frederick Nicolls Collection, Reading; A.P.S. microfilm.

4. Henry A. Muhlenberg, *Peter Muhlenberg* (Phila., 1849), p. 156.

5. Peter M. to Emanuel Schultze, July 28, 1778: Frederick Nicolls Collection, Reading; A.P.S. microfilm.

6. Peter M. to George Washington, September 16, 1778: Correspondence of George Washington (Officers), L.C.

7. James Thacher, *Military Journal* (Boston, 1827), pp. 151-52.

8. *Ibid.*, pp. 188-89.

9. Patrick Henry to Peter M., September 6, 1778: H.M.M.'s Journal, November 22, 1778.

10. George Washington to Peter M., October 28, 1778: *Writings of George Washington* (1937), XIII, 173. Cf. H.M.M.'s Journal, November 22, 1778.

11. H.M.M. to Peter M., November 23, 1778: H.M.M.'s Journal of that date.

12. H.M.M.'s Journal, November 22, 1778.

13. *Ibid.*, March 9, 1779.

14. *Ibid.*, September 27, 1779.

15. *Ibid.*, October 29, 1779.

16. *Ibid.*, October 25, 1779.

17. J. M. Maisch, *Gotthilf Heinrich Ernst Mühlenberg als Botaniker* (N. Y., 1886), pp. 16-17.

18. *Ibid.*

19. H.M.M. to Freylinghausen: H.M.M.'s Journal, October 31, 1778.

20. *Ibid.*

21. Kuntze to H.M.M., November 30, 1778: H.H.M.'s Journal, December 3, 1778.
22. H.M.M.'s Journal, February 15, 1779.
23. *Ibid.*
24. Daniel Hiester to Frederick M., February 28, 1779: H.M.M.'s Journal, March 5, 1779.
25. H.M.M.'s Journal, March 4, 1779.
26. Frederick Nicolls Collection, Reading; A.P.S. microfilm.
27. H.M.M.'s Journal, March 20, 1779.

CHAPTER 19: "WE ARE ALL WELL, THANK GOD"

1. This anecdote was given me by Mr. Charles H. Muhlenberg, 1221 Garfield Avenue, Wyomissing, Pa.
2. Henry Ernest M. to H.M.M., March 23, 1779 (?): H.M.M.'s Journal, Luth. Arch., Mt. Airy.
3. Henry Ernest to H.M.M., March 27, 1779: H.M.M.'s Journal.
4. H.M.M.'s Journal, March 29, 1779.
5. *Ibid.*, April 1, 1779.
6. Henry Ernest M. to H.M.M., April 27, 1779: H.M.M.'s Journal.
7. H.M.M.'s Journal, May 11, 1779.
8. H.M.M. to Emanuel Schultze, April 29, 1779: Frederick Nicolls Collection, Reading; A.P.S. microfilm.
9. Frederick Nicolls Collection, Reading; A.P.S. microfilm.
10. H.M.M.'s Journal, April 7, 1778.
11. *Ibid.*
12. *Ibid.*
13. *Writings of George Washington* (Cong.), XV, 426.
14. Henry A. Muhlenberg, *Peter Muhlenberg* (Phila., 1849), p. 174.
15. George Washington, July 24, 1779: *Writings of George Washington* (Cong.), XV, 474-75.
16. H.M.M.'s Journal, December 9, 1779.
17. *Ibid.*, December 17, 1779.

CHAPTER 20: "I ENTREAT"

1. Correspondence of George Washington (Officers), L.C.
2. *Ibid.*

3. H.M.M.'s Journal, February 29, 1780: Luth. Arch., Mt. Airy.
4. *Ibid.*, March 4, 1780.
5. *Ibid.*, March 10, 1780.
6. *Ibid.*, April 3, 1780.
7. H.M.M. to Henry Ernest M., April 3, 1780: Luth. Arch., Mt. Airy.
8. Correspondence of George Washington (Officers), L.C.
9. George Washington to Peter M., April 20, 1780: Henry A. Muhlenberg, *Peter Muhlenberg* (Phila., 1849), p. 189.
10. Correspondence of George Washington (Officers), L.C.
11. Francis Vinton Greene, *The Revolutionary War and the Military Policy of the United States* (N. Y., 1911), p. 211.
12. Gates Papers, Box 14, New York Historical Society.
13. Henry A. Muhlenberg, *op. cit.*, p. 367.
14. *Writings of George Washington* (Cong.), XIX, 203-5.
15. *Ibid.*, XIX, 194-96.
16. H.M.M.'s Journal, July 4, 1780.
17. H.M.M. to Emanuel Schultze, November 23, 1781: Frederick Nicolls Collection, Reading; A.P.S. microfilm.
18. Luth. Arch., Mt. Airy. The text of this long exercise in mock heroics is in bad condition. I am indebted to Dr. John W. Doberstein for his transcription.
19. July 10, 1780: Luth. Arch., Mt. Airy.
20. Cf. H.M.M.'s Journal, December 10, 1777.
21. H.M.M.'s Journal, January 30, 1780. See also H.M.M. to Frau Weiser, January 24, 1780: H.M.M.'s Journal of that date.
22. H.M.M.'s Journal, August 2, 1780.
23. *Ibid.*, August 20, 1780.
24. *Ibid.*, September 29, 1780.
25. Correspondence of George Washington (Officers), L.C.
26. Peter M. to George Washington, August 1, 1780: Corr. of G.W. (Officers), L.C.
27. Peter M. to George Washington, August 24, 1780: Corr. of G.W. (Officers), L.C.
28. General Gates to Peter M., July 21, 1780: Gates Papers, Box 19, N.Y.H.S.; Henry A. Muhlenberg, *Peter Muhlenberg*, p. 368.
29. General Gates to Peter M., October 12, 1780: Gates Papers, Box 19, N.Y.H.S.

30. September 23, 1780.

31. H.M.M. to Henry Ernest M., September 24, 1780: Luth. Arch., Mt. Airy.

32. H.M.M. to Henry Ernest M., September 29, 1780: Luth. Arch., Mt. Airy.

33. *Ibid.*

34. H.M.M. to Polly, July 25, 1780: H.M.M.'s Journal of same date.

35. Frederick M. to Henry Ernest M., October 11, 1780: Luth. Arch., Mt. Airy.

36. *Ibid.*

CHAPTER 21: BENEDICT ARNOLD

1. *Writings of Thomas Jefferson* (Washington, 1853), I, 265.

2. Peter M. to General Gates, November 7, 1780: Gates Papers, Box 15, N.Y.H.S.

3. Peter M. to General Greene, November 19, 1780: Pierpont Morgan Library, N. Y.; Henry A. Muhlenberg, *Peter Muhlenberg* (Phila., 1849), p. 378.

4. N.Y.H.S.

5. Steuben to George Washington, December 17, 1780: Steuben Letter Book, 1780, N.Y.H.S.

6. *Ibid.*

7. Thomas Jefferson to George Washington, January 10, 1781: *Writings of Thomas Jefferson* (1853), I, 282-84.

8. January 27, 1781: Steuben Papers, Box 2, N.Y.H.S.; copy made for Jared Sparks, Library of Harvard College.

9. Jefferson Papers, L.C. Cf. *Writings of Thomas Jefferson,* I, 289-90; *Works of Thomas Jefferson* (Federal edition, 1904), III, 158-59; *Official Letters of the State of Virginia,* II, 312-13; *Letters of Thomas Jefferson* (1928), pp. 312-13; etc.

10. Isaac Gregory to Peter M., February 23, 1781: Henry A. Muhlenberg, *Peter Muhlenberg,* p. 386.

11. Peter M. to General Steuben, February 18, 1781: N.Y.H.S.; Henry A. Muhlenberg, *op. cit.,* p. 385.

12. Peter M. to Steuben, February 24, 1781: Henry A. Muhlenberg, *op. cit.,* p. 389.

13. February 19, 1781: Steuben Papers, Box 2, N.Y.H.S.

14. *Simcoe's Military Journal* (N. Y., 1844), p. 179.
15. Palmer's *Steuben,* p. 254.
16. Papers of the Continental Congress, Vol. 164, L.C.
17. *Ibid.*
18. Steuben Papers, Box 3, N.Y.H.S.
19. Henry A. Muhlenberg, *Peter Muhlenberg,* p. 394.
20. Col. J. Parker to Peter M., March 2, 1781: Henry A. Muhlenberg, *op. cit.,* p. 393.
21. Peter M. to Col. G. Muter, March 12, 1781: Letters of the Generals of the American Revolution, p. 122, H.S.P.
22. Peter M. to Steuben, March 4, 1781: Steuben Papers, Box 3, N.Y.H.S.; Henry A. Muhlenberg, *op cit.,* pp. 396-97.
23. Steuben Papers, No. 118, Box 13, N.Y.H.S.
24. *Simcoe's Military Journal,* p. 181.
25. *Ibid.*
26. Col. Parker to Peter M., March 2, 1781: Henry A. Muhlenberg, *op cit.,* p. 393.
27. March 10, 1781: *Official Letters of the Governors of Virginia* (Richmond, 1928), II, 400.
28. Executive Letter Book, pp. 185-86, Virginia State Library; *Letters of Thomas Jefferson* (1928), pp. 411-12.
29. Peter M. to Gov. Jefferson, March 20, 1781: Generals of the Revolution, Dreer Collection, H.S.P.
30. Steuben to Peter M., March 23, 1781: Steuben Papers, Box 3, N.Y.H.S.

CHAPTER 22: THE TIDEWATER CAMPAIGN

1. H.M.M.'s Journal, February 2, 1781: Luth. Arch., Mt Airy.
2. H.M.M. to Emanuel Schultze, February 16, 1781: Frederick Nicolls Collection, Reading; A.P.S. microfilm.
3. H.M.M.'s Journal, February 15, 1781.
4. Steuben Papers, Box 3, N.Y.H.S.
5. Gratz Collection, Case 4, Box 13, H.S.P.
6. Steuben Papers, Box 3, N.Y.H.S.; Henry A. Muhlenberg, *Peter Muhlenberg* (Phila., 1849), pp. 407-8.
7. Steuben Papers, Box 3, N.Y.H.S.
8. *Official Letters of the Governors of Virginia,* II, 472.

9. April 15, 1781: Correspondence of George Washington (Officers), L.C.

10. Peter M. to Col. William Davies, April 17, 1781: Generals of the Revolution, Dreer Collection, H.S.P.

11. Peter M. to Steuben, April 20, 1781: Steuben Papers, Box 3, N.Y.H.S.; Henry A. Muhlenberg, *op. cit.*, p. 409.

12. *Ibid.*

13. *Ibid.*

14. Steuben Papers, Box 3, N.Y.H.S.

15. Steuben to George Washington, May 5, 1781, L.C.

16. *Simcoe's Military Journal* (N. Y., 1844), pp. 195-98, contains a description of the "Battle of Blandford," from which this remark is taken.

17. Henry A. Muhlenberg, *op. cit.*, p. 249.

18. *Ibid.*, pp. 249-50.

19. John McAuley Palmer, *General von Steuben* (New Haven, 1937), p. 266.

20. Henry A. Muhlenberg, *op. cit.*, p. 251.

21. *Ibid.*

22. *Ibid.*, p. 252.

23. H.M.M.'s Journal, May 6, 1781.

CHAPTER 23: YORKTOWN: REDOUBT 10

1. Correspondence of George Washington (Officers), L.C.

2. Anthony Wayne to Peter M., June 23, 1781: Wayne Papers, Vol. 13, p. 49, H.S.P.

3. July 30, 1781: Corr. of G.W. (Officers), L.C.

4. July 30, 1781: *Ibid.*

5. July 30, 1781: *Ibid.*

6. Anthony Wayne to Gov. Burke, September 3, 1781: U.S.R., L.C.

7. *Diaries of George Washington,* II, 254.

8. Henry A. Muhlenberg, *Peter Muhlenberg* (Phila., 1849), pp. 266-67.

9. Francis Vinton Greene, *The Revolutionary War and the Military Policy of the United States* (N. Y., 1911), p. 272.

10. *Letters of Lafayette to Washington* (N. Y., 1944), pp. 228-30.

11. *Writings of Thomas Jefferson* (1853), I, 313.

12. Greene, *op. cit.*, p. 271.
13. Correspondence of George Washington (Officers), L.C.
14. *Writings of George Washington* (Cong.), XXIII, 146-48.
15. *P.M. of H.B.*, XXI, 489-90.

CHAPTER 24: ALEXANDER HAMILTON

1. Nevins and Commager, *A Short History of the United States* (N. Y., 1945), p. 116.
2. See *Pennsylvania Journal and Weekly Advertiser*, October 31, 1781.
3. October 15, 1781: Correspondence of George Washington (Officers), L.C.
4. October 16, 1781: *Ibid.*
5. Louis R. Gottschalk, *Lafayette and the Close of the American Revolution* (Chicago, 1942), p. 323.
6. *Letters of Lafayette to Washington* (N. Y., 1944), pp. 234-35.
7. Charlemagne Tower, *The Marquis de La Fayette in the American Revolution* (Phila., 1901), II, 315.
8. J. C. Hamilton, *History of the Republic of the United States of America, as Traced in the Writings of Alexander Hamilton and His Contemporaries* (Phila., 1864), p. 468.
9. Henry Lee, *Memories of the War in the Southern Department of the United States* (Phila., 1812), II, 342.
10. Henry A. Muhlenberg, *Peter Muhlenberg* (Phila., 1849), p. 273.
11. Correspondence of George Washington (Officers), L.C.
12. *Calendar of Virginia State Papers*, II, 550.
13. Henry A. Muhlenberg, *op. cit.*, p. 275.
14. January 31, 1781: Mrs. Jesse Wagner Collection of Muhlenberg Manuscripts, Reading; A.P.S. microfilm.
15. Henry A. Muhlenberg, *op. cit.*, p. 273.
16. Peter M. to George Washington, October 23, 1781: Corr. of G. W. (Officers), L.C.

CHAPTER 25: "OUR GENERAL"

1. Frederick M. to H.M.M., October 24, 1781: Oswald Seidensticker, "Frederick A. C. Muhlenberg," *P.M. of H.B.*, XII, 196-97.
2. Correspondence of George Washington (Officers), L.C.

3. November (?), 1781: Luth. Arch., Mt. Airy.
4. Clements Library, Ann Arbor, Mich.
5. Pierpont Morgan Library, N. Y.; Henry A. Muhlenberg, *Peter Muhlenberg* (Phila., 1849), p. 410.
6. Hand to Muhlenberg, March 14, 1782: Henry A. Muhlenberg, *op. cit.*, p. 411.
7. Henry A. Muhlenberg, *op. cit.*, p. 290.
8. Frederick M. to Henry Ernest M., May 15, 1782: Luth. Arch., Mt. Airy.
9. H.S.P.
10. H.M.M. to Henry Ernest M., January 7, 1783: Luth. Arch., Mt. Airy.
11. Frederick M. to Benjamin Rush, March 21, 1789: Gratz Collection, Case 1, Box 9, H.S.P.
12. H.M.M.'s Journal, November 15, 1783: Luth. Arch., Mt. Airy.
13. *Pennsylvania Packet,* September 4, 1783, H.S.P.
14. Frederick M. to Emanuel Schultze, September 3, 1783: Frederick Nicolls Collection, Reading; A.P.S. microfilm.
15. H.M.M.'s Journal, September 6 and 7, 1783.
16. Oyer and Terminer docket, Supreme Court, 1787, p. 62: City Hall, Philadelphia.
17. *Autobiography of Charles Biddle* (Phila., 1883), p. 232.

CHAPTER 26: OHIO PARADISE

1. Virginia Military Bounty Land Warrants, Vol. IX, p. 74: General Land Office Records, National Archives, Washington, D. C.
2. H.M.M.'s Journal, July 25, 1783: Luth. Arch., Mt. Airy.
3. February 24, 1784: Frederick Nicolls Collection, Reading; A.P.S. microfilm.
4. Henry A. Muhlenberg, *Peter Muhlenberg* (Phila., 1849), pp. 425-53.
5. Frederick M. to Henry Ernest M., June 28, 1784: Luth. Arch., Mt. Airy.
6. Henry Ernest M., *Botanisches Tagebuch,* Vol. I, October 18, 1784: A.P.S.
7. Peter M.'s Journal, March 2, 1784: Henry A. Muhlenberg, *op. cit.*, p. 426.
8. *Ibid.*, March 6: *op. cit.*, p. 427.

9. *Ibid.*, March 31: *op. cit.*, p. 430.

10. Peter M. to Baron Steuben, April 23, 1784: William Henry Smith Memorial Library, Indiana Historical Society, Indianapolis.

11. Peter M.'s Journal, April 18, 1784: Henry A. Muhlenberg, *op. cit.*, p. 438.

12. June 28, 1784: Luth. Arch., Mt. Airy.

13. *Botanisches Tagebuch,* October 18, 1784: A.P.S.

14. *Ibid.*

15. Peter M.'s Journal, April 12, 1784: Henry A. Muhlenberg, *op. cit.*, p. 437.

16. Frederick M. to Henry Ernest M., June 28, 1784: Luth. Arch., Mt. Airy.

17. Indiana Historical Society.

18. Frederick M. to Henry Ernest M., June 28, 1784: Luth. Arch., Mt. Airy.

19. Peter M. to Baron Steuben, September 9, 1784: Steuben Papers, Box 4, N.Y.H.S.

20. Frederick M. to Henry Ernest M., June 28, 1784. Luth. Arch., Mt. Airy.

21. *Ibid.*

22. June 25, 1784.

23. Peter M. to General Mifflin, President of Congress, July 5, 1784: Henry A. Muhlenberg, *op. cit.*, p. 304.

24. Frederick M. to Henry Ernest M., June 28, 1784: Luth. Arch., Mt. Airy.

25. August 3, 1784: *Letters of Members of the Continental Congress,* VII, 579-80.

26. September 9, 1784: Steuben Papers, Box 4, N.Y.H.S.

CHAPTER 27: CANDIDATUS MORTIS

1. Lafayette to George Washington, Feburary 10, 1784: *Letters of Lafayette to Washington* (N. Y., 1944), pp. 310-11; original in Washington Papers, L.C.

2. Wrangel's letter is dated June 15, 1784. A copy of it is in H.M.M.'s Journal for October 21, 1784: Luth. Arch., Mt. Airy.

3. A copy of the reply to Wrangel is in H.M.M.'s Journal for October 22-23, 1784.

4. H.M.M.'s Journal, July 23 and 26, 1784.

5. *Ibid.*, July 23, 1784.

6. August 13, 1784: Frederick Nicolls Collection, Reading; A.P.S. microfilm.

7. H.M.M.'s Journal, August 13, 1784.

8. Emanuel Schultze to Member of Zion Church, August 28, 1784: H.M.M.'s Journal, August 31, 1784.

9. H.M.M.'s Journal, October 20, 1784.

10. H.M.M. to Betsy Schultze, November 16, 1784; Frederick Nicolls Collection, Reading; A.P.S. microfilm.

11. H.M.M.'s Journal, May 26, 1785.

12. *Ibid.*, June 6, 1785.

13. *Ibid.*, August 7, 1784.

14. *Ibid.*, July 26, 1784.

15. *Ibid.*

16. Frederick M. to Henry Ernest M., June 28, 1784: Luth. Arch., Mt. Airy. Part of this letter is printed in Seidensticker, "Frederick A.C.M.," *P.M. of H.B.*, XII, 184-206.

17. September 16, 1784.

18. Minutes of the A.P.S., 1774-87.

19. Frederick Nicolls Collection, Reading; A.P.S. microfilm.

20. Henry A. Muhlenberg, *Peter Muhlenberg* (Phila., 1849), p. 423.

21. Luth. Arch., Mt. Airy.

22. *Ibid.*

23. Frederick Nicolls Collection, Reading; A.P.S. microfilm.

24. *Life, Journals, and Correspondence of Rev. M. Cutler* (Cincinnati, 1888), I, 429.

25. Halle Photostats, H IV, Korrespondenz, 1783-87, pp. 222-25. See also H.M.M.'s Journal, February 7, 1785.

26. Lancaster, 1788.

27. Philadelphia, June 13: L. H. Butterfield, *A Letter from Dr. Benjamin Rush* (Lancaster, 1945).

28. Fabricius (Halle) to Henry Ernest M., December 1, 1787: Luth. Arch., Mt. Airy.

29. Henry Ernest M. to Dr. Benjamin Rush, June 25, 1787; Dubbs, *History of Franklin College.*

30. Luth. Arch., Mt. Airy.

31. H.M.M.'s Journal, June 20, 1777.

32. Elizabeth Schultze to Emanuel Schultze, undated: Frederick Nicolls Collection, Reading: A.P.S. microfilm.

33. William J. Mann, *Life and Times of Henry Melchior Muhlenberg* (Phila., 1888), p. 522.

34. *Ibid.*, p. 523.

CHAPTER 28: MR. SPEAKER

1. Robert L. Brunhouse, *The Counter-Revolution in Pennsylvania 1776-90* (Harrisburg, 1942), p. 208.

2. *Journals of the Continental Congress,* XXXIV, 10.

3. *Autobiography of Charles Biddle* (Phila., 1883), pp. 225-26.

4. Brunhouse, *op. cit.*, pp. 216-18, 343-44.

5. Frederick M. to Benjamin Rush, March 5, 1789: Gratz Collection, Case I, Box 9, H.S.P.

6. *Ibid.*

7. Peter M. to Benjamin Rush, March 18, 1789: Gratz Collection, Case 4, Box 13, H.S.P.

8. March 5, 1789: Gratz Collection, Case I, Box 9, H.S.P.

9. Society Misc. Collection, H.S.P.

10. *P.M. of H.B.*, XXXVIII, 50-51.

11. *Debates and Proceedings in the Congress of the United States* (Wash., 1834), I, 94.

12. Henry A. Muhlenberg, *Peter Muhlenberg* (Phila., 1849), pp. 317-18; Edward W. Hocker, *The Fighting Parson of the American Revolution* (Phila., 1936).

13. Gratz Collection, Generals of the Revolution, Case 4, Box 13, H.S.P.

14. Claude G. Bowers, *Jefferson and Hamilton* (N. Y. 1925), p. 5.

15. Essex Institute, Salem, Mass.

16. Statement signed by Frederick M., Philadelphia, December 13, 1792: *Works of Alexander Hamilton* (1904), VII, 412-13.

17. *Ibid.*

18. Frederick Nicolls Collection, Reading; A.P.S. microfilm.

19. *Ibid.*

20. *Abridgement of the Debates of Congress,* I, 753.

21. Frederick M. to Hon. Thomas Barclay, April 20, 1783: Frederick Nicolls Collection, Reading; A.P.S. microfilm.

22. *Ibid.*

23. City Hall, Philadelphia.

24. *Ibid.*

25. Anne Ayres, *The Life and Work of William Augustus Muhlenberg* (N. Y., 1881), pp. 6-7.

26. Ohio State Archaeological and Historical Society, Ohio State Museum, Columbus.

27. *P.M. of H.B.*, XXI, 490-92.

28. *Pennsylvania Archives,* Ninth Series, II, 1444 (Exec. Min.).

29. *Ibid.,* Ninth Series, III, 1580-81.

30. Mrs. Gerald F. Selinger, Narberth, Pa.

31. Bernard Faÿ, "Early Party Machinery," *P.M. of H.B.*, LX, 386.

32. William Duane to Thomas Jefferson, June 10, 1801: "Letters of William Duane," *Proceedings of the Massachusetts Historical Society,* Second Series, XX, 257-394.

CHAPTER 29: MARCH ON THE CAPITAL

1. Peters Papers, IV, 95, H.S.P.
2. A.P.S.; N.Y.H.S.
3. *Abridgement of the Debates of Congress,* II, 531-32.
4. *Ibid.*
5. *Aurora,* February 16, 1801.
6. Quoted by the *Aurora* of same issue.
7. *Aurora,* February 12, 1801.
8. Letter dated February 16.
9. Gallatin Papers, N.Y.H.S.
10. *Aurora,* February 16, 1801.
11. *Ibid.*
12. *Ibid.,* February 19, 1801.
13. Henry A. Muhlenberg, *Peter Muhlenberg* (Phila., 1849), p. 328; *Correspondence of Thomas Jefferson* (Washington, D. C., 1907), X, 201-2.
14. Henry A. Muhlenberg, *op. cit.,* pp. 329-30.
15. *Debates and Proceedings in the Congress of the United States* (Wash., 1851), *Sixth Congress,* p. 1028.
16. *Aurora,* February 20, 1801.
17. Mrs. Jesse Wagner Collection, Reading; A.P.S. microfilm. A copy of this letter is in the Gallatin Papers, N.Y.H.S.

CHAPTER 30: THE PORT OF PHILADELPHIA

1. "Memoirs of a Senator from Pennsylvania" (Jonathan Roberts), *P.M. of H.B.*, LXII, 92.
2. *Aurora,* February 25, 1801.
3. Gallatin Papers, N.Y.H.S.
4. Peter M. to R. Purviance, November 14, 1803: Chicago Historical Society.
5. Peter M. to Albert Gallatin, June 4, 1804: L.C.
6. Peter M. to Thomas Jefferson, May 20, 1804: Harvard College Library.
7. Peter M. to Thomas Jefferson, June 17, 1807: L.C.
8. Peter M. to Thomas Jefferson, December 27, 1803: Harvard College Library.
9. Thomas Jefferson to Peter M., November 14, 1803: Harvard College Library.
10. Peter M. to Thomas Jefferson, December 29, 1803: Harvard College Library.
11. Peter M. to Thomas Jefferson, February 13, 1804: Harvard College Library. Thomas Jefferson to Peter M., February 24, 1804: L.C.
12. February 28, 1803: Roberts Collection, Haverford College.
13. Mrs. Gerald F. Selinger, Narberth, Pa.
14. Frederick Nicolls Collection, Reading; A.P.S. microfilm.

CHAPTER 31: THE AMERICAN LINNAEUS

1. May 26, 1805: Mrs. Jesse Wagner Collection, Reading; A.P.S. microfilm.
2. April 11, 1791: MS. Letters to Henry Ernest M., 1781-1815, Society Collection, H.S.P.
3. Henry Ernest M. to Palisot de Beauvois, June 14, 1811: MS. Communications to the A.P.S., Vol. I, Natural History, A.P.S.
4. *Floræ Philadelphicæ Prodromus* (Phila., 1815).
5. October 21, 1809: MS. Letters to Henry Ernest M., p. 127, H.S.P.
6. A.P.S.
7. Darlington, *Reliquae Baldwinianae* (Phila., 1843), pp. 51-53.
8. *Ibid.*, pp. 176-78.

9. Luth. Arch., Mt. Airy.

10. Henry Ernest M. to Nebe, September 23, 1800: Halle Photostats, L.C.

11. Henry Ernest M. to William Baldwin, November 4, 1811: Darlington, *op. cit.*, pp. 51-53.

12. Henry Ernest M. to Dr. Baldwin, January 7, 1811: Darlington, *op. cit.*, pp. 15 ff.

13. Henry Ernest M. to Dr. Baldwin, November 28, 1814: Darlington, *op. cit.*, pp. 150-53.

14. Henry Ernest M. to Dr. John Brickell, February 7, 1803: Dreer Collection, Scientists, H.S.P.

15. Bartram Papers, IV, 91, H.S.P.

16. Henry Ernest M. to John Vaughan, April 9, 1807: A.P.S.

17. Henry Ernest M. to Dr. John Brickell, September 10, 1806: Gratz Collection, Case 7, Box 24, American Scientists, H.S.P.

18. Rafinesque to Henry Ernest M., May 9, 1803: MS. Letters to H. E. Muhlenberg, p. 65, H.S.P.

CHAPTER 32: HENRY MUHLENBERG CLOSES HIS JOURNAL

1. Peter Wager to Adam Reigart, September 24, 1805: Society Misc. Coll., H.S.P.

2. *Ibid.*

3. Henry Ernest M. to Dr. George Logan, February 14, 1806: Logan Papers, V, 71, H.S.P.

4. Henry Ernest M. to Emanuel Schultze, April 3, 1807: Frederick Nicolls Collection, Reading; A.P.S. microfilm.

5. Henry Ernest M. to Z. Collins, January 9, 1813: *Botanical Correspondence of Z. Collins*, p. 12, Academy of Science, Phila.

6. *Botanisches Tagebuch*, Vol. III.

7. H.M.M. to Eike and Westphal, September 6, 1785: Luth. Arch., Mt. Airy.

8. Cf. the President's invitation, November 14, 1808: Letters to H. A. Muhlenberg, March 1844-August 1844, p. 552, Mrs. Jesse Wagner Collection, Reading; A.P.S. microfilm.

9. *Ibid.*, pp. 553-54.

10. Thomas Jefferson to Henry Ernest M., March 16, 1814: Huntington Library, San Marino, Calif.

11. Letters to H. E. Muhlenberg, p. 239, H.S.P.
12. Darlington, *Reliquae Baldwinianae* (Phila., 1843), pp. 140-41.
13. October 4, 1814: Darlington, *op. cit.*, pp. 145-47.
14. Darlington, *op. cit.*, pp. 171-74.
15. *Botanisches Tagebuch*, Vol. III, A.P.S.
16. *Botanical Correspondence of Z. Collins*, p. 62, Academy of Science, Phila.
17. Darlington, *op. cit.*, pp. 174-76.
18. *Ibid.*, pp. 176-78.

INDEX

ABBREVIATIONS

FAM: Frederick Augustus (Conrad) Muhlenberg

HEM: (Gotthilf) Henry Ernest Muhlenberg

HMM: Henry Melchior Muhlenberg

PM: Peter (John Peter Gabriel) Muhlenberg